CULTURE OF THE INTERNET

CULTURE OF THE INTERNET

Edited by

Sara Kiesler
Carnegie Mellon University

IEA **Lawrence Erlbaum Associates, Publishers**
1997 **Mahwah, New Jersey**

Lawrence Erlbaum Associates, Inc., Publishers
10 Industrial Avenue
Mahwah, NJ 07430

Cover design by Kathryn Houghtaling
Original painting by Lawrence M. Greene

Library of Congress Cataloging-in-Publication Data

Culture of the internet / editor, Sara Kiesler
      p. cm.
   Includes bibliographical references and index.
    ISBN 0-8058-1635-6 (alk:paper). — ISBN 0-8058-
1636-4 (paper : alk. paper)
    1. Telecommunication—Social aspects. 2. Com-
puter networks—Social aspects.   I. Kiesler, Sara,
1940- .
HE7631.S613   1996
302.23—dc20   96-31388
                                      CIP

Printed in the United States of America
10 9 8 7 6 5 4

Contents

IV. COMPUTER-SUPPORTED COOPERATIVE WORK

V. NETWORKED ORGANIZATIONS

VI. DIFFERENCES IN ACCESS AND USAGE

Preface

Sara Kiesler
Carnegie Mellon University

As we end this century and begin a new one, technological change has dealt another big surprise. Today's surprise is the incredible spread of computer networks in society. Initially designed to help scientists and engineers connect to remote computers, networks spread through universities and technical organizations, then to the business community, and then to the public. The Internet has entered everyday parlance. It is featured in talk shows, in special business "technology" sections of major newspapers, and on the covers of national magazines. Companies offering Internet services that go public, such as Lycos and Yahoo, have seen their stock soar. How-to books on Internet programming are best sellers. Yet at this writing, only a minority of U.S. families are connected to the Internet, and just a tiny percentage of the world's population has been online even once. The Internet lives in imagination more than in reality.

What is so special about this innovation that so few have used? Most observers agree it isn't the technology alone, the devices and machinery that connect computers and run communication applications. It isn't the ready availability of the technology either. Electronic communication (a more general term encompassing all computer networks, including the Internet) can be expensive, time consuming, hard to learn, and difficult for the layperson to understand. Millions of people accessing networks through their work probably would not be online if it were not for the computers and technical support they receive through their employers.

What makes the Internet special is not the technology per se but the social interactions it is inspiring. Every day the Internet supports thousands of experiments in friendship and group formation; in discussion, decision making, publication, and political debate and mobilization; in the creation of advice and social support networks; in geographically distributed teamwork; in business cooperation and coordination; in creating new markets and running existing markets; in digitizing and distributing old forms of information exchange such as library services; and even in crime.

The Internet is a seemingly limitless resource for personal connection and exploration. Networks are always "up," enabling 24-hour asynchronous or synchronous interactions and information exchange among individuals and groups. Organizations, as well, can use electronic communication to keep rich stores of information, often in machine-readable form that permits data exchange for local or remote processing without costly conversion. As a communications medium, the Internet allows people not only to talk with those they know and want to know, but to shop, to play, to sell goods, and to transact business in hundreds of "virtual" forums. Recent developments in software, especially the World Wide Web, have made these possibilities seem more accessible to the average person.

These many experiments in electronic communication, especially in that a large proportion of them are initiated and controlled from the bottom up—by individuals acting alone or in small groups or businesses—constitute a fascinating cultural phenomenon, and perhaps a significant cultural change. The title of this book is recognition that the Internet is not simply a better appliance, but a new domain of human activity. Yet, this is a domain we don't yet understand. Is it an information superhighway? A virtual community? A frontier? It has been called all those things.

If the Internet is a new domain of human activity, it also is a new domain for those who study humans. For social scientists, the Internet raises many questions. First, there is the symbolic force of the Internet even (or, especially) among those who have never used it. This symbolic force seems to have caused significant changes in behavior (big investments by firms; sacrifices by individuals to learn the new technology; legislation; political conflict). Second, inside the world of the Internet itself, some social experiments are evolving into identifiable communities with routines, traditions, and convictions. What has really happened? What do these changes really mean?

This volume is a compendium of essays and research reports representing how researchers are thinking about the social and cultural processes of electronic communication. The chapters were selected to represent a variety of fields, perspectives, and methods, and together comprise an early gathering of social psychological, sociological, and anthropological research on electronic communication and the Internet.

This book is intended primarily for researchers and others who seek exposure to diverse approaches to studying the "people" side of electronic communication and the Internet. For this audience, the book has three purposes: (a) to illustrate how scientists are thinking about evolving social behavior on the Internet, (b) to encourage research-based contributions to current debates on design, applications, and policies, and (c) to suggest, by example, how studies of electronic communication can contribute to social science itself.

Because of space and editorial limitations, much excellent research and some whole areas of work are not represented here. For instance, there are no "ease of use" studies (the chapter by Steve Whittaker and Candy Sidner is a close cousin). A technology that people find hard to use can make the difference between a technology that is used and one that is not used (Card, Moran, & Newell, 1983; Norman, 1988) and usability has social effects (see chap. 19). However, typically such studies address culture indirectly, so they were not included.

The authors of these chapters differ not only by discipline but also by goal. For some, the emergence and use of new technologies represent a new perspective on questions of longstanding interest in their disciplines. Others want to draw on social science theories to understand technology. A third group holds to a more activist program, seeking guidance through research to improve social interventions using technology in domains such as education, mental health, and work productivity. Each of these goals has influenced the research questions, methods, and inferences of the authors and the "look and feel" of the chapters in this book. Editorial influence was not exerted to extract consensus or consistency. Diversity really characterizes this domain of research, and should be reflected in these chapters.

Several themes emerge in the chapters as a whole. One theme across the chapters in this volume is that electronic communication is a politically and personally sensitive technology. The first chapter, by John King, Rebecca Grinter, and Jeanne Pickering, tells how the Internet arose and caused several million people not only to change their routine means of communication but to become emotionally and socially committed to the "Net." Today, denizens of Netville fight to retain open access and free communication on the Internet, whereas others want more regulation. Another conflict rages over the right to personal information and to online documents—for example, whether one's online "publication" of a computer program or document has the same standing as a printed publication. Many people, especially in their roles as employees and consumers, fear loss of control and privacy in electronic communication. Others welcome the means for organizations to "mine" disparate computer databases or even online communications to extract interesting information about people. One persistent finding of research is that both individuals and organizations often discover strategic uses for electronic communication that they did not anticipate when they began using the technology.

An incident occurred in 1991 with extensive discussion of the new Lotus Development Corporation's product *Households*—a "profile" advertising database—on the USENET comp.risks newsgroup. This discussion began when someone close to the development of the product but not working for Lotus leaked a detailed description of the product to his own company's bulletin board. This description was read by another person, and "reposted" with a few keystrokes to the comp.risks bulletin board with its thousands of readers. The subsequent discussion on comp.risks precipitated an electronic protest message-writing campaign directly to the email address of Lotus CEO Joe Manni that produced thousands of email messages decrying the new product. It is reported that this message campaign had a pronounced effect on the Lotus leadership, which subsequently scuttled the product (Culnan, 1991).

Another instance in which people mobilized electronically happened during the Tienamen Square confrontations in June of 1989. The USENET newsgroup soc.culture.china became a highly interactive communications device among Chinese students in the United States and Europe for sharing information and planning action in response to the crisis. This was not simply an electronic version of Tom Paine and the pamphleteers; it was a powerful organizing modality that permitted nearly real-time mobilization and coordination across vast distances. The fact that postings to this newsgroup could not be anonymous meant that participants identified themselves as protesters in a way not common to mass physical demonstrations. Records of the transactions were lasting and widely available.

It is not hard to see why people think electronic communication will change how institutions and individuals exert power through their hold on information. The 1973 Code of Fair Information Practices now serves as the basis for U.S. privacy legislation. However, legal doctrine does not yet clearly answer questions about the privacy of electronic mail, rights to form electronic groups, the responsibility of online services to police networks, and the secondary use of electronic information. In fact, sufficient behavior change has occurred that a whole new practice of electronic communications law has emerged. Because the law tends to change as social expectations and perceptions of fairness change, research bearing on how people and institutions are behaving with respect to information privacy and sharing, control, hierarchy, and the polity is both interesting and important. Many of the chapters in this book address the social processes that determine how people will respond to these new possibilities. Chapter 11, by Peter Carnevale and Tahira Probst, summarizes current research on conflict and explains why electronic communication might change the nature of conflict.

A second theme across the chapters is that electronic communication can have both mundane and significant social effects. Readers can think about the distinction between amplifying and transformative effects. Some technological change is primarily amplifying, making it possible for people to do what they have done before, but more accurately, quickly, or cheaply. In other cases, technology is truly transformative: It leads to qualitative change in how people think about the world, in their social roles and institutions, in the ways they work, and in the political and economic challenges they face. Technologies such as printing, mass production using interchangeable parts, electrification and mechanization of the farm, and the automobile all have the transformative characteristic. Sometimes the amplifying effect is what we see first, never realizing there is a later transformative effect to come, or that the amplifying technology is part of a larger social change. The vacuum cleaner, for example, itself a modest innovation, was a significant part of the revolution in household technology that vanquished servants from the middle-class home (Cowan, 1989). Cleaning was something that people had done, but the new device was so much more efficient that a special class of cleaners was no longer justified. Similarly, amplifying technological change can lead to the rare and esoteric becoming a commonplace part of human existence. Travel as a widespread leisure pursuit, made possible by improved transportation technologies and greater wealth, is an example of this kind of change.

People's behavior, not just the attributes of the technology, determine whether a technology is amplifying or transformative. After they get beyond the hoopla associated with the Internet, people use specific applications of electronic communication differently in different social contexts; in some cases they alter what the technology can accomplish. The result can lead to simple amplification, as discussed by Kraut and Attewell in chapter 15. However, one of the reasons researchers here and elsewhere are fascinated with electronic communication technology is that it clearly has long-term transformative potential. Could the Internet help citizens topple dictatorships? Christopher Kedzie in chapter 10 argues that the correlation of countries' telecommunications capacity with their level of democracy suggests electronic communication can lead to democratization. At a more personal level, in chapter 4 Yitzchak Binik, James Cantor, Eric Ochs, and Marta Meana discuss their research on "smart" computer sex tutors, and whether people could use their computers from home for education and therapy. Most of the other chapters in this book also address issues of amplification and transformation.

A third theme across the chapters is the close connection researchers tend to keep between questions of their disciplines and research on electronic communication. A major incentive for many of the authors represented here is that the Internet can serve as a platform for research on phenomena and processes that have been difficult to observe and study—how markets adapt, what motivates children to learn outside classrooms, how large groups form, and how organizations communicate. The Internet can provide a new means for data collection on communication among individuals, groups, and organizations. The Internet also is being used to conduct psychological experiments, social analyses, and experimental auctions and markets. As a carrier of communication traffic, the Internet can be used to "meter" communications and to collect substantive data as well as transactions. These capabilities show promise for doing new kinds of research with genuine advantages for the social sciences.

Researchers in this domain also face social and conceptual barriers. A major problem is that research (on computer technology, generally, not just on the Internet) occurs in a fast-moving, ideologically sensitive, economically important domain. Vested interests and sacred beliefs affect researchers' thinking and the organizations that provide research support. The climate of optimism that has made the Internet attractive to study also affects researchers and those who support research. For example, assumptions about the benefits of the Internet probably have slowed research on its costs and risks.

Researchers use extant theory to frame what they study. However, electronic communication technology sufficiently changes the context of learning, work, play, and relationships that existing theories often do not address the phenomena under study or suggest appropriate measurements. Studies of networked groups, for instance, have revealed group and organizational behavior that would not be observable, could not happen, or would be unlikely to occur in other environments. For instance, a field experiment conducted by the RAND Corporation suggests that networked organizations might have much more flexible structures than thought possible in organizations.

J. D. Eveland and Tora Bikson (1988) formed two task forces in a large utility firm, each assigned to analyze employee retirement issues and produce a report. Each task force had 40 members, half who had recently retired from the company and half who still worked but were eligible for retirement. The only difference between the two groups was that RAND provided one with networked computer terminals and software. Both task forces created subcommittees, but the task force with electronic communication created more of them. Also, unlike the task force without electronic communication, the electronically connected task force assigned people to more than one subcommittee. It also created a more complex organization of subcommittees, using an overlapping matrix structure, and creating new subcommittees during its work. It also decided to continue meeting even after its official 1-year life span had ended.

Research on organizations that rely heavily on computer networks for employee communications has led to a wave of new work by organization scientists on the "network" organizational form. In the network form, employees have many fluid relationships with individuals across the organization (see Nohria & Eccles, 1992). Employees can use these ties to ~e resources that are unavailable in their immediate work groups r 9 by Barry Wellman and chapter 14, by David Constant, Lee 1 Sara Kiesler).

A fourth theme across the chapters is simply how much we still have to learn. Researchers can't yet say how electronic communication will affect such important social activities as entertainment, commerce, voting, or war. The technology is too new, and research is difficult. A common dictum for researchers is that for a phenomenon to be a focus of research, the question must be framed in researchable ways: The behavior to be observed must be observable, and the theories to be tested must be testable. These requirements, difficult enough to satisfy in traditional areas, pose special problems for those who want to study electronic communication. Hyperbole about the next great upgrade is common, and it can discourage research. Because computer technologies are changing so rapidly, the social phenomena to be studied and understood do represent a moving target. It takes a clever study design to detect when an observed change (or lack of change) is due to technology, to its sheer newness, or to the kinds of users it attracts (see, e.g., Hybels & Barley, 1990). These difficulties have sent more than one graduate student back to "basic research." But the chapters in this volume should prove that interesting and researchable questions can be asked, and even pursued. For those who tolerate ambiguity, it is an endeavor as exciting as any, and if the futurists are right, as important too.

ACKNOWLEDGMENTS

I am grateful to the Markle Foundation for its support of the preparation of this volume. The Markle Foundation has had a long standing commitment to improving and understanding communication technology in society. At the suggestion of the Foundation, and with its support, the Social Science Research Council sponsored an ad hoc panel, Computers in Society, whose purpose was to promote research on the social impact of computers. The panel held a series of occasional workshops from 1984 through 1993. This book is one product of these workshops.

Members of the SSRC panel from 1993 to 1995 were Paul Attewell, Stephen Barley, Tora Bikson, Irv Binik, Terry Connolly, Joel Cooper, Sara Kiesler, John King, Rob Kling, Robert Kraut, Mark Lepper, Keith Nelson, Roy Pea, David Perkins, James Rule, Janet Schofield, Lee Sproull, Gavriel Salomon, and Sharon Traweek. I am grateful to these workshop participants, each of whom contributed expertise and ideas for this volume. I also thank Dr. Aya Betensky, who served as coordinating editor. Rosa Stipanovic performed many important tasks to prepare the book; thank you, Rosa. Finally, Crom and Larry were patient throughout book preparation—though they have no interest in the Internet.

Royalties from the sale of this book will be donated to Computer Professionals for Social Responsibility, the Electronic Frontier Foundation, and Pittsburgh's Hillhouse Association.

REFERENCES

Eveland, J. D., & Bikson, T. K. (1988). Work group structures and computer support: A field experiment. *Transactions on Office Information Systems, 6*, 354–379.

Card, S. K., Moran, T. P., & Newell, A. (1983). *The psychology of human computer interaction.* Hillsdale, NJ: Lawrence Erlbaum Associates.

Cowan, R. S. (1989). *More work for mother: The ironies of household technology from the open hearth to the microwave.* London: Free Association Books.

Culnan, M. J. (1991). The lessons of the Lotus MarketPlace: Implications for consumer privacy in the 1990s. In *Proceedings of the Conference on Computers, Freedom and Privacy.* Palo Alto, CA: Computer Professionals for Social Responsibility.

Hybels, R. C., & Barley, S. R. (1990). Co-optation and the legitimation of professional identities: Human resource policies in high technology firms. In L. R. Gomez–Mejia & M. W. Lawless (Eds.), *Organizational issues and high technology management* (pp. 199–213). Greenwich, CT: JAI.

Nohria, N., & Eccles, R. G. (Eds.). (1992). *Networks and organizations: Structure, form, and action,* Boston: Harvard Business School Press.

Norman, D. A. (1988). *The psychology of everyday things.* New York: Basic Books.

Part I

THE NET AS IT WAS
AND MIGHT BECOME

People always wonder how a seemingly powerful technology will affect their lives and the future of society. The earliest reflections on computer technology polarized around utopian and Orwellian visions of change (e.g., Jacobson & Roucek, 1959; see Dunlop & Kling, 1991). In an influential Harvard Business Review article of 1958, Harold Leavitt and Thomas Whisler predicted that in the 1980s computer information systems would radically restructure and centralize organizations. (In the 1980s, writers were making just the opposite prediction.) Daniel Bell, in his "venture in social forecasting" in 1973, predicted the "knowledge society" would depend on government decision making supported by computer analyses. Virtually all of this writing presented computers as information-processing, computation machines that would affect society through changes in the control of information.

When computers were linked together and carried human writing, people's reflections on computers changed. They started thinking of computers as a communication technology. Among the first empirical studies of computer networks were investigations of group communication—classified experiments sponsored by the Department of Defense on decision making by networked groups. (The idea was that remote networked groups would make more rational judgments than face-to-face groups, but that's another story.) In the 1970s, social scientists in universities and industry research laboratories began to conduct experiments on electronic communication (Chapanis, 1972; Hiltz & Turoff, 1978; Short, Williams, & Christie, 1976). These researchers typically looked at how the technology might be used in work organizations—for tasks such as project organization and decision making. This kind of research remains a strong tradition, as in the research being done on group decision support systems. (Chapter 12, Terry

Connolly's review of research on electronic brainstorming, exemplifies this tradition.)

As the technology of electronic communication matured, researchers began to study people's behavior in situ, and at the same time, they explored new ways of using electronic communication. Soon it became clear that when people talk about electronic communication and the "Internet" they can mean quite different things. Different meanings come both from the symbolic importance of the Internet, and from the quite different activities that the Internet can support. The chapters in this section represent a selection of research perspectives on what the Internet is now and what it might become. John King, Rebecca Grinter, and Jeanne Pickering describe the Internet as a dynamic and historic social institution. Lee Sproull and Samer Faraj discuss the Internet as social gathering place. Michael Mehta and Dwaine Plaza describe the Internet as a market for licit and illicit sexual information exchange. For Yitzchak Binik, James Cantor, Eric Ochs, and Marta Meana, it is a potential health service provider.

That the Internet can be understood from these different viewpoints suggests that electronic communication is a general purpose technology with broad applications and correspondingly diverse social effects. I hope these chapters give readers a sense of the many ways we can think about the culture of the Internet, and encourage them, whatever their discipline, to find interesting questions to ask about it.

REFERENCES

Bell, D. (1973). *The coming of post-industrial society: A venture in social forecasting.* New York: Basic Books.

Chapanis, A. (1972). Studies in interactive communication: The effects of four communication modes on the behavior of teams during cooperative problem-solving. *Human Factors, 14,* 487–509.

Dunlop, C., & Kling, R. (1991). *The dreams of technological utopianism.* In C. Dunlop & R. Kling (Eds.), *Computerization and controversy: Value conflicts and social choices* (pp. 14–30). Boston: Academic Press.

Hiltz, S. R., & Turoff, M. (1978). *The network nation—Human communication via computer.* Reading, MA: Addison-Wesley.

Jacobson, H. B., & Roucek, J. S. (1959). *Automation and society.* New York: Philosophical Library.

Leavitt, H. J., & Whisler, T. L. (1958). Management in the 1980s. *Harvard Business Review, Nov–Dec,* 41–48.

Short, J., Williams, E., & Christie, B. (1976). *The social psychology of telecommunications.* London: Wiley.

1

THE RISE AND FALL OF NETVILLE: THE SAGA OF A CYBERSPACE CONSTRUCTION BOOMTOWN IN THE GREAT DIVIDE

John Leslie King
Rebecca E. Grinter
Jeanne M. Pickering
*Center for Research on Information Technology
and Organizations (CRITO)
University of California, Irvine*

This chapter tells the story of Netville, the virtual society of the Internet. Netville flourished from the 1960s through the 1980s. In that period, Netville's sheltered environment encouraged the development of distinct technical and cultural institutions that were well adapted to the scientific, engineering, and defense communities of the time. Today, as the Internet enters the broader social and commercial world, Netville's future is uncertain.

The challenge of merging technical and social skill bases for the purposes of building effective information technologies has been characterized as the problem of bridging a great divide between technical and social expertise (Bowker, Star, Turner, & Gasser, in press). But truly new technologies often emerge when technologists and their patrons *create* a great divide that shelters technical innovation from the status quo.[1] Invention best arises within a narrow social context, not across all the social contexts it ultimately affects. Perhaps it could not otherwise survive. Yet when ultimately the technology is offered to the broader social world, the divide must be straddled, exposing the community that gave birth to the technology to normal powerful social forces that can destroy it.

This chapter tells the story of the homesteading of the unique virtual settlement of Netville[2] within which the Internet was born. The pioneers of Netville faced the hardships of a technological frontier but they also exploited a great divide—a zone of freedom and opportunity that allowed them to create something truly new. Netville was a community where deeply ingrained institutional values of intellectual curiosity, informal meritocratic reward structures, and egalitarian presumptions enabled a highly disaggregated and distributed population to work together to create an amazing artifact quite unlike any seen before. Through their labors, the people of Netville created cyberspace[3] and a community that was geographically distributed but bound together by a shared interest in a technology that was both the subject and object of their efforts.

As glorious as the rise of Netville has proven to be in retrospect, it was largely unnoticed by the world at large during that rise. From the late 1960s through 1990, the population of Netville grew slowly but steadily in an organic fashion. It drew to itself members of the research and high-technology communities who were willing to learn both the technical procedures and social conventions required for access to and residence in cyberspace. New members of the community found powerful incentives to conform to the social conventions of the earlier settlers, and to a great degree, Netville was a self-governing society with relatively few rules and relatively few rule breakers. This idyllic state began to change around 1990 as the news of Netville and of cyberspace began to spread to new domains—to commercial firms, nonprofit organizations, and most important, the media. Soon the tides of immigration flooded Netville with new settlers, and with them came powerful new institutional interests that displaced the institutional forces that gave life to Netville. Within a few years, Netville had begun to change and the fall of Netville was underway. Cyberspace would survive,

---

[1] The principle of institutionalized order, a key feature of this discussion, can be explored in detail in Meyer and Rowan (1977), DiMaggio and Powell (1983, 1991), March and Olsen (1989), and Scott (1991). A detailed discussion of this is provided in King et al., (1994).

[2] Netville is a name that we have given the community of developers who worked together to provide the technologies that most people using the network today use.

[3] William Gibson first coined this term in his book *Neuromancer* (Gibson, 1984). Faced with trying to describe this space where people meet and talk electronically, a place constructed entirely of electric pulses that does not have any physical existence, he invented the term cyberspace. The book, a science fiction novel, caught the imagination of Netville. Neal Stephenson (1992) in his book *Snow Crash* used the term metaverse to describe the same phenomenon.

after many paleonymic grafts to reshape its meaning and image to fit the interests of the new institutional forces of commerce and entertainment.

Netville emerges from the analysis that follows as a remarkably vital but fragile entity, capable of producing something that would change the world but unable to protect itself from the consequences of its own success. The story, ultimately, involves the clash of institutional interests and values in which the details of technology are critical for marking the progress of Netville and shaping its effect on the world, but play a remarkably subordinate role in the rise and fall of Netville as a community. In this story, Netville's future remains uncertain. It might die the death of many a construction boomtown, leaving empty buildings and the skeletal remains of life. It could as easily be reborn as an entertainment spectacle like Las Vegas, run by those who appreciate the drawing power of money and flesh. The rise and fall of Netville is a modern morality tale of vision, courage, skill, and the nearly inevitable subordination of ideals to material progress.

THE RISE OF NETVILLE

The question of when Netville began is difficult to answer, in part because the history is cloudy, and in part because the definitions of the key terms have evolved over time.[4] As a practical matter, we focus our attention on the Netville era that produced three clear triumphs: demonstration of a robust internetworked system for packet-switched communication (the ARPANET), which evolved into the Internet; electronic mail on that network, which allowed asynchronous text communications between all users of the network; and the hypertext-based World Wide Web, which evolved late in the life of Netville, bringing great new capabilities to the network. Nevertheless, we think it is worthwhile to fix a starting time for Netville. To do so we must at least determine when computer networking and electronic mail first emerged. We provide some historical context to make that challenge a bit easier to understand, and to facilitate our discussion of how Netville as a social community came to be.

Technical Milestones

Perhaps the first technical milestone of Netville was set around 1884 when the U.S. Congress paid Samuel Morse $30,000 to build a telegraph link between Washington, DC, and Baltimore (Thompson, 1947). Telegraphy cannot in any sense be seen as a computer network, but it was the first form of electronic mail, and it operated in a network fashion, with human operators at the nodes. The teletype ushered in a more recognizable form of electronic mail in 1931, providing text output readable directly by some-

---

[4]We thank David Crocker, Einar Stefferud, and John Vittal for their personal insights that provided background and guidance for this discussion.

one other than a telegraph operator (Beniger, 1986). The first remote use of a computer in 1940, using a Bell Laboratories Complex Number Calculator located in New York from a teletype in Hanover, New Hampshire, provides another marker of the beginning of Netville (Williams, 1985). However, none of these systems constituted what we would recognize today as a computer network.

The first true, real-time computer network was the Semi-Automatic Ground Environment (SAGE) air defense system developed in the early 1960s. SAGE was a sensing and process control system that ran over approximately 1 million miles of dedicated communication lines, linking several thousand graphics terminals driven by IBM/MIT AN/FSQ7 computers to AN/FSQ8 weapon control computers (Moreau, 1984). The facsimile machine could be considered a key marker in the electronic mail world, given that it operated on a robust network that (at least now) is computer based, and it transmitted text electronically. The birth of Netville could rightly be tied to any of these events. But none of them contains the key elements of today's Internet: a world in which noncomputer experts communicate with one another through a computer-mediated communications network.

The Internet began with the sharing of messages between users on single-computer, online timesharing systems. Although prosaic by today's standards, these machines represented important conceptual breakthroughs in both computing and communications technology (Moreau, 1984). The first commercial timeshared machine, the IBM 305, allowed up to four users to access shared applications and records almost simultaneously. A much more important breakthrough occurred in the development of the American Airlines/IBM joint project to develop an airline reservations system, SABRE, that allowed simultaneous access by more than 1,000 terminals. Unlike SAGE, which was really a system of sensors and actuators for process control to support the work of specialists, SABRE was an information system that allowed thousands of users with no previous experience with computers to communicate with a shared information resource. However, SABRE did not allow person-to-person communication through the timesharing system.

Email capability of the sort now common emerged in the evolution of sophisticated timesharing systems used in research environments. Remote users of these systems often needed to have the computer operator execute an operation such as a tape mount. Rather than telephone the operator, who was sitting at the computer operations console, it made more sense for the user to create a file that could be attached, via a command, to the operator's "inbox" mail file. It is possible that the first instance of this was the TENEX MAIL command, part of the TENEX operating system built by Bolt, Beranek and Newman Company for the Digital Equipment Corporation's PDP-10 computer in the late 1960s. The ARPANET mail feature grew directly out of this development when it was recognized that the TENEX MAIL command could be used with the recently created File Transfer Protocol feature (FTP), which allowed movement of files across network lines from machine to machine, to append mail files to the inboxes of users on remote machines. The TENEX MAIL command was added to FTP, setting the initial standard for ARPANET MAIL and eventually for the current Internet. It is difficult to say exactly when the first ARPANET message was sent, but it probably occurred around the time of the gala unveiling of the ARPANET at the Washington Hilton in 1972 (Roberts & Kahn, 1972). However, reading mail was an unwieldy affair until the creation of RD (ReaDmail) in 1974. RD was a set of TECO macros to parse inboxes and preset the reader with messages as units of process, rather than just reading the raw file of appended inbox messages. This advance was rapidly followed by many new versions of ARPANET mail handlers that greatly facilitated email use and formed the basis of Netville's most significant practical achievement. From humble beginnings, electronic mail on the Internet has grown to huge proportions. Recently, the Nielsen research corporation estimated that more than 37 million people have ever used the Internet. Probably, electronic mail now supports the work of more than 10 million people, with more joining as regular users each day.

If text-based electronic mail communications over packet-switched computer communication networks marks the early period of Netville, the World Wide Web (WWW) represents the last great technical triumph of the community.[5] The WWW began in 1989 at the European nuclear research center CERN as an inhouse strategy to use computers to help coordinate projects. The essence of the WWW concept was the construction of a "browser" that allowed a user to move across the Internet looking into specially prepared files stored for the purpose of being browsed. The key idea was that the reader went looking for information rather than the user specifically distributing the information. The concept received the name World Wide Web at CERN in 1990. In December of 1991, a poster session on the WWW was presented at the Hypertext conference, marking the first notification by this previously unrecognized group of hypertext developers in the established hypertext community. By late 1992, the WWW was in operation, hosted on computers at major energy laboratories and supporting the work of the global high-energy physics research community. That year, developers at the U.S. National Center for Supercomputer Applications began creating an X-Windows interface for the WWW called XMosaic. Mosaic demonstrated the full potential of the WWW. By late 1993, the WWW began catching on in the popular press. In 1994, Mark Andreessen and other Mosaic developers left NCSA to form Mosaic Communications Corporation, a private firm that later became the firm Netscape. In February

---

[5]Relatively little history of the development of the World Wide Web is available at this point. We appreciate the assistance of Roy Fielding. See http://www.ics.uci.edu/~fielding/socweb/history.html. See also http://www.w3.org/hypertext/WWW/History.html.

of 1995, the WWW was a centerpiece of the G7 meeting of world economic powers.

The Institutional Coalition

The Netville of the ARPANET/Internet era was born of the union of two powerful U.S. institutions, the Department of Defense (DOD) Advanced Research Projects Agency (ARPA)[6] and the academy of research universities and laboratories. Netville grew within an institutional zone of protection that allowed unity to evolve in an otherwise technically and geographically diverse community. The coalition also provided technical and economic incentives to explore the possibilities of the technology, and protected Netville from the interference of other institutions that would have introduced schism and disorder. Two key institutional values held the coalition together and shaped Netville: the demand for technological superiority and the belief in the principle of universal access.

The impetus to develop "internetworking" among organizations can rightly be ascribed to ARPA. ARPA's central institutional value was the maintainence of technological superiority. In the early 1960s ARPA hired the RAND Corporation to conduct a study into methods of building a robust command and control network capable of surviving a major nuclear attack (Newlin, 1995). ARPA's charter under DOD was to direct and fund research that would, when carried to fruition, protect the United States from "technological surprise." ARPA had keen interest in computers. The first computer network system, SAGE, was a DOD effort, and there was widespread belief in DOD that computers held great promise for U.S. defense application (Abbate, 1994).

The notion that a computer-supported communications network might help the country in the event of a nuclear attack was only one reason for ARPA's interest, however. ARPA had founded the Information Processing Techniques Office (IPTO) in 1962 to support cutting-edge computer research projects in areas such as timesharing, artificial intelligence, and graphics. This work required expensive hardware at each research site, and the requests for even more expensive computers were growing.[7] By 1964,

---

[6]During its history, ARPA also has been named DARPA, but we refer to the agency throughout as ARPA. This section draws considerably from Abbate (1994).

[7]Abbate (1994) noted that the main IPTO research centers at that time were Stanford Research Institute (timesharing), Stanford Universtiy (artifical intelligence and timesharing), UC Berkeley (timesharing), University of Utah (graphics), UCLA (timesharing), RAND Corporation (graphics), Systems Development Corporation (timesharing), the University of Illinois (supercomputing), Carnegie-Mellon University (artificial intelligence and timesharing), Bolt, Beranek and Newman Company (BBN) (timesharing), MIT-Lincoln Laboratories (timesharing, artificial intelligence, and graphics), and Harvard (graphics). BBN and RAND played key roles in the early technology endeavors; most of the aforementioned organizations were involved in the first 15-node ARPANET of 1971.

RAND had produced a plan for a spider weblike network with computer nodes at each intersection, and the capacity for messages to be broken into individually addressed packets and shipped out over the network in a seek-and-find manner to be reassembled at the destination's node. IPTO recognized that this concept could address the nuclear attack problem, but as important to its institutional needs, a network could help alleviate the rising demand for computer power among their contractors. Instead of taking computers to each contractor, a network would allow the contractors to come to the computers. Work on the RAND concept was underway soon, and by 1969 the network was named ARPANET after its sponsor.

ARPA had long been in the business of supporting research at leading universities and other academic like research centers such as RAND. After the RAND report, ARPA began a network development effort among its major contractors. ARPA and IPTO had long operated in a collegial, academic-like way, and the IPTO leadership had to work to enlist the efforts of its major contractors who were concerned that the network proposal was just a ploy to interfere with contractor work and deny contractors needed computers (Abbate, 1994). Nevertheless, in time a working agenda for the network projects was built around a plan to connect the key contractor sites together. In effect, the ARPANET was to evolve as a physical map of the existing social network structure of IPTO. Much of the early development effort of the ARPANET illustrates the powerful force of the two key managerial strategies of IPTO: the concept of "layering," which meant dividing complex project tasks up into building blocks to be handled by different contractors; and the decentralized management style for which IPTO was noted.

ARPA's quest for technological superiority was matched by an equally powerful need among its academic partners to maintain open access to scientific and technical knowlege within the academy. A key event in the evolution of the ARPANET was the awarding to faculty in the Computer Science Department at University of California at Berkeley in the early 1970s a large grant to develop what would become the key computing infrastructure of the ARPANET. The early ARPANET was conceived, in part, to allow networking among a hodge-podge collection of machines used by various contractors. This was necessary to accommodate the different contractors, and it was important for IPTO's scheme to reduce computer costs by bringing researchers to computers. But as a practical matter, the heterogeneity of computers made network building and communication more difficult. The Berkeley strategy eventually focused on the AT&T UNIX operating system, which had been developed originally as a single-user version of the powerful MULTICS timesharing system built at MIT with DOD support.

UNIX had a number of advantages as a networking platform, but AT&T was prohibited from exploiting these advantages due to constraints on it as a regulated telephone service provider. AT&T refused to license UNIX to commercial companies at reasonable rates for fear of competition by others using their own creation. But AT&T's attitude toward universities was different. UNIX had been developed at Bell Laboratories, a highly academic research center, with close ties to the university community. AT&T released UNIX, including source code, to universities for essentially no cost, thus making one of the most powerful and innovative timesharing systems available to university researchers. Of equal importance to the future of the ARPANET, Digital Equipment Corporation (DEC) had released a line of powerful minicomputers on which UNIX would run. DEC had been involved in networking research for some time. It also had been started by two academics from MIT, and the company followed very generous policies for donating and discounting their powerful PDP-11 (and eventually VAX) machines.

A confluence of powerful forces thus leveraged Berkeley's role in AR-PANET development. The generally relaxed and collegial IPTO tradition provided researchers with support and left them free to pursue their interests. AT&T provided UNIX source code and licenses at low cost, and permitted modifications and variations on its product as long as they were for educational and research purposes. DEC provided Berkeley and other computer science departments with free or low-cost UNIX-capable computers of great power and flexibility. The Berkeley faculty were already socially networked to other university computer science departments, through the "invisible college" (Crane, 1972; Pickering & King, 1995). These social networks kept communication flowing, including communication related to the evolving ARPANET project. As the Berkeley researchers and developers adapted UNIX for ARPANET support, they distributed their developments to others in the social network. As the computer network itself grew and became more robust, it became the distribution vehicle through the social network, and Berkeley became a key site for distribution of essential technology such as UNIX sources, technical information, and documentation required to keep the existing nodes going and new nodes growing. Before long, a significant virtual community within the invisible college had been built to explore, construct, maintain, and exploit the evolving network. Netville began in the small among the relatively closed community of IPTO contractors, but Berkeley's establishment of UNIX running on DEC machines as the backbone of the network enabled Netville to spread rapidly through university computer science departments. This phenomenon might well have been history's first virtual urban sprawl.

Netville's shared focus on exploration of emergent technological opportunities stands in sharp contrast to most research and development efforts to create an envisioned artifact according to some developmental "life cycle." The Netville developers built their world around themselves, piece by piece, in response to their environment. New developments arose from the continual growth of the network of machines and users, which brought both an almost continuous demand for cooperative work to solve emerging problems and a continuous supply of new talent to solve the problems. Netville was developed by enthusiasts, interested in the technologies of computers and digital communication, working to solve problems they found interesting. Neither the problems nor their solutions were entirely technical; Netville flourished because it evolved solutions to social problems in tandem with solutions to technical problems. This combination of technical and social endeavor provided the core of the concept of cyberspace (RFC 1118, 1989, RFC 1173, 1990).

Collectively, Netville members comprised a diverse geographical and technical group. Members of Netville originally came from research universities and laboratories spread across the United States, and subsequently across continents. Typical members of Netville were socially bound by institutional ties to their emerging discipline of computer science, and to their universities as undergraduates, graduate students, systems administrators, and faculty, or to the military and commercial firms that were part of the evolving ARPA networking scheme. Soon, others such as high school students, former university students, and colleagues in the nondefense commercial sector, managed to persuade systems administrators at these institutions to let them have accounts, and they became members of Netville too. The technical diversity of Netville was due to the great variety of computers and operating systems being used by members of the growing community. This diversity in a planned, top–down implementation effort might have precluded rapid growth. In the loosely structured, flexible community of Netville, the diversity necessitated, and thereby also facilitated, the development of workarounds that allowed distributed work toward a common purpose.

It is tempting to think of Netville diversity as ratification of a libertarian ideology of individualism triumphing over government-imposed order. In fact, the members of Netville were government-supported community participants in a vital coalition of the military/industrial/university (MIU) complex that enabled all coalition members to develop common values and work together, smoothing over the heterogeneity each embodied (cf. Leslie, 1993). This coalition began in 1948 with the collapse of the pacifist wing of the Democrat party and the collapse of the isolationist wing of the Republican party, producing a bipartisan, activist coalition pursuing the newly articulated foreign policy of communist containment. This coalition brought two powerful stimuli to the MIU complex: great sums of money, and an intense expectation of extraordinary performance. The Cold War was being fought in earnest, and the task of the MIU complex was to strengthen and protect the national interest through maintenance of technical superiority. The military and other government agencies enlisted to fight the Cold War provided money to research universities and laboratories. Under this arrangement, the military received products and ideas from the industry and the academy, whereas the industry obtained contracts and the academy obtained funding to undertake interesting and challenging research projects and support bright students. Different government agencies played different roles in the MIU complex, but the primary patron of academic research in computer science was ARPA.

The coalition between ARPA and the academy encouraged Netville to build the network in two ways. First, ARPA provided sufficient equipment and funding to researchers to explore the possibilities of networking technology over an extended period of time, without the hindrance of contract deliverables and deadlines. Netville members were given machines, communication lines, and the time to explore and develop networking. Second, the coalition protected Netville by hiding its developments from other institutions such as the market and regulatory bodies that might have influenced the directions the network took. Netville members did not compete to produce solutions as they might have in a market situation. Instead they shared partial solutions, worked cooperatively on each other's software, and then made the results available to everyone. The standards they adopted were not subject to any external regulations. In contrast to a market/regulation regime, in which anticipatory standards play crucial development roles, standards in Netville developed in an organic manner through informal communications and, eventually, through a generally collegial ARPA-supported authority called the Internet Engineering Task Force (Crocker, 1993).[8] By protecting the borders of the great divide in which Netville worked, special institutional interests within the MIU complex created a temporary and sheltered zone of opportunity in which Netville members themselves defined the criteria of success. In short, the Netville community was given a chance to construct its own reality—an almost unheard of opportunity in the market/regulatory regime.

The character of the ARPA/academy coalition played a critical role in defining the way in Netville conducted networking research. ARPA provided money and a demand for performance, but it was less interested in the process of research than in results. This left the academy free to use ARPA's resources and its demands for performance to define the manner of network research. The leading academic members of Netville soon established as routine the social conventions of "open science" common to academic research institutions. Under the influence of these principles Netville adopted three core values: intellectual curiosity, informal meritocracy, and what we call an egalitarian presumption. Intellectual curiosity meant that finding a new or better solution to a problem was its own reward; cost–benefit analysis was never the first criterion. Status was based on merit, which was based on performance as judged informally by peers:

---

[8]The standards that Netville created and followed began as treaties, which only through their adherence to them turned into standards.

Those who developed solutions that "worked" received distinction within Netville, with rewards such as assignment of "guru"[9] status among the other developers. The egalitarian presumption was embodied in a tradition of accepting any person to the Netville community, from whatever background, as long as the person could do good work. Technical expertise, as measured in comparison to other community members, was the passport for entrants to Netville. These three common values enabled the group, otherwise heterogeneous and distributed, to communicate and work together in an efficient and effective manner.

One consequence of Netville's adherence to these principles was the emergence of an ethos of open access to the network. In part this open access principle was an extension of the open science assumption of easy access to academic literature. In the case of the network, the concept was extended through the meritocratic and egalitarian features of the community that required easy access by all who might contribute to the cause of building superior technology. Access was necessary both to make improvements and to share them, and perhaps as important, access enabled far-flung members to earn respect within the Netville community and thereby gain the social benefits so important to Netville's voluntary contributors. Open access brought problems, however, and required implementing rules of play to govern behavior of community members. Rules of play were the conditions to which all members of Netville should adhere while contributing to the development of the network and benefiting from the work of others. It was the rules of play that ensured that the technologies of the emerging Internet remained interoperable. For example, Netville adopted a rule under which all sites connected to the network would follow a specific format for packaging of electronic mail messages. Rules of play constituted conditions for entry and continued presence, and were not negotiable. Yet the rules themselves had to be maintained flexibly in order to honor the goal of technological superiority. Freezing conventions and standards too solidly would retard adoption and deployment of improvements in the network.

Maintaining effective rules of play in a dynamic and evolving game was perhaps the most daunting of Netville's challenges. A balance had to be struck between imposing the order required to maintain functionality and growth in the community through addition of new members, and the mandate of technological superiority that required constant, disruptive improvements in the network that bound the community together. The balance was achieved only because the collegial governance structure of the community adhered to a "lowest common denominator" principle, in which functionality was maintained by facilitating gateways, workarounds, kludges, and tricks to enable heterogeneous computing and

---

[9]According to the dictionary, a guru is a teacher or a mentor. In the computer science world, anyone with an intimate understanding of a particular system or machine often makes their skills known as a "guru" capabilities. Gurus usually help others with problems related to their topic of special knowledge, and are sometimes widely known for their expertise.

communication systems to interconnect. There was no effort to make the overall network "efficient" in the sense of optimizing performance at the local or global levels. The performance of the local level was left entirely to the locals, who could join the larger Netville community by adopting a relatively simple, albeit changing, regime of technical and social conventions. The global level was heavily subsidized but relatively unconstrained with respect to expectations, so it could respond in a flexible manner to the needs of the locals. The voluntary nature of network membership enabled the powerful streamlining mechanism of self-selection, in which those who wanted to play joined and accepted the rules, and those who did not did not.

In all, the remarkable success of Netville was due to the unlikely but fascinating marriage of institutional interests that were complementary in just the right ways. The impetus and solidarity provided by the Cold War, channeled through the mechanism of ARPA, provided large amounts of money and a strong expectation of performance at the frontier of technological development. However, unlike heavily bureaucratized "procurement" programs, ARPA's patronage left the construction and maintenance of social conventions required to deliver the hoped-for technology to the technological community itself. The dominance of the technical community by academic computer science resulted in the establishment of powerful principles not always found in technical development efforts: intellectual curiosity as a key incentive to the work, suppressing "mission goals" in many cases; informal meritocracy as the core performance evaluation mechanism; and a presumption of egalitarianism that, together with the meritocratic ideal, required open access to the network. The heterogeneity of the Netville community, together with the challenge of maintaining network order while pushing the goal of technological superiority, required the creation of flexible and informal social governance schemes that would probably not have been feasible under a more formally organized program. Although some might argue that the ARPA/Internet succeeded in spite of Netville's "disorganization," it is much more likely that studied disregard for formal organization was the key to its success. Netville was, in fact, highly organized at the lowest levels through powerful social conventions sustained by the key institutional forces of ARPA and the academy. This embedded organizational strength of Netville, brought to bear in a dynamic and evolving manner without the distortions of top–down "corrections," is perhaps the greatest innovation of Netville.

Emblematic Developments in the Rise of Netville

In this section we explore three significant, interrelated developments in cyberspace: the utility of electronic mail, its underlying infrastructure the Transmission Control Protocol and Internet Protocol (TCP/IP), and its superordinate social convention the Domain Name Service (DNS). We demonstrate how the institutional principles and predilections discussed earlier shaped the way in which these systems were built. The examples substantiate our belief that these systems were affected by the institutional coalition in three ways: They were typically built in response to emergent problems, they were not planned, and they were comprised of both technical and social solutions.

Electronic Mail. Person-to-person electronic mail, the most rapidly adopted utility on the ARPA/Internet, was not part of ARPA's original network plan. ARPA had two agendas for the network. From a military standpoint, it sought a robust, distributed, asynchronous, autonomous communication system capable of surviving massive nuclear strikes. This was a "proof of concept" objective, aimed at showing whether or not such a communication system could be built. From a more pedestrian defense research management standpoint, it was searching for a way to aggregate the efforts and costs of geographically dispersed researchers. This was a practical objective, tied to the political chore of justifying ongoing research investments in expensive computing infrastructure for ARPA researchers. The network was seen as a mechanism for cost saving by allowing distributed researchers to share computing resources through file transmission protocol (FTP) and remote login capabilities.

The academic researchers charged with the development of the network had experienced electronic mail on multiuser computers, and saw extension of the utility to different research locations as useful to research across the network. Systems administrators in the research domain had already begun to try to get the computers they ran to communicate so people could send electronic mail locally, but this was difficult due to the variety of different machine platforms. Through sharing of expertise and ideas, researchers at local sites acquired the know-how to connect local machines together, and in time they linked their sites to others across the network. By the early 1970s users of the ARPA/Internet were communicating with each other on a regular basis over the network. The members of Netville, still a small community, used informal agreements to ensure that everyone could read the messages sent across the network.

Over the following 10 years the number of machines connected to the network grew. The decreasing technical costs of joining and the lure of the Netville community brought more machines and more people. By 1983 ARPA split the network up into two parts, MILNET, the military network and the ARPANET for research, together comprising the ARPA Internet.[10] The Netville leadership realized that growth would bring the need to standardize electronic mail formats to allow everyone to communicate with everyone else on the network. Increasing diversity of machine types and

---

[10]An Internet means multiple networks: an Internetwork. At this time there were two, the ARPANET and MILNET.

participants would soon overwhelm the informal standards process, leading to incompatible electronic mail domains. Using the network itself as the platform for discussion, Netville community deliberated for a year before agreeing on the simplest format, the memo (RFC 822, 1982). The memo became a formal rule of play, a lowest common denominator standard to which all mail systems must comply (Crocker, 1993). They recorded this in a working document, the Request for Comments (RFC)[11] that served as an online document of the standards in use (Comer, 1991). This allowed a wide range of mail readers to be built that would run on different kinds of machines, but still be compatible with each other.

By formalizing the rules of play for electronic mail, Netville created the opportunity for individual sites to develop their own systems and principles for electronic mail communications. Different mail handlers including MH, Berkeley Mail and R-Mail were developed and deployed, and the administrators at the distributed sites worked collaboratively with each other to develop state-of-the-art electronic mail applications that they subsequently maintained for multiple sites on the network. New system development was not a condition for continued use of the network, but many systems administrators adhered to the principle that users should help advance the field. In this way the distributed community of Netville members reinforced the principle of seeking technological superiority across the network.

TCP/IP and DNS. The development of electronic mail was crucially dependent on two socially constructed, complementary components of the broad network vision: the Transmission Control Protocol and Internet Protocol, collectively known as TCP/IP; and the Domain Name Service, or DNS. Through TCP/IP and DNS the users of any given machine could inhabit Netville by communication with other machines and other people. Ideally, any would-be Netville member could easily connect his or her platform to the network. This was a "low-barriers-to-entry" vision that required a set of technical rules of play that would specify exactly how all data would travel across the networks, and how addresses were to be constructed and normalized.

TCP/IP was an essential component of the networking vision (Quarterman, 1993). The IP defined the data to be sent across the network by sorting

---

[11] An RFC begins life as a request for comments made by an individual or site concerning a change that they believe should be made to the network. These are then discussed by the developer community, anyone who chooses to have an opinion. Finally, when agreement is reached these documents are kept as the standards documentation that informs Netville of the new change. Everyone is expected to observe the new changes (Crocker, 1987). The history of RFCs is well captured by a quote from Vinton Cerf (1993): "In April 1969, Steve issued the very first Request For Comment. He observed that we were just graduate students at the time and so had no authority. So we had to find a way to document what we were doing without acting like we were imposing anything on anyone. He came up with the RFC methodology to say, "Please comment on this, and tell us what you think.""

information into standard packets that could be transmitted. Under IP each "host" machine was given a unique IP "address," a number to which could be attached attendant routing information. TCP was developed to support IP by providing a reliable mechanism of sending data over the network from one machine to another (Comer, 1991). In addition to the important task of supplying funds to develop the TCP/IP standard, ARPA moved its own machines to TCP/IP. This soon brought other researchers doing work with ARPA to adopt TCP/IP so their systems could link to ARPA systems. Without direct mandates, ARPA influenced the setting and adoption of the TCP/IP regime that became a vital component of Netville's infrastructure. The establishment of TCP/IP as a "standard" occurred with the release of Berkeley Software Distribution (BSD) UNIX 4.2 that incorporated TCP/IP (Quarterman, 1993). BSD made its software available to other research institutions at distribution cost, ensuring the rapid spread of BSD's TCP/IP implementation among academic computer science systems administrators already familiar with and partial to BSD UNIX (Quarterman, 1990; King, 1991). It is estimated that the release of BSD UNIX 4.2 alone resulted in the conversion of 90% of academic computer science departments to TCP/IP (Comer, 1991).

Once TCP/IP was established as the standard for network membership the demand for IP machine addresses went up rapidly. Machines running TCP/IP required an IP address, and this address had to conform to three conditions: It had to conform to an exact format so as to be recognizable throughout the network; it had to be unique so messages would go to the right places; and it had to be formally registered to enable universal and consistent distribution of address tables throughout the network. The distributed Netville community could never expect to exert such exacting control over the vital task of addressing; once again, ARPA aided the Netville cause by assigning the ARPA-supported Network Information Center (NIC) the duty of managing the assignment of IP addresses to new network members (Baker, 1993). Anyone who wished to connect a machine to the network would register their machine with the NIC in order to acquire their unique IP address.

In principle, address control was simple because IP addresses are built from a straightforward numbering scheme that was tractable in network management terms. Unfortunately, an IP address such as *128.10.2.30* did not give much information to Netville members who were trying to communicate with individuals at specific sites. Netville users desired that addresses be accompanied by names: For example, *128.10.2.30* could be called *localhost*, and *localhost* in turn could have other information attached to the name to designate the institutional location of the address (e.g., a specific computer science department in a given university). Adding naming to IP addressing was not a major technical challenge—one simply assigned given addresses specific and unique names, and the resulting tables were used to route messages to the right locations. However although Netville members might be indifferent to the IP address their machines received, they were very particular about the names they used, and they usually wanted to pick their own names. A larger population of names increased the problems of redundancy—a disaster in addressing schemes. In addition, addition of names substantially increased the work involved in updating tables, because every machine linked to the network had to be updated when each new host was added. System administrators at each site bore the brunt of this work, and soon demanded that something be done to reduce the load on them. Netville's solution was to create a new set of rules and principles implemented in part with a technical solution called the Domain Name Service, or DNS (RFC 882, 1983).

DNS structures the assignment of names on the network and converts those names to their unique IP addresses. It enforces a formal naming convention through the concept of domains, which are authority zones within which specific host machines reside. The domains are organized hierarchically when possible: For example, within the "education" domain (edu) a given university is a subdomain, a department within that university another subdomain, and a given machine the local host; for example, *localhost.csdept.stateu.edu*. Table 1.1 shows the common formats agreed to for the types of organizations. For each type of organization, there is a technical system known as a name server that knows about the organizations and machines connected to it.[12] When a packet arrives at the name server the IP address of the machine that correlates to the name is located and required information is sent back up the chain until the address becomes known. These servers work collaboratively to decode the entire name and translate it into the correct address (Krol, 1993). This solution had the advantage of controlling the naming at the higher level of organizations shown in Table 1.1, while allowing choice in names at the lower level domains as long as there were no addressing conflicts identified by the DNS. In the case of conflicts, precedence typically determines the outcome: The first organization to claim a name usually gets to keep it. This has led to controversy, as individuals moved early to register names such as *mtv.com* that could be mistaken for widely recognized company addresses.[13]

Success in the Great Divide

The preceding examples demonstrate how a desire to achieve and maintain technological superiority and universal access shaped the development strategy of Netville. Electronic mail began life as a vision of a technical

---

[12]We have explained DNS in its conceptual format. The technical reality of the system means that each name server actually holds much larger parts of the naming hierarchy than the conceptual model implies (Comer, 1991). The conceptual model makes understanding the relationship between servers much easier to understand.

[13]The cable television network MTV has in fact sued a former employee who retained the Internet name mtv.com before the network had any interest in the Internet, demanding release of the address to the company (cf. New Multimedia Reviews, January 27, 1995).

TABLE 1.1

Internet Addresses for Different Organizations

Extension	Definition
.gov	government organization
.edu	educational organization
.mil	military organization
.com	commercial organization
.net	network organization
.us, .uk, .au, etc....	geographical location
.org	other types of organizations

system to be used by Netville members to build and maintain their community. The drive for electronic mail eventually required Netville to abandon at least some of the dream of local autonomy and develop rules of play by which members at any site with suitable hardware and software could join the community. TCP/IP was created to facilitate ease of access as well as reliability in the network, and the DNS was created to establish and maintain order in the vital area of addressing. These reforms did not simply happen: They were born of the institutional coalition of ARPA and the academy, through the values, guidelines, and protection those institutions offered Netville.

These vital developments occurred as community movements, galvanized through the coordinating authority of key institutional players. None of them followed a software life cycle of development, with extensive requirements analysis, specification, and so on. Indeed, they were created with a remarkable and refreshing lack of concern about "methodology." They arose in response to environmental conditions, most commonly the shared problems of the ever growing community of network users. Somehow the resolution of these problems maintained a balance between the need for community-wide coordination and local autonomy to facilitate innovation. Innovations evolved not by pursuit of a formal planning and development process, but through informal discussion about visions and solutions, supported by a flow of partial solutions through the network. As members learned about the issues they posted questions and suggestions, and when possible sent replies recommending hacks and fixes. Community members designed patches for each other's software, emphasizing a culture of hacker-driven[14] computer-supported cooperative work. What makes Netville particularly fascinating is that it was sui generis: a computer-supported cooperative work (CSCW) project that got its start as an effort to build the

---

[14]We use hacker in the original sense of the meaning, someone who develops code by continually iterating versions and testing. We do not imply that hackers behaved unlawfully or intended harm to other systems, as hacker has come to mean subsequently.

computer support network through which the CSCW would take place. Netville was literally a case of the mechanics making their own tools.

Netville ended up building more than just solutions to technical problems; it also ended up designing solutions to social problems. These social solutions were developed out of necessity through online discussions, through resolutions recorded in RFCs, and through the establishment of rules and principles to govern the actions of their members. Netville members were clearly technically proficient, but they proved to be socially proficient as well, and it seems likely that the technical innovations of Netville could not have occurred without some of the social innovations they developed. But behind every innovation lies a vital context of institutional factors that at the least enabled and arguably encouraged particular social innovations. The curious mix of institutional forces in the MIU nexus, and in the ARPA/academy coalition, sheltered and facilitated the social innovations that make Netville so fascinating.[15]

Star (1993) argues that living in the great divide requires managing the paradox of building a unified community where the prevailing ideology is the maintenance of heterogeneity. Netville accommodated the paradox, and in so doing built the Internet, an "open system" where no one "owns" the fundamental vision and everyone gets to participate, but an ordered and regulated world in which certain rules are enforced with great care (Comer, 1991). The institutional coalition between ARPA and the academy provided the social glue that Netville leveraged in order to create the network. The goals of technical superiority and universal access encouraged individual Netville members to innovate, but within an understood set of constraints required to maintain openness. Netville's rules of play were not unlike Star's distributed passage points that bind heterogeneous actors through a common language, a series of structural and symbolic means of ordering and controlling the action. Using this common language, Netville defined and built technical solutions to problems of transportation, TCP/IP, communication, electronic mail and USENET, and notation systems, DNS, for all network users.

THE FALL OF NETVILLE

Any enterprise that arises in the great divide, even if enabled by the great divide, remains vulnerable to the dangers inherent in that divide. The powerful alliance of ARPA and the academy made life in the great divide sustainable for a time, during which Netville enjoyed an unmolested development domain. The great divide, by Bowker et al.'s (in press) characterization, can be mistakenly seen as a desert, devoid of life. But it is not so

---

[15]Netville's accomplishments are impressive, but they should not be seen as historically unique. Other communities, out of necessity, have developed highly elaborate technical and social solutions to the problems of exchanging information necessary to common enterprise (Forster and King, 1995).

in any a priori sense. The great divide is barren as a matter of choice by those communities that border it; they make it a desert by refusing to occupy it. This disregard for the activity in the divide gives inhabitants of the divide a peculiar freedom. In time, members of adjacent communities become attracted to the activity in the divide, and move into the divide to colonize it. In the late 1980s new and powerful institutional forces that were previously ignorant of, or at least indifferent to, Netville and its accomplishments began the process of colonizing the divide. By 1990 the fall of Netville had begun, illustrated by a mechanism we call "patron swapping."

Institutional patrons such as the DOD, ARPA, NSF (National Science Foundation), and the academy played crucial roles in shaping Netville. But the relationships among these patrons were never very stable, and over time the key financial responsibility for supporting the Netville community wandered from one institutional player to another. In the middle of the 1980s the institutional role of ARPA began to decline. This might sound strange, given that ARPA played such a key role in the creation of Netville. Why did Netville not become a military-dominated bureaucracy, or at least a separately governed bureaucracy subservient to the military's needs, as some of the Department of Energy's laboratories are? The answer, we argue, is that Netville had constructed the desired packet-switched network technology ARPA wanted to see proven. Now ARPA and the DOD establishment could take networking "in house" for their needs without further involvement by Netville.

Equally important, by the mid 1980s it was clear to ARPA that once the researchers were hooked together they would remain connected whether or not ARPA paid for the connection. The ARPANET had become an important vehicle for communication among academics with access to it. From the landmark work of Granovetter (1973) on weak tie social networks, Pickering and King (1995) suggested that strong incentives cause research communities to exploit communication technologies. Electronic mail over networks was an excellent technology for this purpose. The research community, including those working for DOD, would keep their networks operating. Considerable additional impetus was provided for networking in the academic world by the contemporaneous development of grass-roots networking enterprises such as BITNET and CSNET.[16] These network enterprises

---

[16]The story of BITNET and CSNET deserve a full accounting elsewhere. Briefly, BITNET, which stands for "Because It's Time NETwork," grew out of IBM-sponsored network innovations among a number of academic business schools, and eventually grew to encompass a great many academic disciplines. CSNET was an NSF-sponsored program to extend ARPANET-like access to the academic computer science community not formally a part of the ARPA research structure. CSNET is particularly important because it was a key factor in the networking component of the NSF Supercomputer Centers initiatives that located powerful computers at distributed locations throughout the US. The NSFNet backbone of high-speed links that tied these centers together provided the essential trunks for rapidly growing network traffic during the explosive growth in the Internet in the late 1980s and early 1990s. NSF has since backed away from support of the Internet trunks, and the infrastructure at this point is largely privatized.

had emerged to link faculty in business schools, non-ARPA-funded computer science departments, and other university departments. These networks subsequently linked many European research institutions together as well. In the mid-1980s gateways between these networks were created, and over the next half of the decade all of the major network initiatives would be folded into the Internet. By the late 1980s there was a broad cross-section of commercial and research institutions connected together, but still Netville owned the most significant development rights to the network.

In 1990, ARPA, long a vital patron of Netville, signaled its clear intentions to withdraw. The age of the Internet arrived, and with it a new constellation of institutional forces. From this point onward the character of the Internet began a slow and irrevocable change, from a research network to a more commercial successor. Slowly but surely the founding institutional coalition disappeared from the network, leaving Netville's borders open to new influences. Some of these were very much like the earlier academic forces—the noncomputer science academic communities enabled by the big-science networking initiative within NSF and the ancillary expansion of networking into campus computing centers that brought in the humanities, social sciences, and so on. Much more important, however, was the rise of commercial activity on the net. Initially this was in the form of active participation of the research divisions of for-profit corporations as users of the network (Kahin, 1990). In time, however, this grew into a much more serious matter. For one thing, use spread well beyond the research divisions into the general departments of such organizations, so the Internet became a more general-purpose network. Perhaps most significant, commercial companies offering Internet access and services entered the picture, such as Prodigy and America Online, bringing the Internet into the home. Internet began to be advertised as a place to meet people, to ask questions through the bulletin boards and distribution lists, to find answers, and to do business. Many new users joined, inspired by the visions of thousands of users online, and encouraged by the cheap and readily available technologies. The hype of the "information superhighway" finally was crystallized by the newly elected Clinton administration in 1992 (King & Kraemer, 1995).

Some idea of the significance of this growth can be seen in Fig. 1.1. The long-standing use of the educational (edu) domain has continued to grow, but use by the commercial (com) domain has overtaken the educational domain. The new users of cyberspace have had an enormous effect on the character of the network, and in the process they have profoundly changed Netville. The new users often violate social norms long-cherished and adhered to in Netville, either through ignorance, or simply because it is

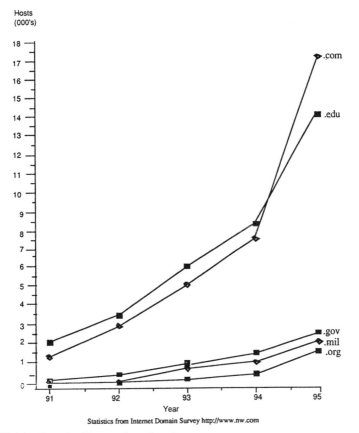

FIG. 1.1.   Growth of Internet host domains.

possible to do so without meaningful penalty. The new users also have
attracted interest from institutional players not traditionally part of the
Netville scene: software development companies, cable TV companies,
telephone companies, Hollywood, and so on who wish to grab a piece of
the market they believe lies dormant in the Internet culture and surrounding cyberspace. These new players have little understanding of and/or use
for the culture of Netville, or the elaborate social conventions and mores
that sustained that culture and enabled the production of the very artifacts
that so entice them. At the same time, the Internet has attracted groups such
as the Computer Professionals for Social Responsibility (CPSR) and the
Electronic Freedom Foundation (EFF) who see it as their mission to contest
these commercial visions of the future of cyberspace, often with ideologies
close to those of the dying Netville. However, these defenders of Netville
values appear to misunderstand the processes that created Netville just as
the new commercial players do, and their arguments about building and
sustaining a viable, Netville-like social enterprise seem naive. The future of

cyberspace now lies clearly "beyond the Internet" (National Academy of Sciences, 1994).

It seems inevitable that as governmental support for Netville's creation decreases and the commercial and market interest increases, Netville itself will come under new institutional directions. There will be changes in governance structures, which will alter what can happen with Netville, and there will be new objectives. For example, the egalitarian spirit will likely be replaced by some form of equity influence, reflective of capitalist enterprise, and the influence of key players will revolve more around successful product development than on clever expressions of intellectual curiosity. Current Netville members may find room to continue their work, possibly in ways close to those they now follow, but they are not likely to experience the same degree and kind of influence over the future of Netville's creations as they enjoyed in the past. The paradigm of exploratory research that Netville grew up with will be replaced by an ideology of efficient production.

There is little doubt that the founding citizens of Netville have lost their ownership of the electronic frontier. Their cozy home in the great divide is rapidly being colonized by commercial organizations, followed closely by regulators who wish to control access, uses, content, and so on. The citizens of Netville will never regain control over cyberspace. Curiously, the citizens of Netville can be said to have manufactured their own downfall. By developing a technically sophisticated network and encouraging universal access for all, they maintained low barriers to entry to a highly desirable resource. The institutional alliance of ARPA and the academy created a vibrant space in the great divide full of resources and freedom. But the institutions involved never intended to create a new world. The Netville enterprise was a project, like many other military/academy projects, that went before. In time, the project had to end. Whether the citizens of Netville "deserve" the fate that has befallen them is an interesting question. Some of the early citizens of Netville have found very lucrative niches in the new commercial order, and have apparently found happiness doing so. In those cases, they are not complaining but some of their colleagues from Netville days who were not so fortunate might. In any case, the whole Netville phenomenon and what it spawned was unforeseen except by a few visionaries who were not taken seriously, so the question of what it means to deserve the fate of Netville is a troublesome question.

Two futures for Netville seem likely at this point, if one considers the future in a superficial way. In one, Netville joins the list of legendary ghost towns with little but relics and ruins to mark what was once a vibrant and progressive social venture. In this vision, the social glue and institutional strengths that held Netville together are slowly eroded by powerful new interests with different visions and goals, and eventually there is nothing left but the empty buildings and dusty streets of a bygone era. Life goes on elsewhere.

In the other vision Netville evolves in the model of Las Vegas. Las Vegas was a sleepy village until the lure of the Dynamo brought can-do engineers and builders, backed by huge sums of federal money, to build a great hydroelectric dam across the Colorado River at Boulder Canyon. Boulder City and Las Vegas were the construction boomtowns of the Hoover Dam Project. Boulder City slipped into oblivion when the dam was done, but Las Vegas did not. Las Vegas capitalized on its rapidly developed infrastructure of vice-filled entertainment, which served the huge dam project, leveraged by the cheap electricity produced by the dam. Brilliant electric lights and a flair for naughty-as-nice brought Las Vegas from construction boomtown to entertainment capital. Few of the old engineers and construction workers were visible in the resulting glitter, but Las Vegas lived on. Some of the Netville wizards have already gone on to their fortunes, having commercialized and exploited those elements to which they could lay claim. It is easy to imagine Netville's future as similar to that of Las Vegas—an icon in a new age of altered social mores and values, released by the power of new technology, in what was once the desert of the great divide. In this view, Netville will live on as a shining but distant and distorted reflection of former glory.

The ghost town and boomtown scenarios are compelling visions of how the future of how Netville will evolve, but they do not offer any specific explanations about the challenges Netville faces if it is to survive in the new order.[17] They also do not reflect some of the nuances that are likely to govern whatever happens. We argue that Netville is much more complex than either of these explanations suggests. It has been a construction boomtown, and probably shares some of the fate of former boomtowns. But it is also a strange and heretofore unseen thing: an online development community that was built around the very artifact it was seeking to build. In this section we outline some of the factors that may work together to affect the fall of Netville.

We are watching the dissolution Netville as it is happening. Much of what we think will be important is necessarily speculative, making it impossible to offer empirical proof to support our claims. We must therefore offer an assessment of the ongoing changes in light of the fact of patron swapping noted earlier, and the implications of this for what we believe to be central values that caused Netville to arise as it has. Presumably, if these change, Netville will change. We focus on phenomena that will produce profound changes in Netville values: proprietary fame, the loss of novelty, and the rise of path dependency.

---

[17]Boomtown is becoming an increasingly popular metaphor for describing how the Internet has grown in the last few years. A recent description of the initial public offering by Netscape Communications Corporation says: "So what exactly was America buying into with such enthusiasm last week? The Internet, of course, that boomtown of the wired world" (Quitner, 1995).

Proprietary Fame

The ARPA/academy nexus of Netville was not concerned with and did not enable a strong connection between genuine equity rights in development of new technology and the fame that might attend such contributions. All the efforts of the enterprise were owned by the institutions that supported the work, not by the individuals involved. And, unlike the field of physical technology developments where fairly sophisticated patenting schemes have evolved to provide rents to inventors, universities, and government from such research, much of the Netville work was in the realm of ideas and software that are not easily patentable. Besides, the focus of the work was anchored by the "public goods" goals of defense and the creation of new knowledge. It is doubtful that many of the early participants in the Netville community realized the downstream commercial potential of their work.

This condition has changed dramatically. Not only has the old ARPA/academy alliance evaporated, the commercial world has stepped in to take the lead role. A host of companies have begun to offer commercial products related to the evolving networks. Netscape is perhaps the most celebrated example of this, wherein a key developer from the traditional Netville community took the knowledge he gained creating the Mosaic network browser—a product owned by the National Center for Supercomputer Applications, a noted Netville entity—and constructed a new proprietary browser with improved performance. He initially distributed this product as shareware, and once it was established, he and his investor partners began selling the product. When a stream of revenues was reached, they created a new public company whose shares increased in value by an order of magnitude in a few months. There are many similar examples. Netville thus departed the era of performance fame and entered the era of proprietary fame. Performance is still a key factor: Netscape's success as shareware was surely due to its superior performance compared to Mosaic. But fame in Netville shifted from recognition of a technical job well done by colleagues who also are developers, to recognition by a consuming public voting with their dollars.

Proprietary fame clashes with core values shared by members of the Netville community. These new technologies are not shared for free, as in the past.[18] It is essentially impossible for a market to emerge where products are shared at no cost to their consumers. An ethic of market choice that depends on price/value comparisons cannot emerge due to lack of pricing. In Netville value was a key focus, and to a remarkable degree value was linked to an amorphous ethic of intellectual curiosity in which clever ways

---

[18]Netscape offers free copies of its browser for academic use. However, despite offering free copies for individual use, the company does not encourage the members of Netville to extend and build upon their product.

to solve problems were cherished. Netville members shared their development efforts around the Internet, not only to end users, but also to other developers who could and did make important additions to and modifications of the products. Ownership was recognized as a matter of professional courtesy rather than as subservience to equity rights that imply authority to collect rents. The advent of proprietary fame deprives Netville members of access to the product itself through imposing the rule of property rights, backed up by a huge institutional establishment that protects them. At the practical level, members who might formerly have jumped in to improve the new products released in Netville face the obstacles common to proprietary software, particularly code that is hidden behind interfaces or otherwise inaccessible to tinkering.

Proprietary fame also deprives members of the Netville community a sense of participation in the vital "cool" new technologies that are being built and released, and destroys the old Netville culture of informal meritocracy through which even otherwise low-status members could find fame quickly. In the past, a clever developer could make a prominent mark in the Netville community simply by providing a technological trump card. There was little concern over the possible theft of the new technology because there was basically nothing to be done with the technology outside the community. This encouraged sharing. There were low barriers to access by other community members, who could request and receive the source codes from their colleagues and hammer on the new products to see how good they really were. Genuine breakthroughs were quickly recognized through such testing, and their developers could gain fame overnight.

Proprietary fame alters the culture of informal meritocracy in key ways. For one thing, it makes it nearly impossible for such a culture to emerge or be sustained. Concern over theft makes it foolish to release new technology without adequate protection of intellectual property, which greatly reduces both provision and access. It also greatly raises the barriers a developer faces in getting innovation into the community. In order to penetrate the wall surrounding the zone of proprietary fame, a developer must acquire financial backing to buy expertise necessary to protect the property and distribute it in a manner that allows rents to be collected. Of course, a developer could still just give away his or her hottest ideas on the grounds that they are good for the community. But without the right protection on those ideas, which can only be created by experts the developer might not be able to afford, there is nothing to prevent an enterprising user from appropriating the ideas and implementing them in a manner that allows the collection of rents. The original developer becomes a chump in such a situation: a factor that discourages such altruism. It is one thing when the community benefits from an idea but no one, including the innovator, gets rich. It is another thing altogether when someone who did not create the innovation gets rich by appropriating it whereas the innovator gets nothing.

This further offends the old ethics of Netville in which technical superiority was respected in ways that clever marketing never could be.[19] Proprietary fame also greatly alters the sensibility of the Netville community by giving developers a stake that they feel they must protect. Unlike in the old Netville community, where costs of innovation diffusion were low and fixation on standards was limited to keeping the vital network running, the new order of proprietary fame creates an incentive for product developers to force standardization as a weapon to freeze innovation around their products and erect barriers to entry by new innovators. This kind of standardization is a great departure from the former, *lassiez innover* ethic in which standards were a necessary evil. Establishment of a proprietary standard can lock in a small group and freeze out a potentially large group of contributors. This can happen even without clever scheming on the part of the proprietary standards providers. Sometimes it simply evolves. A good example is provided by the evolution of the World Wide Web, in which a long-standing community of hypertext researchers who were concentrating on workstation-based systems were displaced by another group that happened to be building an Internet-based implementation of hypertext functionality. Even if the WWW developers had no idea they were displacing the traditional hypertext community by their actions, the traditional community still resents being left out of a revolution they feel, with some justification, they helped to start. Proprietary fame thus creates classes of winners and losers that could not have evolved in the old culture of Netville.

The Loss of Novelty

The Netville community was once the frontier of electronic communication. Members of the community were wildly successful, realizing their visions of a networked world. Although their creation has much room for innovation remaining, as shown by the WWW transforming the character of the Internet by taking it into color, sound, and graphics domains, many of the research questions that drew Netville members have been mined out, and the new questions to be answered have a very different institutional character. They are interesting, but they are not novel. And the loss of novelty will greatly alter the culture of Netville. A good example of this is the shift from concern over how to make the network and its features work to how to deploy network infrastructure at full social scale. The former challenge was basically a research issue, opening the networking frontier. But it was not the first networking frontier to be opened: The networks of electricity,

---

[19]Mark Andreeson, developer of Mosaic and Netscape, is a notable exception to this scenario. He proved his technical prowess before cashing in on it. In the ethics of Netville, he at least deserves what he has gained. It is doubtful that less technically creative people could obtain the respect of the Netville community while getting rich off its innovations.

telephony, and so on were deployed over the past century, and the institutional players in those worlds are deeply established. It is quite likely, in fact, that these players (e.g., the Regional Bell Operating Companies, cable television companies, and so on) will be central service providers as internetworking expands. It would be ironic if the flashy new world of cyberspace is deployed through the institutional structure of "plain old telephone service," but this is a very real possibility.

Those who study the long-term social and economic aspects of technical innovation will not be surprised if cyberspace is eventually subsumed under the umbrella of established infrastructure providers. This is a well-established phenomenon in the history of innovation. To the Netville community, however, such a prospect is anathema to the central value of novelty that mobilized and motivated their work. Netville was about the cutting edge, the truly new. In a profoundly important sense, the Netville vision of novelty was always on a collision course with the success of Netville's efforts. As soon as the networks created by the Netville community went public and started to become commercialized it would be impossible to retain the novelty that characterized the early days. The exciting questions about how to make computers and communications perform this or that interesting feat inspire researchers and engineers. Questions about the character of telecommunications regulatory reform do not. Yet these latter questions address the most important issues that will shape the future of cyberspace. Beyond these, there are the myriad questions related to application, maintainability, and social impact of the networks that typically do not excite engineers, but that are the heart of the future of networking. Loss of novelty, at least as understood by the research and engineering community that gave rise to Netville, is a serious blow to the Netville culture.

Path Dependency

The challenge of creating new infrastructure is often different from the challenge of living with it. In the same way that the success of Netville was on a collision course with the novelty of the enterprise, success is on a collision course with innovation. Earlier we discussed the development of TCP/IP and DNS that were remarkable solutions to the problems of maintaining heterogeneity while at the same time enforcing some uniformity in Netville. These evolved as treaties among Netville members; they were seen as intermediate solutions to critical problems threatening the work of the community. They were not intended to become standards, and they certainly were not seen as future millstones around the collective necks of Netville developers. Yet one can argue that they have become just that, through the process of *path dependency*.

Path dependency is a term coined by Paul David to describe the interesting phenomenon of early technologies becoming so established in use that they cannot be displaced by newer, and clearly better, technologies (see also Levitt & March, 1988). His case in point is the ubiquitous QWERTY keyboard, designed originally to slow down typing so typists would not overdrive the early mechanical typewriter mechanisms. Although ergonomically superior keyboard designs were developed in later years as typewriters improved and allowable typing speed increased, the QWERTY keyboard proved impossible to displace (David, 1985). The economic costs of overcoming the path dependencies generated by the original design were an insurmountable barrier to later designs. This point is relevant to Netville, because treaties and conventions adopted years ago as convenient and temporary solutions to problems have evolved to be ironclad standards that serve powerful commercial interests. Both TCP/IP and the naming conventions that served their purposes well during the Netville era will eventually reach their limits of capacity. Irrespective of whether superior means are available for transferring data, routing messages, and naming systems, the technical infrastructure and the beneficiaries of that infrastructure are locked into TCP/IP and DNS. Even assuming the other changes mentioned previously were irrelevant, this path dependency alone creates a powerful culture clash for the Netville community by limiting the options for creativity.

The loss of novelty, combined with path dependency, run counter to the premise of innovation-above-all that Netville members held when they set about developing the technology. The rise of Netville was the story of pioneers and explorers. The fall of Netville is essentially the story of the end of the frontier that made pioneering and exploration possible and important.

CONCLUSION

The fall of Netville is well underway. The Internet has moved slowly beyond the control of the research world that gave birth to it. America Online, CompuServe, Prodigy, Netscape, and other inheritors of the Netville mantle are fundamentally different, even if they contain some former citizens of Netville. The network that Netville built lives on, and remains an outstanding achievement. Three decades ago the network was a dream, a hazy possibility, a vision in a febright minds. The realization of that dream required the creation of the remarkable boomtown of Netville, located in the great divide that offered sanctuary and protection from the "centers" of other social worlds. The sheltered world of the great divide allowed Netville to prosper in the face of problems and uncertainties. It was not just the skill and patience of the Netville community that brought about cyberspace. It was the enabling condition of Netville's removal from the often overrated incentives and underestimated constraints of the market that allowed those skills and patience to bear fruit. When the payoffs became obvious, the original patrons withdrew because their missions of technological demonstration and proof-of-concept had been established. New patrons seeking to exploit the riches revealed by Netville moved in. In this process of patron swapping, the seeds of the fall of Netville were sown. The final end of Netville will come about through the forces of proprietary fame, loss of novelty, and path dependency that radically alter essential aspects of the Netville culture.

ACKNOWLEDGMENTS

We would like to thank David Harnick-Shapiro, Sam Horrocks, Tim Morgan, and John Romine for the valuable information that they contributed to the start of this chapter, as well as for maintaining our department's commitment to the network. Dave Crocker and John Vittal were instrumental in providing insights not available elsewhere. Roy Fielding was key in our efforts to find information on the history of the World Wide Web. We particularly want to thank Einar Stefferud and Marshall Rose for their vision of networking during their time at the University of California, Irvine, and their collegial insights on the subject. Finally, we thank Lisa Covi, David O'Leary, Ignace Snellen, and Sara Kiesler for their insightful comments.

REFERENCES

Abbate, J. (1994). *From ARPANET to Internet: A history of ARPA-sponsored computer networks, 1966—1988.* Unpublished doctoral dissertation, University of Pennsylvania, Philadelphia.

Baker, S. (1993). The evolving Internet backbone. *UNIX Review, 11*(9), 15.

Beniger, J. (1986). *The control revolution: Technical and economic origins of the information society.* Cambridge, MA: Harvard University Press

Bowker, G., Star, S. L., Turner, W., & Gasser, L. (in press). *Social science, technical systems, and cooperative work: Beyond the great divide.* Mahwah, NJ: Lawrence Erlbaum Associates.

Cerf, V. (1993). How the Internet came to be. As told to Bernard Aboba, *Internaut Magazine*: http://tars5.elte.hu/internt/current.html

Comer, D. E. (1991). *Internetworking with TCP/IP: Vol. 1. Principles, protocols, and architecture.* Englewood Cliffs, NJ: Prentice-Hall.

Crane, D. (1972). *Invisible colleges: Diffusion of knowledge in scientific communities.* Chicago: University of Chicago Press.

Crocker, D. (1987). The origins of RFCS. In RFC1000.

Crocker, D. (1993). Making standards the IETF way. *Standard View, 1*(1), 48–54.

David, P. A. (1985). Clio and the economics of QWERTY. *American Economic Review, 75*(2), 332–337.

DiMaggio, P. J., & Powell, W. W. (1983) The iron cage revisited: Institutional isomorphism and collective rationality in organizational fields. *American Sociological Review, 48*, 147–160.

DiMaggio, P. J., & Powell, W. W. (Eds.). (1991). *The new institutionalism in organizational analysis.* Chicago: University of Chicago Press.

Forster, P. W., & King, J. L. (1995) Information infrastructure standards in heterogeneous sectors: Lessons from the world wide air cargo community. In B. Kahin, & J. Abbate (Eds.), *Standards policy for information infrastructure* (pp. 148–177). Cambridge, MA: MIT Press.

Gibson, W. (1984). *Neuromancer*. New York: Ace Books.

Granovetter, M. (1973). The strength of weak ties. *American Journal of Sociology, 78*, 1360–1380.

Kahin, B. (1990) *Commercialization of the Internet: Summary report*. Electronic document produced following a workshop by that title held by the Science, Technology and Public Policy program at the John F. Kennedy School of Government, Harvard University, March 1–3, 1990, Cambridge, MA.

King, J. L. (1991). What's so great about openess? A dialectical look at the open systems movement. In *Proceedings of NORDDATA '91* (pp. 225–237). Irvine: University of California.

King, J. L., Gurbaxani, V., Kraemer, K. L., McFarlan, F. W., Raman, K. S., & Yap, C. S. (1994). Institutional factors in information technology innovation. *Information Systems Research, 5*(2), 139–169.

King, J. L., & Kraemer, K. L. (1995). Information infrastructure, national policy, and global competitiveness. *Information Infrastructure and Policy, 4*(1), 5–27.

Krol, E. (1993). *The whole Internet: User's guide and catalog*. Sebastopol, CA: O'Reilly and Associates Inc.

Leslie, S. W. (1993).*The Cold War and American science: The military–industrial–academic complex at MIT and Stanford*. New York: Columbia University Press.

Levitt, B., & March, J. G. (1988) Organizational learning. *Annual Review of Sociology, 14*, 319–340.

March, J. G. & Olsen, J. P. (1989). *Rediscovering institutions: The organizational basis of politics*. New York: The Free Press.

Meyer, J. W., & Rowan, B. (1977). Institutionalized organizations: Formal structure as myth and ceremony. *American Journal of Sociology, 83*, 340–363.

Moreau, R. (1984). *The computer comes of age: The people, the hardware, and the software*. Cambridge, MA: MIT Press.

National Academy of Sciences (1994). *Realizing the information future: The Internet and beyond*. Washington, DC: National Academy Press.

New Multimedia Reviews. 1995, January 27. Adam Curry's Metaverse. Online entry seen in the Pathfinder web server: http://www.pathfinder.com/@@cz35xeD38wIAQAgn/ew/950127/multimedia/259mmshorts.html, updated March 3, 1995.

Newlin, D. B., Jr. (1995). Standards and organizations involved in constructing the information superhighway. In B. Kahin & J. Abbate (Eds.), *Standards policy for information infrastructure*. (pp. 531–555). Cambridge, MA: MIT Press.

Pickering, J., & King, J. L. (1995). Hardwiring weak ties: Interorganizational computer-mediated communication, occupational communities, and organizational change. *Organization Science, 6*(4), 479–486.

Quarterman, J. S. (1990). *The matrix: Computer networks and conferencing systems worldwide*. Bedford, MA: Digital Press.

Quarterman, J. S. (1993). The global matrix of minds. In L. Harasim (Ed.), *Global networks: Computers and international communication* (pp. 35–56). Cambridge, MA: MIT Press.

Quittner, J. (1995, August). Browser madness. *Time Magazine, 146* (8).

RFC 822. (1982). Standard for the format of the ARPA Internet text messages. D. Crocker, University of Delaware, August 13.

RFC 882. (1983). Domain names—concepts and facilities. P. Mockapetris, University of Southern California, November.

RFC 1118. (1989). The hitchhikers guide to the Internet. E. Krol, University of Illinois Urbana–Champaign, September.

RFC 1173. (1990). Responsibilities of host and network managers: A summary of the "oral tradition" of the Internet. FTP Software Inc., August.

Roberts, L. G. & Kahn, R. E. (1972). Computer network development to achieve resource sharing. In *Proceedings from AFIPS Spring Joint Computer Conference* (pp. 543–549). New York: Association for Computing Machinery.

Scott, W. R. (1991). Unpacking institutional arguments. In P. J. DiMaggio & W. W. Powell (Eds.), *The new institutionalism in organizational analysis* (pp. 164–182). Chicago: University of Chicago Press.

Star, S. L. (1993). Cooperation without consensus in scientific problem solving: Dynamics of closure in open systems. In S. Easterbrook (Ed.), *CSCW: Cooperation or conflict* (pp. 93–106). Berlin: Springer-Verlag.

Stephenson, N. (1992). *Snow crash.* New York: Bantam.

Thompson, R. L. (1947). *Wiring a continent: The history of the telegraph industry in the United States, 1832–1866.* Princeton, NJ: Princeton University Press.

Williams, M. R. (1985). *A history of computing technology.* Englewood Cliffs, NJ: Prentice-Hall.

2

ATHEISM, SEX, AND DATABASES: THE NET AS A SOCIAL TECHNOLOGY

Lee Sproull
Samer Faraj
Boston University School of Management

Current discussions about network access and use are dominated by a view of people on the net as individual information processors looking for and manipulating information. This perspective views the net as a technology for providing access to information and information tools. This chapter presents an alternative view of people on the net as social beings who are looking for affiliation, support, and affirmation. From this perspective, the net is a social technology that allows people with common interests to find each other, gather, and sustain connections over time. We provide examples of how electronic groups provide support, affiliation, and a sense of community. We conclude with a discussion of how technology policy can be informed from viewing the net as a social technology.

Discussions about network access and use are based on assumptions about people who use the net—who they are, what they want, what they do.[1] Assumptions about users and their motivations influence what metaphors are evoked in planning for change. These metaphors in turn suggest users' behaviors, tools and services to support those behaviors, and policy mechanisms to provide access to those tools and services. A familiar example from

---

[1] In this chapter the "net" is broader than the Internet. It includes all interconnected, interoperating computer networks including commercial services such as Prodigy or CompuServe, and dial-up bulletin board services.

personal computing is the metaphor of the "desktop;" it implies that people do "deskwork" and want tools and services to support that work.

Current discussion about network access is dominated by a view of people as individual information processors who are motivated to contribute to and benefit from the explosion of information found on the net. The first section of this chapter explores that view with its metaphors of the electronic highway and electronic library. The remainder of the chapter offers an alternative view based on a view of people as social beings who need affiliation as much as they need information. We explore the metaphor of an electronic gathering, offer illustrations of electronic gatherings today, and suggest some technical and policy issues that follow from this alternative view of people on the net.

THE NET AS AN INFORMATION TECHNOLOGY

The dominant view of people on the net is that they are individual information processors, looking for and manipulating information. They are continually motivated to find new information and the net always offers more new information for them to discover. The net is viewed fundamentally as a technology for providing access to information and information tools. For example, a popular description of the National Research and Education Network (NREN) noted

> The Network will give researchers and students at colleges of all sizes—and at large and small companies—in every state access to the same
>
> —high performance computing tools
> —data banks
> —supercomputers
> —libraries
> —specialized research facilities
> —educational technology
>
> that are presently available to only a few large universities and laboratories that can afford them. (Coalition for the National Research and Education Network, 1989, p. 9)

An assessment of the changing role of computers suggests that, "By the mid-1990s, people can be expected to view personal computers as knowledge sources rather than as knowledge processors ... gateways to vast amounts of knowledge and information" (Tennant & Heilmeier, 1991, p. 123). Indeed, the workshop preceding the preparation of this volume described the Internet and NREN as an "efficient communications platform and increasingly rich data environment" (Kahin, 1993).[2]

---

[2]See Lynch and Preston (1990) for a history and review leading up to NREN from this perspective.

The metaphors evoked by this information-centered view are the electronic highway and the digital library. People are said to "cruise" or "browse" the net. The pursuit of information—the cruise or the browse—is implicitly solitary; hundreds or thousands of people may search at the same time, but each is independent and unaware of others. The goal is to discover information. These discoveries can range from mildly amusing to enormously helpful, but their value is always determined by the individual searcher. (See column 1 of Table 2.1 for a summary of the dominant view.)

This view of people on the net as individual information searchers and processors underlies ideas about tools to improve information search and manipulation. Early tools relevant to this perspective include the Telnet protocol, which allows users to remotely log onto geographically distant computers, and the File Transfer Protocol (FTP), which allows users to start a session on a remote computer and to transfer files between their machine and the remote one. More recent tools provide a common interface to access large numbers of databases and services on the net. These include archie, a sort of global file location catalogue; gopher, a utility that organizes access to Internet resources through a hierarchical menu system; WAIS, which acts as an electronic reference librarian by searching inside files for requested information; and WWW, a hypertext-based virtual information-searching and -browsing tool.[3]

This dominant view also influences policy discussions about net access and use. If people are primarily searching for and manipulating information, then charging them for accessing and transferring information is sensible. It is appropriate to propose pricing schemes in which people pay varying amounts depending on the value of the information.[4] Protecting intellectual property rights is also important in this view.

A version of the dominant view is found in discussions of extending and increasing network support for scientists. (See, e. g., National Research Council [NRC], 1993.) In this view individual scientists want to find or discover information in databases, journal articles, or other literature that can be made available on the net; they also want to gain access to scarce scientific instruments or apparatus. Increasingly, this view holds, scientists will gain access to these resources through the net. In this view, extending network access and services will let scientists work at a distance from their colleagues, their apparatus, and their data to create and leverage shared knowledge. The metaphor for this view is the virtual scientific laboratory and points to the need to develop tools for locating and sharing data and software for analyzing shared data, tools for controlling remote instru-

---

[3]See Krol (1992) for more information on these tools.

[4]Peak load pricing schemes define value primarily in terms of timeliness of access (e.g., Varian & Mackie-Mason, 1993). Commercial vendors currently offer variable pricing based on time of day.

TABLE 2.1

People on the Net: Alternative Views

	Information Processors	*Social Beings*
Unit	Individual	Group
Place	Highway Library	Gathering
Behaviors	Cruising Browsing	Chatting Arguing
Consequences	Individual knowledge	Affiliation
Tools	Telnet/FTP WAIS/Gopher	Listserv Usenet group visualization
Policies	Information ownership Fee for access	Support for group Fee for membership

ments, and tools for communicating with far-away colleagues (NRC, 1993). It also suggests the need for policy mechanisms to ensure that scientists make data available to others on the net, to ensure that claims of priority for discovery can be registered, and to certify the quality of electronic information much as peer review processes do for journal publications.

The dominant view of people on the net as information seekers and processors is sensible and productive; however, it is also incomplete and misleading in some important ways. An alternative view of the net as a social technology suggests different technical and policy issues.

THE NET AS A SOCIAL TECHNOLOGY

People on the net are not only solitary information processors but also social beings. They are not only looking for information; they are also looking for affiliation, support, and affirmation. Thinking of people on the net as social actors evokes a metaphor of a gathering.[5] Behaviors appropriate at a gathering include chatting, discussing, arguing, and confiding. People go to a gathering to find others with common interests and talk with or listen to them. When they find a gathering they like, they return to it again and again. (See column 2 of Table. 2.1 for a summary of this view.)

If we view people as social actors, then we should view the net as a social technology. Any technology combines artifacts and procedures to apply knowledge for practical ends. A social technology does so to allow people

---

[5]In fact, some networks have created specific metaphorical places, for example, Larry's Bar on The Sierra Net or Roger's Bar on Big Sky Telegraph. Electronic Cafe™ makes the metaphorical gathering real by running real-time events simultaneously in two or more real places connected by electronic networks.

with common interests to find each other, talk and listen, and sustain connections over time. Dinner parties, bowling teams, college reunions, coffeehouses, 12-step programs, neighborhood pubs—all are examples of social technologies. Oldenberg (1989) called these "great good places" that provide a neutral meeting ground where social conventions are democratic and conversation is the main activity. They keep long hours, accommodate people when they are free from their other responsibilities, and are easily accessible. Great good places can be found not only in the real world but also on the net, in the form of electronic groups.

Just as a pub or coffeehouse is recognizable by its exterior decor and name sign, an electronic group is recognizable by its name. At a most basic level a group name labels or signals people who share their common interest using electronic communication.[6] Beyond the name, group structure comes from membership control (whether it is private or public) and editorial control (whether it is moderated or unmoderated). Private groups are open only to people admitted by the owner of the list; public groups are open to anyone with access to a network over which the group can be reached. In moderated groups, all messages are sent to a moderator who may organize or summarize them before posting them to the entire group. In unmoderated groups, each message sent to the group is directly posted.

Electronic gatherings are characterized by three noteworthy social attributes not found in real-world gatherings. First, physical location is irrelevant to participation; if a person has network access, electronic gatherings are accessible. Physical distance has no influence on the size or shape of gatherings and is no longer a barrier for effective participation.

Second, most participants are relatively invisible. If people attend a real-world gathering, their physical presence matters even if they say nothing. They take up space; their movements and nonverbal noises can be interpreted by the speaker and other participants. In an electronic gathering, those who only read messages are entirely invisible because there are usually no reminders or cues to signal how many people, or which people, read a message.[7] In electronic group argot, readers who never post are sometimes called *lurkers*, a term with more sinister connotations than is perhaps warranted. Most electronic groups have a very high proportion of lurkers. For example, on the WELL, a network known for high levels of interaction, about 80% of its 6600 members posted no message during a one-month period (Smith, 1993).

---

[6]The group name may be attached to an email distribution list, in which case a copy of any message mailed to the group name is forwarded to every member's mailbox. The group name may be attached to a bulletin board or newsgroup, in which case any message posted to the group is available to be read by anyone interested in that group.

[7]Some real-time conferences and games do signal the presence of readers. Habitat™ for example, displays a ghost icon if someone enters a room and does not announce his or her identity.

People who do post messages are visible only through the text they write. There is no accompanying visual or aural information about physical appearance, emotional state, social status, or personal situation.[8] People may personalize their messages through typographic conventions for emotion such as the smiley face,[9] or pithy sayings or stylized drawings in the signature block that can be automatically appended at the end of a message. Generally, however, signals and cues are limited to ascii text.

Third, the logistical and social costs to participate in electronic gatherings are quite low. For the most part, people can participate at their own convenience, often from their own office or home. They don't have to get dressed up, drive across town, worry about time zone differences, or schedule a conference room. They can participate for 5 or 10 minutes at a time logging in to check group mail or to read a newsgroup in the interstices between real-world events. People can participate in great social comfort, too. Invisible readers feel no social pressure to justify their presence or to contribute; passive participation impedes an electronic gathering not at all. Posters, who cannot see or be seen by their audience, have few overt reminders that others may be scrutinizing their text and feel secure that only their text can be seen by others. Because they are less aware of their audience, people who "speak" electronically are relatively unbound by social convention. This can result in startlingly intimate revelations that are posted to thousands of people. It can also result in rapid escalation from mild annoyance to "flame wars."

SCOPE AND INSTANCES
OF ELECTRONIC GATHERINGS

Electronic gatherings flourish on all networks. Corporate networks, which are justified for business reasons, support thousands of business-related electronic groups and hundreds of extracurricular electronic groups as well.[10] One large computer manufacturer, for example, supports more than 1,200 business-related groups devoted to such topics as computer-aided manufacturing, specific products, and computer languages. It also supports

---

[8]The main activity in some network-based interactive fantasy games is creating and displaying identity through choice of name and persona, dress and other props, and interaction style. These identities often bear little relationship to their creators' "real" identities. (But see Turkle, chap. 7, this volume, for ways that role playing can help people work through issues of "real" psychological identity.)

[9]A smiley is a combination of two to four characters that approximates a human face when looked at with the viewer's head tilted to the left. A regular smiley, :-), refers to parts of an article or a statement that is meant to be funny. Variations on the basic smiley run in the hundreds. They include ;-), a winky smiley expressing sarcasm and :-(, a frowning smiley expressing unhappiness about something (see Godin, 1993, for an extensive list).

[10]See Finholt and Sproull (1990) for a description of electronic groups at work.

more than 350 extracurricular groups devoted to such topics as Celtic culture, diet support, religion, and four-wheel-drive vehicles. Commercial networks support thousands of groups. The WELL, with about 6,600 subscribers, has more than 220 public conferences; America Online (AOL) has about 350 organized special interest clubs and forums and "countless, countless 'grass roots' interest groups," according to an AOL source. Prodigy supports more than 400 discussion groups, Compuserve supports more than 200, and Delphi supports more than 50 "official" special interest groups and hundreds of personalized groups that are maintained by members. The number of dial-up Bulletin Board Systems (BBS) in the United States exceeds 45,000 and are used regularly by 12 million users (Rickard, 1993). And so does the Internet. Recent estimates show about 2,500 public mailing lists, uncountable numbers of private mailing lists, more than 2,600 newsgroups or bulletin boards, and more than 200 real-time interactive groups.[11]

USENET newsgroups illustrate the popularity and diversity of electronic groups. USENET is a system of distributed electronic bulletin boards (called newsgroups) that are supported by more than 16,000 organizations and have more than 2 million subscribers. USENET is not a computer network; rather, it is a network of bilateral agreements among system administrators to cooperate in managing bulletin boards. A site administrator or system administrator who subscribes to some or all USENET bulletin boards receives all new messages for those boards and forwards them to another site. A person with an account at a subscribing site can read and post to bulletin boards available at that site. Typically, readers and posters are not directly charged for participating in USENET groups. Newsgroups are not representative of all electronic groups on all networks, but do provide an easily accessible view of electronic group behavior that illustrates the function and potential of electronic groups. The USENET community itself collects descriptive statistics and posts them to the newsgroup called news.lists.[12] USENET groups are also relatively accessible to anyone with Internet access.

---

[11]Krol (1993) provided an overview of email lists and newsgroups. See Hardie and Neou (1993) for an annotated description of more than 800 public mailing lists. See "List of Active Newsgroups" and "Publicly-accessible Mailing Lists" on the USENET group, news.lists. Both are periodic multipart listings that are frequently updated.

The real-time groups are a marginal, but fascinating piece of the world of electronic groups. They are called MUDs, for multiuser dungeon games, or MOOs, for muds object-oriented. A person logs on to a MUD, creates an electronic identity, then moves from place to place in a particular electronic world, interacting with other people who are logged on at the same time. Most MUDs are based on adventure and fantasy games. See Curtis, chapter 6, this volume for more information on how MUDs work.

[12]For a more detailed description of USENET, see "What_Is_Usenet" on news.newusers.questions.

More than 19,000 messages are posted each day to USENET newsgroups (50 megabytes of text, equivalent to 20,000 hard copy pages of text). News-groups are organized in broad topic categories, such as "comp" for com-puter-related topics and "rec" for recreational topics. Each category includes as many groups as people wish to create and maintain. More than 100 of the most popular groups have memberships of more than 50,000 people. (See Table 2.2 for descriptions of some popular Usenet groups.) Some of the largest groups function like subscription lists for special interest daily magazines. They exhibit little interaction; messages rarely respond to previous messages. For example, rec.humor and misc.forsale both have more than 100,000 subscribers and receive more than 50 mostly unrelated messages a day. But many large groups look more like gatherings than magazines—they have substantial social interaction with lively discussion sustained over time on many topics including, among others, atheism, sex, and databases.

Table 2.3 displays data drawn from a study investigating the dynamics of electronic group interaction. It describes three groups that discuss social or political topics and three that discuss technical topics. Each group contains a daily mix of solo messages (postings to which no one replies), seed messages (postings that generate replies and thus a discussion thread), and replies. Over half the messages in each group show social interaction; that is, either they induce one or more replies or are themselves replies to previous messages. Like many real-world gatherings, these groups support more than one discussion (or thread) at the same time, which last an average of 3–5 days. These groups exhibit some of the same social dynamics found in real-world gatherings. People take on different roles (e.g., lurker, guru, keeper of archive files); there are comments about the true or intended purpose of the group and about what is or is not appropriate behavior; people give and get help; people come and go. But, unlike real-world gatherings, these groups allow ongoing interaction for thousands of mem-bers.

SOME CONSEQUENCES OF ELECTRONIC GROUPS

In the real world, groups benefit their members (and vice versa) by provid-ing physical, economic, cognitive, and emotional resources. Electronic groups do not provide direct physical or economic resources but they frequently offer information that may lead to them, such as leads or advice about jobs or items for sale. Most electronic groups offer information or cognitive resources for their members. For example, on "comp.databases," one can ask questions such as "I am looking at products for pulling data from an Ingres database running on a VAX (VMS). We currently use PCLINK to get data to PC'sbut [sic] want to access this data through

TABLE 2.2

Popular Usenet Groups[a]

Category # of groups[b]	Description[a]	Popular Groups	Readers[d]	Volume[d] (messages per day)
alternative (alt) 778	Groups that discuss "alternative ways of looking at things."	alt.sex alt.sex.stories alt.activism	140,000 120,000 94,000	5 338 15
computer (comp) 457	Computer science and related topics.	comp.windows.x comp.lang.c comp.graphics	120,000 94,000 93,000	29 38 30
recreation (rec) 276	Groups that discuss hobbies, recreational activities, and the arts.	rec.humor rec.arts.movies rec.music.misc	110,000 71,000 65,000	71 80 59
society (soc) 90	Groups that discuss social issues, where *social* can mean *politically relevant* or *socializing* or anything in between.	soc.culture.indian soc.singles soc.women	73,000 66,000 49,000	104 97 10
science (sci) 69	Groups that discuss scientific research and applications (other than computer science).	sci.electronics sci.math sci.physics	67,000 57,000 53,000	50 3 42
miscellaneous (misc) 39	Anything that does not fit into the foregoing categories or that fits into several categories.	misc.jobs misc.forsale misc.consumers	150,000 120,000 59,000	37 59 37

[a]This table provides an overview of highly popular groups in six domain categories. Groups were selected based on number of readers and volume of messages. Binaries, that is, groups that post images coded in binary form, were excluded due to their specialized nature. Other categories exist but are not included here because of low volume or membership.

[b]Based on an analysis of a .newsrc file at acs@bu.ed on May 20th, 1993. This may understate the total number of groups on the Internet; the numbers are based only on the groups received at Boston University.

[c]From Krol (1992, pp. 129–130).

[d]Derived from Reid (1993).

Ethernet instead of asynch ports. Does anyone have any advice on products from companies like IQ Softwareor [sic] Gupta?? What Ingres products on the PC do I need (Tools for DOS,...)? Any help would be appreciated."

The "comp." groups frequently offer technical advice. On "comp.databases" members exchange opinions about the technical merits of new database packages. On "comp.object," people struggling with trying to write programs using object-oriented methods appeal to the wisdom of more experienced members. On "comp.c++," members discuss the intricacies of the c++ programming language. They post portions of code, saying

TABLE 2.3

Interaction in Usenet Groups (6 Sample Groups)[a]

	soc.culture. lebanon	soc.feminism	alt.atheism	comp. databases	comp.object	comp.c++
Group size	13,000	20,000	53,000	65,000	42,000	82,000
Mean number of messages/day	7.9	8.1	53.3	17.7	9.1	35.8
Message type						
Solo (%)	30.9	24.8	19.0	41.2	31.7	41.7
Seed (%)	18.8	16.4	16.4	18.7	13.4	16.4
Reply (%)	50.4	58.8	64.6	40.1	54.8	41.9
Total lines of text per message	50.0	93.6	47.1	27.2	45.1	45.8
Percentage of new lines per message	85.0	62.0	84.0	38.6	54.8	60.0
Average number of threads per day	4.3	4.9	31.4	4.3	4.7	3.3
Average time length of thread (days)	3.1	7.2	34.4	15.7	8.5	28.7
Mean number of authors posting per day	6.4	7.2	34.4	15.7	8.5	28.7
Domain of author organization (% of total authors)						
Educational	49.9	57.5	44.3	37.1	24.8	21.8
Commercial	16.9	18.6	23.8	24.1	31.4	31.2
International	26.8	15.4	21.4	31.9	34.2	32.7

[a]*Note.* From Faraj and Sproul (1993).

they "think it should work but it does not." These messages challenge other members to identify the problems and post a corrected version. In the technical groups some people expend significant effort to collect and provide technical information. Some people maintain and circulate bibliographies. Members who receive many answers to interesting questions often publish a summary of them.

The social and political groups also offer information. "Soc.feminism," for example, provides impromptu reviews of new feminist books and movie reviews. These reviews are the catalyst for lively discussions regarding current cultural issues. On "soc.culture.lebanon" hard-to-find information is frequently posted the text of U.S. travel advisories to Lebanon, the daily exchange rate of the Lebanese pound, news stories about Lebanon from the UPI and AP news feeds. People exchange advice about how best to prepare Lebanese dishes and suggestions for good bicultural baby names. Jokes, many in poor taste, are frequently posted and either enjoyed or disparaged by readers.

Many electronic groups offer entertainment, which can be an emotional resource. Three of the largest USENET newsgroups, each with more than 100,000 readers, have entertainment as their primary purpose: "alt.sex," "alt.sex.stories," and "rec.humor." The technology policy community sometimes seems mildly embarrassed by such groups. They do not match lofty views of the net as a resource to elevate intellectual discourse; moreover, many people find the contents offensive. Nevertheless, they are extremely popular.

Electronic groups also offer affiliation. Despite the fact that participants in electronic groups may be surrounded by people at work or school, at least some of them feel alone in facing a problem or a situation. If their situation is problematic, it is easy to believe it must be their own fault because no one else around them has the same problem or a similar perspective. Even though electronic groups are usually composed of strangers, because they share a common interest, they are also likely to share common experiences. A result of finding others in the same situation or with the same problem can be the realization that "I am not alone!" Thus, electronic groups can provide emotional support to their members. Here are three examples.

In 1990, a postdoctoral physicist began a public electronic mailing list, the Young Scientists' Network, for scientists like himself, who faced the prospect of being unable to find permanent jobs in physics. The Young Scientists' Network includes weekly messages from the founder on such topics as job tips, funding possibilities, and relevant news stories (Morell, 1992). Subscribers send in their own tips and scoops. Although it was created to provide information to unemployed or underemployed scientists, it rapidly became an informal support group. One physicist said, "The main value was in confirming the trouble I was having finding a job." Another offered, "It helps save your sanity, it helps to know that it's not because of a personal failing that you can't find research work." The Young Scientists' Network, which had about 170 members a year ago, has grown to 3,000 members today.

In 1987, a computer scientist began a private mailing list, Systers, to share information with her colleagues about events and topics in the world of operating systems. Systers expanded to become a "forum for discussion of both the problems and joys of women in [computer science more generally] and to provide a medium for networking and mentoring" (Borg, cited in

Frenkel, 1990, p. 36). There are messages about job openings, book reviews, conferences, and general conversations. One of its members said, "There's a feeling of closeness, so it's easy to talk" (field notes, 1/9/92).[13] She believes that the closeness was established early because the group was private and people were careful to show positive regard for others in their messages. She said that even today, when the interaction starts getting contentious, "somebody always sends mail that's soothing." Systers currently has over 1,500 members in 150 companies, 200 universities, and 18 countries around the world.

"Misc.kids" is a USENET group for discussing the joys and sorrows of kids and parenting. It's a mix of information, jokes, discussion, and debate, with topics ranging from diaper rash to corporal punishment. One reader describes misc.kids as "a support organization, a debate-team, an encyclopedia of information, and a social group all rolled into one. Even the people I never agree with, I care about" (field notes, 5/92). Another confided, "When I had problems in pregnancy (the baby had a chromosome abnormality), I posted about it and received support from all over the world—an amazing experience" (field notes, 5/92). Misc.kids sees about 60 messages a day and has about 48,000 subscribers worldwide.

These electronic groups do much more than provide information. They offer the opportunity to make connections with other people. They provide support and a sense of community. To be sure, they also provide information. But, as one group member said, it is "information with an attitude."

In the real world, mutual benefit is the social glue that sustains face-to-face groups over time; members who benefit from others reciprocate. Direct reciprocity is difficult if not impossible in the electronic context, but more generalized altruism is relatively easy to sustain. When one person asks for help, it is very likely that one or more group members will provide a helpful or supportive response. (A much larger proportion might be able to help but might be too busy, too diffident, or too selfish to respond.) With membership of thousands, the proportion responding can be extremely small and still yield one or more beneficial responses. Furthermore, responses can be seen by all group members, thereby helping others who had the same question or problem but did not post a message about it. Moreover, even people who receive no direct benefit from any particular helpful message see the process of helping behavior modeled in the group. And finally, with large groups, no one person need spend much time being helpful. A small number of small acts can sustain a large community because each act is seen by the entire group.

The benefits provided by electronic groups often extend beyond the direct participants when members act as conduits of information to people

---

[13]Quotations whose source is "field notes" are from electronic group participants who preferred to remain anonymous.

outside the group. Requests for information are frequently posted to a group "for a friend who doesn't have net access." Group members sometimes forward pertinent posts to friends or colleagues. In the case of technical groups at least, we hypothesize that employers benefit from their employees' group membership when information gleaned from the group is applied or passed on in the workplace. Note in Table 2.3 that users from commercial organizations represent a larger fraction of posters in the technical groups than in the social groups.

Of course the consequences of electronic group membership are not all positive, just as the consequences of affiliations in the real world are not all positive. Erroneous or poor information can be promulgated as easily as high-quality information. People can spend a lot of time reading group messages. Lively discussion can degenerate into frustrating conflict and rancor. But, for several million members, the benefits apparently outweigh the costs.

TECHNOLOGY AND POLICY ISSUES

Ideas about tools and policies for the net are influenced by one's view of people on the net. An information-centered view calls for tools to find and manipulate information and policies to protect it. People are building and using information tools such as gopher, WAIS, and World Wide Web. As the amount of information increases and the number of people wishing to find and use it continues to expand, more and better information tools should be developed. An information-centered view leads to policy goals for limiting unauthorized access to information, for protecting the integrity of information, and for preventing the misuses of information. Access and use restrictions and legal restraints are important topics for current policy debate.

What tools and policies are suggested by viewing the net as a social technology?

Tools for Groups

Electronic groups have not been the major focus for network tool development to date, although a few helpful tools exist. DIGEST and DLIST help support moderated lists in digest format. Listserv programs help maintain and archive group membership lists. But for the most part electronic groups have flourished under conditions of benign neglect, much as email flourished in its early days with relatively low levels of technology support or policy attention.

Tools and services that help people find, join, participate in, and derive benefit from groups are important. Some tools might help people differentiate among groups and remind them of what group they are in. These may encompass tools for group visualization, group identity, and group memory—various ways to evoke the "character" and charter of a group. For example, some tools might represent different groups by using icons or graphics to display images of relevant places, people, or symbols. They might use behaviors (such as the number of messages a day) or attributes (such as the number of readers or posters with particular characteristics) to create representations that reflect the changing nature of the group.

Tools are also needed to help people offer services targeted to groups, rather than to individuals. Such services might include digesting or indexing group messages, matchmaking, toast mastering, hosting, mediation and conflict resolution. Nascent examples of these and other services can be found in some electronic groups today. But typically they are ad hoc efforts that are difficult to sustain, leverage, or generalize.

Electronic groups depend on the talent and goodwill of thousands of support people system operators, system administrators, Usenet site administrators, people who create lists and newsgroups, group moderators, and group archivists. Group maintainers also need better tools and services. Moreover, we need to understand how such people can be recruited, supported, sustained, and recognized. Economic analyses of networks that consider only equipment and transmission costs ignore the extraordinary value contributed by volunteers. Developing, sustaining, and recognizing the people who support the net is crucial.

Policy Issues for Groups

We have had relatively little experience with electronic group governance. The most important policy issue is how to balance people's rights and responsibilities in electronic gatherings. Every group creates and sustains a shared understanding of the rights and responsibilities of membership—a social contract. The social contract guides both individual behavior and collective response to that behavior. In the real world, social contracts take a variety of familiar forms formal legal codes, professional codes of conduct, association bylaws, community standards. Their enforcement mechanisms are equally rich and varied, ranging from socialization of the novice member, to warning signs and signals, to gestures of solidarity, to penalties for noncompliance.

Social contracts in the electronic world are extremely problematic. Because electronic groups are both diverse and ephemeral, attempts to directly apply codes of conduct from the real world often go awry. Social influence is played out in a world that is rich in imagination and diversity and impoverished in means of communication—ascii text.

Electronic groups currently lack subtle ways to convey expectations about behavior. In the real world, training, practice, and socialization are offered in probationary periods and sheltered environments such as driver's education class, moot court, and clinical internships; there are no electronic equivalents. In the real world, objects such as traffic signals, judicial robes and a raised bench, and party decorations remind people of appropriate behavior for particular situations; there are no equivalents in electronic groups. In the real world small transgressions can evoke small rebukes; in electronic groups, there is no easy equivalent of the raised eyebrow or "tsk-tsk" if someone misbehaves, so small transgressions typically go unremarked. But a large number of small transgressions can create an unpleasant environment.

Electronic groups currently have few ways to deal with blatant misbehavior. Sometimes people use a tool to filter out other peoples' messages that they deem obnoxious. Filters exemplify the consequences of thinking about people on the net as individual information processors—in this case, individuals who want to ignore messages with particular attributes. Although a filter may benefit the individuals who use it, it may be socially dysfunctional for the group; it does not inform the miscreant that his or her behavior has been identified as objectionable, nor does it inform the larger group that someone finds particular behavior objectionable. Thus it cannot educate either the individual or the group about objectionable behavior. It also gives people an easy technological way to avoid social responsibility.

Extremely disruptive behavior in electronic groups, often justified by the perpetrator in terms of freedom of speech, can generate endless debate over how to respond. Both the disruption and the debate can disenchant members who want to pursue the designated topic of the group, rather than issues of social control. Ejecting members from groups, removing groups from sites, or closing down groups are complicated and contentious undertakings.

It is much easier to suggest tools for groups than it is to suggest policies for how to balance people's rights and responsibilities. We need much more discussion within groups themselves as well as in the broader policy community about group governance. We also need research that documents implicit codes of behavior and social influence mechanisms across a wide variety of group types.

CONCLUSION

One might ask why it is necessary to attend directly to electronic groups and to the net as a social technology. Is it possible that social benefits will occur simply as a by-product of information-centered technology and policies? As the number, size, and heterogeneity of groups continue to grow, the need for group tools does also. So does the need to understand group governance. Tools and policies directed at individual information processors are not necessarily responsive to group needs.

The human need for affiliation is at least as strong as the need for information. Often, both needs are met simultaneously in human association. Many electronic groups provide both information and affiliation, and the value of information received in groups derives, at least in part, from its being offered by people who have chosen to affiliate. The motivation to offer information also derives, in part, from the obligation and affirmation of membership. And, of course, the value of groups goes beyond information.

Even those who wish to design electronic highways and libraries for individual information processors can incorporate ideas about membership and affiliation. On a real highway, each vehicle carries few passengers. On the electronic highway we can run tour buses with hundreds of passengers and dozens of tour guides. People who like the people they meet on a tour can take another journey with them. In a real library, "no talking" is the rule. In the electronic library, we can have sociable gatherings around every document. People can give their opinions about something they have read; authors can rejoin or elaborate; readers and writers can become discussers and collaborators. If we remember that access to the net means not only access to information, but access to people, we can provide tools and policies to promote both.

ACKNOWLEDGMENTS

This chapter is reprinted, with slight changes, from B. Kahin & J. Keller (Eds.) (1995). *Public access to the Internet*, Cambridge, MA: MIT Press. Reprinted by permission.

REFERENCES

Coalition for the National Research and Education Network. (1989). *NREN The National Research and Education Network*. Washington, DC Author.

Faraj, S. & Sproull. L. (1994). *Interaction dynamics in electronic groups*. Unpublished manuscript, Boston University, Boston.

Finholt, T. & Sproull, L. (1990). Electronic groups at work. *Organization Science, 1,* 41–64.

Frenkel, K. (1990) November. Women and computing. *Communications of the ACM,* 34–46.

Godin, S. (1993). *The smiley dictionary*. Berkeley, CA Peachpit Press.

Hardie, E. T. L., & Neou, V.(Eds.). (1993). *INTERNET Mailing lists*. Englewood Cliffs, NJ: Prentice-Hall.

Kahin, B. (1993). Public access to the Internet Call for papers. Electronic message.

Krol, E. (1992). *The whole INTERNET*. Sebastopol, CA: O'Reilly and Associates, Inc.

Lynch, C. A., & Preston, C. M. (1990). Internet access to information resources. *Annual Review of Information Science and Technology, 25,* 263–312.

Morell, J. (1992, May 1). E-mail links science's young and frustrated. *Science*, p. 606.

National Research Council. (1993). *National collaboratories Applying information technology for scientific research.* Washington, DC National Academy Press.

Oldenberg, R. (1989). *The great good place.* New York Paragon House.

Reid, B. (1993). *USENET readership report for Feb 93.* Article 2370 of news.lists.

Rickard, J. (1993, September/October). Home-grown BBS. *Wired.*

Smith, M. A. (1993). *Voices from the WELL The logic of the virtual commons.* Unpublished manuscript, University of California, Los Angeles, Department of Sociology.

Tennant, H., & Heilmeier, G. H. (1991). Knowledge and equality Harnessing the tides of information abundance. In D. Leebaert (Ed.), *Technology 2001 The future of computing and communications,* (pp. 117–149). Cambridge, MA. MIT Press.

Varian, H., & Mackie-Mason, J. (1993, May). *Cost and pricing models for different levels of functionality and service.* Paper presented at Workshop on Public Access to the Internet, John F. Kennedy School of Government, Cambridge, MA.

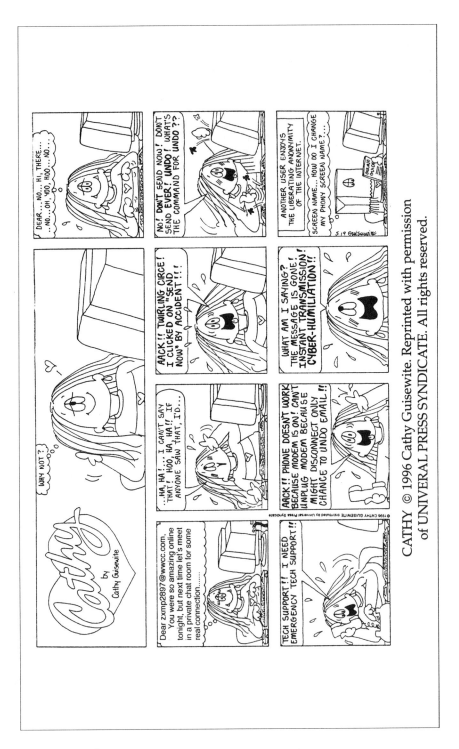

3

PORNOGRAPHY IN CYBERSPACE: AN EXPLORATION OF WHAT'S IN USENET

Michael D. Mehta
Queens University

Dwaine E. Plaza
York University

Although there have been content analyses of sexually explicit magazines (Winick, 1985), pornographic comics (Palmer, 1979; Scott & Cuvelier, 1993), soft-core magazines (Malamuth & Spinner, 1980), and erotic videos (Garcia & Milano, 1990; Palys, 1986), hardly any research examines pornography on computer networks. We describe a study of pornographic images located in public access USENET newsgroups before the wide-scale commercialization of the Internet. We compare the type of pornographic images posted by anonymous, noncommercial users with material posted by commercial vendors to illustrate how rapid growth of Internet commercial participation also leads to changes in Internet content and culture.

A recently published paper by Rimm (1995) raised public awareness that pornographic material is widely available on adult bulletin board services and USENET groups. His study involved analyzing the descriptions given to 917,410 images found primarily on private bulletin board services rather than in USENET or the World Wide Web. Using what he called "linguistic parsing software," Rimm analyzed pornographic images based on their descriptions. His study coded only the presence of a theme. Because most images contain multiple themes (e.g., oral sex with bondage and the use of a foreign object in the same image), Rimm's study, by coding for dominant single themes alone, tended to inflate the prevalence of acts that he defined, using the current issue of the *Diagnostic and Statistical Manual for Mental Disorders (DSM–IV)*, as pedophilic, hebephilic, and paraphilic. Moreover, Rimm's paraphilic category combined a wide variety of acts including bondage, sadomasochism, urination, defecation, and bestiality, which also could have exaggerated the degree of "obscenity" in these images.

Our study focuses on the content of pornographic images in USENET, a public computer network forum for electronic groups called "newsgroups." We examine a random sample of 150 images from 17 alternate newsgroups available on April 18, 1994. The findings of the study described here were presented at a symposium on free speech and privacy issues.[1] The present chapter is an updated version of the original paper (Mehta & Plaza, in press). Here we incorporate ideas stimulated by publication of the Rimm paper in June 1995. Many of the weaknesses of Rimm's study are addressed in our study.

PORNOGRAPHY AND THE INTERNET

The Internet has evolved over the past 25 years from a U.S. Department of Defense network for assisting with engineering and scientific research to a commercially oriented communications network. As a research tool, the Internet helps users to share information with minimal costs. Calem (1992) described the Internet as:

> ... an enormous computer network in which any existing network can participate. It encompasses satellites, cable, fiber and telephone lines, and it seems to have grown exponentially. Now, everyone from ...students to commercial enterprises can get access through the Internet to vast amounts of information on other computer systems around the world. (p. 11)

One of the biggest benefits of using this network for employees of academic and engineering organizations has been that long-distance charges do not apply. Until recently, the costs of the network infrastructure were absorbed by the U.S. National Science Foundation in its administration of the central "backbone" of the Internet. However, this form of administration is now changing, and privatization is expected to proceed very quickly. The quasi-public "information superhighway" is now facing new challenges as the first stage of privatization begins. An ever increasing proportion of the Internet's rapid growth consists of commercial traffic.

---

[1]The symposium on Free Speech and Privacy in the Information Age was held at the University of Waterloo (Waterloo, Canada) on November 26, 1994.

Commercial interests are rapidly transforming the face of the network from a research tool to a facility for profit, that is, a market.

The Internet is changing markedly for individuals too. Branwyn estimated in 1993 that the number of computer networks linked through the Internet was approximately 1.3 million worldwide, with an estimated 14 million to 15 million individual users, growing at a rate of 25% every 3 months. This rapid growth and increased interconnectivity is providing users with access to multitudinous sources of information and products. No longer is it necessary for computer users to procure software from retail outlets like computer and software stores. The Internet allows users the opportunity to download software without ever leaving the comfort and privacy of their homes and offices, thus ensuring the anonymity of users retrieving software such as pornographic material.

In short, computers are no longer exclusively the domain of researchers, large corporate firms, or computer "hackers." Decreasing costs, user-friendly software, and inexpensive access to online services such as CompuServe and America Online have greatly increased the number of everyday users of computers in general, and of the Internet in particular. This rapid growth has, in part, been due to the widescale commercialization of the Internet, where online services provide value-added information such as stock market quotes, travel information, real estate services, and inexpensive electronic mail. On the other hand, the Internet also enables individuals and groups to exchange information that can include hate literature, instructions on how to make a nuclear bomb and other weapons, and both written and visual pornographic material. The widescale availability of pornography on the Internet has raised concern about what constitutes acceptable use of a medium that crosses borders with impunity and may supersede community standards and mores.

Social scientists and feminist social commentators have conducted substantial research on the effects of pornography on attitudes of men toward women (Zillmann & Bryant, 1984), sexual aggression against women (Baron & Straus, 1989; Donnerstein, Linz, & Penrod, 1987; Padgett, Brislin-Stutz, & Neal, 1989), and the role that pornography plays in perpetuating sexual discrimination (Dworkin & MacKinnon, 1988; Dworkin, 1985). Taken as a body, this work is inconclusive and often contradictory. Furthermore, debate and consternation regarding the effects of pornography exist. If pornography is the portrayal of persons as sexual objects for the pleasure of others, then pornography objectifies individuals in a sexualized, eroticized manner. According to Catherine MacKinnon (1995):

> Pornography in cyberspace is pornography in society—just broader, deeper, worse, and more of it. Pornography is a technologically sophisticated traffic in women; electronically communicated pornography traffics women in a yet more sophisticated form.... As pornography comes ever more into the open, crossing new boundaries, opening new markets, and pioneering new harms, it also opens itself to new scrutiny. (p. 1959)

Computer pornography, in this view, represents the ultimate in erotic fragmentation. Not only are individuals reduced to bytes and pixels, their images are subject to mass distribution, electronic manipulation, and commercial exploitation.

The potential of the Internet to disseminate vast amounts of pornographic material within an unregulated marketplace with a large, international audience is of great concern to those who feel that it does harm. If so, computer pornography has important consequences not because it is new and different from that in erotic magazines and videos, but rather because the distribution of pornography via computer networks can reduce its costs dramatically, reducing barriers to both publish and receive. This pornography also represents an unexpected use for the technology of the "global village." For those who do not believe pornography is harmful, the issue of computer pornography is important because it represents a domain of deep social and political controversy and possibly the main domain for contention over network regulation.

Nature of Computer Pornography

Computer pornography has moved from simple images composed of alphanumeric characters to more sophisticated digitized, moving images. A variety of computer pornography including soft-core "erotic" images of male and female models, animated serials, sexually explicit moving images, interactive sex games, and virtual reality-based types of cybersex is available (Robinson & Tamosaitis, 1993). Essentially, pornographic images that can be viewed on a computer screen are no different in type or nature from images readily available in erotic magazines or videos. In fact, many images come directly from such magazines and videos. However, because users select which images are posted, pornographic images on the Internet will reflect the taste of consumers and might not have the same frequency of themes as images in sexually oriented magazines and videos. Access to pornography through USENET newsgroups is relatively simple and straightforward. These newsgroups are organized collections of text, images, and computer software that cater to specific users. Access to the main news menu allows users to retrieve or post letters, computer programs, or graphic image files. The vast majority of newsgroups are associated with societies, organizations, gopher servers, and computer user groups. However, several thousand so-called "alternative" newsgroups also exist. Such groups are unable to mobilize sufficient support from "mainstream" newsgroups. As a result, their status is ambiguous, semipermanent, and dubious. Because newsgroups belonging to this hierarchy often are stigmatized and are not carried by many Internet servers, groups that provide electronic community support (e.g., alt.sex.abuse.recovery) can have more members if they move from the alt.* hierarchy to one that is more accessible like the misc.* or soc.* hierarchies.

Pornographic images may be posted on newsgroups in two ways. In one way, material may be posted anonymously by individual users from any location. That is, individuals with access to a scanner or a digital camera can scan images from pornographic magazines and videos or take photographs that can then be posted in one or more newsgroups. Alternatively, images may be posted by businesses such as bulletin board services, software companies, "sex shops," or graphic design firms. Perhaps commercial vendors believe that public domain space like newsgroups provides a good opportunity to advertise their products or services.

Although the Internet has the potential to overcome many of the traditional systemic barriers to access, an individual still needs a computer and modem, a telephone line, access to an Internet host, and leisure time to learn the intricacies of navigating a complex labyrinth of computer networks. Because such barriers still exist, it makes sense, intuitively, that most users of the Internet are somewhat technical, well-educated, high-income, White men between the ages of 20 and 40 years. It should be no surprise, then, that those who use the Internet most frequently are posting pornographic material that suits the predilections of young men. Commercial services also respond to this demand. The unregulated nature of the Internet coupled with a high potential for profit has a profound effect on how pornographic images are marketed on the Internet.

Assuming that commercial distributors have greater awareness of the legal implications of distributing explicit pornographic material, and that responsibility for posting such material can be directly traced to them, we hypothesized that there would be a greater likelihood of finding explicit material posted by anonymous, noncommercial users. Although the rapid growth of the Internet has created many regulatory gaps, we believe that commercial vendors will not risk arousing public concern, precisely because the new regulations that are bound to accompany increased commercialization of the network may eventually prove to be overly restrictive. Recent attempts in the United States to regulate content available to U.S. Internet users in the form of the Communications Decency Act is an illustration of a strong response to what some perceive as a social problem. A real threat of criminal prosecution for possession and distribution of pornography—which is deemed illegal in some jurisdictions—may be a sufficiently strong disincentive for commercial distributors to reconsider posting material that could result in such prosecutions (Branscomb, 1995).

In Canada, the Criminal Code respecting Canadian laws on child pornography was changed in 1993 to define more explicitly what acts constitute a breach of the law. Section 163.1 of the Criminal Code makes it illegal to possess, produce, distribute, or import "child pornography." The Code stipulates that any photograph, film, video, or other visual representation, made by electronic or mechanical means, that depicts a person as being under the age of 18 years, and engaged in explicit sexual activity, or where there is an emphasis on a sexual organ or the anal region, is child pornography. Therefore, in Canada, individuals who download pornography from the Internet may possess and import material that is a violation of the law. Tracing the flow of such material into Canada via the Internet to specific users is a time-consuming, expensive, and technically demanding task. Individuals who download such material are developing sophisticated cloaking techniques for maintaining their anonymity. For example, some users deliberately construct complex access paths criss-crossing the globe to post and download such material. Other users use public and private key encryption software like "Pretty Good Protection" (PGP) to accomplish the same objective. Finally, some users subscribe to anonymous servers like anon.penet.fi in Finland to post and download pornographic material. Such servers guarantee their clients anonymity with no questions asked. These arguments support our hypothesis that anonymous, noncommercial users of the Internet are more likely to post explicit pornography in USENET than are commercial services.

METHOD

Sample

A sample of 150 randomly selected pornographic images was downloaded from newsgroups on the Internet. Newsgroups were selected based on our interpretation of whether the name assigned to such groups suggested that sexually oriented material was present (e.g., alt.binaries.pictures. erotica, alt.sex.pictures). Our sample was taken from 4,937 newsgroups available at our university as of April 18, 1994. This group represents only a fraction of the more than 15,000 newsgroups available on the Internet.

Because few Internet providers offer complete access to all these groups, our sampling procedure is likely to include many of the largest and most active groups. As a rule, Internet providers such as universities must select, for technical and nontechnical reasons, which newsgroups they will sub-scribe to. Technical reasons include limitations on hard-drive capacity, processing power, and other factors affecting operating costs. Nontechnical reasons are based on subjective criteria determined, in part, by university policy, committees, and individuals who are responsible for systems man-agement. It is likely that such considerations will attempt to use a wide range of criteria, including legal and ethical considerations. For example, many services and firms restrict the number of groups within the alt.bina-ries.* hierarchy, or do not get them at all.

Our sample was obtained from 17 alternate newsgroups, including alt.binaries.pictures.erotica, alt.binaries. pictures.erotica.* (children, blondes, cartoons, female, male, orientals, anime, bestiality, bondage, nud-ism), alt.sex.pedophilia, alt.sex.pictures, alt.tasteless.pictures, alt.sex.pic-tures.* (female, male, and children). Images from these groups were selected using proportionate random sampling. The size of the newsgroup in proportion to the total number of graphic files available in all 17 news-groups determined the relative frequency of files selected from each news-group. A random number table was then used to select specific graphic files from the available pool of images.

Measures

Frequency and Percentage of Features and Themes. Because each image may contain multiple combinations of themes, the number of images containing specific themes plus the percentage of themes present within the sample were calculated. We also compared the frequency of variables from our findings with the frequencies from other content analyses on porno-graphic magazines and videos, and with Rimm's (1995) study of adult bulletin boards. We used a two-tailed test of significance for comparing differences between commercially and noncommercially distributed por-nography.

Intercoder Reliability. Because images were dichotomously coded and nominally scaled, we used kappa as a measure of agreement. Kappa values greater than .75 indicate excellent agreement beyond chance, values be-tween .40 and .75 indicate fair to good agreement beyond chance, and values less than .40 indicate poor agreement beyond chance (Landis & Koch, 1977). Mean kappas for each variable by each pair of coders was then calculated. Variables with mean kappas below .40 were dropped from subsequent analysis.

Procedure

We developed a coding scheme by adapting several content analysis cate-gories used in previous research to analyze erotic videos, magazines, and cartoons (e.g., Garcia & Milano, 1990; Palys, 1986; Winick, 1985; Palmer, 1979). In addition, new categories related to how computer pornography is displayed were also developed (e.g., color vs. black-and-white images, relative quality of images, digitized or animated images). Each category is briefly described in Table 3.1.

A two-stage coding procedure was used in this study. In the first stage, we individually rated the sample of 150 images by assigning one or more content categories, based on central themes, to each image in the sample. Content categories were coded for either their presence or their absence. Concern about intercoder reliability led to a second round of coding of a random subsample of 35 images. We and two female graduate students in the social sciences worked independently to code this subsample. The two female coders were not told about the study but were made aware of coding procedures by both oral and written instructions. Neither coder had sub-stantial prior exposure to pornography in any form.

TABLE 3.1

Pornographic Features and Themes Used in Content Analysis

Mode of distribution	Commercial images are those that are posted for business purposes. Typically, bulletin board services place images in USENET as business cards to attract new customers. Non-commercial images are those posted anonymously without charge.
Type of image	Images that are digitized from photographs or animated (cartoons).
Color	Images that are displayed either in color or black and white.
Image quality	Images that have resolutions that are low, medium, or high. This assessment includes the amount of screen occupied by image, sharpness, and color rendition or separation.
Frontal nudity	Shows a full display of male or female genitalia.
Close-up	Content involving a high emphasis on human genitalia ("zoomed in").
Erect penis	Shows an erect penis.
Fetishes	Shows sexual activity or poses where there is a central fetishistic dimension (e.g., lingerie, leather, rubber, boots, etc.).
Masturbation	Content involving manual stimulation of the genitals. Such stimulation may or may not include the use of foreign objects like dildos.
Homosexuality	Content involving two or more men or two or more women interacting sexually.
Use of foreign object	Content in which "sex toys" are shown or used (e.g., dildos, vibrators, bananas, etc.).
Fellatio	Content involving oral stimulation of the penis.
Children/adolescents	Images depicting nude children or adolescents. Images giving the illusion of someone being under the age of 18 years also fall into this category. Text stating age, props such as "teddy bears" and clothing are included in this variable.
Vaginal penetration	Shows vaginal penetration with a penis, finger, object, etc.
Group sex	Shows more than two people interacting sexually.
Bondage and discipline	Content in which at least one person is relatively immobile and subject to discipline usually as a result of being tied.
Ejaculation	Content involving copious amounts of male or female ejaculate.
Cunnilingus	Shows oral stimulation of the vagina.
Urination	Shows explicit depictions of urination.
Incest	Shows or alludes to undisguised incestuous relations between kin (explicitly stated in text) accompanying image.

RESULTS

Kappa reliability coefficients were calculated for each variable among the four coders on a sample of 35 images. The overall mean kappa for all raters across the 22 themes is .67, indicating a good to fair degree of intercoder reliability (Landis & Koch, 1977). Disagreement between male and female coders on the variables for quality, close-ups, homosexual sex, use of a foreign object, images of children/adolescents, anal penetration, bondage and discipline, and ejaculation was noted. We hypothesized that these discrepancies arose from limited coder training and possible distress in viewing explicit images that one female coder particularly mentioned. Nevertheless, the mean intercoder reliability fell below .40 only for the quality and frontal nudity variables, which we dropped from the analysis, as they fall into Landis and Koch's poor agreement category.

Table 3.2 shows the percentage of features and themes found in our sample of pornographic images from the identified USENET newsgroups.

TABLE 3.2

Percentage of Features and Themes in a Sample of Pornographic Images on USENET

	Number	Percentage
IMAGE & DISTRIBUTION		
Commercial distribution	53	35
Color images	122	81
Type of image		
Digitized	138	92
Animated	12	8
THEMES		
Close-up	65	43
Erect penis	53	35
Fetishes	50	33
Masturbation	32	21
Homosexuality	27	18
Use of foreign object	26	17
Fellatio	23	15
Children/adolescents	23	15
Vaginal penetration	23	15
Group sex	17	11
Bestiality	15	10
Bondage and discipline	15	10
Ejaculation	11	7
Cunnilingus	8	5
Anal penetration	5	3
Urination	5	3
Incest	2	1

Note. N = 150. Percentages will not add to 100 because individual images may contain multiple variables. All values are rounded to whole numbers.

Of the 150 pornographic images analyzed, 65% were distributed noncommercially by anonymous network users, 81% were in color, and 92% were digitized. The most prevalent themes are close-ups (43%), erect penises (35%), fetishes (33%), and masturbation (21%).

We compared our results with other content analyses to determine whether computer pornography differed in theme from magazine and video pornography. We found that fellatio was present in 15% of our sample, compared with Garcia and Milano's (1990) finding of 8.1% for fellatio. Homosexual sex was present in 18% of our sample whereas Winick (1985) and Garcia and Milano (1990) obtained much lower levels in the 2%–4% range. Finally, group sex appeared in 11% of computer pornography but in only 1%–3% of other pornography (Winick, 1985; Garcia & Milano, 1990). These results suggest that the criteria for selecting what material to post on the Internet are different from those used by magazine and video producers.

When our results are compared with Rimm's (1995) study on pornography available through adult bulletin board services, several similarities emerge. Rimm's classification system makes direct comparison with our results difficult. However, certain trends can be gleaned from the data. For example, Rimm reported that 15.6% of images were pedophilic/hebephilic. We find very similar results, in that 15% fall into the children/adolescents category. Of the other themes common to both studies we found bondage and discipline (10%), foreign objects (17%), incest (1%), bestiality (10%), and urination (3%). The sum of these percentages is not dissimilar from Rimm's 32.8% for "paraphilia." Overall, our findings indicate that pornography in the bulletin board services studied by Rimm, appears close to what we found available in USENET newsgroups.

Our study showed some significant differences in the kind of images posted by commercial and noncommercial users of the Internet. A two-tailed test of significance using mode of distribution as an independent variable revealed the following results: fellatio [$F(1,149) = 5.88, p < .05$], children/adolescents [$F(1,149) = 7.02, p < .05$], and use of a foreign object [$F(1,149) = 10.60, p < .01$]. These tests reflect a tendency for commercial pornography on the Internet to be more focused on younger subjects and explicit sexual acts like fellatio and the use of foreign objects such as dildos. (See Table 3.3.)

DISCUSSION

Our examination of the nature and content of 150 randomly selected pornographic images available through 17 alternate newsgroups on the Internet suggests that pornography on the Internet is readily available in a large quantity to any determined user. We also found differences in the type of material posted by commercial and noncommercial users. Commercial users appear to be more likely to post explicit pornographic material in

TABLE 3.3

**Comparison of Commercial and Noncommercial Pornographic Images Reporting
Percentage of Distribution, F Statistic, and Significance Level**

	Percentage of Commercial	Percentage of Noncommerical	F	Significance Level
IMAGE				
Color	79	82	.17	_____
Digitized image	96	90	1.86	_____
THEMES				
Close-up	54	37	4.12	_____
Erect penis	46	29	4.72	_____
Fetishes	38	31	.94	_____
Masturbation	15	23	1.35	――――
Homosexuality	17	18	.03	_____
Use of foreign object	31	10	10.60	.003**
Fellatio	25	10	5.88	.033*
Children/adolescents	25	9	7.02	.017*
Vaginal penetration	17	13	.44	_____
Group sex	15	9	1.29	_____
Bestiality	12	9	.21	_____
Bondage and discipline	13	8	1.05	_____
Ejaculation	8	6	.13	_____
Cunnilingus	0	7	3.95	_____
Anal penetration	4	3	.06	_____
Urination	0	5	2.76	_____
Incest	2	1	.21	_____
n =	52	98		

Note. N = 150. Significance levels were calculated using a two-tailed analysis of variance.

*Significant at $p < .05$

**Significant at $p < .01$

public access newsgroups. This finding fails to support our hypothesis that there is a greater likelihood of finding explicit pornographic material posted by anonymous, noncommercial users.

We speculate that our result reflects the attempt of distributors of pornography on the Internet to post material to attract new customers to private, pay-per-use bulletin board services. The Internet is a weak regulatory environment and a fiercely competitive market. In such a marketplace, commercial vendors need to provide users with services that are not only superior to those provided by their competitors, but also with services not available "free of charge" by others. Consequently, commercial vendors advertising their services and products in newsgroups would attract more attention by posting sexually explicit pornography. It appears as though the lack of regulation on the Internet makes taking these risks worthwhile.

Although commercial vendors are more likely to post sexually explicit images than are noncommercial distributors, we did not find that they posted a statistically significant different amount of material depicting illegal sexual acts such as bestiality. Perhaps commercial vendors are willing to take minor risks posting images that depict explicit material showing the use of foreign objects, fellatio, and images of children or adolescents but do not take larger risks. We believe that the reason commercial vendors are more likely to post images showing children and adolescents might be that the nature of the medium is attractive to users with interests in this area who may have difficulty or face greater risks obtaining such material in more conventional adult book stores and similar venues. This result can be explained somewhat by our coding procedure too. If an image was accompanied by text suggesting that subjects were under the age of 18 years, we coded this image as a "hit." In other words, models in such coded images may be technically adults by age, but props or descriptors give the illusion of being an adolescent. In Canada the cultivation of such an illusion is illegal under the Criminal Code. As a qualifier, the vast majority of the small number of such images depicting children and adolescents probably come from nudist magazines or were taken by those who have visited such communities. We never came across an image depicting a sexual act between an adult and a child/adolescent, or acts between children. We did, however, come across some images that were electronically altered, using software designed for desktop publishing and photo retouching to juxtapose the faces and bodies of children and adults and give the impression of sexual interaction.

Limitations of This Research

Our analysis is limited to USENET newsgroups, although several others sources of computer pornography exist. A more thorough approach for assessing computer pornography, in general, would involve examining not only newsgroups but also bulletin board services (see Rimm, 1995), file transfer protocol (FTP) servers, pornographic software (e.g., "Leisure Suit Larry"), virtual reality games (e.g., "Midnight Stranger") and commercially available software on CD-ROM and diskettes (e.g., *Playboy* and *Penthouse* photo collections). Nevertheless, the simplicity associated with perusing newsgroups probably means that the Internet is the lowest cost means for retrieving a constantly changing repertoire of pornographic material.

A second limitation of our study is that we selected only images from newsgroups with names suggesting that sexually related material is present. Therefore, newsgroups with words like *sex, pictures, homosexual*, and *bestiality* in their name were automatically included in our sample. Unfortunately, other newsgroups with names that are cryptic or nonspecific may also contain sexually related material. Unless one searched through every possible newsgroup (approximately 15,000 and growing), it would be impossible to ensure that all pornography is accounted for.

A third limitation of our study is that we analyzed only single-series graphic image files (e.g., gif, jpeg). In addition to these types of graphic images, there are also more advanced types of image files that simulate movement (e.g., mpegs). To view these moving images, users require computers with fast central processing units and larger amounts of random access memory. Our limited access to such equipment restricted this study to only single-series graphic image files. Additionally, few moving picture files are currently available in USENET groups. The large amounts of memory required for such applications usually mean that such files are not practical for posting or downloading. This shortcoming, however, presents little threat to the validity of our findings because most images currently available on Internet newsgroups tend to be gif and jpeg files.

Most images in our sample appear to be taken directly from magazines and videos. Apparently, noncommercial users select these images, unfettered by editorial considerations or local obscenity laws. In this respect, they differ from magazine and video producers, who need to include a wide variety of sexual content to sell their product to as large a market as possible, or who must develop and maintain niche markets. Users of the Internet who post sexually explicit material, however, do not have to worry about such promotional considerations, because they are uploading images irrespective of sequencing, editing, or layout. This selection process suggests that pornographic images on the Internet tend to represent the dominant interests of network users. As we speculated earlier, such content probably reflects the values, tastes, preferences, and mores of young White, upper middle-class men. Perhaps such an electronic community also creates a chilly climate for women, non-White, and older users. More study on this question is needed.

Future researchers in this area should examine a multitude of related issues: Will increasing commercialization of the Internet lead to a change in the type of pornography available? How does computer pornography differ, if at all, from other types of pornography? How is computer pornography being used, and by whom? As more people spend greater amounts of their time using computers and navigating through computer networks, these questions need to be addressed.

In conclusion, not only does the Internet possess the potential to overcome geographical, social, and political barriers and to act as a medium for the exchange of ideas, but it also has the potential to undermine local laws, customs, and mores in its current form. For now, the Internet is being regulated on a local, microlevel by access providers who restrict and censor information. On a larger scale, such practices have profound implications for individuals and corporations wishing to partake in the freedoms offered by a global information infrastructure. The Internet has outpaced current rules and regulations regarding intellectual property rights, definitions of obscenity, publication bans, and government excise mechanisms, and the Internet changes again even as groups try to bridge these gaps. As a result researchers will have to repeat our study to document how computer pornography is changing. Over time, we expect that the content of computer pornography will reflect both changes in the balance of commercialization in the Internet and changes in how local and international groups attempt to regulate technology and to develop standards. All of these changes, in turn, will change the culture of the Internet.

REFERENCES

Baron, L., & Straus, M. A. (1989). *Four theories of rape in American society*. New Haven, CT: Yale University Press.

Branscomb, A. W. (1995). Internet Babylon? Does the Carnegie Mellon study of pornography on the information superhighway reveal a threat to the stability of society? *The Georgetown Law Journal, 83*(5), 1935–1957.

Branwyn, G. (1993). Compu-sex: Erotica for cybernauts. *The South Atlantic Quarterly, 92*, 779–791.

Calem, R. E. (1992, December 6). The network of all networks. *New York Times*.

Donnerstein, E., Linz, D., & Penrod, S. (1987). *The question of pornography*. New York: The Free Press.

Dworkin, A. (1985). Against the male flood: Censorship, pornography, and equality. *Harvard Women's Law Journal, 8*, 1–19.

Dworkin, A., & MacKinnon, C. A. (1988). *Pornography and civil rights*. Minneapolis, MN: Organizing Against Pornography.

Garcia, L. T., & Milano, L. (1990). A content analysis of erotic videos. *Journal of Psychology and Human Sexuality, 3*, 95–103.

Landis, J. R., & Koch, G. G. (1977). The measurement of observer agreement for categorical data. *Biometrics, 33*, 159–174.

MacKinnon, C. A. (1995). Vindication and resistance: A response to the Carnegie Mellon study of pornography in cyberspace. *The Georgetown Law Journal, 83*(5), 1959–1967.

Malamuth, N., & Spinner, B. (1980). A longitudinal content analysis of sexual violence in the best-selling erotic magazines. *The Journal of Sex Research, 16*, 226–237.

Mehta, M., & Plaza, D. (in press). A content analysis of pornographic images on the Internet. *The Information Society*.

Padgett, V. R., Brislin-Stutz, J., & Neal, J. A. (1989). Pornography, erotica, and attitudes toward women: The effects of repeated exposure. *The Journal of Sex Research, 26*, 479–491.

Palmer, C. E. (1979). Pornographic comics: A content analysis. *The Journal of Sex Research, 15*, 285–298.

Palys, T. S. (1986). The social content of video pornography. *Canadian Psychology, 27*, 22–34.

Rimm, M. (1995). Marketing pornography on the information superhighway: A survey of 917,410 images, descriptions, short stories, and animations downloaded 8.5 million times by consumers in over 2000 cities in 40 countries, provinces, and territories. *The Georgetown Law Journal, 83*(5), 1849–1934.

Robinson, P., & Tamosaitis, N. (1993). *The joy of cybersex: An underground guide to electronic erotica*. New York: Brady.

Scott, J. E., & Cuvelier, S. J. (1993). Violence and sexual violence in pornography: Is it really increasing? *Archives of Sexual Behavior, 22,* 357–371.

Winick, C. (1985). A content analysis of sexually explicit magazines sold in an adult bookstore. *The Journal of Sex Research, 21,* 206–210.

Zillmann, D., & Bryant, J. (1984). Effects of massive exposure to pornography. In N. Malamuth & E. Donnerstein (Eds.), *Pornography and sexual aggression* (pp. 115–138). Orlando, FL: Academic Press.

Erotica on the Internet: Early Evidence From the HomeNet Trial

Jane Manning
William Scherlis
Sara Kiesler
Robert Kraut
Tridas Mukhopadhyay
Carnegie Mellon University

Is the average American family devouring pornographic materials on the Internet? HomeNet, a panel study at Carnegie Mellon University of how ordinary families use the Internet concludes that families aren't big consumers of sexual information on computer networks. Few seem likely to become avid readers.

At the start of the HomeNet field trial in February 1995, a panel of 50 families in the Pittsburgh area received Macintosh computers, a full Internet connection, and Internet services including electronic mail and a World Wide Web browser. The families were also encouraged to explore electronic newsgroups, or discussion groups, on hundreds of topics where anyone can read and post messages to others. Detailed electronic audit trails are being collected by the researchers to understand how the 150 individuals in these families use the Internet. (Research participants all signed consent forms. No results will be reported that could in any way attribute specific behaviors to specific individuals in the study.)

So, what do ordinary people do with the Internet, and with USENET newsgroups in particular, when they're there?

The sample of ordinary people in Pittsburgh is far less interested in using the net as a way to access erotica than publicity from popular magazines would seem to predict. And their interest is mostly transient: Nearly half of the people who have, in fact, looked at sexually oriented newsgroups during the entire first year of the study have done so only once or twice.

Those who looked at any particular sexually oriented newsgroup more than twice constitute less than one fourth of the sample. And even for these people, their usage of sexually oriented groups was a relatively small portion of their overall activity with newsgroups.

Mostly, people browse groups specific to their interests. Because there are so many newsgroups fitting diverse interests, few such groups show up in the "top 40." But in the aggregate, they far outrank the sexually oriented groups in popularity. Local groups that allowed users to exchange information relevant to their day-to-day lives (e.g., "where's the easiest place in Pittsburgh to take the driver's license exam?") were by far the most popular in the first year of the study.

We created four large categories of newsgroups—sex, music, sports and religion—that together were read by roughly 60% of the HomeNetters who read newsgroups. Forty-two percent read a sexually oriented newsgroup and/or a music oriented newsgroup at least once, 34%, a sports oriented newsgroup, and 10%, a religion oriented newsgroup. The group that sampled sexually oriented newsgroups included three fourths of the teenage boys, almost half of the teenage girls, a third of the adult men, and a fifth of the adult women. Controlling statistically for their overall Internet usage, men more than women, and teenagers more than adults, sampled these newsgroups. The same bias applies to sports and religious categories but not to music oriented newsgroups, which women and teenage girls read as much as men and teenage boys.

"Lurking": Sometimes HomeNet followers of a newsgroup (defined as reading the group three times or more) also post to these groups, but the median ratio of posting to reading is 1:2 (i.e., among people who both read and post, people tend to post to about half as many groups as they read). If we include people who have never posted in the calculation, then the ratio drops to 1:10 (and in case you're wondering, after 12 months on the Internet only four HomeNet users had ever posted to a sexually oriented newsgroup).

The HomeNet trial is expected to last 3 years. For more information about HomeNet research, see HomeNet's web page, http://home-net.andrew.cmu.edu/progress.

4

FROM THE COUCH TO THE KEYBOARD: PSYCHOTHERAPY IN CYBERSPACE

Yitzchak M. Binik
McGill University and Royal Victoria Hospital

James Cantor
Eric Ochs
Marta Meana
McGill University

In this chapter we review research on computerized automated psychotherapy, computer-mediated therapy, and computer-created virtual realities for therapy. We discuss the different theoretical, practical, and ethical issues that result from computer involvement in the psychotherapeutic process. One central focus to our discussion is the ability of computer technology to support a therapeutic alliance. To the extent this is possible, we believe that computerized psychotherapy will be successful therapeutically. Moreover, the attempts to create suitable forms of computerized psychotherapy will provide us with novel experimental opportunities to investigate the necessary elements required in therapeutic relationships.

Psychotherapy must rank high, perhaps just after motherhood and friendship, on the list of domains least likely to be taken over by machines. therapy is generally defined as a series of contacts between a professionally trained person and someone seeking help for problems that interfere with his or her emotional well-being. Every major school of therapy places a high premium on the emotive aspects of this relationship. In the psychoanalytic approach, derived mainly from the writings of Sigmund Freud, the therapist's neutrality and uncritical acceptance of the client are the foundation for the development of a strong emotional attachment to the therapist. It is through this emotive link (at times positive, at others negative) that the patient works through the difficulties of his or her other relationships. In the client-centered approach initiated by Carl Rogers, the therapist's function is to create optimal conditions of permissiveness and to convey unconditional positive regard for the client. Because the client finds himself or herself in a nonjudgmental and yet caring relationship, maladaptive defenses become unnecessary. Although the cognitive–behavioral approach to therapy focuses more specifically on rule-governed techniques to effect behavior change through rewards, cognitive–behavioral therapists stress that the warmth and empathic capacity of the therapist are important in producing constructive change (Barnlund, 1990).

Must you be in the presence of a therapist to improve? Could one design a virtual reality system to create unconditional positive regard? Can the rule-governed process of cognitive–behavioral therapies be captured by an expert system and still convey the required measure of empathy? In other words, can a computer provide the emotionally corrective experience everyone agrees is key to psychotherapeutic change? If so, could this be done on the Internet?

The answers to these questions will no doubt shed light on central issues in psychotherapy. If the psychotherapeutic alliance between therapist and client can be simulated by a computer, it will have been rendered programmmable. This is of particular relevance, because the single best predictor of psychotherapy outcome with a human therapist is not his or her experience, school of thought, training, or physical appearance, but the strength of the therapeutic alliance (e.g., Horvath, Gaston & Luborsky, 1993). We generally conceptualize the therapeutic alliance as having three constituent parts: (a) an agreement between patient and therapist about therapeutic tasks or interventions, (b) an agreement about therapeutic goals, (c) an affective bond between patient and therapist based on trust, acceptance, and confidence (cf. Muran, Segal, Samstag, & Crawfore, 1994). Such a conceptualization potentially allows for easing the requirement that psychotherapy requires a human therapist.

Despite the general resistance to the idea of an inanimate therapist, especially one acting at a distance, psychotherapeutic processes that dispense with the human therapist are not entirely new. Self-help books and videos have been on the market for over two decades and are now widely used. There is adequate research to suggest that the "therapy" provided by self-help books and videos is sometimes as effective as that provided by human therapists (Jacobs & Goodman, 1989).

Further, computers have made some very significant inroads into the realm of psychotherapy, both as a medium connecting two or more individuals and as a software proxy for the psychotherapist. There is even initial work attempting to use virtual reality technology for therapeutic purposes. Part of this phenomenon has evolved from academic research, part has been market-driven, and part has sprung spontaneously from laypeople reaching out to each other in the new cyber-community.

The possibility of a developing a therapeutic alliance with a computer was inadvertently raised by Weizenbaum's (1976) attempt to write a computer program to understand natural language. This early and unsuccessful attempt to simulate natural language comprehension resulted in a program called ELIZA, which performed somewhat like a Rogerian therapist. The following excerpt (Weizenbaum, 1976) exemplifies a "conversation" in which a young woman (lower case type) is speaking with ELIZA (capitals):

Men are all alike.

IN WHAT WAY

They're always bugging us about something or other.

CAN YOU THINK OF A SPECIFIC EXAMPLE

Well, my boyfriend made me come here.

YOUR BOYFRIEND MADE YOU COME HERE

He says I'm depressed much of the time.

I AM SORRY TO HEAR YOU ARE DEPRESSED

It's true. I am unhappy.

DO YOU THINK COMING HERE WILL HELP YOU NOT TO BE UNHAPPY

I need some help, that much seems certain.

WHAT WOULD IT MEAN TO YOU IF YOU GOT SOME HELP

Perhaps I could learn to get along with my mother.

TELL ME MORE ABOUT YOUR FAMILY

My mother takes care of me.

WHO ELSE IN YOUR FAMILY TAKES CARE OF YOU

My father.

YOUR FATHER

You are like my father in some ways.

WHAT RESEMBLANCE DO YOU SEE (pp. 3–4)

Weizenbaum (1976) was startled at how quickly and how deeply people became involved with ELIZA and how deeply they resented any intrusion on their interactions with the program. Some 30 years later, a large number of similar programs sell very well despite their still relatively primitive conversational abilities. Their widespread appeal is perhaps illustrated by the following excerpt from Lodge's (1984) novel, *Small World* :

HALLO, HOW ARE YOU FEELING TODAY, says ELIZA

Terrible, Robin Dempsey types.

WHAT EXACTLY DO YOU MEAN BY TERRIBLE?

Angry.incredulous.jealous.

WHAT HAS CAUSED YOU TO HAVE THESE FEELINGS?

Something i have read in the newspaper about Philip Swallow

TELL ME ABOUT PHILIP SWALLOW.

Robin Dempsey types for twenty-five minutes without stopping, until Josh Collins wanders over from his glass walled cubicle, nibbling a Kit-Kat, upon which Robin stops typing and covers the computer with its plastic hood.

"Want some?" says Josh, offering a piece of the chocolate-covered biscuit.

"No, thank you," says Robin without looking at him.

"Getting some interesting stuff from ELIZA, are you?"

"Yes."

"You don't think you're overdoing it? ... [I]t fair gives me the creeps to see you hunched over that VDU, day in and day out. You're becoming dependent upon it."

"I'm simply doing my research."

"It's called transference. I looked it up in a psychology book."

"Rubbish!" shouts Robin Dempsey.

"If you ask me, you need a proper psychiatrist," says Josh Collins, trembling with anger. "You're off your trolley. That thing"—he points a quivering finger at ELIZA—"Can't really talk, you know. It can't actually think. It can't answer questions. It's not a bloody oracle."

"I know perfectly well how computers work, thank you," says Robin Dempsey, rising to his feet. "I'll be back after lunch." (pp. 242–243)

The Eliza phenomenon strongly suggested that the nature of the interaction between a computer and willing client could possibly result in a therapeutic alliance. The following pages review our work and that of others in examining this question.

COMPUTER-CONDUCTED PSYCHOLOGICAL INTERVENTION

The 30 years since ELIZA have seen much activity in the field of computer-conducted intervention. We are aware of at least four full-length monographs (Baskin, 1990; Hand, 1985; Lieff, 1987; Romanczyk, 1986) and two scholarly journals (*Computers in Human Behavior; Computers in Human Services*) devoted totally or in large part to describing and summarizing developments in computerized psychological intervention. Most major clinical psychological or psychiatric conferences have at least one major session devoted to this topic. Bloom's (1992) review article listed over 200 relevant references, and there have been at least 50 additional publications since then.

Computer-Conducted Assessment and Therapy

Testing. Almost every major psychological assessment instrument, from tests of vocational interest to projective personality tests, has a computerized administration format. Most of these can also be scored by the computer that administers them, and a growing number of programs generate an interpretive report. Although there was much initial debate over the potential reaction of clients to these testing methods, research has been unanimous in indicating that most individuals find taking computerized tests acceptable, with some clients even preferring it to human administration (Bloom, 1992). There is more controversy about the validity of computerized interpretation; however, it seems only a matter of time before acceptable norms for computerized interpretation are developed and before programs with high interpretive validity are available. These developments are likely to end the traditional role of psychologists and psychometrists as administrators and interpreters of tests.

Interviewing. Although psychological tests are frequently used for many kinds of clinical assessment, the clinical interview is still the cornerstone of most psychological diagnosis. In fact, a variety of computer-administered interviews has been developed for initial psychiatric screening interviews (e.g., Lieff, 1987; McCullough, Farrell, & Longabaugh, 1986). Some of these interviews generate official psychiatric diagnoses based on the *DSM–IV (Diagnostic and Statistical Manual,* American Psychiatric Association, 1994), in addition to diagnostic summary reports. Patient acceptance of computerized interviewing has been very high, and concordance between diagnoses made by a computer-administered interview and that of a clinician is similar to that between two clinicians.

There appear to be at least two sources of discordance between computer- and human-administered assessment interviews. First, even the most experienced clinicians tend to "forget" to ask some relevant questions and therefore reach conclusions based on inadequate information. Second, individuals report more pathology to a computer than to a human interviewer, especially concerning "socially unacceptable" behaviors such as use of drugs, alcohol, and "deviant" sexual behavior (e.g., Erdman, Klein, & Greist, 1985). Available research and common sense suggests that computer-elicited reports are more likely to approximate the truth. However, there is no simple way to verify this. Interestingly, both sources of discordance tend to suggest that clinicians may be underestimating certain kinds of pathology.

It seems only a matter of time before hospitals, clinics, and individual practitioners offer an initial assessment interview or a battery of psychological tests over the Internet. The information obtained through this type of assessment might then serve as the basis for referrals, reassurance, or explicit instructions to seek immediate help. Individuals in crisis might soon be able to dial into the psychiatric emergency room computer for screening and advice about what to do.

Vocational and Behavioral Counseling.   Probably the most widespread use of computerized counseling has been in the realm of vocational advice. These programs assess individuals' aptitudes, skills, and attitudes and provide advice about appropriate career choices. The most well known of these programs, SIGI, was originally developed at the Educational Testing Service (cf. Katz, 1993); however numerous others exist (Sampson, Reardon, Humphreys, & Peterson, 1990). Although exact figures are difficult to obtain, it seems likely that these vocational counseling programs are used in hundreds of North American high schools and universities. Controlled research about the quality of the advice given by these programs or the long-term effects of this advice is limited (Sampson, 1991).

An early but well-developed and researched counseling system called PLATO DCS was initiated by Wagman (1988) and his colleagues at the University of Illinois. This system, designed for university students, asks them to translate their problems and solutions into if–then statements and leads them through an evaluation of the potential positive and negative consequences of choosing one course of action over another. The theory behind this system has been well worked out, and a variety of outcome studies have been completed demonstrating the effectiveness of the program. To the best of our knowledge, PLATO DCS is not available outside the University of Illinois.

Two other "everyday problems, " weight control and smoking cessation, have been the subject of recent computer-conducted counseling applications. Burnett and his colleagues (e.g., Taylor, Agras, Losch, Plante, & Burnett, 1991) have developed a hand-held microchip that computes calories, makes menu suggestions, charts weight, and provides information and general advice about a variety of food intake issues. The outcome data from this project are no different from the outcome data from most non-computer-based weight control programs. A series of studies by Schneider and his colleagues (e.g., Schneider, Walker, & O'Donnell, 1990) has demonstrated that an entire computer-based smoking cessation program can be presented on a computer network. Several thousand individuals were given access to this program via CompuServe, and Schneider demonstrated that this method of access was acceptable to users, potentially inexpensive, and somewhat effective. These studies are particularly important because they probably herald the future use of computer networks as vehicles for computerized intervention.

Psychotherapy.   Researchers have developed a number of computer-conducted psychotherapy programs (cf. Plutchik & Karasu, 1991, for a review). Other than briefly discussing two therapeutically promising programs that have been compared to human clinicians and/or other forms of self-help, our discussion focuses on a sex therapy program we have been developing and testing over the last few years.

The first computer program was developed by Marks and his colleagues in the context of an ongoing behavioral treatment regimen for phobias. The treatment, a series of graded exposures to the phobic stimulus, is the standard for phobias. Because the treatment is so well defined, Marks has written a self-help book that outlines the program in detail, which was adapted to computer presentation. A controlled study of 71 phobics compared the computer-administered treatment with therapist-administered treatment and the self-help book . All treatment groups showed significant clinical improvement, but mode of delivery made no difference (Ghosh & Marks, 1987). Interestingly, Marks decided on this basis that there was little reason to use a computer-administered format and further development was abandoned (I.M. Marks, personal communication, July, 1990).

A second project, initiated by Selmi, Klein, Greist, Sorrell, and Erdman (1990), developed a program called Morton that simulated the cognitive–behavioral treatment of depression. This program, written originally in the 1970s, instructs clients on the relationship between cognitive errors in understanding everyday events and resulting emotions, particularly depression. It monitors depression levels and provides didactic examples and suggestions about altering cognitive style to improve mood. In a striking study of patients with clinical depression, Morton performed as well as a therapist.

Although these studies need to be replicated, they strongly suggest that computer-conducted therapy, at least in the behavioral realm, may be highly effective in comparison to human therapists and self-help books.

However, none of the developed programs has undergone rigorous testing outside their developers' laboratories and none, to our knowledge, is commercially available.

Sexpert   Our work has involved the development of an expert system to interview, assess, counsel, and provide therapy to couples with sexual dysfunctions. Although our initial choice of sex therapy was accidental (Binik, Ochs, & Meana, in press), there was adequate practical and theoretical justification for working in this area. Sex therapists had long used and recommended self-help materials such as books and videos. We felt that an expert computer system could extend the individualization of such self-help tools and promote self-disclosure and compliance with therapeutic recommendations. It was also possible to design a computer system that could be used together by a couple. Moreover, we believed that because interaction with a computer is potentially a more active process, it could be more effective than reading a book or viewing a video. With the projected increase in the number of home computers and computer networks users, easy access to help at minimal expense seemed likely. We hoped that such increased availability would result in early consultation, which could have an important preventative function. Finally, we felt that the domain of sexual problem diagnosis and therapy was among the more defined and delimited areas in clinical psychology, which would facilitate computerization.

From the outset, our work was also directed by a set of requirements we believed were necessary for all "personal advice systems." These requirements were based on the premise that a computer must react according to user expectations of normal social discourse in counseling situations, in order to create the effective illusion of an understanding and intelligent caregiver. The importance of this requirement was illustrated by one of our earliest pilot subjects, who, when questioned about her interaction with Sexpert, said it was "terrible" despite the fact that Sexpert had understood her situation perfectly and given her reasonable advice. When we asked her why the experience was terrible she replied, "I told Sexpert something very important to me and it answered too quickly! No human could respond that fast."

Taking into account our experience and those of others with ELIZA and similar programs (DeMuth, 1984), we also felt it was crucial to simulate the process of therapeutic dialogue (cf. Servan-Schreiber & Binik, 1989). Although we could not construct an intelligent system that would accept natural language, we could simulate this by structuring dialogue plans to follow the expectations of normal social intercourse and to present accurate feedback in natural language. Another important requirement was that our system be able to shift focus based on users' answers rather than plod ahead trying to solve its internal goals. We also tried to construct a system that would monitor when it lacked adequate knowledge and inform the user accordingly. In addition, we required the system to allow users to backtrack and change previous answers without having to repeat the entire interaction. Finally, we believed it necessary to develop a system that could inform the user about the reasons behind a particular conclusion.

The following dialogue illustrates a couple's interaction with Sexpert on the topic of everyday sexual repertoire. Other examples of dialogues can be found in the following papers: Binik, Servan-Schreiber, Freiwald and Hall, 1988; Servan-Schreiber and Binik, 1989; Binik, Meana, and Sand, 1994; Ochs, Meana, Mah, and Binik, 1993; Ochs, Meana, Paré, Mah and Binik, 1994. This excerpt begins with feedback about the couple's current foreplay. Sexpert then investigates potential changes:

Sexpert begins the session by introducing itself and asking for the couple's names, ages, and other general background information. Then Sexpert provides information about how it was developed, and discusses its areas of expertise. Here, Sexpert begins to find out more details about the couple's sexual life.

Eva, who usually initiates sex?
1: You always initiate (100%)
2: You usually initiate (75% or more)
3: You each initiate about equally often (about 50% of the time)
4: Adam usually initiates (75% or more)
5: Adam always initiates (100%)
>>>>3

Adam, do you agree with Eva about who usually initiates sex?
>>>>Y

Adam, who would you LIKE to initiate sexual activities?
1: You more often
2: You like it as it is now
3: Eva more often
>>>>2

And you, Eva, who would you LIKE to initiate sexual activities?
1: Adam more often
2: You like it as it is now
3: You more often
>>>>1

Adam, would you like to have sex with Eva:
1: less frequently
2: as frequently as you do now (about 4 times a month)
3: more frequently
>>>>3

Adam, are you pleased with the way Eva lets you know she would like to have sex?
1: it's fine
2: there is room for improvement

3: you would like it to change
>>>>2

Eva, are you pleased with the way Adam lets you know he would like to have
sex?
1: it's fine
2: there is room for improvement
3: you would like it to change
>>>>1

Adam, when you make sexual advances, how does Eva usually respond?
1: accepts with pleasure
2: accepts reluctantly
3: often refuses at first but then gives in
4: refuses or ignores me
>>>>1

Eva, when you make sexual advances, how does Adam usually respond?
1: accepts with pleasure
2: accepts reluctantly
3: often refuses at first but then gives in
4: refuses or ignores me
>>>>1

Eva, would you like to have sex with Adam:
1: less frequently
2: as frequently as you do now (about 4 times a month)
3: more frequently
>>>>3

Both of you want to increase your frequency of sex. I take this as a sign that
you both see a lot of potential for enjoying sex more often. Why not try? You
probably will also want to consider the quality of your sexual repertoire and
I'll try to give you some feedback about that in a minute.

With respect to your pattern of initiation, there seems to be some discrepancy
between the two of you in terms of who you feel should have the responsibility for initiating sex. You, Adam, are happy with the situation as it is now,
whereas you, Eva, would like Adam to initiate more. Adam, since you feel
that you are having sex less often than you would like, it is difficult for me to
understand why you are not initiating more often, especially in view of the
fact that Eva would like you to do just that. In fact, she too has expressed a
desire to have sex more often. The real issue may be not so much the actual
frequency of sex but that Eva would like you, Adam to be more active in your
love making.

Even though there is no right or wrong way to initiate sex, everyone has his
own likes and dislikes. Eva, you are very pleased with the manner in which
Adam lets you know he is interested in having sex. Unfortunately, Adam, is
not as pleased.

It's not clear to me how this situation developed. Perhaps Eva has let you know, Adam, how she would like you to initiate, and you took her preferences to heart. Perhaps you figured it out on your own. Perhaps it was just luck, but I doubt it since most couples I speak with aren't able to have good sex by chance.

I would like to congratulate you both on the enthusiasm with which you each respond to the other's sexual advances despite some of the problems we have already discussed about who has the responsibility for initiating sex.

Adam, since you would like Eva to change how she initiates sex, let me make a suggestion. Sit down at a quiet and relaxed time, make believe you're strangers, and ask each other how you would like your ideal lover to initiate sex. Even if you keep your description simple, I'm willing to bet that at the very least, the discussion will be interesting as well as informative. In a little while, I'll also try to help you along, by asking you some very detailed questions about how you initiate sex.

From this point, Sexpert begins to inquire in detail about the couple's foreplay and intercourse activities, and provides feedback at appropriate times. This session ends when the couple's entire sexual repertoire has been covered.

Empirical Studies

We have carried out four separate empirical studies of Sexpert involving approximately 250 individuals or couples (Binik, Westbury, & Servan-Schreiber, 1989; Ochs et al., 1993; Binik et al., 1994; Ochs et al., 1994). Because all of these studies followed a similar pattern, we summarize the major procedures and results of the research program rather than summarizing each study in detail. Couples volunteering to participate were randomly assigned in a between-groups design to interact for 20–60 minutes with a source of advice about their sexuality (e.g., Sexpert, a self-help book, a video, a therapist, etc.). Before and after this interaction, couples provided information about their attitudes toward each source of information and reported on their sexual behavior. Our two general goals were to demonstrate empirically that Sexpert's style of interaction was engaging and positive for couples and that Sexpert would motivate behavior change.

Attitudes Toward Sexpert.   Generalizing over all our studies, Sexpert was rated just as good as, if not better than, other sources of self-help such as books or videos. Interaction with a therapist, however, is still considered the ideal. Our most recent, as yet unpublished study, in which we included for the first time a one-hour session with a therapist as one of the experimental manipulations, indicated that a therapist is rated more highly than Sexpert on most measures. Nonetheless, the overall data suggest that Sexpert is on the right track in simulating therapeutic dialogue and has the ability to engage couples in positive interactions.

This interpretation is confirmed by answers to open-ended questions in our studies indicating that subjects, much to their surprise, found Sexpert to be intelligent, humanlike, and engaging. We believe that with multiple sessions, couples would begin to form attachments to Sexpert similar to those they form with a therapist. This impression is confirmed by several videotapes we made of couples interacting with Sexpert. In viewing these tapes, it became clear to us that the richness of the couple interaction while they were responding to Sexpert is not being adequately recorded on the keyboard and is similar in a number of respects to a therapy session.

Behavior Change.   Demonstrating behavior change has proved to be a more difficult task than transforming attitudes. At present, there is no definitive evidence that Sexpert is effective in inducing behavior change. Data from two studies (Ochs et al., 1993; Binik et al., 1994) using a daily self-monitoring strategy were unable to demonstrate any significant behavior change resulting from interaction with Sexpert or, for that matter, with any other source of information and advice (e.g., video or self-help books).

Retrospective reports of behavior change, on the other hand, indicated that interaction with Sexpert, videos, or books resulted in significant behavior change as well as improved communication about sexuality, satisfaction with the relationship, and learning about sexuality. In these studies (Ochs et al., 1993; Binik et al., 1994), Sexpert was less successful than a therapist and equally successful (or unsuccesful) at inducing behavior change as the more traditional self-help methods, all of which were superior to no-treatment controls. We are confident, however, that if future studies are able to remedy certain procedural and methodological problems in measuring sexual behavior change (Binik et al., 1996), we will be able to demonstrate such change with Sexpert.

What We Have Learned

The major practical lesson we have learned from our work on Sexpert and our review of the literature is that computer-conducted assessment, psychotherapy, and counseling is an active area of development, is acceptable to patients and nonpatients, and probably will become widely available in the future, independent of whether or not its efficacy is formally demonstrated. To the extent that assessment and treatment efficacy are demonstrated, computer programs may become another important clinical technology.

These developments open up the possibility for a variety of new theoretical directions in research on human–computer interaction. To what extent and under what conditions are individuals willing to anthropomorphize computers (cf. Nass, Steuer, Henriksen, & Dryer, 1994)? Research is starting to formulate an answer to the key question "can an individual develop transference or a therapeutic alliance with a computer?" Weizenbaum's early reports, our data concerning attitude change with Sexpert, and the potential therapeutic efficacy of counseling and psychotherapy programs suggest that this is possible. The technology and empirical tools exist to carry out this research, and it has the potential to change our basic ideas about the nature of psychotherapy and the nature of emotional attachment.

For example, if one can develop positive transference to a computer program, one can systematically vary potentially crucial elements in the program and study the effects on the therapeutic alliance. Will adding color, sound, video imagery and so forth, help or hinder this process (cf. Sproull, Subramani, Kiesler, Walker, & Waters, in press) ? It is possible that transference may even be enhanced when there are no visual obstacles to the association between the therapist and, say, the client's father. The tabula rasa quality of the computer may allow for a wider range of transferences; for example, the gender of the therapist would become a nonissue. Finally, the issue of client–therapist compatibility would probably not be very different. Different psychotherapy programs would appeal to different users. Ultimately, it will be much easier to manipulate psychotherapy program characteristics than it is to manipulate those of a therapist. Once the novelty of a computer therapist has lost some of its sheen, it will become very interesting to deconstruct the process and attempt to determine the ingredients key to a successful therapeutic alliance between user and computer program.

Computer-conducted psychotherapy also raises the issue of commitment and responsibility on the part of the client. Will the absence of a human being in the room and the knowledge that there is no one waiting to hear about your progress remove the urgency of applying the techniques suggested by the therapist? In addition, computer-conducted psychotherapy allows for interesting new research concerning the importance of nonverbal cues in the therapeutic process. Current computer systems cannot process these cues; humans cannot avoid processing them.

Finally, the data suggesting that individuals are willing to admit more pathology to a computer than to a human assessor may reflect an important and basic aspect of the process of self-disclosure. If "talking to a machine" or communicating on a network disinhibits or relaxes typical social constraints as suggested by Kiesler and Sproull (1986), then it would be important to investigate why and to what extent. It may also be that interacting with a "faceless screen" is similar in some respects to interacting with a neutral analyst sitting behind you and facilitates the self-investigatory process that Freud suggested was crucial to psychoanalysis.

One unexpected result of the project was our discovery that expert systems may be a highly effective training tool. A variety of trainees at our hospital spent a considerable amount of time interacting with Sexpert because it gave them the opportunity to simulate and experience a relatively large number of cases without having to actually see them. We believe that the training potential of most expert systems has been left unexploited.

In addition, the existence of such systems also opens the possibility of empirically testing long-standing issues in psychotherapy research concerning the essential nature of the therapeutic alliance and the importance of nonverbal cues in diagnosis.

The diagnostic portion of the project has also confirmed our view that, to a large extent, the diagnosis of sexual problems is a social construction with large gray areas unsupported by data. It seems unlikely to us that it will be ever be possible to write a set of formal rules to define most sexual dysfunctions, because such definitions are dependent on social expectations that change over time and across cultures. Modern sexual diagnostic systems such as the *DSM–IV* or the multiaxial problem-oriented system (Schover, Friedman, Weiler, Heiman, & LoPiccolo, 1982) indirectly acknowledge this by leaving much to the judgment of the therapist or by using arbitrary diagnostic cut-off points. The most recent diagnostic module of Sexpert deals with this necessary uncertainty by telling couples whose sexual behavior falls into these gray areas that they have to decide whether or not to consider their sexual behavior problematic.

TUNE IN, TURN ON, LOG OUT:
COMPUTER-MEDIATED PSYCHOTHERAPY

Despite the advances made by computer-conducted psychotherapy, no working system has been widely distributed beyond the laboratory. However, many computer-mediated forms of psychotherapy have appeared online on various networks. That is, rather than the computer itself serving as the psychotherapist, there now exist forums through which people coping with emotional or behavioral concerns can communicate with each other, in self-help group style, or with human therapists, using the computer as an intermediary tool. Such uses of computers in psychotherapy have sparked their own controversies and present their own theoretical concerns.

Many of the issues presented by computer-mediated psychotherapy are not new. One set of potential hazards and advantages of communication technology was originally discussed with regard to the use of telephones (Fish, 1990). Both media allow for greater accessibility of therapeutic support regardless of distance. However, each also removes the use of posture, gestures, tones of voice, and facial expressions. Therapists are deprived of the opportunity to observe the behavior of the client and clients no longer so easily perceive the empathetic and supportive gazes and gestures of the therapist, although they know there is actually a human being on the other end.

In practice, however, telephone communication has proven to be a valid adjunct to standard psychotherapy. Research studies have shown the equivalence and reliability of telephone versus face-to-face interviews in the diagnosis of psychological disorders (Lanska, Schmitt, Stewart, & Howe, 1993; Paulsen, Crowe, Noyes, & Pfohl, 1988). Telephone communication provides immediate crisis counseling and suicide hotlines (Glatt, Sherwood, & Amisson, 1986; Hornblow, 1986) when inperson contact is not feasible or desired by the client. Psychologists have already reported experiences conducting psychotherapy by telephone when circumstances required (Mermelstein & Holland, 1991), and argued for their legitimacy as an adjunctive tool (Lester, 1973, 1974; Rosenblum, 1969). In fact, Sims and Sims (1973) reported that emotionally insecure adolescents discussed a greater number of personal and school-related problems with a therapist over a telephone than they did in person. The mechanism for this increase in problem reporting over the phone may be similar to the one resulting in increased reports of pathology to a computer-interviewer. As compared with the telephone, computer-mediated psychotherapy removes one more human element (the voice), and there is little reason to believe that it should fare any worse than telephone therapy.

Virtual Support Groups

The introduction of self-help support groups such as Alcoholics Anonymous, encounter groups, and professionally led therapy groups sparked its own debate decades ago. The fear expressed by some elements of the psychotherapy community was that these groups would diffuse the therapist's focus on the client, damage or annihilate the therapeutic alliance, and impede behavior change. Despite this trepidation, group therapy and self-help groups have become an accepted and, at this point, traditional form of psychotherapy (Jacobs & Goodman, 1989).

The Internet has become a new home for a growing number of these groups. Internet sites provide forums for thousands of interest groups from the most popular to the most obscure. Given their widespread use for the discussion of highly specialized topics, facility in providing anonymity, and propensity to elicit rather daring comments from participants, one should not be surprised that users have formed Virtual Support Groups (VSGs) over networks. In much the same way as occurs in traditional 12-step groups, members relate their experiences, share their coping strategies, and offer each other feedback and encouragement (King, in press).

Through Listservers, members post email messages that are received by all other group members. Any member who chooses may respond with his or her own messages to the group or with a private email sent only to the original person. Such groups often have closed memberships, with new members being added (or removed) only by action of the group leader, who controls the electronic facilities providing the Listserver. The size of the cyberworld, with an estimated population of 7 million USENET users alone (Pfaffenberger, 1995), allows specialized groups to form easily. Just as specialized hobby and interest groups proliferate in the cyber community, the population can support groups of people coping with dozens of physical and emotional difficulties. Table 4.1 provides only a partial listing of those currently available.

The widespread use of support groups seems to indicate both the need for such groups and the willingness of network participants to avail themselves to those groups, revealing details of their lives protected by the anonymity of the network. *Alt.support.depression* has an estimated readership of nearly 10,000 with monthly postings approaching 2,000, whereas *alt.sexual.abuse.recovery* currently maintains a readership of over 37,000 (Pfaffenberger, 1995).

Postings on these newsgroups vary from jokes in poor taste, to commercial advertisements, to requests for information, to bona fide requests for help. One of the best uses of the various networks, as well as one of the most

TABLE 4.1

Selected Psychology-Related Newsgroups Available on USENET

Issues Discussed	Newsgroup
Recovery for abuse offenders/perpetrators	alt.abuse.offender.recovery
Recovering from all types of abuse	alt.abuse.recovery
Recovering from sexual abuse (moderated)	alt.abuse-recovery
Alternate models of dealing with abuse	alt.abuse.transcendence
Angst	alt.angst
Hypnosis discussion	alt.hypnosis
Fibromyalgia fibrosis	alt.med.fibromyalgia
General help with psychological problems	alt.psychology.help
General topics in recovery	alt.recovery
Recovery and Alcoholics Anonymous	alt.recovery.aa
Recovering from sexual addictions	alt.recovery.addiction.sexual
Adults from dysfunctional families	alt.recovery.adult-children
Codependency	alt.recovery.codependency
Recovery and Narcotics Anonymous	alt.recovery.na
Recovering from the effects of religion	alt.recovery.religion
Self-improvement tips & techniques	alt.self-improve
Recovering from sexual abuse	alt.sexual.abuse.recovery
General discussion of suicide & techniques	alt.suicide.holiday
Other support topics & questions	alt.support
Partners of sexual abuse survivors	alt.support.abuse-partners
Anxiety and panic disorders	alt.support.anxiety-panic
Attention-deficit disorders	alt.support.attn-deficit

continued

common, is a request for and the dissemination of information. Writers share recommendations—about books, films, and even inperson support groups—such as in the following post from *alt.support.shyness:*

> My problem is not so much shyness but more a lack of knowing what to say to people. I work for a firm of solicitors and have no trouble talking to clients about their case, but I find it impossible to start idle conversation with them. I had a similar problem with the girls I went to college with. I could speak to them about the stuff that we were learning but other than that-silence. What I was hoping was that somebody out there could give me advice on how to conduct idle conversations, or point me to a book, available in the U.K. that could help.

[signature deleted]

Issues Discussed	Newsgroup
Fat-acceptance with no dieting talk	alt.support.big-folks
Depression & mood disorders	alt.support.depression
Manic depression & bipolar disorders	alt.support.depression.manic
Seasonal Affective Disorder (SAD)	alt.support.depression.seasonal
Developmental delay	alt.support.dev-delays
Divorce/marital breakups	alt.support.divorce
Eating disorders (anorexia, bulimia, etc.)	alt.support.eating-disord
Former cult members & family & friends	alt.support.ex-cult
Issues of grief and loss	alt.support.grief
Loneliness	alt.support.loneliness
Obesity (moderated)	alt.support.obesity
Obsessive–Compulsive Disorder (OCD)	alt.support.ocd
For people with personality disorders	alt.support.personality
Schizophrenia	alt.support.schizophrenia
Shyness	alt.support.shyness
Sleep disorders & problems sleeping	alt.support.sleep-disorder
General discussion of AIDS & HIV	misc.health.aids
Medicine & related products & regulations	sci.med
General psychology	sci.psychology
Self-acceptance for fat people/no diet talk	soc.support.fat-acceptance
Transgendered & intersexed persons	soc.support.transgendered
Gay youths helping each other (moderated)	soc.support.youth.gay-lesbian-bi

Note. Constructed from a list kept by J. M. Grohol and advertised on the Internet.

Other VSG users take advantage of the ability to contact others who have shared similar problems. The following posting from *alt.support.divorce* echoes emotions one could easily hear during a face-to-face support group such as Parents without Partners:

> Hi All,
>
> I have been divorced for 6 mo now and still feel great pain when I see my X. We have a 2 year old son and have to still try and get along.. My questions to you is how can I let go?? I keep fooling myself every day!! Deep down I still am in love with her. Why?? I have read some good books to boot. It hurts the most when my son tells me he will be back for me.. I really miss the family life ever so much.. Also hits the most on Sundays that's when my son goes with his mom..
>
> Thanks for hearing me out.
>
> [signature deleted]

This person's need for support was met by the following response, which was made soon after the original post:

> It sounds like on an intelectual [sic] level you have accepted that it is over, but on an emotional level you still feel love of your ex and are having a hard time letting go of the marriage. The emotional part is very hard, I had the same problem for about a year after my divorce, one thing that you might try and keep in mind is that love cannot be one sided, true love has to come from both partners, true love is a union, once that union has been broken, eventually your love for her will die. One thing that you might try is to think of the reasons that you loved her for when you first married and while the marriage was going good, then try and take a honest look at her now and ask your self if this is the same person now, or are you possibly still in love with the image of who she used to be. Unfortunately people change, part of the reason we love someone is usually they also love us, when your partner changes and no longer loves you, it don't mean that they are a bad person but what it does mean is that they are no longer that person that was in love with you, they have become someone else.
>
> The fact that you can still feel love is very good, many people at your stage feel nothing but hate and contempt. Once you get past the pain and the hurt and run across someone that can love you as much as you love them your ability to love will bring you and her much happiness.
>
> Hang in there and best of luck.
>
> [signature deleted]

However, just as a person can be in despair in a therapy session, so too can a person send a posting to *alt.support.depression* or one of the suicide newsgroups:

well.. here it is.. my re-entry to a.s.h. yet another hopeless fucking whine. skip it if you want.

sitting here breaking one of my cardinal rules.. getting drunk on a weeknight. in the eight years since i started drinking, i've only broken that rule once before tonight. i am very far down. i'm trying to recover emotionally from a suicide attempt last sunday (the 14th.. mother's day.. how awesomely ironic.) and not having any luck. if anything, i keep wishing that i had succeeded.

and so i sit here downing shots of vodka (it's still early enough so i shouldn't have a hangover tomorrow.. i'll stop in another shot or two; just enough to make me comfortable and not care. but not completely trashed.). i've downed three so far. i think two more will do the trick.

metallica's "two of one" playing in the background, razor blades close at hand. it's gonna be a lovely evening. when i'm done with this, i'll throw in my marillion video and then perhaps if i'm still awake, _dead_ringers_. actually, i want to get drunk enough to cut myself without pain. i want to see my blood tonight. it's been entirely too long....

ah.. now it's kicking in. not eating dinner (not hungry) helps it hit the bloodstream that much faster....

the outside bleeding reflecting the inner wounds that won't fucking heal no matter how hard i try to bind them.

the speed at which my blood is clotting tells me i'm up on all my vitamins, in spite of the food i haven't been eating lately..

fuck it.. i'm out of here.

night.

Postings such this one are not uncommon and often elicit from readers responses of considerable support (King, in press). However, no data currently exist regarding the frequency of either attempted or completed suicides associated with electronic suicide threats. The effect of the support that other readers provide to writers such as the one just quoted is likewise unknown.

However, there is reason to suspect that the ability to express frustration and hopelessness through any forum may have therapeutic value. The energy and time a person takes in the very act of formulating and expressing his or her distress may provide at least some release from tension and anxiety. Students who keep diaries show lower levels of anxiety (Burt, 1994) and even improved physical health (Pennebaker, Colder, & Sharp, 1990) as compared to control groups. The improvement can become dramatic when the topics are meaningful to the writer. Pennebaker and Beall (1986) assigned two groups of students to record life events for 4 consecutive days, one group writing about personally traumatic events, the second group, trivial events. The group disclosing the more difficult information showed better physical health outcomes 6 months after the experience, as reflected by fewer visits to health centers. Regardless of the peer responses or even professional responses the aforementioned writer receives, the very act of writing may be of help to him.

Professional Psychotherapy Online

In using public access newsgroups, there is a general principle of caveat emptor; no one is expert, and all information and advice transmitted are taken with a grain of salt. However, a new set of issues arises when the source of the support is a professional psychotherapist communicating with the expressed purpose of assisting the client, possibly for monetary reimbursement. One-on-one psychotherapy of this sort resembles traditional therapy sessions in that there is a single client at any given moment with the full attention of a professionally trained therapist. The two may be exchanging anecdotes, questions, and advice in sequences of email, pen-pal style, or they may be using one of the real-time talk channels, analogous to a scheduled telephone conversation.

The *Montreal Gazette* carried the story of Ian Silver, who provides support and counseling on the Internet (Cribb, 1995). Silver related experiences where he was able to save people from suicide by sending police, as well as those where he received a good-bye message such as, "Thank you for all of your help, but by the time you receive this, I'll be dead." A group that has been providing suicide prevention hotlines in Great Britain since 1945, The Samaritans, began providing assistance by email in 1994 (King, in press). Both Silver and the Samaritans independently describe the openness of those who contact them. The privacy of the medium, they reported, allows the users to express emotions that are not easily expressed in person, even with the traditional therapists that so many of the users also consult.

Another resource, *Shrink-Link*, represents the first for-profit venture into psychology practice on the Internet by professional counselors. Network users contacting their World Wide Web site, http://www.west-net.com/shrink, pose a short, 200-word question to a panel of expert psychologists and psychiatrists who return their answers within 24–72 hours. The users include their credit card information and are charged $20 per query. The providers of *Shrink-Link*, Cyberlink Consulting Inc., emphasize that their service does not replace face-to-face counseling. However, it may allow people to become somewhat more educated about issues important to them without committing to more indepth therapy. There certainly seems to be a market for this type of therpeutic delving, because the service received between 10–30 paid users each day of its first month in business (Resnick, 1995).

Computer networks allow users several advantages. Through their "virtual mobility," they permit contact between would-be consumers of psychological services and therapists with whom they would not ordinarily have the opportunity to interact. The American Psychological Association (APA) has documented the continuing shortage of therapists in rural areas (Hutner & Windle, 1991; Murray & Keller, 1991), despite efforts to lure them from more central areas. Some clients have physical disabilities that limit their ability to travel to a therapist's office or that impair their use of spoken language. Additionally, many clients prefer to use therapists who share a particular cultural background (Sue, Zane, & Young, 1994) or possess particular expertise that is not commonly available. Although computer-mediated therapy may indeed prove to be suboptimal, the client's choice may be between suboptimal therapy and no therapy at all.

Paradoxically perhaps, the anecdotal reports of Ian Silver, the Samaritans, and others are that users in emotional distress find it easier to relate over a terminal. The anonymity appears to ease the process of asking for help. This would be especially true for individuals who generally find face-to-face situations anxiety provoking, a group that often makes up a substantial proportion of those in therapy. This increased ease of relating over a terminal is supported by research indicating that individuals are willing to take more risks (McGuire, Kiesler, & Siegel, 1987) and are less likely to be affected by differences in status of conversation partners over networks (Dubrovsky, Kiesler, & Sethna, 1991). That is, the ideas written on the computer screen take greater importance over the prestige of the person making the comments, a factor that often influences face-to-face interactions.

What We Have Learned

Although there are no systematic data, there now appear to be large numbers of individuals using computer networks for psychotherapeutic support. There also appear to be a growing number of therapists who are willing and perhaps eager to dispense advice over the Internet. From the information available to us, it appears quite likely that the relationships formed over computer networks can be emotionally charged and that this medium can be used to foster therapeutic alliances. If the "disinhibiting effects" (Sproull & Kiesler, 1991) of communication over networks generalize to therapeutic relationships over networks, then this should have significant effects on the process of psychotherapy and the formation of therapeutic alliances. A comparative study of network and "inperson" therapists is now possible and perhaps warranted.

Psychotherapy on the Internet also poses a series of practical questions for both governmental and professional regulatory bodies. All American states and Canadian provinces require licenses for individuals practicing psychotherapy. Psychotherapists licensed in one state, however, cannot use their licenses in another. Yet the client and therapist communicating electronically may not live in the same region. Where, exactly, is the therapy taking place? Additionally, the confidentiality of psychotherapeutic information is a legal and ethical requirement. Finally, communication over computer networks allows not only for the anonymity of the client in therapy, but even of the therapists themselves. To require accurate and honest disclosure of the credentialing of computer therapists would be to permit the regulation of electronic communication that has already proven so controversial. As far as we are aware, these issues have not been directly addressed by appropriate professional bodies. The APA ethics committee has indirectly reacted to the issue of psychotherapy on the Internet in a recent statement on telephone therapy:

> The Ethics Code is not specific with regard to telephone therapy or teleconferencing or any electronically provided services as such and has no rule prohibiting such services ... the use of telephone for purposes such as educative information, suicide hot lines, or brief crisis contact and referral are reasonably well establishd. The use of telephone for the provision of regular ongoing therapy or for diagnosis is not established, nor are such services as teleconferencing, *internet* or similar methods. (APA Ethics, 1995, p.15, italics added)

FLYING AT HOME:
VIRTUAL REALITY THERAPEUTIC EXPERIENCES

Virtual reality (VR) has been described as a computer-generated environment in which the user feels present (Biocca, 1992). We are interested here in the implications of this new kind of "environment" for helping people to deal with psychological issues. From the technological standpoint, VR represents the amalgamation of a number of technologies, principally the digital computer, software capable of processing visual and auditory information, and a means of presenting this information to the user. The use of miniature television monitors in front of each eye combined with stereo earphones produces the impression in the user of occupying an actual space. Thus, the potential to create sensory worlds that mimic the real world now exist (Durlach & Mavor, 1994; Shapiro & McDonald, 1992). Indeed, it is also possible to produce actual physical sensations directly by mechanical stimulation of the skin of appropriate areas. Research to determine exactly what features are required to produce a realistic experience is still in its infancy (Kozak, Hancock, Arthur, & Chrysler, 1993). However, VR technology is currently being applied in such diverse areas as medicine, architecture, rehabilitation, engineering, and scientific visualization. In the near future, entertainment applications will likely figure prominently in VR development (Rheingold, 1991). As a result of the progress in these areas, we can expect ongoing improvements in VR technology. At this time there are a few VR applications dedicated to helping solve psychological problems.

What Can a VR Therapist Do?

Before delving into the ways VR could be a therapeutic aid, it is necessary to review the role of imagination and fantasy in the therapeutic process until now. In some sense, VR represents the entrance into a fantasy world with the addition of powerful means to control its content. At least as early as Freud's travels down the royal road to the unconscious, a patient's own fantasies figured prominently in the psychotherapeutic process (much earlier, if one includes shamanistic rituals). Much later, therapists began asking clients seated in their offices to imagine activities that would lead to learning new behaviors. For example, Meichenbaum (1985) described how imagery rehearsal is used by patients to rehearse coping efforts during training sessions that approximate a stressful situation. During this process the patient and therapist together generate a hierarchy of stressful scenarios, and the patient then imagines coping with the progressively more threatening scenarios while in a relaxed state of mind.

A major drawback of this technique is that it depends in part on a patient's ability to imagine the stressful scenarios vividly. Even though the first part of therapy may occur in the patient's imagination, a more realistic confrontation with the feared stimulus is eventually required. The key to success is developing coping strategies for fear, and gradually increasing the intensity of the exposure to the feared object, so that the patient can learn to interact with the object without experiencing debilitating fear (the phobic response).

Ralph Lamson (1995) recently utilized VR environments to help treat phobias. In a VR simulation, Lamson allows patients to learn to cope with fear of heights. In VR, his patients walk over a bridge that crosses a rushing stream far below. When they can complete this exercise without developing symptoms of panic (racing heart, perspiration, etc.), they are ready to move onto the real-world part of the therapy. Lamson has also used this kind of virtual exposure to treat fear of blood and agoraphobia with great success. In principle, graduated exposure to any feared stimulus (snakes, crowds, dogs, heights, etc.) could be accomplished in VR. The advantages are obvious: Some kinds of therapy sessions are made possible or greatly simplified because all the needed stimuli are virtual (you won't have to climb to a cliff edge or find a large snake), virtual stimuli cannot directly harm a client, and there is no need to rely on the imagination of patients because they will have a vivid experience! Finally, direct therapist control of the exact characteristics of the exposure experience is vastly increased. This therapeutic control means not having to wait for the real world to deliver situations that will be optimally helpful. In addition, it will be possible to produce multiple variations of challenging situations or stimuli to maximize the learning. Thus, VR combines the control previously possible only in a laboratory with at least some of the salient characteristics of the real world. The best of both virtual and real worlds!

In addition to VR's potential to allow patients to confront a feared object, VR constructed social interactions could allow patients to learn how to cope with social phobias. For example, patients trying to cope with giving public speeches and performing in front of audiences, or with mundane social phobias like difficulty urinating in a crowded men's room or writing a check in front of a bank clerk (Marks & Gelder, 1966), could learn to handle these situations in VR. Consider how salient these interactions could be made: The therapist (or computer program) could tailor the content and degree of difficulty while simultaneously adapting to the patient's own coping in order to optimize the therapy. The characteristics of virtual persons could also be controlled to allow an individual optimal challenge and potential for learning new skills, behaviors, attitudes, and so on.

It is conceivable that under conditions of rapid and appropriate feedback in a VR environment, a patient could begin to experience what Csikszentmihalyi and Csikszentmihalyi (1988) described as a flow experience. Everyone experiences flow at some times and can recognize it by the following characteristics: They feel strong, alert, in effortless control, un-self-conscious, and at the peak of their abilities. This transcendent feeling is experienced when our challenge is neither too difficult for our abilities, nor so easy it is boring. The possibility of optimizing an experience for an individual in VR so that a formerly anxiety-provoking situation becomes intrinsically rewarding holds out great promise for stimulating the growth of personal competencies as well as overcoming dysfunctional responses.

VR's ability to provide a powerful therapeutic environment would be enhanced by including inputs like heart rate, blood pressure, galvanic skin response, and pupil dilation to the computer program controlling the VR environment. Thus, a VR virtual therapist would have direct access to some of the emotional experience of the patient. This kind of information, appropriately used, could allow a computer program to fine tune a treatment program for panic attacks, agoraphobia, social phobia, and so forth, in a way no human could hope to match. In addition, let us consider what could be done by reversing the flow of information about emotional states. A VR therapist could teach a patient how to be more sensitive or aware of the emotional experiences of others by modeling facial expressions (Ekman, 1989) in specific social-emotive contexts so that the patient would learn about subtle cues that he or she may not have been attending to before.

We have been discussing the potential of VR to treat various kinds of phobias, and to learn new skills and coping behaviors. One last example illustrates the applications of VR in what will likely be a controversial arena: sex therapy. As discussed earlier, one of the advantages of interacting with a machine is the increased willingness to disclose information (e.g., Erdman et al., 1985) by users who feel they are not being judged by the machine. A VR environment would have the potential to provide useful information about sexual functioning in a highly salient way, allow very precise control by the therapist (human or computer) of potentially very sensitive material concerning sexual behavior, and finally, allow a user to engage in sexual activity (therapy exercises) with a virtual partner when connected to the appropriate mechanical devices. A VR sex partner would be useful for the many persons suffering sexual problems and lacking a real partner with whom to work on difficult, emotionally charged issues.

In the past, this rationale led to the use of so-called sex surrogates in sex therapy (Masters & Johnson, 1970). Sex surrogates are educated in the sexual dysfunctions and are trained to engage patients in sexual activity prescribed by their therapist. Currently, this practice is deemed problematical for various ethical reasons (Bancroft, 1989), which primarily concern the problem of role confusion between a therapist and a surrogate, and the similarity of surrogate work to prostitution. These issues are moot if the patient is having sex with a construct in VR. Of course, there may be other ethical issues surrounding the promotion of sexual activity with a machine even for ostensibly therapeutic ends.

What Are the Risks of VR Therapy?

In the preceding section we have focused on the potential benefits to patients who might interact in VR to attain therapeutic goals. Many of the procedures outlined earlier require the computer to generate a stressful situation for the patient to grapple with; will patients develop computer phobias because of the association of strong negative emotions with proximity to the computer? Who would be responsible if this did occur and who would deal with it? On the other hand, will some patients (or anyone else who uses VR) become addicted to risk-free reality? With only virtual consequences to their actions, will patients be able to have the kinds of powerful learning experiences that result from facing fear and overcoming it? Moreover, could playing VR "games" trivialize the real experiences that are being simulated, thereby preventing patients from facing reality? In principle, patients could use VR to hide from reality as easily as to face it.

One "nightmare" scenario is that truly vivid VR technology will create an epidemic of false memory syndromes. Therapists have always been aware that the line between fantasy and reality is not a clear one for certain individuals, and one can't help but be worried that VR technology will help to redraw this line for those who are already susceptible. While this possibility may provide for ground-breaking research concerning the perception of reality and the creation of memory, it raises serious ethical concerns.

More generally, we need to consider the ethics of controlling a person's experience directly in VR, and of allowing a computer program to exercise that power. Do we know enough about what makes a human therapist act responsibly to codify it in a computer program's actions?

Allowing for the possibility that VR therapy produces no deleterious side-effects, we should ask if a successful VR experience actually prepares a patient for coping with reality. Do the experiences of VR have any generalizability to patients' real lives and the real world? In general, how will we assess the outcomes of these new kinds of therapy? Although preliminary studies show great potential, they need to be followed up with further work. It would be disturbing if economic factors or a simple desire to see if it could be done were the main or only impetus behind the development of VR therapy.

What We Have Learned

We have learned very little about VR therapy because the technology is still in its infancy. Our lack of knowledge, perhaps, inflates the potential benefits and risks. The major source of data is still science fiction, but there seems to be little reason not to believe that individuals will form therapeutic alliances with virtual (or bionic) therapists even when they know they are not dealing with a real human. Whether this knowledge makes any difference would consititute an interesting study.

WHEN THE MICROCHIPS ARE DOWN: CONCLUDING COMMENTS

A popular but not unreasonable approach to evaluating the strength of a therapeutic alliance might be to ask the question, "have you fallen in love with your therapist yet?" Is this a reasonable question in the context of computerized psychotherapy? We think so. Although our sensibilities may be violated by the idea of falling in love with the current square box computer, there are definite signs of marked attachment exhibited by large numbers of "hackers" who show striking symptoms of lovesickness when separated from their favorite operating system. Communicating with one's therapist by email should not interfere with and may even promote the formation of therapeutic alliances. Literary theorists have suggested that imposing the constraint of written communication may heighten the potential for highly charged emotional communication (cf. Altman, 1982, for a fascinating discussion of the epistolary love novel). Exchanging "love letters" has been a classic means of keeping relationships alive especially when real encounters were disappointing. It would seem to matter little whether therapeutic communication occurs by email or snail mail. Finally, it would seem at least as easy to fall in love with your virtual reality fantasy as your present life reality. Such a phenomenon could give new meaning to the concept of Platonic love. At the risk of oversimplifying, we suggest that computerized psychotherapy will come of age when we begin hearing reports of individuals who have "fallen hopelessly in love" with their computer therapist.

Although the market will no doubt determine the future of computer-conducted, computer-mediated, and VR psychotherapy, social scientists have an important role to play in both in the optimization of this new technology and in the regulation of ethical and practical issues to which this new technological application gives rise. We strongly believe that the current caveat emptor approach to self-help should not be extended to computerized intervention. The social science community should take the lead in establishing empirical and ethical guidelines for the publication and distribution of computerized psychotherapy. Although this view may appear to conflict with the principle of free speech, we already limit the free speech of those who wish to give professional advice by imposing significant training and licensing requirements. Computer simulations of the psychotherapy process may inform us as to the adequacy of our current standards and training requirements and will empirically address issues that were heretofore not testable. Ultimately, it is not what the computer can do but what the computer cannot do that will be the key to rethinking some tightly held assumptions about the human element in the psychotherapeutic process.

REFERENCES

Altman, J. G. (1982). *Epistolarity: Approaches to a form*. Columbus: Ohio State University Press.

American Psychiatric Association. (1994). *Diagnostic and Statistical Manual of Mental Disorders* (4th ed., rev.). Washington, DC: Author.

APA Ethics Committee adopts statement on telephone therapy. (1995, October). *APA Monitor*, p. 15.

Bancroft, J. (1989). *Human sexuality and its problems* (2nd ed.). New York: Churchill Livingstone.

Barnlund, D. C. (Ed.). (1990). Therapeutic communication. In G. Gumpert & S. Fish (Eds.), *Talking to strangers: Mediated therapeutic communication*. (pp.10–28). Norwood, NJ: Ablex.

Baskin, D. (Ed.). (1990). *Computer applications in psychiatry and psychology*. New York: Bruner/Mazel.

Binik, Y. M., Meana, M., & Sand, N. (1994). Interaction with a sex-expert system changes attitudes and may modify sexual behavior. *Computers in Human Behavior, 10*, 395–410.

Binik, Y. M., Ochs, E. P., & Meana, M. (1996). A (S)expert computer in the bedroom: Fact or fantasy. In M. Miller, M. Hile, & K. Hammond (Eds.), *Mental health computing* (pp. 17–33). New York: Springer-Verlag.

Binik, Y. M., Servan-Schreiber, D., Freiwald, S., & Hall, K. S. (1988). Intelligent computer-based assessment and psychotherapy: An expert system for sexual dysfunction. *Journal of Nervous and Mental Disease, 178*, 387–400.

Binik, Y. M., Westbury, C. F., & Servan-Schreiber, D. (1989). Interaction with a "sex-expert" system enhances attitudes towards computerized sex therapy. *Behavior Research and Therapy, 27*, 303–306.

Biocca, F. (1992). Communication within virtual reality: Creating a space for research. *Journal of Communication, 42*(4), 5–22.

Bloom, B. L. (1992). Computer assisted psychological intervention: A review and commentary. *Clinical Psychology Review, 12*, 169–198.

Burt, C. D. B. (1994). Prospective and retrospective account-making in diary entries: A model of anxiety reduction and avoidance. *Anxiety, Stress & Coping: An International Journal, 6*(4), 327–340.

Cribb, R. (1995, March 13). Computer counsellor goes on-line to help troubled Internet users. *The Montreal Gazette*, p. A-5.

Csikszentmihalyi, M., & Csikszentmihalyi, I. S. (Eds.). (1988). *Optimal experience: Psychological studies of flow in consciousness.* New York: Cambridge University Press.

DeMuth, P. (1984). "Eliza and her offspring." In M. D. Schwartz (Ed.), *Using computers in clinical practice* (pp. 321–327). New York: Haworth.

Dubrovsky, V., Kiesler, S., & Sethna, B. (1991). The equalization phenomenon: Status effect in computer-mediated and face-to-face decision making groups. *Human–Computer Interaction, 6*(2), 119–146.

Durlach, N. I. & Mavor, A. S. (Eds.). (1994). *Virtual reality: Scientific and technological challenges.* Washington, DC: National Academy Press.

Ekman, P. (1989). The argument and evidence about universals in facial expressions of emotion. In H. Wagner & A. Manstead (Eds.), *Handbook of psychophysiology: Emotion and social behavior* (pp. 143–164). London: Wiley.

Erdman, H. P., Klein, M. H., & Greist, J. H. (1985). Direct patient computer interviewing. *Journal of Consulting and Clinical psychology, 53*, 760–773.

Fish, S. L. (1990). Therapeutic uses of the telephone: Crisis intervention vs. traditional therapy. In G. Gumpert & S. L. Fish (Eds.), *Talking to strangers: Mediated therapeutic communication* (pp. 154–169). Norwood, NJ: Ablex.

Ghosh, A., & Marks, I. M. (1987). Self-treatment of agoraphobia by exposure. *Behavior Therapy., 18,* 3–16.

Glatt, K. M., Sherwood, D. W., & Amisson, T. J. (1986). Telephone helplines at a suicide site. *Hospital & Community Psychiatry, 37*(2), 178–180.

Grohol, J. M. (1995, May 3). *Psychology & support groups newsgroup pointer* [Online]. Available: http://www1.mhv.net/~grohol Archive-Name: finding-groups/psychology-and-support. [jgrohol@alpha.acast.nova.edu]

Hand, D. J. (1985). *Artificial intelligence and psychiatry.* New York: Cambridge University Press.

Hornblow, A. R. (1986). The evolution and effectiveness of telephone counseling services. *Hospital & Community Psychiatry, 37*(7), 731–733.

Horvath, A., Gaston, L., & Luborsky, L. (1993). The therapeutic alliance and its measures. In N. E. Miller, L. Luborsky, J. P. Barber, & J. P. Docherty (Eds.). *Psychodynamic treatment research: A handbook for clinical practice* (pp. 247–273). New York: Basic Books.

Hutner, M., & Windle, C. (1991). NIMH support of rural mental health. *American Psychologist, 46*(3), 240–243.

Jacobs, M. K., & Goodman, G. (1989). Psychology and self-help groups. *American Psychologist, 44*(3), 536–545.

Katz, M. R. (1993). *Computer-assisted career decision making: The guide in the machine.* Hillsdale, NJ: Lawrence Erlbaum Associates.

Kiesler, S., & Sproull, L. (1986). Response effects in the electronic survey. *Public Opinion Quarterly, 50,* 402–413.

King, S., (in press). Suicidal ideation in virtual support groups [75 paragraphs]. *Virtual Psychology* [Online serial].

Kozak, J. J., Hancock, P. A., Arthur, E. J., & Chrysler, S. T. (1993). Transfer of training from virtual reality. *Ergonomics, 36*(7), 777–784.

Lamson, R. J. (1995). Virtual therapy: The treatment of phobias in cyberspace. *Behavioral Healthcare Tomorrow, 4*(1), 51–53.

Lanska, D. J., Schmitt, F. A., Stewart, J. M., & Howe, J. N. (1993). Telephone-assessed mental state. *Dementia, 4*(2), 117–119.

Lester, D. (1973). Role of psychologists in crisis telephone services. *American Psychologist, 28*(5), 448–449.

Lester, D. (1974). The unique qualities of telephone therapy. *Psychotherapy: Theory, Research & Practice, 11*(3), 219–221.

Lieff, J. D. (1987). *Computer applications in psychiatry.* Washington, DC: American Psychiatric Association Press.

Lodge, D. (1984). *Small world.* Markham, Ontario: Penguin Books Canada.

Marks, I. M., & Gelder, M. G. (1966). Different ages of onset in varieties of phobias. *American Journal of Psychiatry, 1123,* 218–221.

Masters, W. H., & Johnson, V. E. (1970). *Human sexual inadequacy.* Boston: Little, Brown.

McCullough, L. Farrell, A. D., & Longabaugh, R. (1986). The development of a microcomputer-based mental health information system. *American Psychologist., 41,* 207–214.

McGuire, T., Kiesler, S., & Siegel, J. (1987). Groups and computer-mediated discussion effects in risk decision making. *Journal of Personality and Social Psychology, 52*(5), 917–930.

Meichenbaum, D. (1985). *Stress innoculation training.* pp. 76–78. New York: Pergamon Press.

Mermelstein, H. I., & Holland, J. C. (1991). Psychotherapy by telephone: A therapeutic tool for cancer patients. *Psychosomatics, 32*(4), 407–412.

Muran, J. C., Segal, Z. V., Samstag, L. W., & Crawford, C. E. (1994). Patient pretreatment interpersonal problems and therapeutic alliance in short-term cognitive therapy. *Journal of Consulting and Clinical Psychology, 62,* 185–190.

Murray, J. D., & Keller, P. A. (1991). Psychology and rural America: Current status and future directions. *American Psychologist, 46*(3), 220–231.

Nass, C., Steuer, J., Henriksen, L., & Dryer, D. C. (1994). Machines, social attributions and ethopoeia: Performance assessments of computers subsequent to "self" or "other" evaluations. *Human Computer Studies, 40*(3), 543–559.

Ochs, E. P., Meana, M., Mah, K., & Binik, Y. (1993). The effects of exposure to different sources of sexual information on sexual behavior: Comparing a "sex-expert system" to other educational material. *Behavior Research Methods, Instruments, & Computers, 25,* 189–194.

Ochs, E. P., Meana, M., Paré, L., Mah, K., & Binik, Y. M. (1994). Learning about sex outside the gutter: Attitudes toward a computer sex-expert system. *Journal of Sex and Marital Therapy, 20,* 86–102.

Paulsen, A. S., Crowe, R. R., Noyes, R., & Pfohl, B. (1988). Reliability of the telephone interview in diagnosing anxiety disorders. *Archives of General Psychiatry, 45*(1), 62–63.

Pennebaker, J. W., & Beall, S. K. (1986). Confronting a traumatic event: Toward an understanding of inhibition and disease. *Journal of Abnormal Psychology, 95*(3), 274–281.

Pennebaker, J. W., Colder, M., & Sharp, L. K. (1990). Accelerating the coping process. *Journal of Personality & Social Psychology, 58*(3), 528–537.

Pfaffenberger, B. (1995). *The USENET book: Finding, using, and surviving newsgroups on the Internet.* Reading, MA: Addison-Wesley.

Plutchik, R., & Karasu, T. B. (1991). Computers in psychotherapy: An overview. *Computers in Human Behavior, 7,* 33–44.

Resnick, R. (1995, March 27). Shrink-Link & beyond. *The Miami Herald,* p. 32.

Rheingold, H. (1991). *Virtual reality.* New York: Summit Books.

Romanczyk, R. G. (1986). *Clinical utilization of microcomputer technology.* New York: Pergamon.

Rosenblum, L. (1969). Telephone therapy. *Psychotherapy: Theory, Research & Practice, 6*(4), 241–242.

Sampson, J. P. (1991). The place of the computer in counseling research. In C. E. Watkins & L. J. Schneider, *Research in counseling* (pp. 261–284). Hillsdale, NJ: Lawrence Erlbaum Asociates.

Sampson, J. P., Reardon, R. C., Humphreys, J. K., & Peterson, G. W. (1990). A differential feature-cost analysis of nine computer-assisted career guidance systems. In: Evaluating computer-assisted career guidance systems. [Special issue]. *Journal of Career Development*, *17*, 81–111.

Schneider S. J., Walker, R., & O'Donnell, R., (1990). Computerized communication as a medium for behavioral smoking cessation treatment: Controlled evaluation. *Computers in Human Behavior, 6*, 141–151.

Schover, L., Friedman, J. M., Weiler, S. J., Heiman, J. R., & LoPiccolo, J. (1982). Multiaxial problem-oriented system for sexual dysfunctions: An alternative to DSM–III. *Archives of General Psychiatry, 39*, 614–619.

Selmi, P. M., Klein, M. H., Greist, J. H., Sorrell, S. P., & Erdman, H. P. (1990). Computer-administered congitive–behavioral therapy for depression. *American Journal of Psychiatry, 147*, 51–56.

Servan-Schreiber, D., & Binik, Y. M. (1989). Extending the intelligent tutoring system paradigm: Sex therapy as intelligent tutoring. *Computers in Human Behavior, 5*, 241–259.

Shapiro, M. A., & McDonald, D. G. (1992). I'm not a real doctor, but I play one in virtual reality: Implications of virtual reality for judgments about reality. *Journal of Communication, 42*(4), 94–114.

Sims, G. K., & Sims, J. M. (1973). Does face-to-face contact reduce counselee responsiveness with emotionally insecure youth? *Psychotherapy: Theory, Research & Practice, 10*(4), 348–351.

Sproull, L., & Kiesler, S. (1991). *Connections: New ways of working in the networked organization.* Cambridge, MA: MIT Press.

Sproul, L., Subramani, M., Kiesler, S., Walker, J., & Waters, K. (1996). When the interface is a face. *Human-Computer Interaction, 11*, 97–124.

Sue, S., Zane, N., & Young, K. (1994). Research on psychotherapy with culturally diverse populations. In A. E. Bergin & S. L. Garfield (Eds.), *Handbook of psychotherapy and behavior change* (4th ed., pp. 783–817). New York: Wiley.

Taylor, C. B., Agras, W. S., Losch, M., Plante, T. G., & Burnett, K. (1991). Improving the effectiveness of computer-assisted weight loss. *Behavior Therapy, 22*, 229–236.

Wagman, M. (1988). *Computer psychotherapy systems: Theory and research foundations.* New York: Gordon and Breach Science Publishers.

Weizenbaum, J. (1976). *Computer power and human reason: From judgment to calculation.* San Francisco: Freeman.

Part II

ELECTRONIC GROUPS

In chapter 2, Lee Sproull and Samer Faraj argued that electronic groups that form and meet using electronic communication are a compelling feature of this technology. The authors in this section explore the behavior and relationships of people in electronic groups. A central feature of many electronic groups is that they exist completely within the network, having no external counterpart outside of the messages and other electronic information the members exchange by computer. This feature makes these relationships somewhat like those of the time-honored "pen pals," but unlike pen pals, a person's electronic group relationships can include tens, hundreds, or thousands of people.

The most common electronic group until a few years ago was one in which employees in a corporation with access to a company network or the Internet formed a group online (Sproull & Kiesler, 1991). Although the group members had normal organizational duties and responsibilities in the organization of their employment, these duties could extend through the network to people in other such organizations with whom the employee had work-related needs for discourse and discussion. Collaboratively authored documents flowed back and forth through the network, residing in different versions here or there in various host machines, eventually wending their way to dissemination or publication. Employees often had extensive discussion as well via private person-to-person electronic mail.

With the rise of commercial online services and electronic communication from homes, people have begun to participate in electronic groups just for personal communication, pleasure, and help. The chapters in this section are a sample of the growing body of research about the personal exchanges that take place in electronic groups. In chapter 5, Nancy Baym studies the communications and norms of an electronic group over time. She uses the method of ethnography (a collection of participant observation techniques originally developed by anthropologists and sociologists). She shows how the group extends the functionality of television technology through the exchange by members of TV soap digests and reviews. More important, however, is the feeling of community that builds in this group of people who have never met face-to-face. In chapters 7 and 8, two researchers from quite different perspectives write about MUDs, or multiuser domains (also called multiuser dungeons and MOOs—multiuser object-oriented domains). MUDs are electronic meeting places where people gather to talk and play simultaneously. Pavel Curtis, a computer scientist, discusses the operation and governance of the largest existing MUD; Curtis' observations are unique because he is the creator and moderator of the MUD. Sherry Turkle, an anthropologist, discusses MUDs as they affect individuals' perceptions of others and themselves. Chapter 8, by Kristin Mickelson, continues the discussion of the effects of electronic groups on individuals. Her survey research on how parents of exceptional children seek social support on the Internet was a fortuitous consequence of being unable to find enough ordinary research participants. Turning to the Internet for research subjects not only increased her sample size but also allowed her to observe some tantalizing differences between parents who participate in social support groups on the Internet and those who don't.

Chapter 9, by Barry Wellman, discusses the use of sociological social network theory to understand electronic groups. The concept of "group" needs to be reconsidered and possibly redefined in light of our observations of large electronic groups. Electronic groups with highly fluid membership, obscure boundaries, and very large size don't fit theories of small groups very well. Wellman argues that social network theories and techniques, which have been used successfully to study diffuse neighborhoods and communities, might be a useful approach to understand such groups.

REFERENCE

Sproull, L. S., & Kiesler, S. (1991). *Connections: New Ways of Working in the Networked Organization.* Cambridge, MA: MIT Press.

5

INTERPRETING SOAP OPERAS AND CREATING COMMUNITY: INSIDE AN ELECTRONIC FAN CULTURE

Nancy K. Baym
Wayne State University

This chapter examines the traditions of a very successful newsgroup, rec.arts.tv.soaps (r.a.t.s). R.a.t.s has created a folklore with some similarities to other newsgroups, and some traditions uniquely its own. Posters in the group have adapted features of electronic communication, such as subject lines and punctuation marks, to demark subgroups, define genres, and express emotion. Members of r.a.t.s are rewarded for humorous, insightful, individualistic, and considerate performances. Though dispersed in space and time, they are a true community that sustains relationships and keeps members interested, even when the soaps themselves are boring.

Early conceptions of the folk group required shared location and unmediated interaction. This chapter examines a highly successful electronic discussion group, or "newsgroup," about American day-time television soap operas—Rec.arts.tv.soaps. ("r.a.t.s"). R.a.t.s is a group with a distinct folklore, yet it is distributed in the form of electronic messages through the USENET network of groups on the Internet. More recent conceptions of the folk group require only that groups share a common factor and unique traditions (Dundes, 1965), or that traditions are grounded in distinct shared rules for the conduct and interpretation of speech (Hymes, 1986). Computer-mediated groups share the topics around which they organize, the system that links them, and the communication that passes between them.

These three sets of resources seem sufficient to create distinct ways of speaking, and hence distinctive folk groups and folkloric traditions.

This chapter begins with an overview of my own relationship to the group and my methods of inquiry. Second, I turn to the group's technical and participatory structure, looking in particular at the ways these structures mitigate the spatial–temporal separation of group members. Third, I look at some of the emergent traditions in r.a.t.s. Finally, I look at performance in r.a.t.s, asking how performance is evaluated.

METHOD

R.a.t.s is one of the oldest and most successful USENET newsgroups. It began in 1984 when it split off from the television newsgroup (then called "net.tv"). Non-soap fans became annoyed at the excessive soap opera discussion, and the soap opera fans moved to create their own group, "net.tv.soaps." "Rec.arts" was substituted for "net" a few years later as newsgroups multiplied and the hierarchical system used to name them expanded. R.a.t.s now ranks between 200th and 300th in estimated readership (of many thousands of newsgroups). R.a.t.s was one of the first groups to pass the 100,000 article mark.

The work discussed here is part of an ongoing ethnographic study of communication in the r.a.t.s newsgroup community. My positions in the group are those of a participant and a researcher. As a longtime fan of soap operas, I was thrilled to discover this group. It was only after I had been reading daily and participating regularly for a year that I began to write about it. As the work has evolved, I have shared its progress with the group members and found them exceedingly supportive and helpful.

The data for this study were obtained from three sources. In October 1991, I saved all the messages that appeared on r.a.t.s; I collected more messages in 1993. Eighteen participants responded to a questionnaire I posted to r.a.t.s. Personal email correspondence with 10 other r.a.t.s participants provided further information. I posted two notices to the group explaining the project and offering to exclude posts by those who preferred not to be involved. No one declined to participate.

GROUP STRUCTURE

USENET. R.a.t.s is shaped by its host, USENET (see chap. 2). For instance, because the number of messages passing through USENET is enormous, many sites store messages for only a few days or weeks. This ethereal quality of messages in many ways makes them more like talk than like writing. The conversationality of USENET also is fostered by newsreader designs and accompanying normative conventions that invoke social contexts for messages. I focus in particular on the role of the quotation system and headers in overcoming spatial and temporal separation and thus facilitating the creation of social context and community.

When one responds to a message in a newsgroup, most newsreaders make it easy to quote, cut, or edit the entire earlier post. Social conventions across USENET groups dictate that one should quote posts to which one is replying, and then cut quotes to the minimal length necessary to ground one's remarks. The ability to imbed previous talk in new contributions allows people to understand responses to posts they have not yet seen (Raymond, 1991). The quotation system also allows ideas to remain attributed to their original writers. Ownership and attribution of ideas associate discourse with particular individuals. Context is created anew in each post that uses quotation. Messages are thus situated in ongoing streams of personalized discussion, much like face-to-face talk. Context also is created by headers appearing at the top of every post.[1]

Participation. R.a.t.s participants are primarily women. Judging from the headers of 1 month's r.a.t.s posts, of the 492 people who contributed, 60% were clearly women, 20% were clearly male, and another 20% had addresses that left gender ambiguous. Assuming r.a.t.s is approximately 72% female and 28% male, the group reflects the gender demographics of American soap opera viewers (Alexander, Carveth, Ryan, & Bohrer, 1992). The r.a.t.s participants claim for the most part to be between the ages of 20 and 50 years.

R.a.t.s participants are well educated, as in most of the Internet (see chap. 19). Many who responded to the questionnaire and email have or are pursuing advanced degrees. Most read newsgroups while at work or school, often checking in several times each day. That they are at work means, of course, that they are not at home watching soap operas. They videotape soaps and save them for evenings and weekends, if they watch them at all.

There are two ways to participate in any newsgroup, including r.a.t.s. Lurking involves reading without ever contributing; posting means writing messages. Of 492 posters in October 1991, 187 posted only once during the month, 185 posted 2 to 5 times, 73 posted 6 to 10 times, and 45 posted more than 10 times. The 187 one-time posters sent 9% of the total messages, whereas those 45 who posted more than 10 times sent 44%. This demonstrates that a small group of people does most of the performing. Furthermore, the most prolific on r.a.t.s tend to maintain that position over time, and play powerful roles in shaping group tradition. They generate most of the discourse and carry the highest name recognition. Norms implied by and embedded in their messages carry a good deal of persuasiveness.

---

[1]Not all networks are equally hospitable to the processes needed to allow distinct speech communities to emerge. For instance, if posters cannot include parts of previous postings in their posts, it is much more difficult to carry on a discussion over time.

TRADITION

Traditionalization occurs through a group's communicative practice. As traditional ways of speaking emerge, so do conventions about how to mark speech. Conventionalized markings and groupings of discourse determine how speech is to be interpreted, yet are usually highly efficient and minute in comparison to the discourse as a whole (Hymes, 1975). Two of the conventionalized systems in r.a.t.s use marking components in the subject line to frame messages.

Indicating message type with conventionalized subject line components is common across USENET groups. Talk is often differentiated into an unmarked category and one or more marked categories. "Rec.food.recipes," for instance, distinguishes posted recipes from requests for recipes with the inclusion of "REQUEST:" or "RECIPE:" in the subject line. Almost all groups have a subject line labeled "FAQ" (Frequently Asked Questions) to explain group norms and facilitate new users' entry. Subject line conventions allow people to make informed choices about what to read, and hence in which events to participate.

Cueing Soap Opera.   Participants in r.a.t.s use the initials of each soap opera in the subject lines to subdivide the group internally. Identifying which soap opera one is addressing is the first rule of competent communication. One respondent's claim that "the thing most people have a hang-up about is using subject initials in your heading" exemplifies the group's awareness that not using these initials is likely to irritate others and to result in posts that "flame" or scold violators for the omission. FAQs tell newcomers how to address their messages (see Table 5.1). Because the initialing system allows people to avoid posts about soap operas they do not follow, r.a.t.s actually hosts almost a dozen subgroups, each of which discusses one serial. The initialing system thus marks not only the soap opera of reference but also the community, and each subgroup of soap opera fans may have its own traditions.

Genres.   Other conventionalized markers are used to cue particular kinds of talk, or genres. Hymes' (1975) and Bauman's (1992a) original formulations of genres suggested they were meaningful structures maintained through communicative activity. Bakhtin, however, has argued for a more dynamic conception, in which genre includes the process of strategically using tradition to endow discourse with dimensions of personal and social meaning (see Bauman, 1992a).

R.a.t.s discussants have traditionalized a number of genres. In this section I discuss the subgroup, "All My Children" (AMC), because it has been the subject of most of my research and because it has the most subject line marked genres of the r.a.t.s subgroups. Over 2 weeks of postings (380 posts), I noted seven categories of discussion, six marked and one un-

TABLE 5.1

Message to the Newsgroup rec.arts.tv.soaps
Explaining How Posters Should Mark Subject Lines

One of the following abbreviations should be used at the beginning of the subject line of all postings to rec.arts.tv.soaps. For example:

Subject: DOOL—Update for Thursday or Subject: SB: CC and Sophia

This will allow those who use rn or any other method of pre-selecting articles to determine whether they wish to read the article or not. For information on these methods see the monthly NEWCOMERS posting by sally@pixies.proton.com. Remember that if you want to write about

ALL—To be seen by all readers of r.a.t.s

ABC—All ABC daytime soaps (LOV

CBS—All CBS daytime soaps (Y&R

NBC—All NBC daytime soaps (DOOL

AMC—All My Children

AW—Another World

ATWT- As the World Turns

B&B—The Bold & the Beautiful

DOOL- Days of Our Lives

GH—General Hospital

GL—Guiding Light

LOV—Loving

OLTL—One Life to Live

SB—Santa Barbara

Y&R—The Young & the Restless

HF—Homefront

KL—Knot's Landing

marked. The marked genres, from least to most common, are trivia, unlurkings, sightings, and spoilers (each with fewer than 5% of the total posts), updates (16%) , and tangents (20%). The seventh category, with over 60% of the posts, is unmarked. Drawing on the networkwide use of the term *thread* to describe lines of conversation, I call this genre *new threads*.

Each of the genres has distinct structural features and serves different social functions. Posts with "trivia" in the subject line repeat published trivia questions (or answers), usually from trivia cards, games or books, and magazines about "All My Children." For instance, one quiz began as follows:

Since there was a request for another trivia quiz, here is a new one.

1. What little nothing has Phoebe been known to wear to bed to entice Langley? . . .

Trivia games and game shows have formalized a genre of interactive play based on testing one's store of minute and trivial bits of information. Aside from providing a game for participants to play, the answers to these historical questions occasionally spin off into highly evaluative and extended discussions of the show's past.

Unlurking, marked by the use of the term *unlurking, unlurk,* or *lurker* in the subject line, are posts in which a new or rare poster introduces herself to the group, as shown in this excerpt:

> I wanted to introduce myself. My name is Kari Banning. I am a PhD. student at Carnegie Mellon University in Pittsburgh. I have been watching AMC for several years. At first, it was during the summers in the mid to late 70's-back when Erica was involved with Nick and her marriage to Tom (this was while I was in high school). Then I watched during my lunch hour. With the help of my faithful VCR, I have not missed an episode in about 4 years....

These posts usually specify the poster's name, how long she has been lurking in r.a.t.s, her occupation, often the species and names of pets (especially cats, which seem to be a common link among AMC participants), and almost always general opinions about AMC. This genre is almost exclusively relational in purpose, as unlurkings flag the entry of a new member into the community. Responses to unlurkings work as a welcoming committee, encouraging new or returning participants to remain active.

Posts marked as sightings in the subject line are reports of having seen a current or former soap opera actor in another context, such as live public appearances, roles in movies, and televised appearances on talk shows, prime time shows, and commercials. For example: "Yep! It's another one of those alumni sightings. I saw Lanie in a commercial for a new kind of Reebok's that has pads in the soles .... "

One of the more striking genres, spoilers, are previews culled from magazines, sightings, and other computer networks. This spoiler begins :

> Here's a treat you guys that enjoy spoilers! For next week's AMC:

> Mon: Altho Trevor has pulled back from their kiss, Nat asks him to stay. When Adam finds Brian strangling the life out of Will, he realizes he should intervene à shouldn't he? . . .

This posting ends, "Wow! Sounds like a great action-packed week!"

Magazines cited in spoilers include *Soap Opera Digest, Soap Opera Weekly, Soap Opera Monthly,* and *Soap Opera Now.* The two commercial networks referenced are Prodigy and GEnie. Credibility is a key issue underlying spoilers. Those from less reputable sources, such as the supermarket tabloid, *The Star,* are explicitly marked as dubious, as are those that appear in reputable sources as "predictions" rather than as "previews." Discussions of spoilers are highly evaluative.

Spoilers and their subsequent discussion must be identified so they can be avoided. As one longtime r.a.t.s participant explained, "I have found that reading the 'spoilers' every week detracts from my enjoyment of the show. I like being surprised by the show, not by the group! . . ." On the other hand, many people like spoilers. "If there is a spoiler and I already know what's going to happen, I feel more free to do chores while I'm 'watching.'. . ." Spoilers also provide r.a.t.s readers with status in their interactions with soap opera fans who do not have access to the network. That many of r.a.t.s participants know the plots of forthcoming shows suggests that Brundson (1989) may be right in her claim that viewers watch soap operas not to see what will happen, but how it will happen.

Posts marked by "update" and the show's date in the subject line are retellings of the week's daily episodes. Updates are unique in that they are posted only by preselected members of the community. The first AMC updater recalls that when she decided to do updates in 1984 no one else was doing them. She began of her own initiative and, when she received grateful email in response, decided to continue. When she tired of it, others volunteered and she handed off each day. The incumbent updater continues to select a successor. Updating is a time-consuming task, and updaters make a substantial commitment to the group.

Updates are by far the longest posts, averaging 172 lines each as opposed to posts in other genres, which average only 24 lines. Updaters retell each episode in tremendous detail. Evaluations and opinions are embedded in the updates but are clearly framed as separate from the retelling. This is done by stating opinions up front, then using transitions such as "And now on to the update." A more common technique is to embed commentary in brackets with or without the prefix "Ed. note:" to separate it clearly from the story.

Updates allow people who are not able to watch shows to keep up with them. The almost daily pleas for updates continually reinforce the need for them. The discussion they stimulate involves using the update to frame one's own commentary. Although people occasionally modify an update, more commonly they excerpt the relevant section and offer an opinion.

Tangents, marked by "TAN" in the subject line, are a default category into which falls all discussion no longer directly related to the soap operas. Tangents reveal people as individuals. As one person says, "I also like the AMC TANS, because it gives you a chance to get to know the poster.... " The TANS also allow those who have developed social relationships to enrich them by increasing the breadth of their interaction. A particularly sociable participant explains, "I find the subjects brought up as tangents almost as interesting as the soaps—for example, the cross section of r.a.t.s who are cat lovers, star trekkers, etc. Some of us have shared our birthdays, our taste in beer and our butt size.... We know who has read GWTW. We know who has PMS.... " Tangents are used as a forum for discussing issues of particular concern to women, including experiences with violence against women, worst dates, whether or not to change names when marrying, and more. Less gender-bound topics are about when to put up the Christmas tree, other television shows, and notorious court cases.

Tangents are the most recently marked form of discourse. In fall 1991, when traffic on the newsgroup began to expand dramatically, people who barely had time to read posts pertaining to the soap operas began to voice irritation with having to weed through unrelated messages. Someone proposed that the convention of marking a subject line with TAN, used in other USENET newsgroups, be imported, a suggestion that was almost instantaneously adapted with little explicit discussion. This compromise allows people who do not want to read TANs to edit them out fairly simply, while granting those who want them the public ground on which to stray. The genesis of the TAN convention in r.a.t.s exemplifies the interactive and functional nature of traditionalization on r.a.t.s and, I suspect, in other electronic cultures.

The final category, new threads, is unmarked. It includes posts that first raise topics related to the soap opera. Subject lines usually identify the topic by character or characters, as with "AMC: Dixie and Brian" but can contain any of a range of components. New threads pool opinion, criticize, predict, and parody. Duranti (1988) wrote that "although the presence of a lexical term for a given activity or 'strip of interaction' is only one level of local organization of experience—perhaps the most obviously ideological—the lack of a term for any given such 'strip' is an interesting clue for fieldworkers" (p. 220). That new threads and their subsequent discussions are not explicitly named in the subject lines suggests that interpretive evaluation of the soap opera is considered the norm, and that the named genres indicate perceived variations from that norm.

New threads are explicit interpretations. As interpretations, they make few claims to authority. In fact, r.a.t.s participants actively discourage the claiming of authority. Trivia, sightings, spoilers, and updates, on the other hand, are genres invoked in part to invest a message with external authority—primarily that of the soap opera press and the soap opera itself. The flip side of claiming such authority is excluding or bracketing one's own perspective. The lack of a subject line marker for new threads is a clue to the fact that the community's primary mission is as a forum for publicly negotiating soap opera interpretations.

PERFORMANCE

If genre is the "what" of recurrent forms of speech, performance is the "how" (Hymes, 1975). In this section I turn from tradition as embodied in subject line conventions to performance in the sense of framing one's communicative activity as open for evaluation of competence. In newsgroups all posts are open to evaluation. Given that the option of lurking always exists, those who contribute feel they have something of significance either to add or to ask. R.a.t.s is characterized in part by a politeness norm against wasting readers' time. I suspect that the responsibility to be stimulating characterizes most newsgroup participation, though standards of what is "stimulating" vary wildly. A lurker alluded to this responsibility when she responded to a post that thanked her for unlurking to post a New Yorker magazine article about AMC: "I'm also glad for the chance to add something to this ongoing stimulating dialogue!! I've been lurking for several weeks now, but rarely post, since you all seem to already have so many fun things to say!"

Keying Performance.   Like genres, performances are keyed through conventional cues including "a wink, gesture, posture, style of dress ..." (Hymes, 1986, p. 62). The computer medium seems at first glance to eliminate just these kinds of cues, but given time, participants respond to this deprivation by creating new ways to convey crucial metacommunicative information. Emoticons (or "smiley faces") are pictorial representations of emotional expressions using punctuation marks. Meant to be viewed sideways (left is up), they have been used commonly in electronic interaction since 1980 (Raymond, 1991). The most common are :-) = smile, :-(= frown, and ;-) = wink. People also use brackets of nonverbal expressions such as *yawn* and [g] for grin, and capital letters as in: "[w]hen he handed her that BOULDER of a diamond.... "

Evaluating Performance.   A culture's analysis of what constitutes "skill" and "effectiveness" in its own talk is a privileged entryway into the underlying interests that organize group life (Bauman, 1992b). Participants in r.a.t.s use three methods to compliment skilled performances: They respond to them, they thank their senders, and they offer explicit praise. Receiving responses is considered flattering and fairly exciting, and the hope of receiving responses often motivates performance. In response to one man's question as to whether or not he ought to feel foolish for being so excited at having received a response to his first post, an active poster assured him: "I can tell you that when I made *my* first posts (and they were rather brief) I wanted nothing more than a lengthy reply. In fact, lots of lengthy replies. The worst feelings I ever had was when I thought I was bringing up something interesting and got *no* replies. That bothered me.... " As this suggests, without replies there is no way of assessing whether others found one's contribution worthwhile or competent, let alone skilled. Not all competent performances receive responses. Particularly skilled performances, however, are almost always rewarded with explicit praise.

Participants in r.a.t.s differ in what they want from r.a.t.s posts and hence in how they evaluate their merits. Though there are occasional innovative exceptions, four ways of living up to the group's performative potential consistently emerge in r.a.t.s. These criteria of skilled performance are humor, insight, distinctive personality, and politeness.

Everyone agrees that r.a.t.s is first and foremost meant to be fun. As one participant said, "I don't read [r.a.t.s] to get job-related information or anything to help me in my daily life (well, just to get my daily 'soap fix,' but I don't think that counts :-); it's just a fun way to pass a few minutes and hopefully hear some news about my two soaps (GH and OLTL)." Soap operas often bring to mind images of characters wrapped in constant melodrama, crisis, and emotional torment. Except for the laugh with which they are often dismissed, soap operas are rarely taken to evoke humor. However, there is little praise higher on r.a.t.s than to be told you made someone laugh, and being a funny poster is a particularly effective way to forge a known identity in the group. When I asked what makes a poster successful, I often received answers along the lines of "Well, a good sense of humor, definitely. I love the posts from people who are funny!"

Much of the humor on r.a.t.s achieves its impact at the soap opera's expense. That fans would seek to transform the show's shortcomings into a form of humor for group pleasure is understandable on two counts. First, fans have a strong need to grapple with the show's weaknesses and transform them into something worthwhile. Second, humor provides a way to enhance social affiliation, which is especially vulnerable when the show fails to entertain (Jenkins, 1992).

One conventionalized form of humor is "aptonyms," or nicknames appropriate to a character (Nilsen, 1993, p. 68). The AMC group, for example, nicknamed the naive and stupid Dixie, "Ditsie"; her sleazy brother Will, "Swill"; and the controlling Dimitri, "Dementri" then "Dimwit." The DOOL group, too, savors the creative use of nicknames creating, in one case, a contestlike quality to the ever-changing nicknames of Isabella (called "Izzy-B" by her onscreen lover), including "Izzamomma2B" when her pregnancy was announced, and "Izzachameleonlivingonmyhead" in criticism of her ever-changing hair color.

"Soap opera laws" are another conventionalized form of humor. Accompanied with absurdly high or precise numbers, such as "Soap Opera Law 462n" or "Soap Opera Law N-533-2a," these laws include soap opera truisms, such as "If you only have sex once you will certainly become pregnant," and "If a figure referred to in someone's past who never had a name suddenly gets a name they will soon show up in town." These principles are based on advanced expertise in reading the genre, and their humor affirms the group's extended soap opera competence. Because these laws so often point out soap opera's absurdity, their articulation also helps members establish an explicit awareness of its absurdity that distances them from it and, indeed, makes that absurdity a source of humor in its own right.

Humorous lists are another genre of humor on r.a.t.s. Borrowing a humor genre from David Letterman, some participants write Top 10 Lists, such as the top 10 bad acting performances on "General Hospital." People have also created Top 40 song lists attributing real recorded songs to characters to whom the titles are relevant. New lyrics to familiar songs are also a popular form of humor, especially in the DOOL group. During a particularly dull period of AMC, Natalie's insane sister Janet (known on the net as "JaNut") left her down a well for over a month in an effort to steal her fiancé, Trevor (nicknamed "Porkchop" by his onscreen niece), by pretending to be Natalie. A few AMC regulars collaborated on the song "Nat's in the Well" to be sung to the tune of "The Farmer in the Dell":

> And Nat's in the well
> And Nat's in the well
> Hi Ho the dreary-o
> Nat's in the well

The verses that followed summarized the story line and r.a.t.s discussions of it, as well as offered a few comical resolutions of the story line:

> Trevor takes a "wife"...
> The "wife" is a nut...
> The viewers are not pleased....

The complete version of this song was posted to rec.arts.tv.soaps, October 7, 1991. Over a year later, when Erica was left in a crypt to die, one AMC participant reprised the first verse of the song with the lyrics "Erica's in the crypt."

The use of humor as a criterion in evaluating performance on r.a.t.s is directly related to important functional concerns in the group. It helps keep fans entertained during times when a soap opera may fail to do so, and it helps to create an accepting and caring group atmosphere (Morreall, 1983). R.a.t.s. is above all a forum for the pooling of evaluative interpretations. Humor helps to create a friendly and open environment that encourages participants to leap in and voice their own opinions.

Humor acts as a standard for evaluating performance in many other electronic cultures as well. In fact, it is common enough that conventional ways of acknowledging humorous performances have emerged across the electronic subculture. The acronym ROTFL or ROFL, for instance, is used across many networks to mean "rolling on the floor laughing." In r.a.t.s, praise for humor often appears as variations on two themes: "I laughed so hard everyone in my office knew I wasn't working," and "I laughed so hard I spit on my screen."

The second criterion applied in evaluating r.a.t.s performance is its degree of insightfulness into the soap opera. To be involved in r.a.t.s at all one has to be aware of what is happening on the soap opera. Without knowledge of the latest characters, twists, and turns, one cannot follow even the simplest of r.a.t.s discussions. For the participants who do not have the time or means to watch the soap, then, the "good" posts are the ones that enable them to keep up with both the soap opera and the discussion. They emphasize retelling (or pretelling) over interpreting. As one woman says, "My favorite r.a.t.s posters are the ones who post summaries and interesting tidbits about 'my' two soaps, since I don't generally tape or watch them and that's my only way of keeping track of what's happening on them. :-)" Hence, the most often praised informative post is the update, whose writers have been praised by others in poetry and song.

Another informative posting is the retelling of a show's deep history. Some soap operas have been on the air for over 50 years: "As the World Turns" and "Guiding Light" predate television; "Days of Our Lives," "All My Children," "General Hospital," and "One Life to Live" have all been broadcast for over 20 years. Although soap operas continually repeat themselves in order to bring new viewers up to date, it would be impossible to repeat this entire history. Retellings of and reminiscing about a show's past provide deep history that allows participants more insight into the current episodes (Whetmore & Kielwasser, 1983). When the character, Brooke, on "All My Children" hired a man who had served time for stalking his ex-wife to work at her magazine, many r.a.t.s participants were dismayed. Those who knew the show's history were especially certain Brooke would never have done this and, to support their claim, retold for the others how Brooke herself had been victimized by a stalker many years earlier.

Confused viewers who have missed something in either deep or recent soap history frequently ask for history lessons when they do not understand something. They thus encourage those with good memories to perform. Answers are usually posted within a few days at the most. Longtime watchers with good memories and/or electronic soap opera archives are able both to answer these questions and to stake out roles as resident history experts. This "Santa Barbara" fan demonstrated his ability to retell deep history in this excerpt:

> pamela & cc were married & had mason. pamela had an affair with hal clark (scott's uncle). she & cc divorced but she was carrying cc's child (the writers never quite explained why it wasn't hal's kid). nevertheless, unbeknownst to cc, pamela had his daughter, elena. she was raised by dr. alex nikolas (cc's enemy who always loved pamela). cc finds out about her about 30 years later when she starts terrorizing the acknowledged capwell children (esp. eden L mason). this story gets really convoluted so i'll just point out the highlights. around the same time jeffrey & alex came to town for revenge on cc (because of his treatment of pamela) jeffrey & kelly fell in love & married & divorced. elena was shot & cruz was accused & turned out she comitted suicide. alex left town after he realized he could never have pamela (BTW, pamela showed up during cruz' trial). i hope this helps....

Finally, participants in r.a.t.s pool information culled from their own areas of expertise, usually to assess (and often to criticize) a show's realism. Once Adam, on "All My Children," revealed that Erica and he were never

legally divorced 7 years earlier because his identical twin, Stuart, imperson-
ated him at the proceedings (a plot twist that had been predicted by
history-oriented AMC posters many months earlier). Viewers researched
the legal implications of the scenario and posted their findings, for example:

> Bigamy is defined as follows: the criminal offense of willfully and knowingly
> contracting a second marriage(or going through the form of a second mar-
> riage) while the first marriage, to the knowledge of the offender is still
> subsisting and undissolved.

> Translation: Adam is the criminal here; Erica is the innocent victim....

Finally, insight into the show can be offered without informing others of
anything but one's own reading of the soap opera text. Insightful perspectives are favorites in the group. Says one poster, "Usually the best [posts]
are ones that are either people's own views on what happened on a soap
opera, or new plot ideas." Soap operas are what Allen (1985) called an "over
coded" form, meaning that they offer more possible interpretations that are
necessary to move the narrative forward. Because of this, the text can
support multiple legitimate interpretations. Part of the pleasure of being a
soap opera fan is negotiating these interpretations with others. Indeed it
can be argued that this pleasure is one of the major modes of engaging with
the soap opera narrative. "Half the fun of watching," says one participant,
"is comparing notes and speculations with others!" One social consequence
of pooling this insight is the creation of a vast body of public knowledge
and opinions to which all group members share access. The fact that they
are so well informed moves them out of the class of most soap opera fans
in their local communities and aligns them instead with other r.a.t.s users.

A third criterion for assessing performative skill on r.a.t.s is the degree
of individuality with which one invests one's posts. Most scholars of
electronic communication have argued that, in addition to reducing the
conventional cues used to frame talk, the lack of visual and auditory
information in electronic talk reduces most cues to status, appearance
identity, and gender (Kiesler, Siegel, & McGuire, 1984; Cheseboro & Bonsall,
1989; Raymond, 1991; Reid, 1991). Some hold that this lack of information
reduces the communicators to anonymity, which would seem to prevent
the formation of true community. Further, most r.a.t.s interactants, in Dundes' (1977) words are "part-time folk." Regular posters, however, can create
personalities, and differential identity can be seen as a creative accomplishment resulting from intentional efforts to create a community populated by
distinctive personalities.

Individualizing is a desirable accomplishment in r.a.t.s, as illustrated by
such comments as "the most successful r.a.t.s posters are the ones who
interject their own personalities into theirs posts, whether by a .sig [signa-
ture] file that reveals things about them, or by making comments about their
personal lives. A "Days of Our Lives" participant described what makes a

good poster: "The willingness to express their feelings and opinions, and stand behind them. Uniqueness of posting style (so long as it's positive uniqueness). A sense of humor. A nongrating personality." The quest to establish distinct (and nongrating) personalities in a sea of similar-looking posts is also manifested in users' frequent references to one another by name and even occasional "roll calls" urging both lurkers and posters to introduce themselves to the group at large. It can also be seen in the traditionalization of unlurkings and TANS, both of which are designed to allow room for personal discussion that goes beyond the soap opera.

Another route to establishing a public identity on the group is the use of self-disclosure. Because of the issues around which soap operas revolve, self-disclosures are often highly personal. African Americans, Asian Americans, and gays have described their own experiences as victims of racism and homophobia when similar events are depicted on the shows. Women have told of being raped or beaten when discussing story lines dealing with these traumas. For example, in this post, a known personality in the AMC group used a personal narrative to justify her view of the show's portrayal of the wife-beating villain, Carter Jones (who was masquerading under the pseudonym "Kyle"):

> Friday's episode was very difficult to watch. I am a bit upset with the writers for turning Carter/Kyle into this wild maniac....

> I was on the receiving end just ONCE—but it was enough to make me get an immediate annulment from a mistake-of-a-marriage. AMC portrayed my ex to a "T" (professional, likable)—but completely lost me when they started this ridiculous story with Nat....

The personal narrative is used to ground the poster's criticism of the show in real-life expertise and thus could be evaluated in terms of the insight it provides. At the same time, it works at a personal level, helping to replace the anonymity of the newsgroup with real people living real lives.

Over time, these cues to personality fill in the identities of active participants so that shared knowledge goes far beyond the soaps and into other aspects of each other's lives. R.a.t.s participants have turned to the group for support during such frightening events as being robbed, harassed, or divorced, and such positive events as getting married, having children, and even being reunited with children given up for adoption decades earlier. The personalism brought into the group thus not only allows for richer interpretations, but also allows the group to function as a supportive community in which people are able to share their own experience as well as to dissect the experiences of the soap opera's fictional communities.

The valuing of individuality, just like the prizing of humor and insight, therefore relates to the need of soap opera fans to share and compare personalized interpretations of the show. The creation of a community of real people through disclosure, TANS, unlurkings, and the many other cues mentioned is the creation of a community in which it is easy for people to share their personalized interpretations. The value of personality can also be seen as a way to encourage people to be funny or insightful. Funny people, clever people, and even those who simply take the time to type in articles and tidbits from magazines are able to establish identities for themselves on the strength of such performances. Being recognized as an individual, known by name within the community, is an end toward which many participants strive.

The emergence of particular individuals within a community brings with it the potential for tension with those who are less known. In the DOOL group, for instance, a heated argument was prompted by a new poster who felt he was not granted the status he deserved for his inside connection to the show and the spoilers he shared. He argued he was being excluded by a tight-knit clique whose dominance squelched dissenting voices. The emergence of apparent "ingroups" within the r.a.t.s community would seem to make personal interpretations posted by known identities more authoritative than others and hence more difficult to discount publicly. Because the group exists largely to compare viewpoints, such potential authority can actually work against the group's coherence, pushing out those who would disagree with big-name posters. The potential interpretive authority of the well known r.a.t.s participants is actively discouraged, however, through the basic standard of politeness that cuts across r.a.t.s.

Although humor, insight, and personality contribute to making a post stand out as particularly good, politeness is a criterion of communicative competence that keeps posts from standing out as particularly bad. Posts are never commended for being especially polite, but those considered rude are quickly reprimanded. Negative comments and opinions are tolerated (and even encouraged) as long as another person is not attacked. A poster can seem rude simply by implying that others should see things as she does. "I like the summaries and the comments that come across as *comments* not forced opinions," one woman told me. She continued, "I enjoy reading ones that let you think what you want and ask for opinions and other thoughts."

Although there is pleasure in the voicing of multiple interpretations, there is always the potential for conflict, especially given the emotional attachments viewers form with soap opera characters and the emotional issues around which soap opera story lines revolve. If conflicts were to become personal (or degenerate into "flame wars"), people would be inhibited from contributing potentially controversial opinions, and the primary function of the group as an interpretive forum would be disrupted. After a flame war among the followers of "Days Of Our Lives," one longtime participant posted a lengthy "netiquette" post that explicated the nuances of the tolerance norm and the reasoning behind it. Excerpts follow:

FIRST AND FOREMOST remember that the net is populated by PEOPLE not computers. What you say CAN hurt. It is very difficult to judge someone's feelings when you can't see their face, so you have to be extra careful about EVERYTHING you post....

If something makes you angry, take a break before you reply or post a response. Then COUNT TEN and reread your reply or follow up before you send it....

Remember that opinions are OPINIONS, not facts....

Conversely, don't take things that people write to you or post PERSON-ALLY....

Remember, FLAMES BEGET FLAMES....

Being rude, as this post explains, is accomplished through personal attacks or self-righteousness. Being polite rests largely on the use of qualifiers that explicitly locate interpretations as personal perceptions. These qualifiers include "I thought that..." "my take was...," and the ever-popular network-wide acronyms IMHO (in my humble opinion) and IMNSHO (in my not-so-humble opinion). Other politeness strategies including preceding interpretive disagreements with explicit agreements and providing extended reasoning to justify such disagreements.

This overwhelming regard for the right to have one's own opinion is quite different from some of the groups on USENET that hurl insults over even the most minor of disagreements. The friendliness engendered by adherence to the norm of tolerance on r.a.t.s is one of the features participants find particularly compelling. Indeed, the only group any participant described as friendlier is that devoted to dog ownership, rec.pets.dogs. As a participant in both groups said, "The group in which I find the most flame wars (thus the least friendly and supportive in my opinion) is a local group uw.general for posting things mainly affecting our school or community. There are others I just read for information, for example, rec.food.recipes, comp.object. I would put rec.arts.tv.soaps right under rec.pets.dogs, for friendliness, support, warm, lack of flame wars (in Y&R anyway, which is the only soap I watch and read about), in general, overall enjoyment."

Politeness in r.a.t.s as a criterion of performance is intricately interwoven with the three other criteria of performance of humor, insight, and individuality. Fun, history, interpretation, and individuality require safety. From this need for safety comes the norm of tolerance and the efforts at personalization and humor. As well, humor and social support in r.a.t.s keep viewers interested when the soaps are not as good as they would like.

CONCLUSION

This chapter makes clear that technology in the form of computer networks is certainly no threat to folklore. Networks also are far more than a medium of transmission or a rich topic for new jokes. R.a.t s demonstrates that these networks can serve as the site for complex, interwoven, and personalized communities. These communities exist in asynchronous time and without shared location. As a result they rely more than ever on the traditionalization of communicative practice. In such a context, folklore is the only means to transform individual users from an anonymous collection of voices into a group.

The dramatic proliferation and growth of electronic communities has broad implications for how one thinks about the effects of technology on culture. Often one views television and computers as leading to a society increasingly involved with machines and decreasingly involved in community. However, these groups show that for an ever-growing number of people, the need for community has transformed working alone at a desk with only a computer as a companion into an excuse to spend time chatting away in vibrant communities of cyberspace neighbors.

ACKNOWLEDGMENTS

This chapter is an abridged version of Baym, N. (1993), Interpreting soap operas and creating community: Inside a computer-mediated fan culture. *Journal of Folklore Research, 30,* 143–176. Copyright 1993 by Indiana University Folklore Institute. Adapted by permission.

REFERENCES

Alexander, A., Carveth, R., Ryan, G., & Bohrer, M. S. (1992). Investigating gender differences in college student soap opera viewing. In S. Frentz (Ed.), *Contemporary. soap opera criticism* (pp. 19–32). Bowling Green, OH: Bowling Green State University Popular Press.

Allen, R. C. (1985). *Speaking of soap operas.* Chapel Hill: University of North Carolina Press.

Bauman, R. (1992a). Contextualization, tradition, and the dialogue of genres: Icelandic legends of the Kraftaskald. In A. Duranti & C. Goodwin (Eds.), *Rethinking context language as an interactive phenomenon* (pp. 125–146). New York: Cambridge University Press.

Bauman, R. (1992b). Performance. In R. Bauman (Ed.), *Folklore, cultural performances, and popular entertainments: A communications-centered handbook* (pp. 41–49). New York: Oxford University Press.

Brundson, C. (1989). Text and audience. In E. Seiter, H. Borchers, G. Kreutzner et al. (Eds.), *Remote control: Television, audiences, and cultural power* (pp. 116–129). New York: Routledge.

Cheseboro, J. W., & Bonsall, D. G. (1989). *Computer-mediated communication: Human relationships in a computerized world.* Tuscaloosa: University of Alabama Press.

Dundes, A. (1965). *The study of folklore.* Englewood Cliffs, NJ: Prentice-Hall.

Dundes, A. (1977). Who are the folk? In W. Bascom (Ed.), *Frontiers of folklore* (pp. 17–35). Boulder, CO: Westview.

Duranti, A. (1988). Ethnography of speaking: Toward a linguistics of the praxis. In F. P. Newmeyer (Ed.), *Language: The socio-cultural context* (pp. 210–228). New York: Cambridge University Press.

Hymes, D. (1975). Folklore's nature and the sun's myth. *Journal of American Folklore, 88,* 345–369.

Hymes, D. (1986). Models of the interaction of language and social life. In J. J. Gumpen & D. Hymes (Eds.), *Directions in sociolinguistics: The ethnography of speaking* (pp. 35–71). New York: Basil Blackwell.

Jenkins, H. (1992). *Textual poachers: Television fans and participatory cultures.* London: Routledge.

Kiesler, S., Siegel, J., & McGuire, T. J. (1984). Social psychological aspects of computer-mediated communication. *American Psychologist, 39,* 1123–1134.

Morreall, J. (1983). *Taking laughter seriously.* Albany: State University of New York Press.

Nilsen, D. L. F. (1993). *Humor scholarship: A research bibliography.* Westport, CT: Greenwood.

Raymond, E. S. (Ed.). (1991). *The new hacker's dictionary.* Cambridge, MA: MIT Press.

Reid, B. (1991). *USENET readership summary report.* [Monthly posting to *news.lists.,* USENET.]

Whetmore, E. J., & Kielwasser, A. P. (1983). The soap opera audience speaks: A preliminary report. *Journal of American Culture, 6,* 110–116.

6

MUDDING: SOCIAL PHENOMENA IN TEXT-BASED VIRTUAL REALITIES

Pavel Curtis
Xerox PARC

A MUD (Multiuser Dungeon or, sometimes, Multiuser Dimension) is a network-accessible, multiparticipant, user-extensible virtual reality whose user interface is entirely textual. Participants (usually called players) have the appearance of being situated in an artificially constructed place that also contains those other players who are connected at the same time. Players can communicate easily with each other in real time. This virtual gathering place has many of the social attributes of other places, and many of the usual social mechanisms operate there. Certain attributes of this virtual place, however, tend to have significant effects on social phenomena, leading to new mechanisms and modes of behavior not usually seen "IRL" (in real life). In this chapter, I relate my experiences and observations from having created and maintained a MUD for over a year.

A BRIEF INTRODUCTION TO MUDDING

> *The Machine did not transmit nuances*
> *of expression. It only gave a general*
> *idea of people—an idea that was good*
> *enough for all practical purposes.*
> *—E. M. Forster (1928/1973)*

A MUD is a software program that accepts connections from multiple users across some kind of network (e.g., telephone lines or the Internet) and

121

provides to each user access to a shared database of "rooms," "exits," and other objects. Each user browses and manipulates this database from "inside" one of those rooms, seeing only those objects that are in the same room and moving from room to room mostly via the exits that connect them. A MUD, therefore, is a kind of virtual reality, an electronically represented place that users can visit.

MUDs are not, however, like the kinds of virtual realities that one usually hears about, with fancy graphics and special hardware to sense the position and orientation of the user's real-world body. A MUD user's interface to the database is entirely text based; all commands are typed in by the users and all feedback is printed as unformatted text on their terminal. The typical MUD user interface is most reminiscent of old computer games like "Adventure" and "Zork" (Raymond, 1991); a typical interaction is shown in Table 6.1. Three major factors distinguish a MUD from an "Adventure"-style computer game, though:

1. A MUD is not goal oriented; it has no beginning or end, no score, and no notion of winning or success. In short, even though users of MUDs are commonly called players, a MUD isn't really a game at all.

2. A MUD is extensible from within; a user can add new objects to the database such as rooms, exits, "things," and notes. Certain MUDs, including the one I run, even support an embedded programming language in which a user can describe whole new kinds of behavior for the objects they create.

TABLE 6.1

A Typical MUD Database Interaction

look
Corridor
The corridor from the west continues to the east here
but the way is blocked by a purple-velvet rope
stretched across the hall. There are doorways leading
to the north and south.
You see a sign hanging from the middle of the rope here.
read sign
This point marks the end of the currently-occupied
portion of the house. Guests proceed beyond this point
at their own risk.
— The residents
go east
You step disdainfully over the velvet rope and enter
the dusty darkness of the unused portion of the house.

3. A MUD generally has more than one user connected at a time. All of the connected users are browsing and manipulating the same database and can encounter the new objects created by others. The multiple users on a MUD can communicate with each other in real time.

This last factor has a profound effect on the ways in which users interact with the system, transforming the interaction from a solitary activity into a social activity.

Most interplayer communication on MUDs follows rules that fit within the framework of the virtual reality. If players "say" something (using the say command), then every other player in the same room will "hear" them. For example, suppose that a player named Munchkin typed the command

> say Can anyone hear me?

Then Munchkin would see the feedback

> You say, "Can anyone hear me?"

and every other player in the same room would see

> Munchkin says, "Can anyone hear me?"

Similarly, the emote command allows players to express various forms of nonverbal communication. If Munchkin types

> emote smiles.

then every player in the same room sees

> Munchkin smiles.

Most interplayer communication relies entirely on these two commands.[1]

There are two circumstances in which the realistic limitations of say and emote have proved sufficiently annoying that new mechanisms were developed. It sometimes happens that one player wishes to speak to another player in the same room, but without anyone else in the room being aware of the communication. If Munchkin uses the whisper command

> whisper "I wish he'd just go away..." to Frebble

then only Frebble will see

> Munchkin whispers, "I wish he'd just go away..."

---

[1] In fact, these two commands are so frequently used that single-character abbreviations are provided for them. The two example commands would usually be typed as follows:

"Can anyone hear me?

:smiles

The other players in the room see nothing of this at all.

Finally, if one player wishes to say something to another who is connected to the MUD but currently in a different and perhaps "remote" room, the page command is appropriate. It is invoked with a syntax very like that of the whisper command and the recipient sees output like this:

You sense that Munchkin is looking for you in The Hall.

He pages, "Come see this clock, it's tres cool!"

Aside from conversation, MUD players can most directly express themselves in three ways: by their choice of player name, by their choice of gender, and by their self-description.

When players first connect to a MUD, they choose a name by which the other players will know them. This choice, like almost all others in MUDs, is not cast in stone; players can rename themselves at any time, though not to a name currently in use by other players. Typically, MUD names are single words, in contrast to the longer full names used in real life.

Initially, MUD players appear to be neuter; automatically generated messages that refer to such a player use the family of pronouns including *it, its,* and so on. Players can choose to appear as a different gender, though, and not only male or female. On many MUDs, players can also choose to be plural (appearing to be a kind of "colony" creature: "ChupChups leave the room, closing the door behind them"), or to use one of several sets of gender-neutral pronouns (e.g., *s/he, him/her* and *his/her,* or *e, em* and *eir*).

Every object in a MUD optionally has a textual description that players can view with the look command. For example, the description of a room is automatically shown to players when they enter that room and can be seen again just by typing "look." To see another player's description, one might type "look Bert." Players can set or change their descriptions at any time. The lengths of player descriptions typically vary from short one-liners to 12-line paragraphs.

Aside from direct communication and responses to player commands, messages are printed to players when other players enter or leave the same room, when others connect or disconnect and are already in the same room, and when objects in the virtual reality have asynchronous behavior (e.g., a cuckoo clock chiming the hours).

MUD players typically spend their connected time socializing with each other, exploring the various rooms and other objects in the database, and adding new such objects of their own design. They vary widely in the amount of time they spend connected on each visit, ranging from only a minute to several hours; some players stay connected (and almost always idle) for days at a time, only occasionally actively participating.

This very brief description of the technical aspects of mudding suffices for the purposes of this chapter. It has been my experience, however, that it is difficult to properly convey the sense of the experience in words. Readers desiring more detailed information are advised to try mudding themselves, as described in the final section of this chapter.

SOCIAL PHENOMENA OBSERVED ON ONE MUD

Man is the measure.
E. M. Forster (1928/1973)

In October of 1990, I began running an Internet-accessible MUD server on my personal workstation here at PARC. Since then, it has been running continuously, with interruptions of only a few hours at most. In January of 1991, the existence of the MUD (called LambdaMOO[2]) was announced publicly, via the Usenet newsgroup rec.games.mud. As of this writing, well over 3,500 different players have connected to the server from over a dozen countries around the world and, at any given time, over 750 players have connected at least once in the last week. Recent statistics concerning the number of players connected at a given time of day (Pacific Standard Time) appear in Fig. 6.1.

LambdaMOO is clearly a reasonably active place, with new and old players coming and going frequently throughout the day. This popularity has provided me with a position from which to observe the social patterns of a fairly large and diverse MUD clientele. I have no formal training in sociology, anthropology, or psychology, however, so I cannot make any claims about methodology. What I relate below are merely my personal observations made over a year of mudding. In most cases, my discussions of the motivations and feelings of individual players are based on in-MUD conversations with them; I have no means of checking the veracity of their statements concerning their real-life genders, identities, or (obviously) feelings. On the other hand, in most cases I have no reason to doubt them.

I have grouped my observations into three categories: phenomena related to the behavior and motivations of individual players, phenomena related to interactions between small groups of players (especially observations concerning MUD conversation), and phenomena related to the behavior of a MUD's community as a whole. Cutting across all of these categories is a recurring theme to which I would like to draw the reader's attention. Social behavior on MUDs is in some ways a direct mirror of behavior in real life, with mechanisms being drawn nearly unchanged from real life, and in some ways very new and different, taking root in the new opportunities that MUDs provide over real life.

---

[2]The "MOO" in "LambdaMOO" stands for "MUD, Object-Oriented." The origin of the "Lambda" part is more obscure, based on my years of experience with the Lisp programming language.

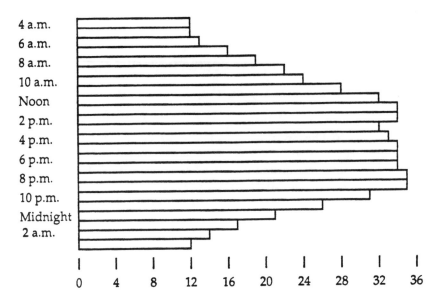

FIG. 6.1. Average number of connected players on the LambdaMOO, by time of day.

Observations About Individuals

The Mudding Population. The people who have an opportunity to connect to LambdaMOO are not a representative sample of the world population; they all read and write English with at least passable proficiency and they have access to the Internet. Based on the names of their network hosts, I believe that well over 90% of them are affiliated with colleges and universities, mostly as students and, to a lesser extent, mostly undergraduates. It appears to me that no more than half (and probably fewer) of them are employed in the computing field; the increasing general availability of computing resources on college campuses and in industry appears to be having an effect, allowing a broader community to participate.

In any case, it appears that the educational background of the mudding community is generally above average and it is likely that the economic background is similarly above the norm (see Chap. 19). Based on my conversations with people and on the names of those who have asked to join a mailing list about programming in LambdaMOO, I would guess that over 70% of the players are male.

Player Presentation. As described in the introduction to mudding, players have a number of choices about how to present themselves in the MUD; the first such decision is the name they will use. Table 6.2 shows some of the names used by players on LambdaMOO. One can pick out a few common styles for names (e.g., names from or inspired by myth, fantasy, or other literature, common names from real life, names of concepts, animals, and everyday objects that have representative connotations, etc.), but it is clear that no such category includes a majority of the names. Note that a significant minority of the names are in lower case; this appears to be a stylistic choice (players with such names describe the practice as "cool") and not, as might be supposed, an indication of a depressed ego.

Players can be possessive about their names, resenting others who choose names that are similarly spelled or pronounced or even that are taken from the same mythology or work of literature. In one case, for example, a player named "ZigZag" complained to me about other players taking the names "ZigZag!" and "Zig."

The choice of a player's gender is, for some, one of great consequence and forethought; for others (mostly males), it is simple and without any questions. For all that this choice involves the fewest options for the players (unlike their names or descriptions, which are limited only by their imagination), it is also the choice that can generate the greatest concern and interest on the part of other players.

The great majority of players who are male generally choose to present themselves as such. Some males, however, taking advantage of the relative rarity of females in MUDs, present themselves as female and thus stand out to some degree. Some use this distinction just for the fun of deceiving others, some of them going so far as to try to entice male-presenting players into sexually explicit discussions and interactions. This is such a widely noticed phenomenon, in fact, that one is advised by the common wisdom to assume that any flirtatious female-presenting players are, in real life, males. Such

TABLE 6.2

A Selection of Player Names From LambdaMOO

Toon	Gemba	Gary_Severn	Ford	Frand
li'ir	Maya	Rincewind	yduJ	funky
Grump	Foodslave	Arthur	EbbTide	Anathae
yrx	Satan	byte	Booga	tek
chupchups	waffle	Miranda	Gus	Merlin
Moonlight	MrNatural	Winger	Drazz'zt	Kendal
RedJack	Snooze	Shin	lostboy	foobar
Ted_Logan	Xephyr	King_Claudius	Bruce	Puff
Dirque	Coyote	Vastin	Player	Cool
Amy	Thorgeir	Cyberhuman	Gandalf	blip
Jayhirazan	Firefoot	JoeFeedback	ZZZzzz...	Lyssa
Avatar	zipo	Blackwinter	viz	Kilik
Maelstorm	Love	Terryann	Chrystal	arkanoiv

players are often subject to ostracism based on this assumption.

Some MUD players have suggested to me that such transvestite flirts are perhaps acting out their own (latent or otherwise) homosexual urges or fantasies, taking advantage of the perfect safety of the MUD situation to see how it feels to approach other men. Although I have had no personal experience talking to such players, let alone the opportunity to delve into their motivations, the idea strikes me as plausible given the other ways in which MUD anonymity seems to free people from their inhibitions. (I say more about anonymity later on.)

Other males present themselves as female more out of curiosity than as an attempt at deception; to some degree, they are interested in seeing "how the other half lives," what it feels like to be perceived as female in a community. From what I can tell, they can be successful at this.

Female-presenting players report a number of problems. Many of them have told me that they are frequently subject both to harassment and to special treatment. One reported seeing two newcomers arrive at the same time, one male-presenting and one female-presenting. The other players in the room struck up conversations with the putative female and offered to show her around but completely ignored the putative male, who was left to his own devices.

In addition, probably due mostly to the number of female-presenting males one hears about, many female players report that they are frequently (and sometimes aggressively) challenged to "prove" that they are, in fact, female. To the best of my knowledge, male-presenting players are rarely if ever so challenged. Because of these problems, many players who are female in real life choose to present themselves otherwise, choosing either male, neuter, or gender-neutral pronouns. As one might expect, the neuter and gender-neutral presenters are still subject to demands that they divulge their real gender.

Some players apparently find it difficult to interact with those whose true gender has been called into question; because this phenomenon is rarely manifest in real life, they have grown dependent on "knowing where they stand," on knowing what gender roles are "appropriate." Some players (and not only males) also feel that it is dishonest to present oneself as being a different gender than in real life; they report feeling "mad" and "used" when they discover the deception. I encourage the interested reader to look up Van Gelder's (1991) fascinating article for many more examples and insights, as well as the story of a remarkably successful deception via electronic transvestism.

The final part of a player's self-presentation, and the only part involving prose, is the player's description. This is where players can, and often do, establish the details of a persona or role they wish to play in the virtual reality. It is also a significant factor in other players' first impressions, because new players are commonly looked at soon after entering a common room.

Some players use extremely short descriptions, either intending to be cryptic (e.g., "the possessor of the infinity gems") or straightforward (e.g., "an average-sized dark elf with lavender eyes") or, often, just insufficiently motivated to create a more complex description for themselves. Other players go to great efforts in writing their descriptions; one moderately long example appears in Table 6.3.

A large proportion of player descriptions contain a degree of wish fulfillment; I cannot count the number of "mysterious but unmistakably powerful" figures I have seen wandering around in LambdaMOO. Many players, it seems, are taking advantage of the MUD to emulate various attractive characters from fiction.

Given the detail and content of so many player descriptions, one might expect to find a significant amount of role playing, players who adopt a coherent character with features distinct from their real-life personalities. Such is rarely the case, however. Most players appear to tire of such an effort quickly and simply interact with the others more-or-less straightforwardly, at least to the degree one does in normal discourse. One factor might be that the roles chosen by players are usually taken from a particular creative work and are not particularly viable as characters outside of the context of that work; in short, the roles don't make sense in the context of the MUD.

A notable exception to this rule is one particular MUD I've heard of, called "PernMUSH." This appears to be a rigidly maintained simulacrum of the world described in Ann McCaffrey's celebrated *Dragon* books. All players there have names that fit the style of the books and all places built there are consistent with what is shown in the series and in various fan materials devoted to it. PernMUSH apparently holds frequent "hatchings" and other social events, also derived in great detail from McCaffrey's works. This exception probably succeeds only because of its single-mindedness; with every player providing the correct context for every other, it is easier for everyone to stay more-or-less in character.

Player Anonymity.   It seems to me that the most significant social factor in MUDs is the perfect anonymity provided to the players. There are no

TABLE 6.3

A Moderately Long Player Description

You see a quiet, unassuming figure, wreathed in an oversized, dull-green Army jacket which is pulled up to nearly conceal his face. His long, unkempt blond hair blows back from his face as he tosses his head to meet your gaze. Small round gold-rimmed glasses, tinted slightly grey, rest on his nose. On a shoulder strap he carries an acoustic guitar and he lugs a backpack stuffed to overflowing with sheet music, sketches, and computer printouts. Under the coat are faded jeans and a T-Shirt reading 'Paranoid CyberPunks International.' He meets your gaze and smiles faintly, but does not speak with you. As you surmise him, you notice a glint of red at the rims of his blue eyes, and realize that his canine teeth seem to protrude slightly. He recoils from your look of horror and recedes back into himself.

commands available to the players to discover the real-life identity of each other and, indeed, technical considerations make such commands either very difficult or impossible to implement. It is this guarantee of privacy that makes players' self-presentation so important and, in a sense, successful. Players can only be known by what they explicitly project and are not locked into any factors beyond their easy control, such as personal appearance, race, and so forth. In the words of an old military recruiting commercial, MUD players can "be all that you can be."[3]

This also contributes to what might be called a shipboard syndrome, the feeling that because one will likely never meet anyone from the MUD in real life, there is less social risk involved and inhibitions can safely be lowered. For example, many players report that they are much more willing to strike up conversations with strangers they encounter in the MUD than in real life. One obvious factor is that MUD visitors are implicitly assumed to be interested in conversing, unlike visitors in most real-world contexts. A deeper reason, though, is that players do not feel that very much is at risk. At worst, if they feel that they've made an utter fool of themselves, they can always abandon the character and create a new one, losing only the name and the effort invested in socially establishing the old one. In effect, a new lease on life is always a ready option.

Players on most MUDs are also emboldened somewhat by the fact that they are immune from violence, both physical and virtual. The permissions systems of all MUDs (excepting those whose whole purpose revolves around adventuring and the slaying of monsters and other players) generally prevent any player from having any kind of permanent effect on any other player. Players can certainly annoy each other, but not in any lasting or even moderately long-lived manner.

This protective anonymity also encourages some players to behave irresponsibly, rudely, or even obnoxiously. We have had instances of severe and repeated sexual harassment, crudity, and deliberate offensiveness. In general, such cruelty seems to be supported by two causes: The offenders believe (usually correctly) that they cannot be held accountable for their actions in the real world, and the very same anonymity makes it easier for them to treat other players impersonally, as other than real people.

Wizards. Usually, societies cope with offensive behavior by various group mechanisms, such as ostracism, and I discuss this kind of effect later. In certain severe cases, however, it is left to the authorities or police of a society to take direct action, and MUDs are no different in this respect. On MUDs, it is a special class of players, usually called wizards or (less

---

[3]Kiesler, Siegel, and McGuire (1991) investigated the effects of this kind of electronic anonymity on the decision-making and problem-solving processes in organizations; some of their observations parallel mine given here.

frequently) gods, who fulfill both the authority and police roles. A wizard is a player who has special permissions and commands available, usually for the purpose of maintaining the MUD, much like a system administrator or "superuser" in real-life computing systems. Players can only be transformed into wizards by other wizards, with the maintainer of the actual MUD server computer program acting as the first such.

On most MUDs, the wizards' first approach to solving serious behavior problems is, as in the best real-life situations, to attempt a calm dialogue with the offender. When this fails, as it usually does in the worst cases of irresponsibility, the customary response is to punish the offender with "toading." This involves either (a) severely restricting the kinds of actions the player can take or preventing the player from connecting at all, (b) changing the name and description of the player to present an unpleasant appearance (often literally that of a warty toad), and (c) moving the player to some very public place within the virtual reality. This public humiliation is often sufficient to discourage repeat visits by the player, even in a different guise.

On LambdaMOO, the wizards as a group decided on a more low-key approach to the problem; we have, in the handful of cases where such a severe course was dictated, simply "recycled" the offending players, removing them from the database of the MUD entirely. This is a more permanent solution than toading, but also lacks the public spectacle of toading, a practice none of us was comfortable with.

Wizards, in general, have a very different experience of mudding than other players. Because of their palpable and extensive extra powers over other players, and because of their special role in MUD society, they are frequently treated differently by other players. Most players on LambdaMOO, for example, upon first encountering my wizard player, treat me with almost exaggerated deference and respect. I am frequently called "sir" and players often apologize for "wasting" my time. A significant minority, however, appear to go to great lengths to prove that they are not impressed by my office or power, speaking to me bluntly and making demands that I assist them with their problems using the system, sometimes to the point of rudeness.

Because of other demands on my time, I am almost always connected to the MUD but idle, located in a special room I built (my "den") that players require my permission to enter. This room is useful, for example, as a place in which to hold sensitive conversations without fear of interruption. This constant presence and unapproachability, however, has had significant and unanticipated side-effects. I am told by players who get more circulation than I do that I am widely perceived as a kind of mythic figure, a mysterious wizard in his magical tower. Rumor and hearsay have spread word of my supposed opinions on matters of MUD policy. One effect is that players are often afraid to contact me for fear of capricious retaliation at their presumption.

Although I find this situation disturbing and wish that I had more time to spend out walking among the "mortal" members of the LambdaMOO community, I am told that player fears of wizardly caprice are justified on certain other MUDs. It is certainly easy to believe the stories I hear of MUD wizards who demand deference and severely punish those who transgress; there is a certain ego boost to those who wield even simple administrative power in virtual worlds and it would be remarkable indeed if no one had ever started a MUD for that reason alone. In fact, one player sent me a copy of an article, written by a former MUD wizard, based on Machiavelli's *The Prince*; it details a wide variety of more-or-less creative ways for wizards to make ordinary MUD players miserable. If this wizard actually used these techniques, as he claims, then some players' desires to avoid wizards are understandable.

Observations About Small Groups

MUD Conversation. The majority of players spend the majority of their active time on MUDs in conversation with other players. The mechanisms by which those conversations get started generally mirror those that operate in real life, though sometimes in interesting ways.

Chance encounters between players exploring the same parts of the database are common and almost always cause for conversation. As mentioned earlier, the anonymity of MUDs tends to lower social barriers and to encourage players to be more outgoing than in real life. Strangers on MUDs greet each other with the same kinds of questions as in real life: "Are you new here? I don't think we've met." The very first greetings, however, are usually gestural rather than verbal: "Munchkin waves. Lorelei waves back."

The @who (or WHO) command on MUDs allows players to see who else is currently connected and, on some MUDs, where those people are. An example of the output of this command appears in Table 6.4. This is, in a sense, the MUD analog of scanning the room in a real-life gathering to see who's present.

Players consult the @who list to see if their friends are connected and to see which areas, if any, seem to have a concentration of players in them. If more than a couple of players are in the same room, the presumption is that an interesting conversation may be in progress there; players are thus more attracted to more populated areas. I call this phenomenon "social gravity"; it has a real-world analog in the tendency of people to be attracted to conspicuous crowds, such as two or more people at the door of a colleague's office.

It is sometimes the case on a MUD, as in real life, that one wishes to avoid getting into a conversation, either because of the particular other player involved or because of some other activity one does not wish to interrupt. In the real world, one can refrain from answering the phone, screen calls

TABLE 6.4

Sample Output From LambdaMOO's @who Command

Player name	Connected	Idle time	Location
Haakon (#2)	3 days	a second	Lambda's Den
Lynx (#8910)	a minute	2 seconds	Lynx' Abode
Garin (#23393)	an hour	2 seconds	Carnival Grounds
Gilmore (#19194)	an hour	10 seconds	Heart of Darkness
TamLin (#21864)	an hour	21 seconds	Heart of Darkness
Quimby (#23279)	3 minutes	2 minutes	Quimby's room
koosh (#24639)	50 minutes	5 minutes	Corridor
Nosredna (#2487)	7 hours	36 minutes	Nosredna's Hideaway
yduJ (#68)	7 hours	47 minutes	Hackers' Heaven
Zachary (#4670)	an hour	an hour	Zachary's Workshop
Woodlock (#2520)	2 hours	2 hours	Woodlock's Room

Total: 11 players, 6 of whom have been active recently.

using an answering machine, or even, in copresent situations, pretend not to have heard the other party. In the latter case, with luck, the person will give up rather than speak up more loudly.

The mechanisms are both similar and interestingly different on MUDs. It is often the case that MUD players are connected but idle, perhaps because they have stepped away from their terminal for a while. Thus, it often happens that one receives no response to an utterance in a MUD simply because the other party wasn't really present to see it. This commonly understood fact of MUD life provides for the MUD equivalent of pretending not to hear. I know of players who take care after such a pretense not to type anything more to the MUD until the would-be conversant has left, thus preserving the apparent validity of their excuse.

Another mechanism for avoiding conversation is available to MUD players but, as far as I can see, not to people in real-life situations. Most MUDs provide a mechanism by which each player can designate a set of other players as "gagged"; the effect is that nothing will be printed to the gagging player if someone they've gagged speaks, moves, emotes, and so on. There is generally no mechanism by which the gagged player can tell a priori that someone is gagging him; indeed, unless the gagged player attempts to address the gagging player directly, the responses from the other players in the room (who may not be gagging the speaker) may cause the speaker never even to suspect that some are not hearing him.

We provide a gagging facility on LambdaMOO, but it is rarely used; a recent check revealed only 45 players out of almost 3,000 who are gagging other players. The general feeling appears to be that gagging is rude and is only appropriate (if ever) when someone persists in annoying you in spite of polite requests to the contrary. It is not clear, though, how universal this feeling is. For example, I know of some players who, on being told that some other players were offended by their speech, suggested that gagging was the solution: "If they don't want to hear me, let them gag me; I won't be offended." Also, I am given to understand that gagging is much more commonly employed on some other MUDs.

The course of a MUD conversation is remarkably like and unlike one in the real world. Participants in MUD conversations commonly use the emote command to make gestures, such as nodding to urge someone to continue, waving at player arrivals and departures, raising eyebrows, hugging to apologize or soothe, and so forth. As in electronic mail (though much more frequently), players employ standard "smiley-face" glyphs, e.g., :-), :-(, and :-|, to clarify the tone with which they say things. Utterances are also frequently addressed to specific participants, as opposed to the room as a whole (e.g., Munchkin nods to Frebble. "You tell 'em!").

The most obvious difference between MUD conversations and those in real life is that the utterances must be typed rather than simply spoken. This introduces significant delays into the interaction and, like nature, MUD society abhors a vacuum.

Even when there are only two participants in a MUD conversation, it is very rare for there to be only one thread of discussion; during the pause while one player is typing a response, the other player commonly thinks of something else to say and does so, introducing at least another level to the conversation, if not a completely new topic. These multitopic conversations are a bit disorienting and bewildering to the uninitiated, but it appears that most players quickly become accustomed to them and handle the multiple levels smoothly. Of course, when more than two players are involved, the opportunities for multiple levels are only increased. It has been pointed out that a suitable punishment for truly heinous social offenders might be to strand them in a room with more than a dozen players actively conversing.

This kind of cognitive time sharing also arises due to the existence of the page command, which allows a player to send a message to another room. It is not uncommon (especially for wizards, whose advice is frequently sought by "distant" players) to be involved in one conversation "face-to-face" and one or two more conducted via page. Again, although this can be overwhelming at first, one can actually come to appreciate the relief from the tedious long pauses waiting for a fellow conversant to type.

Another effect of the typing delay (and of the low bandwidth of the MUD medium) is a tendency for players to abbreviate their communications, sometimes past the point of ambiguity. For example, some players often greet others with "hugs" but the meanings of those hugs vary widely from recipient to recipient. In one case the hug might be a simple friendly greeting, in another it might be intended to convey a very special affection. In both cases, the text typed by the hugger is the same (e.g., "Munchkin hugs Frebble."); it is considered too much trouble for the hugger to type a description of the act sufficient to distinguish the kind of hug intended. This leads to some MUD interactions having much more ambiguity than usually encountered in real life, a fact that some mudders consider useful.

The somewhat disjointed nature of MUD conversations, brought on by the typing pauses, tends to rob them of much of the coherence that makes real-life conversants resent interruptions. The addition of a new conversant to a MUD conversation is much less disruptive; the flow being disrupted was never very strong to begin with. Some players go so far as to say that interruptions are simply impossible on MUDs; I think that this is a minority impression, however. Interruptions do exist MUDs; they are simply less significant than in real life.

Other Small-Group Interactions. I would not like to give the impression that conversation is the only social activity on MUDs. Indeed, MUD society appears to have most of the same social activities as real life, albeit often in a modified form. PernMUSH holds large-scale, organized social gatherings such as "hatchings" and they are not alone. Most MUDs have at one time or another organized more or less elaborate parties, often to celebrate notable events in the MUD itself, such as an anniversary of its founding. We have so far had only one or two such parties on LambdaMOO, to celebrate the "opening" of some new area built by a player; if there were any other major parties, I certainly wasn't invited!

One of the more impressive examples of MUD social activity is the virtual wedding. There have been many of these on many different MUDs; we are in the process of planning our first on LambdaMOO, with me officiating in my role as archwizard.

I have never been present at such a ceremony, but I have read logs of the conversations at them. As I do not know any of the participants in the ceremonies I've read about, I cannot say much for certain about their emotional content. As in real life, they are usually very happy and celebratory occasions with an intriguing undercurrent of serious feelings. I do not know and cannot even speculate about whether or not the main participants in such ceremonies are usually serious or not, whether or not the MUD ceremony usually (or even ever) mirrors another ceremony in the real world, or even whether or not the bride and groom have ever met outside of virtual reality.

In the specific case of the upcoming LambdaMOO wedding, the participants first met on LambdaMOO, became friendly, and eventually decided to meet in real life. They have subsequently become romantically involved in the real world and are using the MUD wedding as a celebration of that fact. This phenomenon of couples meeting in virtual reality and then pursuing a real-life relationship is not uncommon; in one notable case, one of them lived in Australia and the other in Pittsburgh!

It is interesting to note that the virtual reality wedding is not specific to the kinds of MUDs I've been discussing; Van Gelder (1991) mentioned an online reception on CompuServe and weddings are common on Habitat (Morningstar & Farmer, 1991), a half-graphical, half-textual virtual reality popular in Japan.

The very idea, however, brings up interesting and potentially important questions about the legal standing of commitments made only in virtual reality. Suppose, for example, that two people make a contract in virtual reality. Is the contract binding? Under which state's (or country's) laws? Is it a written or verbal contract? What constitutes proof of signature in such a context? I suspect that our real-world society will have to face and resolve these issues in the not-too-distant future.

Those who frequent MUDs tend also to be interested in games and puzzles, so it is no surprise that many real-world examples have been implemented inside MUDs. What may be surprising, however, is the extent to which this is so.

On LambdaMOO alone, we have machine-mediated Scrabble, Monopoly, Mastermind, Backgammon, Ghost, Chess, Go, and Reversi boards. These attract small groups of players on occasion, with the Go players being the most committed; in fact, there are a number of Go players who come to LambdaMOO only for that purpose. I say more about these more specialized uses of social virtual realities later on. In many ways, though, such games so far have little, if anything, to offer over their real-world counterparts except perhaps a better chance of finding an opponent.

Perhaps more interesting are the other kinds of games imported into MUDs from real life, the ones that might be far less feasible in a nonvirtual reality. A player on LambdaMOO, for example, implemented a facility for holding food fights. Players throw food items at each other, attempt to duck oncoming items, and, if unsuccessful, are "splattered" with messes that cannot easily be removed. After a short interval, a semianimate "Mr. Clean" arrives and one-by-one removes the messes from the participants, turning them back into the food items from which they came, ready for the next fight. Although the game was rather simple to implement, it has remained enormously popular nearly a year later.

Another player on LambdaMOO created a trainable Frisbee, which any player could teach to do tricks when they threw or caught it. Players who used the Frisbee seemed to take great pleasure in trying to outdo each other's trick descriptions. My catching description, for example, reads "Haakon stops the frisbee dead in the air in front of himself and then daintily plucks it, like a flower." I have also heard of MUD versions of paint-ball combat and fantastical games of Capture the Flag.

Observations About the MUD Community as a Whole

MUD communities tend to be very large in comparison to the number of players actually active at any given time. On LambdaMOO, for example, we have between 700 and 800 players connecting in any week but rarely more than 40 simultaneously. A good real-world analog might be a bar with a large number of "regulars," all of whom are transients without fixed schedules.

The continuity of MUD society is thus somewhat tenuous; many pairs of active players exist who have never met each other. In spite of this, MUDs do become true communities after a time. The participants slowly come to consensus about a common (private) language, about appropriate standards of behavior, and about the social roles of various public areas (e.g., where big discussions usually happen, where certain "crowds" can be found, etc.).

Some people appear to thrive on the constant turnover of MUD players throughout a day, enjoying the novelty of always having someone new to talk to. In some cases, this enjoyment goes so far as to become a serious kind of addiction, with some players spending as many as 35 hours out of 48 constantly connected and conversing on MUDs. I know of many players who have taken more-or-less drastic steps to curtail their participation on MUDs, feeling that their habits had gotten significantly out of control.

One college-student player related to me his own particularly dramatic case of MUD addiction. It seems that he was supposed to go home for the Christmas holidays but missed the train by no less than 5 hours because he had been unable to tear himself away from his MUD conversations. After calling his parents to relieve their worrying by lying about the cause of his delay, he eventually boarded a train for home. However, on arrival there at 12:30 A.M. the next morning, he did not go directly to his parents' house but instead went to an open terminal room in the local university, where he spent another 2 1/2 hours connected before finally going home. His parents, meanwhile, had called the police in fear for their son's safety in traveling.

It should not be supposed that this kind of problem is computer addiction; the fact that there is a computer involved here is more-or-less irrelevant. These people are not addicted to computers, but to communication; the global scope of Internet MUDs implies not only a great variety in potential conversants, but also 24-hour access. As Figure 6.1 shows, the sun never really sets on LambdaMOO's community.

Although it is at the more macroscopic scale of whole MUD communities that I feel least qualified to make reliable observations, I do have one striking example of societal consensus having concrete results on LambdaMOO.

From time to time, we wizards are asked to arbitrate in disputes among players concerning what is or is not appropriate behavior. My approach generally has been to ask a number of other players for their opinions and to present the defendant in the complaint with a precis of the plaintiff's grievance, always looking for the common threads in their responses. After many such episodes, I was approached by a number of players asking that a written statement on LambdaMOO manners be prepared and made available to the community. I wrote up a list of those rules that seemed implied by the set of arbitrations we had performed and published them for public comment. Very little comment has ever been received, but the groups of players I've asked generally agree that the rules reflect their own understandings of the common will. For the curious, I have summarized our rules in Table 6.5; the actual "help manners" document goes into a bit more detail about each of these points.

It should be noted that different MUDs are truly different communities and have different societal agreements concerning appropriate behavior. There even exist a few MUDs where the only rule in the social contract is

TABLE 6.5

The Main Points of LambdaMOO Manners

Be polite. Avoid being rude. The MOO is worth participating in because it is a pleasant place for people to be. When people are rude or nasty to one another, it stops being so pleasant.

"Revenge is ours," sayeth the wizards. If someone is nasty to you, please either ignore it or tell a wizard about it. Please don't try to take revenge on the person; this just escalates the level of rudeness and makes the MOO a less pleasant place for everyone involved.

Respect other players' sensibilities. The participants on the MOO come from a wide range of cultures and backgrounds. Your ideas about what constitutes offensive speech or descriptions are likely to differ from those of other players. Please keep the text that players can casually run across as free of potentially offensive material as you can.

Don't spoof. Spoofing is loosely defined as "causing misleading output to be printed to other players." For example, it would be spoofing for anyone but Munchkin to print out a message like "Munchkin sticks out his tongue at Potrzebie." This makes it look like Munchkin is unhappy with Potrzebie even though that may not be the case at all.

Don't shout. It is easy to write a MOO command that prints a message to every connected player. Please don't.

Only teleport your own things. By default, most objects (including other players) allow themselves to be moved freely from place to place. This fact makes it easier to build certain useful objects. Unfortunately, it also makes it easy to annoy people by moving them or their objects around without their permission. Please don't.

Don't teleport silently or obscurely. It is easy to write MOO commands that move you instantly from place to place. Please remember in such programs to print a clear, understandable message to all players in both the place you're leaving and the place you're going to.

Don't hog the server. The server is carefully shared among all of the connected players so that everyone gets a chance to execute their commands. This sharing is, by necessity, somewhat approximate. Please don't abuse it with tasks that run for a long time without pausing.

Don't waste object numbers. Some people, in a quest to own objects with "interesting" numbers (e.g., #17000, #18181, etc.) have written MOO programs that loop forever creating and recycling objects until the "good" numbers come up. Please don't do this.

that there is no social contract. Such "anarchy" MUDs have appeared a few times in my experience and seem to be popular for a time before eventually fading away.

THE PROSPECTS FOR MUDDING IN THE FUTURE

> *The clumsy system of public gatherings had*
> *been long since abandoned; neither Vashti nor her*
> *audience stirred from their rooms. Seated in her*
> *arm-chair, she spoke, while they in their arm-chairs*
> *heard her, fairly well, and saw her, fairly well.*
> *—E. M. Forster (1928/1973)*

A recent listing of Internet-accessible MUDs showed almost 200 active around the world, mostly in the United States and Scandinavia. A conservative guess that these MUDs average 100 active players each gives a total of 20,000 active mudders in the world today; this is almost certainly a significant undercount already and the numbers appear to be growing as more and more people gain Internet access.

In addition, at least one MUD-like area exists on the commercial CompuServe network in the United States and there are several more commercial MUDs active in the United Kingdom. Finally, there is Habitat (Morningstar & Farmer, 1991), a half-graphical, half-textual virtual reality in Japan, with well over 10,000 users.

I believe that text-based virtual realities and wide-area interactive "chat" facilities (Reid, 1992) are becoming more and more common and will continue to do so for the foreseeable future. Like CB radios and telephone party lines before them, MUDs seem to provide a necessary social outlet.

The MUD model is also being extended in new ways for new audiences. For example, I am currently involved in adapting the LambdaMOO server for use as an international teleconferencing and image database system for astronomers. Our plans include allowing scientists to give online presentations to their colleagues around the world, complete with "slides" and illustrations automatically displayed on the participants' workstations. The same approach could be used to create online meeting places for workers in other disciplines, as well as for other nonscientific communities. I do not believe that we are the only researchers planning such facilities. In the near future (a few years at most), I expect such specialized virtual realities to be commonplace, an accepted part of at least the academic community.

On another front, I am engaged with some colleagues in the design of a MUD for general use here at Xerox PARC. The idea here is to use virtual reality to help break down the geographical barriers of a large building, of people increasingly working from their homes, and of having a sister research laboratory in Cambridge, England. In this context, we intend to investigate the addition of digital voice to MUDs, with the conventions of the virtual reality providing a simple and intuitive style of connection management: If two people are in the same virtual room, then their audio channels are connected. Some virtual rooms may even overlap real-world rooms, such as those in which talks or other meetings are held.

Of course, one can expect a number of important differences in the social phenomena on MUDs in a professional setting. In particular, I would guess that anonymity might well be frowned upon in such places, though it may have some interesting special uses, for example in the area of refereeing papers.

Some of my colleagues have suggested that the term, "text-based virtual reality," is an oxymoron, that virtual reality refers only to the fancy graphical and motion-sensing environments being worked on in many places. They go on to predict that these more physically involving systems will supplant the text-based variety as soon as the special equipment becomes a bit more widely and cheaply available. I do not believe that this is the case.

Although I agree that the fancier systems are likely to become very popular for certain applications and among those who can afford them, I believe that MUDs have certain enduring advantages that will save them from obsolescence.

The equipment necessary to participate fully in a MUD is significantly cheaper, more widely available, and more generally useful than that for the fancy systems; this is likely to remain the case for a long time to come. For example, it is already possible to purchase palm-size portable computers with network connectivity and text displays, making it possible to use MUDs even while riding the bus, and so on. Is similarly flexible hardware for fancy virtual realities even on the horizon?

It is substantially easier for players to give themselves vivid, detailed, and interesting descriptions (and to do the same for the descriptions and behavior of the new objects they create) in a text-based system than in a graphics-based one. In McLuhan's (1964) terminology, this is because MUDs are a "cold" medium, whereas graphically based media are "hot"; that is, the sensorial parsimony of plain text tends to entice users into engaging their imaginations to fill in missing details whereas, comparatively speaking, the richness of stimuli in fancy virtual realities has an opposite tendency, pushing users' imaginations into a more passive role. I also find it difficult to believe that a graphics-based system will be able to compete with text for average users on the metric of believable detail per unit of effort expended; this is certainly the case now and I see little reason to believe it will change in the near future.

Finally, one of the great strengths of MUDs lies in the users' ability to customize them, to extend them, and to specialize them to the users' particular needs. The ease with which this can be done in MUDs is directly related to the fact that they are purely text based; in a graphics-based system, the overhead of creating new moderate-quality graphics would put the task beyond the inclinations of the average user. Whereas, with MUDs, it is easy to imagine an almost arbitrarily small community investing in the creation of a virtual reality that was truly customized for that community, it seems very unlikely that any but the largest communities would invest the greatly increased effort required for a fancier system.

CONCLUSIONS

> Vashti was seized with the terrors of direct
> experience. She shrank back into her
> room, and the wall closed up again.
> —E. M. Forster (1928/1973)

The emergence of MUDs has created a new kind of social sphere, both like and radically unlike the environments that have existed before. As they become more and more popular and more widely accessible, it appears likely that an increasingly significant proportion of the population will at least become familiar with mudding and perhaps become frequent participants in text-based virtual realities.

It thus behooves us to begin to try to understand these new societies, to make sense of these electronic places where we'll be spending increasing amounts of our time, both doing business and seeking pleasure. I would hope that social scientists will be at least intrigued by my amateur observations and perhaps inspired to more properly study MUDs and their players. In particular, as MUDs become more widespread, ever more people are likely to be susceptible to the kind of addiction I discuss in an earlier section; we must, as a society, begin to wrestle with the social and ethical issues brought out by such cases.

Those readers interested in trying out MUDs for themselves are encouraged to do so. The USENET newsgroup rec.games.mud periodically carries comprehensive lists of publicly available, Internet-accessible MUDs, including their detailed network addresses. My own MUD, LambdaMOO, can be reached via the standard Internet telnet protocol at the host lambda.parc.xerox.com (the numeric address is 13.2.116.36), port 8888. On a UNIX machine, for example, the command

    telnet lambda.parc.xerox.com 8888

will suffice to make a connection. Once connected, feel free to page me; I connect under the names "Haakon" and "Lambda."

ACKNOWLEDGMENTS

I was originally prodded into writing down my mudding experiences by Eric Roberts. In trying to get a better handle on an organization for the material, I was aided immeasurably by my conversations with Françoise Brun-Cottan; she consistently brought to my attention phenomena that I had become too familiar with to notice. Susan Irwin and David Nichols have been instrumental in helping me to understand some of the issues that might arise as MUDs become more sophisticated and widespread. The reviewers of this chapter provided several pointers to important related work that I might otherwise never have encountered. Finally, I must also give credit to the LambdaMOO players who participated in my online brainstorming session; their ideas, experiences, and perceptions provided a necessary perspective to my own understanding.

REFERENCES

Forster, E. M. (1973). The machine stops. In B. Bova (Ed.), *The science fiction hall of fame* (Vol. IIB, pp.248–279). New York: Avon. (Original work published 1928)

Kiesler, S., Siegel, J., & McGuire, T. (1991). Social psychological aspects of computer-mediated communication. In C. Dunlop & R. Kling (Eds.), *Computerization and controversy* (pp. 330–349). New York: Academic Press.

McLuhan, M. (1964). *Understanding media.* New York: McGraw-Hill.

Morningstar, C., & Farmer, F. R. (1991). The lessons of Lucasfilm's Habitat. In M. Benedikt (Ed.), *Cyberspace* (pp.273–302). Cambridge, MA: MIT Press.

Raymond, E. S. (Ed.). (1991). *The new hacker's dictionary.* Cambridge, MA: MIT Press.

Reid, E. M. (1992). Electropolis: Communication and community on Internet Relay Chat. *Intertek, 3.3,* 7–13.

Van Gelder, L. (1991). The strange case of the electronic lover. In C. Dunlop & R. Kling (Eds.), *Computerization and controversy* (pp. 364–375). New York: Academic Press.

7

CONSTRUCTIONS AND RECONSTRUCTIONS OF SELF IN VIRTUAL REALITY: PLAYING IN THE MUDS

Sherry Turkle
Massachusetts Institute of Technology

There are over 300 multiuser games based on at least 13 different kinds of software on the international computer network known as the Internet. Here I use the term "MUD" to refer to all the various kinds. All provide worlds for social interaction in a virtual space, worlds in which you can present yourself as a "character," in which you can be anonymous, in which you can play a role or roles as close or as far away from your "real self" as you choose.

In the MUDs, the projections of self are engaged in a resolutely postmodern context. Authorship is not only displaced from a solitary voice, it is exploded. The self is not only decentered but multiplied without limit. There is an unparalleled opportunity to play with one's identity and to "try out" new ones. MUDs are a new environment for the construction and reconstruction of self.

In an interactive computer game designed to represent a world inspired by the television series "Star Trek: The Next Generation," over a thousand players spend up to 80 hours a week participating in intergalactic exploration and wars. They create characters who have casual and romantic sex, who fall in love and get married, who attend rituals and celebrations. "This is more real than my real life," said a character who turns out to be a man playing a woman who is pretending to be a man. In this game the rules of social interaction are built not received.

In another, more loosely structured game, each player creates a character or several characters, specifying their genders and other physical and psychological attributes. The characters need not be human and there are more than two genders. All interactions take place "in character." Beyond this, players are invited to help build the computer world itself. Using a relatively simple programming language, they can make a "room" in the game space where they can set the stage and define the rules. That is, they make objects in the computer world and specify how they work. Rachel, an 11-year-old, built a room she calls "the condo." It has jewelry boxes containing magical pieces that transport her to different places and moments in history. When Rachel visits the condo, she invites her friends, she chats, orders pizza, and flirts. Other players built TVs showing scenes taking place in the rooms of the game, a transportation system to navigate the space, and a magical theater that replays past game events. Some have built robots, for example a program named "Julia" that "pretends" to be a person as she offers directions and helps to locate your friends.

Both worlds exist on international computer networks, which of course means that in a certain sense, a physical sense, they don't exist at all.

The first game, Trek Muse, and the second, LambdaMOO, are examples of a class of virtual worlds known as MUDs—an acronym for "Multiuser Dungeons."[1] In the early 1970s, a role-playing game called "Dungeons and Dragons" swept the game cultures, a game in which a "dungeon master" created a world in which people created characters and played out complex adventures. Several years later, "Dungeons and Dragons" was interpreted for computational space in a program called "Adventure." There, players proceeded through a maze that was presented to them through text description on a computer screen. The term "dungeon" has persisted in both the games and hi-tech culture, and in the case of MUDs, refers to a virtual social space that exists on a machine.

There are over 300 multiuser games based on at least 13 different kinds of software on the international computer network known as the Internet. Here I use the term "MUD" to refer to all the various kinds. All provide worlds for social interaction in a virtual space, worlds in which you can present yourself as a "character," in which you can be anonymous, in which you can play a role as close or as far away from your "real self" as you choose. Where they differ is in how constrained that world is. It can be built

---

[1]For a general introduction to LambdaMOO and mudding, see Pavel Curtis, chap. 6, this volume, and Amy Bruckman, "Identity Workshops: Emergent Social and Psychological Phenomena in Text-Based Virtual Reality," unpub ms. March, 1992. On virtual community in general, see Allucquere Rosanne Stone, "Will the Real Body Please Stand Up?: Boundary Stories about Virtual Cultures" in Michael Benedikt, ed., *Cyberspace: First Steps* (Cambridge: MIT Press, 1992).

around a medieval fantasy landscape in which there are dragons to slay and gold coins and magical amulets to collect, or it can be a relatively open space in which you can play at whatever captures your imagination, both by playing a role and by participating in building a world.

In the MUDs, the projections of self are engaged in a resolutely postmodern context. There are parallel narratives in the different rooms of the MUD; one can move forward or backward in time. The cultures of Tolkien, Gibson, and Madonna coexist and interact. Authorship is not only displaced from a solitary voice, it is exploded. The MUDs are authored by their players, thousands of people in all, often hundreds of people at a time, all logged on from different places. And the self is not only decentered but multiplied without limit. There is an unparalleled opportunity to play with one's identity and to "try out" new ones.

My past research into the experiences of individuals working with computers has led me to underscore the power of this technology not only as a medium for getting things done but for thinking through and working through personal concerns (Turkle, 1984). Engagement with computational technology facilitates a series of "second chances" for adults to work and rework unresolved personal issues and more generally, to think through questions about the nature of self, including questions about definitions of life, intentionality, and intelligence.

What is true of individuals working alone with a computer is raised to a higher power when people use computers to communicate with other people as they do on the MUDs. In the first case, the person alone with the computer, I have found that individuals use computers to work through identity issues that center around control and mastery; in the second, where the computer is used as a communications medium, there is more room to use the control provided by the computer to develop a greater capacity for collaboration and even intimacy. The medium enables the self to explore a social context as well as to reflect on its own nature and powers.

My method of investigation of MUDs has been ethnographic and clinical: Play the games, "hang out" with games players in virtual as well as real space, interview game players in person both individually and in groups. Some of my richest data came from a series of weekly "pizza parties" for mudders within the Boston area.[2] There the topic was open and conversation turned to what was on the players' minds: most often love, romance, and what can be counted on as real in virtual space.

I begin my report from this new social and psychological world by taking one step back to general considerations of how role-playing games enable people to work through issues of identity and then move on to the form this takes in MUDs, which enhance the evocative potential of tradi-

---

[2]Amy Bruckman, a graduate student at MIT's Media Laboratory, was my research assistant and dialogue partner during a summer of intensive work on the MUD phenomena; my understanding of this activity and its importance owes much to our collaboration.

tional games by further blurring the line between the game and what players refer to as RL, "real life," or TRW, "the real world."[3]

Traditional role playing prompts reflection on personal and interpersonal issues, but in games that take place in ongoing virtual societies such as MUDs, the focus is on larger social and cultural themes as well. The networked computer serves as an "evocative object" for thinking about community. Additionally, people playing in the MUDs struggle toward a new, still tentative discourse about the nature of a social world that is populated both by people and by programs. In this, life in the MUD may serve as a harbinger of what is to come in the social spaces that we still contrast with the virtual by calling the "real."

ROLE-PLAYING GAMES

As identity workshops, MUDs have much in common with traditional role-playing games, for example, the role-playing games played by Julee, a 19-year- old who has dropped out of Yale after her freshman year. Part of the reason for her leaving college is that she is in an increasingly turbulent relationship with her mother, a devout Catholic, who turned away from her daughter when she discovered that she had had an abortion the summer before beginning college.

From Julee's point of view, her mother has chosen to deny her existence. When asked about her most important experience playing role-playing games, Julee described a game in which she had been assigned to play a mother facing a conflict with her daughter. Indeed, in the game, the script says that the daughter is going to betray, even kill, the mother.

In the role-playing game, played over a weekend on the Boston University (BU) campus, Julee and her "daughter" talked for hours: Why might the daughter have joined her mother's opponents, how could they stay true to their relationship and the game as it had been written? Huddled in a corner of an empty BU classroom, Julee was having the conversation that her mother had not been willing to have with her. In the end, Julee's character chose to ignore her loyalty to her team in order to preserve her daughter's life.

Clearly, Julee projected feelings about her "real" mother's choice onto her experience of the game, but more was going on than a simple reenactment. Julee was able to reexperience a familiar situation in a setting where she could examine it, do something new with it, and revise her relationship toward it. In many ways, what happened was resonant with the psychoanalytic notion of "working through."

---

[3]For more material on the contrast with traditional role playing see Gary Alan Fine, *Shared Fantasy: Role-Playing Games as Social Worlds* (Chicago: The University of Chicago Press, 1983). Henry Jenkins' study of fan culture, *Textual Poachers: Television Fans and Participatory Culture* (New York: Routledge, 1992), illuminates the general question of how individuals appropriate fantasy materials in the construction of identity.

Julee's experience stands in contrast to images of role-playing games that are prevalent in the popular culture. A first popular image portrays role-playing games as depressing and dangerous environments. It is captured in the urban legend that describes an emotionally troubled student disappearing and committing suicide during a game of "Dungeons and Dragons." Another popular image, and one that has been supported by some academic writing on role-playing games, turns them into places of escape. Players are seen as leaving their "real" lives and problems behind to lose themselves in the game space. Julee's story belies both stereotypes. For her the game is psychologically constructive rather than destructive. And she uses it not for escape but as a vehicle for engaging in a significant dialogue with important events and relationships in her "real" life.

Role-playing games are able to serve in this evocative capacity precisely because they are not simple escapes from the real to the unreal, but because they stand betwixt and between, both in and not in real life. But in the final analysis, what puts Julee's game most firmly in the category of game is that it had an end point. The weekend was over and so was the game.

MUDs present a far more complicated case. In a certain sense, they don't have to end. Their boundaries are more fuzzy; the routine of playing them becomes part of their players' real lives. The virtual reality becomes not so much an alternative as a parallel life. Indeed, dedicated players who work with computers all day describe how they temporarily put their characters to "sleep," remain logged on to the game, pursue other activities, and periodically return to the game space.

Such blurring of boundaries between role and self present new opportunities to use the role to work on the self. As one experienced player put it, "you are the character and you are not the character both at the same time." And "you are who you pretend to be." This ambiguity contributes to the games' ability to be a place in which to address issues of identity and intimacy. They take the possibilities that Julee found in role-playing games and raise them to a higher power.

VIRTUAL REALITIES:
ROLE-PLAYING TO A HIGHER POWER

The notion "you are who you pretend to be" has a mythic resonance. The Pygmalion story endures because it speaks to a powerful fantasy: that we are not limited by our histories, that we can be re-created or can re-create ourselves. In the real world, we are thrilled by stories of self-transformation. Madonna is our modern Eliza Doolittle; Ivana Trump is the object of morbid fascination. But of course, for most people such re-creations of self are difficult. Virtual worlds provide environments for experiences that may be hard to come by in the real.

Not the least of these experiences is the opportunity to play an "aspect of your self" that you embody as a separate self in the game space.[4]

Peter is a 23-year-old physics graduate student at the University of Massachusetts. His life revolves around his work in the laboratory and his plans for a life in science. He says that his only friend is his roommate, another student whom he describes as being even more reclusive than he. This circumscribed, almost monastic life does not represent a radical departure for Peter. He has had heart trouble since he was a child; his health is delicate; one small rebellion, a ski trip when he first came up to Boston, put him in the hospital for 3 weeks. His response has been to circumscribe his world. Peter has never traveled. He lives in a small compass.

In an interview with Peter he immediately made it clear why he plays on MUDs: "I do it so I can talk to people." He is logged on for at least 40 hours a week, but it is hard to call what he does "playing" a game. He spends his time on the MUDs constructing a life that in only a seeming paradox is more expansive than his own. He tells me with delight that the MUD he frequents most often is physically located on a computer in Germany: "And I started talking to them [the inhabitants of the MUD] and they're like, 'This costs so many and so many Deutschmarks.' And I'm like, 'what are Deutschmarks? Where is this place located?' And they say: 'Don't you know, this is Germany.'"

It is from MUDs that Peter has learned what he knows of politics, of economics, of the differences between capitalism and welfare state socialism. He revels in the differences between the styles of Americans and Europeans on the MUDs and in the thrill of speaking to a player in Norway who can see the Northern lights.

On the MUD, Peter shapes a character, Achilles, who is his ideal self. Life in a University of Massachusetts dorm has put him in modest and unaesthetic circumstances. Yet the room he inhabits on the MUD is elegant, romantic, out of a Ralph Lauren ad.

Peter's story illustrates several aspects of the relationship of mudding and identity. First, the MUD serves as a kind of Rorschach inkblot, a projection of inner fantasies. Second, unlike a Rorschach, it does not stay on a page. It is part of Peter's everyday life. Beyond expanding his social reach, MUDs have brought Peter the only romance and intimacy he has ever known. At a social event held in virtual space, a "wedding" of two regular players on his favorite Germany-based MUD, Peter met Winterlight, one of the three female players. Peter who has known little success with women, was able to charm this most desirable and sought after player. Their

---

[4]"The Well" has a "topic" (discussion group) on "On Line Personae." In a March 24, 1992 posting to this group F. Randall Farmer noted that in a group of about 50 Habitat users, about a quarter experienced their online personae as a separate creature that acted in ways they do in real life, and a quarter experienced their online personae as a separate creature that acted in ways they do not in real life.

encounter led to a courtship in which he was tender and romantic, chivalrous and poetic. One is reminded of Cyrano who could only find his voice through another's persona. It is Achilles, Peter's character on the MUD, who can create the magic and win the girl.

While people work one-on-one with the computer, the machine becomes an evocative object for thinking through issues of identity that tend to be centered on control and mastery. But Peter's experience (where the computer is a mediator to a reality shared with other people) has put computation more directly in the service of the development of a greater capacity for friendship, the development of confidence for a greater capacity for intimacy.

But what of the contrast between Peter and Julee? What can we say about the difference between role playing games in the corridors of BU and on computer virtual worlds?

Julee and Peter both use games to remake the self. Their games, however, are evocative for different reasons. Julee's role playing has the powerful quality of real-time psychodrama, but on the other hand Peter's game is ongoing and provides him with anonymity, invisibility, and potential multiplicity. Ongoing: He can play it as much as he wants, all day if he wants, every day if he chooses as he often does. There are always people logged on to the game; there is always someone to talk to or something to do. Anonymous: Once Peter creates his character, that is his only identity on the game. His character need not have his gender or share any recognizable feature with him. He can be who he wants and play with no concern that "he, Peter," will be held accountable in "real life" for his characters actions, quarrels, or relationships. The degree to which he brings the game into his real life is his choice. Invisible: The created character can have any physical description and will be responded to as a function of that description. The plain can experience the self-presentation of great beauty; the nerdy can be elegant; the obese can be slender. Multiplicity: Peter can create several characters, playing out and playing with different aspects of his self. An ongoing game, an anonymous personae, physical invisibility, and the possibility to be not one but many, these are the qualities at the root of the holding power and evocative potential of MUDs as "identity workshops."[5] Faced with the notion that "you are what you pretend to be," Peter can only hope that it is true for he is playing his ideal self.

Peter plays what in the psychoanalytic tradition would be called an "ego ideal." Other players create a character or multiple characters that are closer to embodying aspects of themselves that they hate or fear or perhaps have not ever consciously confronted before. One male player described his role playing as:

> daring to be passive. I don't mean in having sex on the MUD. I mean in letting other people take the initiative in friendships, in not feeling when I am in character that I need to control everything. My mother controlled my whole

---

[5]This felicitous phrase was coined by Amy Bruckman. See Bruckman, "Identity Workshops: Emergent Social and Psychological Phenomena in Text-Based Virtual Reality."

family, well, certainly me. So I grew up thinking "never again." My "real life" is exhausting that way. On MUDs I do something else. I didn't even realize this connection to my mother until something happened in the game and somebody tried to boss my pretty laid-back character around and I went crazy. And then I saw what I was doing.

The possibilities the medium offers for projecting both conscious and unconscious aspects of the self suggests an analogy between MUDs and psychotherapeutic milieus. The goal of psychotherapy is not of course to simply provide a place for "acting out" behavior that expresses one's conflicts, but to furnish a contained and confidential environment for "working through" unresolved issues. The distinction between acting out and working through is crucial to thinking about MUDs as settings for personal growth. For it is in the context of this distinction that the much-discussed issue of "MUDs addiction" should be situated. The accusation of being "addicted" to psychotherapy is only made seriously when friends or family suspect that over a period of time, the therapy is supporting repetitions and reenactments rather than new resolutions. Mudding is no more "addictive" than therapy when it works as a pathway to psychological growth.

Robert is a college freshman who in the months before beginning college had to cope with his father's having lost his job and disgraced his family because of alcoholism. The job loss led to his parents' relocation to another part of the country, far away from all of Robert's friends. For a period of several months, Robert, now at college, mudded over 80 hours a week. Around the time of a fire in his dormitory that destroyed all his possessions, Robert was playing over 120 hours a week, sleeping 4 hours a night, and only taking brief breaks to get food, which he would eat while playing.

At the end of the school year, however, Robert's MUD experience was essentially over. He had gotten his own apartment; he had a job as a salesman; he had formed a rock band with a few friends. Looking back on the experience he thought that mudding had served its purpose: It kept him from what he called his "suicidal thoughts," in essence by keeping him too busy to have them; it kept him from drinking ("I have something more fun and safe to do"); it enabled him to function with responsibility and competency as a highly placed administrator; it afforded an emotional environment where he could be in complete control of how much he revealed about his life, about his parents, even about something as simple for other people as where he was from. In sum, MUDs had provided what Erik Erikson would have called a "psychosocial moratorium." It had been a place from which he could reassemble a sense of boundaries that enabled him to pursue less bounded relationships.[6]

---

[6]Of course, taking the analogy between a therapeutic milieu and virtual reality seriously means that incidents when players lose their anonymity are potentially psychologically damaging. In therapy, the transference is to the person of the therapist or to the therapy group; in virtual space the transference is to the "body" of the MUD as often as represented by its "wizards" or system administrators.

Through theories that stress the decentered subject and through the fragmented selves presented by patients[7], contemporary psychology confronts what is problematic in traditional notions of a unitary self. MUDs have become a new context that provokes reflection on such questions. Virtual communities such as MUDs are the most dramatic example of the way the culture of simulation challenges traditional notions of human identity. Indeed, they make possible the construction of an identity that is so fluid and multiple that it strains the very limits of the notion. Identity, after all, literally means *one*. When we live through our electronic self-representations we have unlimited possibilities to be *many*. People become masters of self-presentation and self-creation. The very notion of an inner, "true self" is called into question.

These remarks have addressed MUDs as privileged spaces for thinking through and working through issues of personal identity. Additionally, when role playing moves from circumsciribed "weekend encounters" such as those Julee participated in onto a sustained virtual stage, a new social world grows up too. The development of virtual social life is of signal importance: It makes MUDs very special kinds of evocative objects.

EVOCATIVE OBJECTS:
GENDER, COMMUNITY, AND "BOTS"

In *The Second Self* (Turkle, 1984), I called the personal computer an evocative object because it provoked self-reflection and stimulated thought. It led to reevaluations and reconsiderations of things taken for granted, for example, about the nature of intelligence, free will, and our notions of what is alive. And I found that the computer did this not just because it presented people with ideas as did traditional philosophy, but because it presented them with experiences, an ongoing culture of personal computing that provoked a new philosophy in everyday life.

The same kind of process, this provocation of new discourse and reflection, is taking place around computer-mediated communications in virtual realities such as MUDs. But the emphasis of the new discourse and reflection is on social and cultural issues as well as individual ones.

One dramatic example is the novel and compelling discourse that surrounds the experience of "gender swapping" in virtual reality. In the MUDs, men may play the roles of women and women the roles of men, a common practice known as gender swapping. As MUD players talked to me about their experiences with gender swapping, they certainly gave reason to

---

[7]Perhaps most dramatically the increasing numbers of patients who present with multiple personality disorder, literally "divided selves."

believe that through this practice they were working through personal issues that had to do with accepting the feminine and/or the masculine in their own personalities. But they were doing something else as well that transcended the level of individual personality and its dynamics. People were using gender swapping as a firsthand experience through which to form ideas about the role of gender in human interactions. In the ongoing culture of MUDs, these issues are discussed both within the space of the games and in a discussion group on USENET called "rec.games.mud."

Discussion on USENET about gender swapping has dealt with how female characters are besieged with attention, sexual advances, and unrequested offers of assistance that imply that women can't do things by themselves. It has dealt with the question of whether women who are consistently treated as incompetent may start to believe it. Men playing women on role-playing games have remarked that other male players (read male characters) sometimes expect sexual favors in return for technical assistance. In this case, offering technical help, like picking up the check at dinner, is being used to purchase rather than win a woman's regard. Although such expectations can be subtly expressed, indeed sometimes overlooked in real life, when such things happen in MUDs, they are more visible, often widely witnessed, and openly discussed. As this takes place, the MUD becomes an evocative object for a richer understanding not only of sexual harassment but of the social construction of gender.

Mudding throws issues of the impact of gender on human relations into relief and brings the issue home; the seriousness and intensity of discussions of gender among mudders speaks to the fact that the game allows its players to experience rather than merely observe what it feels like to be the opposite gender or to have no gender at all.

MUDs are evocative objects for thinking about gender, but there are similar stories to tell about discussions in MUD environments about violence, property, and privacy. Virtual communities compel conversations about the nature of community itself.

On an early MUD known as Habitat, which ran as an experiment in the United States and has become a successful commercial venture in Japan, players were originally allowed to have guns. However, when you are shot, you do not cease to exist but simply lose all the things you were carrying and are transported back to your virtual home. For some players, thievery and murder became the highlight of the "game." For others, these activities were experienced as a violent intrusion on their peaceful world. An intense debate ensued (for more detail, see Morningstar & Farmer, 1992).

Some players argued that guns should be eliminated; unlike in the real world, a perfect gun ban is possible with a few lines of code. Others argued that what was damaging was not the violence but the trivializa-

tion of violence, and maintained that guns should persist, but their consequences should be made more real: When you are killed, your character
should cease to exist and not simply be sent home. Still others believed that
because Habitat was "just a game," and playing assassin was part of the
fun, there could be no harm in a little virtual violence.

As the debate raged, a player who was a priest in real life founded the
"Order of the Holy Walnut" whose members pledged not to carry guns.
In the end, the game designers divided the world into two parts: In town,
violence was prohibited. In the wilds outside of town, it was allowed.
Eventually a democratic voting process was installed and a sheriff
elected. Debates then ensued about the nature of Habitat laws and the
proper balance between individual freedom and law and order. What is
remarkable is not just the solution, but the quality of the debate that led
up to that solution. The denizens of Habitat were spending their leisure
time debating pacifism, the nature of good government, and the relationships between representations and reality.

Virtual reality is not "real," but it has a relationship to the real. By
being betwixt and between, it becomes a play space for thinking about
the real world. It is an exemplary evocative object.

When a technology serves as an evocative object, old questions are
raised in new contexts and there is an opportunity for fresh resolutions.
I conclude with a final example of how MUDs are able to recast some
old questions about personhood and program.

When in the context of "traditional" computation, people meet a
program that exhibits some behavior that would be considered intelligent if done by a person, they often grant the program a "sort of"
intelligence, indeed a "sort of" life, but then insist that what the essence
of human intelligence or indeed of human uniqueness is what "the
computer cannot do." Computers cannot have intentions, feelings, the
sense of an "I" (see Turkle, 1984).

In MUDs, however, intelligent computational entities are present in a
context that gives new saliency to questions about their status. Some of
the inhabitants of these virtual worlds are artificial intelligences, robots,
affectionately referred to as "bots," which have been built by enterprising players. When you wander about in a MUD, you find yourself in
conversations with them, asking them for directions, thanking them for
being helpful, ordering drinks from them at a virtual bar, telling them a
joke. And you find yourself doing all of these things before you know
that they are not people but "things." (Of course, you may be a person
"playing" the role "an intelligent Batmobile" or "a swarm of bees.") The
"thingness" of the bots is not part of your initial encounter or the
establishment of your relationship with them. You have unintentionally
played out a Turing test in which the program has won.

Reaction to such experiences is strong, much of it still centered on the
question of human uniqueness and "whether a program can be an 'I.'" (For

example, within the Narrative Intelligence electronic discussion group centered at MIT, there was heated debate about bots and the question of the "I." In this debate, sophisticated programmers of, and players in, virtual worlds admitted to being nonplussed when they first realized that they had unknowingly participated in casual social conversation with these virutally "ambulatory" artificial intelligences [AIs]). But another way of talking about the bots has grown up as well, a discourse marked by two new themes.

First, instead of dwelling on the essence of bots, conversation among mudders turns to the ethics of whether "they" (the bots) should or should not be required to announce their artificiality. This discussion of "full disclosure" is of course taking place in the context of a virtual world where changing gender, race, and species is the norm. With people playing robots, there is a new level of self-consciousness about the asymmetry of demanding that robots not play people.

In the film, *Blade Runner*, sophisticated androids almost indistinguishable from humans have been given the final defining human qualities: childhood memories and the knowledge of their mortality. This is a world obsessed with the Turing test; the film's hero, Decker, makes his profession diagnosing the real from the artificial. But by the end of the film, Decker, who has spent his life tracking down and destroying androids, is less concerned with whether he is dealing with an artificial being and more concerned with how to thank one of them for saving his life and how to escape with another of them with whom he has fallen in love. The film speaks to an increasing tension in our traditional notions of the real and the artificial. As we live in a world of cyborgs, the important distinctions may not follow from a priori essences but from ongoing relationships.

And indeed, the second new theme in MUD-based conversations about bots turns discussion away from questions of essence and towards the most practical matters. How exactly should the AIs function within the community? Are specific bots disruptive or facilitating? Are they rude or are they kind? In this sense, MUDs may be harbingers of the discourse about the artificial in a post-Turing test world.

There is a lot of excitement about virtual reality. In both the popular and academic press there is enthusiasm and high expectation for a future in which we don gloves and masks and bodysuits and explore virtual space and sensuality. However, from the point of view of how we think about identity and community, there is reason to feel great excitement about where we are in the present. In the text-based virtual realities that exist today, people are exploring, constructing, and reconstructing their identities. They are doing this in an environment infused with a postmodern ethos of the value of multiple identities and of playing out aspects of the self and with a constructionist ethos of "Build something, be someone." And they are creating communities that have become privileged contexts for thinking about social, cultural, and ethical dilemmas of living in constructed lives that we share with extensions of ourselves we have embodied in program.

Watch for a nascent culture of virtual reality that underscores the ways in which we construct gender and the self, the ways in which we *become* what we play, argue about, and build. And watch for a culture that leaves new space for the idea that he or she who plays, argues, and builds might be doing so with a machine.

ACKNOWLEDGMENTS

This chapter is reprinted from Turkle, S. (1994), Constructions and reconstructions of self in virtual reality: Playing in the MUDs. *Mind, Culture, and Activity, 1*, 158–167. Copyright by LCHC. Reprinted by permission.

REFERENCES

Bruckman, A. (1992). *Identity workshops: Emergent social and psychological phenomena in text-based virtual reality.* Unpublished manuscript.

Fine, G. A. (1983). *Shared fantasy: Role-playing games as social worlds.* Chicago: University of Chicago Press.

Jenkins, H. (1992). *Textual poachers: Television fans and participatory culture.* New York: Routledge.

Morningstar, C., & Farmer, F. R. (1991). The lessons of Lucasfilm's Habitat. In M. Benedikt (Ed.), *Cyberspace: First steps* (p. 289). Cambridge, MA: MIT Press.

Stone, A. R. (1992). Will the real body please stand up?: Boundary stories about virtual cultures. In M. Benedikt (Ed.), *Cyberspace: First steps.* Cambridge, MA: MIT Press.

Turkle, S. (1984). *The second self: Computers and the human spirit.* New York: Simon & Schuster.

"*On the Internet, nobody knows you're a dog.*"

8

SEEKING SOCIAL SUPPORT: PARENTS IN ELECTRONIC SUPPORT GROUPS

Kristin D. Mickelson
Harvard Medical School and
University of Michigan

The Internet contains hundreds of electronic groups and mailing lists whose ostensible purpose is to discuss problems and to provide social support (e.g., alt.support.depression). Thousands of other special interest groups also may provide social support indirectly. Social support is the transaction of empathy and concern, information and advice, or tangible aid (i.e., goods and services) between two or more individuals. Social support is an important process; when encountering a stressful life event such as illness, unemployment, or bereavement, social support can shield people from the negative consequences of these events (see Cohen & Wills, 1985, for a review). Though we know social support is useful, even necessary, researchers do not fully understand how it works. For instance, do people seek out support for all types of stressful events, and if so, do they always receive it? A key question in my research is whether an observable stigma such as obesity, physical deformity, or use of a prosthetic device discourages people from seeking support or prevents them from receiving support.

I describe data from a larger research study on social support. These data bear on how interactions in electronic groups influence social support processes. The study was not intended, at the outset, to address questions of electronic support. However, because I solicited participants—parents of children with special needs—from a nonelectronic population and from electronic support groups, I am able to compare the responses of these two groups to a survey about how they seek social support. My data show how people in electronic support groups differ from others with similar problems, and how the process of exchanging support electronically may differ from the support process people experience in "real life." My study also indicates that the Internet is a social setting in which strangers can exchange useful support.

Most researchers interested in social support have focused on the mediating or moderating role of social support in the stress-adjustment relation. That is, given an amount of social support, does it reduce the impact of stress on people's adjustment? Few researchers have examined the effect of stress on how much support people receive. For instance, do some kinds of stressful events enhance social support whereas others inhibit it? My research addresses this question by examining the effect of a problem's visibility on seeking and receiving social support. Visibility refers to problems or side-effects of problems that are observable to others such as scars, bruises, hair loss, or drastic weight loss. Some research suggests that as a problem's visibility increases, social support from family and friends also increases (e.g., Chesler & Barbarin, 1984; Dunkel-Schetter, 1984; Fontana, Kerns, Rosenberg, & Colonese, 1989; Levy, Herberman, Lee, Lippman, & d'Angelo, 1989). Other research suggests the opposite, namely that as visibility increases, social support from family and friends decreases (e.g., Dunst, Trivette, & Cross, 1986; Kiecolt-Glaser, Dyer, & Shuttleworth, 1988; Turner, Hayes, & Coates, 1993; Wolcott, Namir, Fawzy, Gottlieb, & Mitsuyasu, 1986). One way to resolve these contradictory findings is to consider the role perceived stigma plays in this relation.

Perceived stigma is defined here as a mark of shame, disgrace, or taboo attached by people to their problem and, hence, to themselves.[1] There are two components to this definition: (a) people's personal feelings about their problem, such as embarrassment, fear, disgust, or confusion, and (b) people's projection of these feelings onto others. People interpret others' actions and words through their filter of perceived stigma. Hence, people's perceptions of stigma may or may not accurately reflect network members' feelings about the problem. Only a few studies have examined the influence of perceived stigma on social support. Except for one study that failed to find a relation between perceived stigma and perceived social support (Mansouri & Dowell, 1989), the other studies report a negative association between perceived stigma and social relationships. Perceived stigma was related to less favorable perceptions of others (Crandall & Coleman, 1992; Gibbons, 1985) and lower participation in social activities (Lennon, Link, Marbach, & Dohrenwend, 1989; MacDonald & Anderson, 1984).

I hypothesized that if people perceive a stigma is attached to their problem, increased visibility of the problem will be detrimental to their

---

[1] This definition is different from Goffman's (1963) definition of stigma as "an attribute which is deeply discrediting." In his seminal book, and the majority of research to follow, stigma has been examined from the perspective of what *society* deems a stigma rather than what the individual with the "stigma" actually perceives. I have not ignored the contributions of this research, instead I have used them to address issues about the individual's perceptions of stigma. In the confines of this chapter, I am not able to adequately review the expansive literature on "social stigma"; therefore, I have restricted my discussion to the few studies that specifically address "perceived stigma."

social support. But, if they do not perceive a stigma is attached to their problem, increased visibility will be beneficial to their social support. Three aspects of social support were examined in this study: perceived availability of support, willingness to seek support, and support seeking. With respect to the first two aspects, I predicted that perceived stigma and problem visibility would interact, such that for those with low perceived stigma, increased visibility would be related to an increase in people's perceptions of support availability and willingness to seek support whereas the opposite result would be found for those with high perceived stigma (see Fig. 8.1). This prediction was based on the idea that increased visibility of nonstigmatized problems would enhance unsolicited support from family and friends. As family and friends give more unsolicited support, people should perceive more support to be available in the future and also should be more willing to seek support in the future. However, when perceived stigma is entered into the equation, increased visibility should intensify people's fear of rejection and negative interactions with family and friends. People would then perceive support to be less available and they would be less willing to seek support. I also predicted a main effect for perceived stigma: As perceived stigma increases, perceived support availability and willingness to seek support should decrease, regardless of the problem's

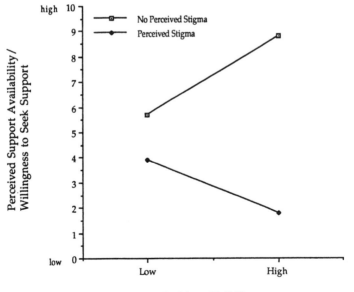

FIG. 8.1. Hypothesized model of visibility and perceived stigma for perceived support availability and willingness to seek support.

visibility.

For actual support seeking, I predicted main effects for visibility and perceived stigma such that both would be related to decreased support seeking (see Fig. 8.2), but for different reasons. On the one hand, for nonstigmatized problems, the unsolicited support accompanying increased visibility should eliminate people's need to seek support. On the other hand, for stigmatized problems, a fear of rejection and negative interactions accompanying increased visibility should inhibit people's support seeking.

FIELD STUDY

To examine a chronic problem for which people would seek social support and one that demonstrated sufficient variance in both visibility and perceived stigma, I studied parents of children with special needs, specifically mental retardation, autism, or developmental delays. Mental retardation is the presence of significantly below average intellectual functioning, with Down syndrome being the most common condition (Marsh, 1992). Children with mental retardation are classified as mild, moderate, severe, or profound. They often experience delays in other developmental areas (e.g.,

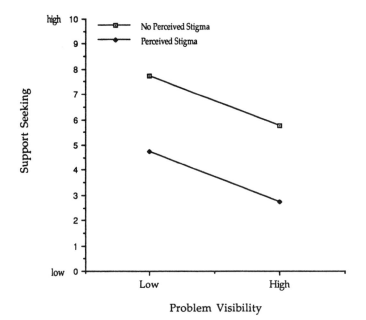

FIG. 8.2. Hypothesized model of visibility and perceived stigma for support seeking.

language and social skills) as well as physical health problems such as chronic ear infections, eye problems, and heart defects. The prominence of physical features, including slanted eyes, flattened nose bridge, protruding tongue, or smaller body size, varies from child to child. Visibility of these features, however, does not necessarily correlate with severity of the mental retardation.

Autism has been defined in many different ways and even today experts cannot agree on one definition. One common definition was stated best by a parent on an autism electronic bulletin board: "Autism is a life-long developmental disability that prevents individuals from properly understanding what they see, hear, and otherwise, sense. This results in severe problems of social relationships, communications, and behaviour." Children range from high-functioning, which often means they have high IQs but lack social skills or language, to having significant delays in most areas of development. Autistic children do not have distinct physical features; rather autism tends to vary in behavioral and emotional visibility. Some children exhibit self-abusive behaviors, frequent tantrums, or catatoniclike states whereas other children exhibit minimal or infrequent bouts of behavioral abnormalities.

Developmental delays are normally diagnosed in children between 30 and 60 months of age. Most evaluations are performed by therapists associated with local school districts. To be diagnosed as developmentally delayed, children must show significant delays in one or more developmental areas. This diagnosis often is applied when it is unclear if the delay will be persistent or short-term. These children can vary in physical and behavioral visibility. Behaviorally, these children may lack speech or proper social skills. Physical visibility stems from other contributing problems such as cerebral palsy, which has distinct physical characteristics.

Parents of children with these diagnoses vary in how much stigma they attach to the condition. Often these parents feel isolated and alienated; at the time of their child's diagnosis they often do not know of any other parents in their situation. There are four sources of perceived stigma for these parents: (a) realization that their children are not "normal" by society's standards, (b) recollection of stigmatized views that they held regarding "these types of kids" prior to their own child's birth or diagnosis, (c) feeling embarrassed, ashamed, or responsible for their child's condition, and (d) actions of family, friends, and acquaintances toward the parent or child. The following quotes, taken from parents' posts on electronic bulletin boards, demonstrate the variability of stigma perceptions:

> For me autism isn't a diagnosis that's any more dreaded or stigmatizing than any other; it's just more confusing ....

> Did you ever have a friend just cut-off communication with you?? Did you ever wonder if it had anything to do with your relations with a person having

DS [Down syndrome]?? My son is 3 years old and has DS .... do you think he has anything to do with it??

The one thing I did notice was that when my son was born and word got out that he had DS, nobody asked me about my new baby; whether he was a boy or a girl, what we'd named him, whether I had any pictures, etc. This did upset me some, and I couldn't decide if I should just ignore them or whether I should be overly pushy talking about my baby in an attempt to let them know that I didn't consider this a complete tragedy ... I just stayed quiet.

Some parents take years to come to terms with their feelings of stigma, whereas other parents rebound quickly and develop an attitude that "if our friends cannot handle the fact about [our child] well then that's O.K. with me" (quote from parent posting on a bulletin board).

METHOD

Parents in this study were recruited through local community health organizations and on electronic bulletin boards. I interviewed these parents twice about their perceptions of stigma attached to their child's special needs, visibility of those special needs, and relationships with others (spouse, parents, and a casual friend). A casual friend was defined as someone with whom the person had regular contact, such as a coworker, neighbor, or church friend, but who was not a close or best friend. I expected the spouse to be a greater source of support than the parents, and the parents to be a greater source of support than the casual friend. I tested the perceived stigma and visibility hypotheses separately for each support source.

One hundred and nine parents (77 females, 32 males) participated in an initial interview and 102 parents (72 females, 30 males) in a second interview, 4 months later. To be eligible to participate, a parent had to have a child between birth and 7 years of age with a diagnosis of mental retardation, autism, or developmental delays. In order to obtain independent data, only one parent in each household was interviewed. All but two parents had just one child with one of the aforementioned diagnoses. One parent had triplets with autism (one girl and two boys) and the other parent had identical twins and an older child diagnosed with autism (all three children were boys). One child was adopted and all the rest were biological offspring. There were 83 (73%) boys and 30 (27%) girls in the initial sample. This distribution of child gender is not unusual when dealing with children with mental retardation, autism, and developmental delays. Because U.S. society expects greater competence in intellectual functioning in males than in females, boys are more likely to be diagnosed with any one of these conditions, whereas girls are simply labeled as slow (Levinson & Starling, 1981; Marsh, 1992).

Local Recruitment

Local parents were recruited via letters sent through Pennsylvania's Allegheny County Mental Health/Mental Retardation chapter agencies, which register children diagnosed with significant delays. Two local Pennsylvania chapters of the Arc (formerly known as the Association for Retarded Citizens) mailed letters to eligible parents. The Arc also distributed approximately 350 cover letters and consent forms to parents in 10 different infant–toddler groups.

Letters contained the investigator's phone number and an addressed, stamped postcard for interested parents to return with their phone number and name on the back. If a parent agreed to participate, the investigator obtained an address to mail out a consent form. The consent form explained the study, its risks and benefits, confidentiality, and rights of participants to withdraw, as well as the name, address, and phone number of the primary investigator. Of approximately 600 mailed letters, 56 parents (approximately 9%) responded with a call or postcard. Of these parents, two decided not to participate, two were not eligible (child was too old; foster parent to child). One interview was terminated because the parent did not understand the questions, and five parents were unreachable (disconnected phone, no telephone number, not home after five contact attempts). The remaining 44 (80%) parents agreed to participate in the study and the initial interview was successfully completed.

Internet Recruitment

Parents also were recruited through electronic groups on the Internet. A brief description of the study (similar to the one used in the letters) and eligibility requirements were posted twice during a 3-month interval in four USENET groups: netnews.alt.education.disabled, netnews.alt.support.dev-delays, netnews.bit.listserv.autism, and netnews.bit.listserv.down-syn. Interested parents were asked to reply directly to the post, at which point a more detailed message about the study's purposes, confidentiality, and participation was sent. If a parent agreed to participate, further contact was made electronically to schedule a day and time for a telephone conversation. After this contact, the consent form was mailed to the parent. It is not possible to determine how many parents were reached by the electronic bulletin boards. These boards are transmitted nationally as well as internationally. Approximately 95 replies were received via the Internet. Of these replies, 65 parents (68%) were contacted and interviewed. Of the remaining 30 replies, two thirds were eligible parents with whom I was not able to schedule an interview after three contacts. The other one third were either ineligible parents or professionals inquiring about the project. Some of these people provided me with names of parents who were interested but not on the Internet, some told me of other bulletin boards to post my request, and still others were therapists or academics interested in hearing more about the study.

Interview and Measures

The initial interview lasted approximately 45 minutes. After a brief introduction, parents were asked to provide some demographic information. This interview included measures of perceived stigma, problem visibility, perceived support availability, willingness to seek support, actual support seeking, depression, unsolicited support, perceived stress, fear of rejection, and attitudes about help seeking. The follow-up interview 4 months later lasted approximately 30 minutes. (A final questionnaire will be mailed to parents 12 months after the initial interview.)

Perceived Stigma.   Perceived stigma associated with the child's diagnosis was assessed with an eight-item measure adapted from two previously used measures (Crandall, 1991; Levinson & Starling, 1981). Parents were asked to indicate how true or false the following statements were for them on a 5-point scale (1 = *definitely false*; 3 = *neither true nor false*; 5 = *definitely true*):

1. I feel that I am odd or abnormal because of my child's special needs.
2. There have been times when I have felt ashamed about having a child with special needs.
3. I *never* feel self-conscious about my child's special needs.
4. People treat me differently when they find out that I have a child with special needs.
5. I *never* feel embarrassed about my child's special needs.
6. People look down on me because I have a child with special needs.
7. I have found that people say negative or unkind things about me behind my back because I have a child with special needs.
8. I have been excluded from social gatherings because I have a child with special needs.

Scores on items 3 and 5 were reversed. These eight items had a Cronbach's alpha of .76. Therefore, these items were summed to obtain a perceived stigma score for each subject with higher scores indicating more perceived stigma. Parents' scores ranged from 8 to 36, with a mean of 20.18 ($N = 109$).

Visibility of the Special Needs.   Parents were asked to assess the physical, behavioral, and overall visibility of their child's diagnosis on a 5-point scale (1 = *not at all*; 5 = *definitely*) using the following three questions: (a) "If a complete stranger were to *see a snapshot* of your child, would they be able to tell by looking at the picture that something is different about your child?"; (b) "If a complete stranger were to *interact or talk* to your child, would they be able to tell that something is different about your child?"; (c) "How visible do you feel your child's condition is to the public?". Cronbach's alpha for these three questions was .60. The questions were summed to obtain a visibility score for each child with higher scores indicating greater visibility of the special need. Parents' scores ranged from 3 to 15, with a mean of 8.08 ($N = 109$).

Perceived Support Availability.   Perceived support availability was assessed individually for each of the three network members (spouse, parents, casual friend) by an adapted version of the UCLA -Social Support Inventory (Dunkel-Schetter, Feinstein, & Call, 1986). Parents were asked to rate the perceived availability of three types of support (emotional, informational, tangible) on 5-point scales (1 = *not at all*; 5 = *extremely*). Emotional support was defined as love, caring, understanding, or reassurance regarding the child and his or her diagnosis. Informational support was defined as information or advice about the child and his or her diagnosis. Tangible support was defined as help with household tasks, errands, or child care. Separate questions were asked to assess each type of support. Parents were asked to indicate the extent to which they could turn to each source for each of the three kinds of support. Thus, there were nine questions in total. Cronbach's alpha for the three kinds of support was .70 for spouse, .78 for parents, and .60 for friend. An index of the items was computed separately for spouse, parents, and casual friend. Higher scores indicate more perceived support availability.

Perceived support availability also was defined as how approachable, receptive, and withdrawn parents perceive their network members to be. I adapted a perceived social support scale by Lepore, Allen, and Evans (1993) to assess parents' perceptions of each support source with respect to their child's diagnosis. Parents rated each support source on seven bipolar traits; the latter two I added because I felt they were relevant to the assessment of perceived support availability in this study (supportive–unsupportive, close–distant, rejecting–accepting, warm–cold, unhelpful–helpful, approachable–unapproachable, and unreceptive–receptive). These traits were rated on 5-point scales (e.g., 1 = *rejecting* to 5 = *accepting*). Scores for supportive–unsupportive, close–distant, warm–cold, and approachable–unapproachable were recoded to parallel the other traits. Cronbach's alpha for the seven traits was computed separately for spouse, parents, and friend. The alphas were .81, .92, and .88, respectively. The seven traits were summed for each support source to reflect subjects' trait perception of their spouse, parents, and friend. Higher scores indicate a more favorable trait perception.

Willingness to Seek Support.   Participants rated how willing they were to seek help from the three different network members. Willingness to disclose information and accompanying emotions as well as willingness to make specific requests for help were assessed. Parents were asked: "How willing are you to tell your spouse (parents, friend) about your feelings about your child and his or her diagnosis?" and "How willing are you to tell your spouse (parents, friend) about your difficulties in daily living due to your child's diagnosis?". To assess willingness to seek the three kinds of support, parents were asked: "How willing are you to seek understanding or reassurance about your child from your spouse (parents, friend)?", "How willing are you to seek information or advice about your child from your spouse (parents, friend)?", and "How willing are you to seek physical support, such as help with household tasks, errands, or childcare from your spouse (parents, friend)?". All five questions were answered on 5-point scales from (1) "not at all" to (5) "a lot." Cronbach's alpha for these five questions was .78 for spouse, .86 for parents, and .83 for friend. An index of the five items was computed separately for spouse, parents, and casual friend. Higher scores indicate greater willingness to seek support.

Actual Support Seeking. Parents' actual support seeking was assessed for the previous 3 months in the initial interview and the prior 4 months in the follow-up interview. The questions paralleled those for willingness to seek support. Two questions asked about disclosure: "How often in the last 3 months have you told your spouse (parents, friend) about your difficulties in daily living due to your child's diagnosis?"; "How often in the last 3 months have you told your spouse (parents, friend) about your feelings about the child and his or her diagnosis?". Three questions asked about seeking informational, emotional, and tangible support from each of the network members. Parents responded to each question on a 5-point scale (1 = *never*; 3 = *sometimes*; 5 = *very often*). Cronbach's alpha for these five questions was .75 for spouse, .84 for parents, and .79 for friend. An index of the items was computed separately for spouse, parents, and casual friend. Higher scores indicate greater support seeking.

Other Items. Three questions were asked about *expectations* for emotional, information, and tangible support from each support source (e.g., "How much understanding and reassurance regarding your child do you expect from your spouse?"). Parents responded to each question on a 5-point scale (1 = *none*; 5 = *a lot*). Cronbach's alpha for these three questions were modest (.49 for spouse, .63 for parents, .63 for friend). An index of the items was computed separately for spouse, parents, and casual friend. Higher scores indicate higher support expectations. However, because of the modest reliabilities of these three scales, caution should be used in interpreting their results.

Unsolicited support was assessed for the previous 3 months by asking parents to rate how often they received emotional, instrumental, and informational support from their spouse, parents, and friend without asking for it. All three questions were responded to on 5-point scales (1 = *never*; 3 = *sometimes*; 5 = *very often*) and summed to obtain an unsolicited support score for each support source. Cronbach's alpha for the three questions was .74 for spouse, .73 for parents, and .56 for casual friend.

Parents' *fear of rejection* by others was assessed by one question: "How concerned are you that your requests for help or support regarding your child might be rejected or ignored by your spouse (parents, friend)?" (1 = *not at all*; 5 = *very*).

Parents' *perceived stress* was assessed with one question: "How serious is the stress you are experiencing with respect to your child's special needs?" (1 = *not at all*; 5 = *very*).

Parents rated on 5-point scales (1 = *not at all*; 5 = *a lot*) the extent to which they believed four *attributions* (heredity, fate/God's will, behaviors during pregnancy, genetics) each contributed to their child's special needs.

The Center for Epidemiologic Studies Depression Scale (CES–D; Radloff, 1977) was included in the interview to assess the relation of perceived stigma and problem visibility to parents' *depression*. It was thought that depression may play a role in the relation of perceived stigma to social support. However, no specific predictions were made concerning the role of depression; this measure was included for exploratory purposes only. Cronbach's alpha for the 20-item scale was .89. These items were summed to obtain a score of depressive symptomatology with higher scores indicating more depressive symptoms. Parents' scores ranged from 0 to 42, with a mean of 12.77 (N = 109).

A measure of one's general attitude toward *help seeking*, Eckenrode's (1983) Efficacy of Help-Seeking Scale, was included at the beginning of the initial interview. I included this measure as a dispositional control variable that could influence parents' help seeking, willingness to seek help, or perceptions of family and friends. Cronbach's alpha for this scale was .62 in the initial interview; this alpha was deemed satisfactory. The six items were summed to obtain a help-seeking score for each subject with higher scores indicating a more positive attitude toward help seeking. Parents' scores ranged from 11 to 24, with a mean of 19.09 (N = 109).

General Findings From the Field Study

Parents' attitudes about help seeking in general were highly correlated with their professed willingness to seek support and perceptions of support availability; therefore, these attitudes were used as a covariate in all analyses of stigma and support. I did not find the predicted relation of visibility to social support, but perceived stigma was an important variable. One surprising finding was that whereas perceived stigma was related to perceptions of *less* support availability and *less* willingness to seek support (from spouse and parents), people who perceived their children's problem to be stigmatized reported actually seeking *more* support from spouse and casual friend. Also, as in Coyne, Aldwin, and Lazarus (1981), people who were depressed sought more support (from spouse and casual friend).

TABLE 8.1

Profile of Parents From Electronic Support Groups and the Local Community

	Electronic Parents	Local Parents
Gender	34 mothers (52.3%)	43 mothers (97.7%)
	31 fathers (47.7%)	1 father (2.3%)
Avg. Age	35.5 years	33.4 years
Marital Status	96.9% married	88.6% married
	1.5% divorced	4.5% divorced
	1.5% single	6.8% single
Race	92.3% White	86.4% White
	3.1% African-American	11.4% African-American
	3.1% Asian-American	2.3% Hispanic
	1.5% Hispanic	
Religion	49.2% Protestant	34.1% Protestant
	32.3% Catholic	59.1% Catholic
	6.2% Jewish	2.3% Jewish
	12.3% none	4.5% none
Education	35.4% postgraduate	15.9% postgraduate
	21.5% some college/vocational	36.4% some college/vocational
	4.6% completed high school	9.1% completed high
	1.5% some high school	6.8% some high school
Employment	63.1% full-time	34.1% full-time
	9.2% part-time	15.9% part-time
	4.6% self-employed	6.8% self-employed
	16.9% homemakers	31.8% homemakers
	6.1% unemployed	11.3% unemployed
Special Needs Children		
Gender	54 boys (78.3%)	29 boys (65.9%)
	15 girls (21.7%)	15 girls (34.1%)
Avg. Age	45.9 months	33.0 months
Diagnosis	46.2% autism	9.1% autism
	40.0% Down syndrome	22.7% Down syndrome
	7.7% developmental delays	43.2% developmental delays
	6.2% other mental retardation	25.0% other mental retardation
Avg. Delay	35.3% delay	38.8% delay

PARENTS FROM ELECTRONIC GROUPS
COMPARED WITH OTHER PARENTS

Parents recruited from electronic support groups differed from other parents across a variety of demographic characteristics: age, marital status, race, religion, education level, occupational status, child's age and diagnosis, and, most of all, gender (see Table 8.1). Parents from electronic groups were slightly older and more likely to be married, White, Protestant, have completed college, and be employed full-time than the other parents. In addition, their special needs children were slightly older and more likely to have autism or Down syndrome; children of the other parents were more likely to have developmental delays. Only one parent in the nonelectronic sample was male.

Differences in Support Seeking

To constrain the number of comparisons in this exploratory analysis (so as not to inflate the significance of findings), I present only two comparisons: (a) parents from electronic support groups versus other parents (i.e., mothers) and (b) mothers from electronic support groups versus other mothers. The latter comparison controls for gender. Lastly, I present results from the 4-month follow-up study.

Parents solicited from electronic support groups differed from mothers solicited from the local community on one of the main independent variables of my field study, visibility, and several social support variables (see Table 8.2). Parents from electronic support groups rated the visibility of their child's special needs higher than did nonelectronic mothers. Social support differences were limited to parents and casual friend, but the direction of these differences was consistent: Parents from electronic support groups viewed their parents and casual friends less favorably than non-electronic mothers. These parents expected less support from their parents and casual friends, perceived their casual friends less favorably, and reported receiving less unsolicited support from their parents than did nonelectronic mothers. (Parents solicited from electronic groups were unlikely to name as a "casual friend" someone they met online. Thus, the differences between parent samples on the casual friend support variables cannot be attributed to their choice of casual friend.)

A second analysis, controlling for gender effects, compared mothers solicited from electronic support groups with those solicited from the local community. These two groups differed on social support variables and on variables related to the child's special needs (perceived stigma, attributions for the child's special needs). Mothers in electronic groups perceived more stigma attached to their child's special needs and were more likely to admit they avoid being in public with their child than other mothers. Mothers in electronic groups also were more likely to attribute the cause of their child's

TABLE 8.2

Comparison of Electronic Parents With Nonelectronic Mothers

	Electronic Fathers	Electronic Mothers	Nonelectronic Mothers
Perceived Stigma	20.23^{ab}	22.41^a	18.56^b
Avoid Being in Public With Child	1.32^b	2.00^a	1.16^b
Visibility	8.68^a	8.62^a	7.19^b
Support Expectations			
Spouse	11.91^b	12.10^a	13.39^a
Parents	7.26^b	8.30^b	9.70^a
Casual Friend	6.73^b	7.44^b	8.76^a
Trait Perception			
Spouse	32.55^a	30.76^a	31.39^a
Parents	27.39^a	27.18^a	30.00^a
Casual Friend	28.87^b	30.09^b	32.79^a
Unsolicited Support			
Spouse	13.27^a	10.06^b	11.03^b
Parents	6.77^b	7.33^b	8.84a
Casual Friend	5.78^b	6.41^{ab}	7.12^a
Attributions			
Heredity	2.29^{ab}	2.59^a	1.86^b
Fate/God's Will	2.97^{ab}	2.82^b	3.53^a
Behavior During Pregnancy	1.52^{ab}	1.24^b	1.72^a

Note. Common superscripts indicate that the means do not significantly differ at $p < .05$. Superscripts are arranged such that "a" represents the highest mean.

special needs to hereditary factors whereas other mothers were more likely to attribute the cause to fate or God's will, or to their behaviors during pregnancy.

Differences in Social Support Processes

I developed a model of perceived stigma and support seeking from the results of the study. In this post-hoc model, perceived stigma is related to support seeking through three variables: perceived support availability, willingness to seek support, and depression. This post-hoc model was tested through structural equation modeling with the initial test of the model failing to fit the data. However, after adding a direct link between perceived stigma and support seeking, the revised model did provide a good fit to the data for support seeking from spouse but not as well for parents or casual friend.

Testing this model separately on the two groups of mothers would suggest whether their processes for seeking support from spouses are the same or different.[2] The revised post-hoc model provided a good fit to the data for mothers in electronic support groups, overall χ^2 (5, N = 33) = 1.61, $p > .10$ (Bentler-Bonnett fit index [BBFI] - normed = .97; BBFI - non-normed

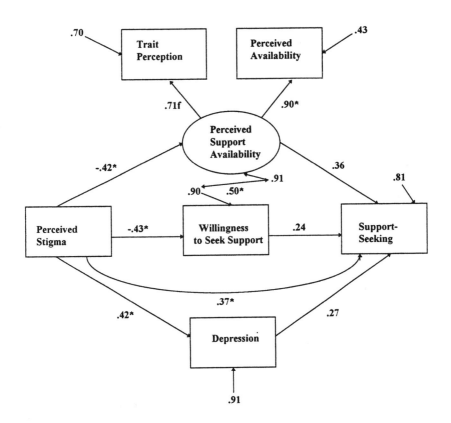

FIG. 8.3. Standardized structural equation model results for mothers from electronic support groups. N = 33 Internet mothers.
*Parameter estimate significant at $p < .05$. A superscript "f" indicates a parameter set

---

[2]Because the post-hoc models for support seeking from parents and casual friend did not fit the overall population, I only compared the two groups of mothers on the model for support seeking from spouse.

= 1.25). This model is presented in Fig. 8.3. Perceived stigma is related directly to support seeking and indirectly through perceived support availability, willingness to seek support, and depression. The direct relation accounted for 13.7% of the variance in the model, whereas the indirect relations accounted for a total of 36.8% of the model's variance. When this model for spouse was tested on mothers from the local community, however, it failed to fit the data. Even after adding and dropping several links suggested by the program, the model still did not provide a good fit to the data for these mothers. The only link that was significant in the model indicated that perceived stigma was related to higher levels of depression.

FOLLOW-UP INTERVIEW

From the electronic and nonelectronic samples, 95% and 91%, respectively, completed the follow-up interview. Except for a few measures (e.g., support expectations, trait perceptions), excluded to shorten the interview, the follow-up interview contained the same questions as the initial interview.

Differences in Support Seeking

Some of the differences between the parent samples persisted in the follow-up interview. Parents from electronic support groups reported receiving less unsolicited support from their parents and casual friends than did mothers in the nonelectronic sample (see Table 8.3). They also were less willing to seek support from their parents and actually sought less support from them than did mothers in the nonelectronic sample.

Comparisons involving just mothers showed that mothers from electronic support groups reported receiving less unsolicited support from their spouse, perceived their spouse as less available, and were less willing to seek support from their spouse than were nonelectronic mothers. Also, as in the initial interview, they perceived more stigma attached to their child's special needs than did nonelectronic mothers.

Internet Use and Social Support

Several questions were added to the follow-up interview to examine whether reading and posting publicly or privately was differentially related to social support perceptions, as well as to perceived stigma, visibility, and depression. Parents who read electronic bulletin boards can obtain comparison information or vicarious support without having to disclose anything about themselves. This "lurking" (Sproull & Kiesler, 1991) also may allow parents to obtain validation for their feelings of stigma without having to communicate those feelings to others. Reading about or posting to parents having similar problems may allow parents to receive social

TABLE 8.3

Comparison of Electronic Parents With Nonelectronic Mothers: Follow-Up Interview

	Electronic Fathers	Electronic Mothers	Nonelectronic Mothers
Perceived Stigma	17.66[ab]	20.85[a]	17.10[b]
Unsolicited Support			
Spouse	12.93[a]	10.00[b]	11.59[a]
Parents	6.43[b]	7.34[b]	8.87[a]
Casual Friend	5.07[b]	5.97[b]	7.29[a]
Perceived Support			
Availability			
Spouse	13.52[a]	11.78[b]	13.03[a]
Parents	8.07[b]	9.00[ab]	10.51[a]
Casual Friend	8.32[b]	9.00[ab]	10.26[a]
Willingness to Seek Support			
Spouse	21.76[ab]	21.16[b]	23.00[a]
Parents	13.61[b]	15.59[b]	18.18[a]
Casual Friend	14.25[b]	18.23[a]	17.48[a]
Actual Support Seeking			
Spouse	19.17[a]	17.28[a]	17.81[a]
Parents	10.14[b]	11.13[b]	13.18[a]
Casual Friend	8.82[b]	11.09[a]	12.32[a]

Note. Common superscripts indicate that the means do not significantly differ at $p < .05$. Superscripts are arranged such that "a" represents the highest mean.

support from their electronic support group without having to confront family and friends about potential or experienced conflicts.

Parents in electronic support groups were asked three questions in the follow-up interview: (a) "How often in the last 4 months have you read the [newsgroup] where this study was posted or any [electronic group] pertaining to your child's special needs?"; (b) "How often have you posted publicly on the [newsgroup] in the last 4 months?"; (c) "How often have you posted privately [sent electronic mail] to one or more individuals in the last 4 months?". Answers were coded into one of seven categories: never, less than once a month, monthly, two times per month, weekly, more than once a week, daily. Only those support variables that were significantly correlated with one of the three questions are shown in Table 8.4. The only variable that was consistently correlated with support perceptions was how often parents publicly posted messages on the electronic newsgroups. The more parents posted publicly, the more stress they perceived they were experiencing with respect to their child's special needs and the less available they

TABLE 8.4

Correlations of Reading and Posting on the Internet With Support Variables

	Reading	Posting Publicly	Posting Privately
Perceived Stress	.11	.25[+]	.06
Fear of Rejection:			
Casual Friend	.18	.28[*]	.12
Perceived Support Availability:			
Spouse	−.03	−.27[*]	−.25[*]
Support Seeking:			
Casual Friend	.10	.27[*]	.14
Unsolicited Support:			
Spouse	−.13	−.19	−.29[*]

$+p < .10$

$p < .05$

perceived their spouse to be. Furthermore, posting publicly was related to greater fear of being rejected by their casual friend, but, surprisingly, it also was related to more support seeking from their casual friend.

Sending private electronic mail to one or more individuals in the electronic group was correlated negatively with perceived availability of spouse and unsolicited support from spouse. That is, the more parents sent electronic mail to one or more individuals in the electronic groups, the less available they perceived their spouse to be and the less they reported receiving unsolicited support from their spouse. The amount parents read electronic newsgroups was not correlated with any of the social support variables.

DISCUSSION

What do these results tell us about those who use electronic support groups to obtain social support for stressful events? Although the results of this study are preliminary, they are consistent. Parents solicited from electronic support groups were, first of all, a higher socioeconomic status group and much more likely to include fathers than those solicited from the local community. Second, parents from electronic support groups reported more stress and perceived stigma associated with having a special needs child, and perceived family and friends as less supportive than did the mothers in the non-electronic sample. Why do these parents perceive their family and nonelectronic friends less well than other parents? One reason may be that by relying on parents reached through the Internet with similar problems, they are not communicating with their spouses, parents, or casual friends. In other words, these parents may be withdrawing from their traditional social networks when they access electronic support groups. Alternatively, parents who use electronic support groups may do so because they feel misunderstood or rejected within their local social networks.

Mothers in electronic groups perceived more stigma attached to their child's special needs than other mothers. This finding was stable over two interviews. Why do these mothers perceive more stigma than other mothers? First, by exchanging stories with other parents, the electronic group may have promoted in these mothers a greater self-awareness and acceptance of social stigma. Second, because of their higher education, these mothers may be more aware of the feelings held by society toward delayed children and they may have had higher expectations for their child than other mothers. When these expectations are shattered by a diagnosis of mental retardation or autism, parents in electronic support groups may experience more stress than other parents. Another explanation could be the different diagnoses in the two samples: Parents from the electronic groups were more likely to have a child diagnosed as autistic or having Down syndrome whereas nonelectronic parents were more likely to have a child diagnosed as developmentally delayed. Autism and Down syndrome may be perceived as more stigmatizing than developmental delays. However, an analysis of the three main diagnoses (autism, Down syndrome, developmental delays), controlling for parent type and help seeking, failed to reveal any significant difference in perceived stigma among these three diagnoses. Therefore, greater perceptions of stigma by mothers in electronic groups cannot be explained by the different diagnoses in the two samples.

Structural equation modeling suggested that mothers in electronic groups may actually engage in a different process of seeking support from their spouses than other mothers. Their process of seeking and perceiving support from their spouse appeared to be strongly related to their stigma perceptions unlike nonelectronic mothers. Longitudinal studies need to be done to determine the causal direction of the process as well as whether the difference between electronic and nonelectronic mothers persists over time.

There are a few limitations to this study. Most notably, there was a possible self-selection bias in the study. Because the study focused on perceived stigma and social relationships, those perceiving the most stigma and/or those who had the poorest social relationships may have been less likely to participate in the study. Because of confidentiality rules and lack of information about Internet users, I was not able to assess the differences, or lack thereof, between those who did and did not choose to participate in the study. Thus, the relation of perceived stigma and visibility to social support for this sample may not be representative of the general population of parents with special needs children. This problem of selection bias is common to field research on the Internet.

Second, because the samples differed demographically, it is hard to distinguish demographic from communication effects in this study. The role of demographic differences among parents in social support needs to be further examined. For example, demographic differences may explain the attributional differences between the two groups of mothers. Mothers in the electronic group were more likely to attribute their child's special needs to heredity (which students in higher education may study), whereas other mothers were more likely to attribute the cause to fate or God's will, or to their behaviors during pregnancy. Parents who are unaware of the biological aspects of these diagnoses may be more likely to attribute the special need to their own behavior or to God. Of course, mothers using the electronic support groups also may have received different information about the causes of the disability than mothers from the local community. So, communication effects also could explain the differences in attributions.

A third limitation to this study is the absence of fathers in the community sample; all but one of the fathers were solicited via the Internet. The presence of so many fathers in the electronic sample could reflect differential Internet usage by men (Times Mirror, 1995; chap. 19). Online support groups may be particularly attractive for men because they provide anonymity and do not demand self-disclosure. One can lurk in these support groups, unlike traditional support groups, which by their very nature do not allow for much anonymity or nondisclosure. Prior research has shown that women have a tendency to attend traditional support groups more than men (Taylor et al., 1988). Future research would benefit from comparing the social support processes of fathers and mothers using electronic support groups with fathers and mothers in local, face-to-face support groups, as well as the support processes of fathers in particular.

Conclusion

This research has shown that those using electronic support groups do differ from those using more traditional forms of support. Parents accessing electronic support groups perceive their family and friends less favorably than do other parents. Although electronic parents have online a ready resource for support, information, and sympathy, they, in fact, may be using it as a way to avoid communicating better with family and friends. It is unclear from these results which comes first: Do electronic support groups increase the isolation of these people from their traditional support networks? Or, are those with poor traditional support networks more likely to access Internet support groups? This issue is especially important as the Internet becomes easier to access.

ACKNOWLEDGMENTS

Preparation of this chapter was supported 'n part by Training Grant T32-MH16806 from the National Institute of Mental Health. I am grateful to Sara Kiesler for her comments on an earlier draft of this chapter as well as to all the parents who so generously gave their time to be interviewed.

REFERENCES

Chesler, M. A., & Barbarin, O. A. (1984). Difficulties of providing help in a crisis: Relationships between parents of children with cancer and their friends. *Journal of Social Issues, 40*(4), 113–134.

Cohen, S., & Wills, T. A. (1985). Stress, social support, and the buffering hypothesis. *Psychological Bulletin, 98*(2), 310–357.

Coyne, J. C., Aldwin, C., & Lazarus, R. S. (1981). Depression and coping in stressful episodes. *Journal of Abnormal Psychology, 90,* 439–447.

Crandall, C. S. (1991). AIDS-related stigma and the lay sense of justice. *Contemporary Social Psychology, 15,* 66–67.

Crandall, C. S., & Coleman, R. (1992). AIDS-related stigmatization and the disruption of social relationships. *Journal of Social and Personal Relationships, 9,* 163–177.

Dunkel-Schetter, C. (1984). Social support and cancer: Findings based on patient interviews and their implications. *Journal of Social Issues, 40*(4), 77–98.

Dunkel-Schetter, C., Feinstein, L., & Call, J. (1986). *UCLA social support inventory.* Los Angeles: University of California.

Dunst, C. J., Trivette, C. M., & Cross, A. H. (1986). Mediating influences of social support: Personal, family, and child outcomes. *American Journal of Mental Deficiency, 90*(4), 403–417.

Eckenrode, J. (1983). The mobilization of social supports: Some individual constraints. *American Journal of Community Psychology, 11,* 509–528.

Fontana, A. F., Kerns, R. D., Rosenberg, R. L., & Colonese, K. L. (1989). Support, stress, and recovery from coronary heart disease: A longitudinal causal model. *Health Psychology, 8*(2), 175–193.

Gibbons, F. X. (1985). A social–psychological perspective on developmental disabilities. *Journal of Social and Clinical Psychology, 3,* 391–404.

Goffman, E. (1963). *Stigma: Notes on the management of spoiled identity.* Englewood Cliffs, NJ: Prentice-Hall.

Kiecolt-Glaser, J. K., Dyer, C. S., & Shuttleworth, E. C. (1988). Upsetting social interactions and distress among Alzheimer's disease family care-givers: A replication and extension. *American Journal of Community Psychology, 16*(6), 825–837.

Lennon, M. C., Link, B. G., Marbach, J. J., & Dohrenwend, B. P. (1989). The stigma of chronic facial pain and its impact on social relationships. *Social Problems, 36,* 117–134.

Lepore, S. J., Allen, K. A. M., & Evans, G. W. (1993). Social support lowers cardiovascular reactivity to an acute stressor. *Psychosomatic Medicine, 55,* 518–524.

Levinson, R. M., & Starling, D. M. (1981). Retardation and the burden of stigma. *Deviant Behavior, 2,* 371–390.

Levy, S. M., Herberman, R. B., Lee, J. K., Lippman, M. E., & d'Angelo, T. (1989). Breast conservation versus mastectomy: Distress sequelae as a function of choice. *Journal of Clinical Oncology, 7*(3), 367–375.

MacDonald, L. D., & Anderson, H. R. (1984). Stigma in patients with rectal cancer: A community study. *Journal of Epidemiology and Community Health, 38,* 284–290.

Mansouri, L., & Dowell, D. A. (1989). Perceptions of stigma among the long-term mentally ill. *Psychosocial Rehabilitation Journal, 13,* 79–91.

Marsh, D. T. (1992). *Families and mental retardation: New directions in professional practice.* New York: Praeger.

Radloff, L. S. (1977). The CES–D scale: A self-report depression scale for research in the general population. *Applied Psychological Measurement, 1*(3), 385–401.

Sproull, L., & Kiesler, S. (1991). *Connections: New ways of working in the networked organization.* Cambridge, MA: MIT Press.

Taylor, S. E., Falke, R. L., Mazel, R. M., & Hilsberg, B. L. (1988). Sources of satisfaction and dissatisfaction among members of cancer support groups. In B. H. Gottlieb (Ed.), *Marshaling social support: Format, processes, and effects* (pp. 187–208). Newbury Park, CA: Sage.

Times Mirror Center for The People and The Press. (1995, October). *Technology in the American household*. Washington, D C: Author.

Turner, H. A., Hays, R. B., & Coates, T. J. (1993). Determinants of social support among gay men: The context of AIDS. *Journal of Health and Social Behavior, 34*, 37–53.

Wolcott, D. L., Namir, S., Fawzy, F. I., Gottlieb, M. S., & Mitsuyasu, R. T. (1986). Illness concerns, attitudes towards homosexuality, and social support in gay men with AIDS. *General Hospital Psychiatry, 8*, 395–403.

9

AN ELECTRONIC GROUP
IS VIRTUALLY A SOCIAL NETWORK

Barry Wellman
Centre for Urban and Community Studies,
University of Toronto

When a computer network connects people, it is a social network. Just as a computer network is a set of machines connected by a set of cables, a social network is a set of people (or organizations or other social entities) connected by a set of socially meaningful relationships. I show how social network analysis might be useful for understanding how people relate to each other through computer-mediated communication (see also Wellman & Gulia, in press; Wellman et al., 1996).

Social network analysis conceives of social structure as the patterned organization of these network members and their relationships. Social network analysts work at describing underlying patterns of social structure, explaining the impact of such social structures on other variables, and accounting for change in social structures. Social network analysis has developed procedures for detecting structural patterns, seeing how patterns of different types of relationships interrelate, analyzing the implications that structural patterns have for the behavior of network members, and studying the impact on social structures of the characteristics of network members and their social relationships. In the past three decades, social network analysis has produced a range of concepts, findings, and methods in the social sciences (Berkowitz, 1982; Wellman, 1988b; Scott, 1991; Wasserman & Faust, 1993). For example, analysts have demonstrated the role of social networks in providing interpersonal support (Wellman, 1992), structuring riots and other political contentions (Tilly, 1984), channeling the flow and settlement of immigrants (Salaff, Fong, & Wong, in press), linking seemingly disparate personnel at work, and connecting ostensibly independent organizations (Nohria & Eccles, 1992).

The social network approach provides ways for analysts to think about social relationships that are neither groups nor isolated duets. Instead of an either/or distinction between group membership and social isolation, researchers can bring to bear in their analysis a set of structural variables, such as the density and clustering of a network, how tightly it is bounded, and whether it is diversified or constricted in its size and heterogeneity, how narrowly specialized or broadly multiplex are its relationships, and how indirect connections and positions in social networks affect behavior. For example, the fact that Person A and Person B interact online may have to be interpreted in the light of the offline reporting relationship of Person B to Person C, the company president. Thus thinking about relationships in social networks rather than in groups can allow analysts to take into account the contexts within which relationships operate.

Although all studies have to start somewhere with some populations, many network analyses do not treat formal group boundaries as truly social boundaries, be they departments in organizations or officially designated neighborhoods in cities. Instead they trace the social relationships of those they are studying, wherever these relationships go and whomever they are with. Only then do network analysts look to see if such relationships actually cross formal group boundaries. In this way, formal boundaries become important analytic variables rather than a priori analytic constraints.

The distinction between groups and social networks opens up consideration of how the characteristics of computer-supported social networks affect the behavior of the people using them and the social systems in which these networks are embedded.[1] Just as a local area network is only one kind of a computer network, a group is only one kind of a social network. More precisely, a group is a social network whose ties are tightly bounded within a delimited set and are densely knit so that almost all network members are directly linked with each other. To be sure, there are densely knit and tightly bounded work groups and community groups. Yet there are other kinds of work and community networks whose relationships are sparsely knit with only a minority of members of the workplace or community directly connected with each other. These relationships tend to ramify out in many directions like an expanding spider's web rather than curling back on themselves into a densely knit tangle.

For example, a bunch of people who hang out together—at work, in a café, or on an Internet discussion group—can studied as either a group or a social network. Those who study them as groups assume that they know

---

[1]Although both "group" and "network" are really social networks, the linguistic distinction is well established in everyday discourse.

the membership and boundaries of the groups. They might ask how important each group is to its members, how the groups are governed and make decisions, and how the groups control members. Yet, in all but laboratory situations, researchers will be faced with the real-world problem that members are entering and leaving a group over time. By contrast, those who study such entities as social networks can treat their membership and boundaries as open questions. For example, frequent participation in an Internet discussion group might be treated as the basis for membership but so might be the indirect connections (and resource flows) that discussion group members provide to others outside the group. The patterns of relationships become a research question rather than a given.

By definition, people who use computer networks have social relationships with each other that are embedded in social networks. Yet much of the analysis of online relationships via the study of "computer-mediated communication" has focused on two-person dyads rather than on the broader social networks in which these dyads are connected. People's relationships with others strongly affect their social resources, mobility, happiness, work habits, and many other important things about them. Hence it makes sense to use social network analysis to understand the patterns of relationships that people have online in addition to fine-grained analyses of online dyads.[2]

To collect information about computer social networks, analysts must first decide whether they are doing whole network or ego-centered network analyses. The more common whole network analyses gather information about relevant relationships within some population, where both the relevance of the relationship and the population are defined by the investigator. For example, our research group is studying relationships online and offline among a set of university computer scientists (Haythornthwaite, Wellman, & Mantei, 1995; Haythornthwaite & Wellman, 1996b) and a small organization (Garton, 1995). We collected information before and after the adoption of videoconferencing. At each wave, we asked all the members of the organization to report on how frequently they were interacting at that time with every other network member. We asked about such interactions for a score of different relationships, such as "supervising work" or "socializing after work." We asked separately about the frequency of interaction with each network member in each kind of relationship (supervising, etc.) for a number of different modes of communication used by these participants: email, videoconferencing, informal unscheduled inperson encounters, and formally scheduled inperson meetings.[3] We are now using a variety of network analytic techniques, coupled with field notes from ethnographic

---

[2]I am grateful to Sara Kiesler for suggesting the argument in the preceding two paragraphs.

[3]It is noteworthy that in these two organizations there was little telephoning, faxing, or circulation of paper memos.

observation and indepth interviews, to analyze these data.[4]

We also study the ego-centered (or personal) networks of each participant: a set of ties defined from the standpoint of the person at its center.
Rather than showing the whole network from the God-like standpoint of
an external observer, ego-centered analyses are Ptolemaic views of networks as experienced by each individual (Wellman, 1993). Typically, network analysts use standard survey techniques to ask a sample of
respondents to describe each member of their networks: the members'
social characteristics (such as age and gender), the characteristics of the
relationship between each member and the respondent (e.g., kin or friend,
frequency of contact, kinds of support provided), and (less reliably) the
characteristics of the relationship (if any) between two members of each
respondent's network.

In thinking about how to use the social network approach to study
patterns of interaction online, two linked questions are relevant for this
chapter:

1. How do different social network patterns of relationships affect interactions, online and offline?
2. How does computer-mediated communication affect patterns of social relationships?

My objectives are to discuss how computer networks support a variety
of social networks at work and in the community. I consider first the
implications for computer-supported social networks of two opposing
ideal types: dense, bounded groups and sparse, unbounded networks.
Then, I show how some of the key concepts of social network analysis apply
to understanding relationships online. To conclude, I work from a social
network approach to suggest research questions for future studies of computer-mediated communication and computer-supported social networks.

GROUPS AND NETWORKS
OF COMMUNITY AND WORK

Social scientists and the public alike have tended to see dense, bounded
groups as the desirable form of community and work while fearing that
technological change, industrialization, and urbanization have so isolated
people to create alienated individuals, standing alone in mass societies (e.g.,
Nisbet, 1962). Such fears continue to be expressed as analysts try to antici-

---

[4]The most widely used software package tailored for doing social network analysis is
UCINet (Borgatti, Everett, & Freeman, 1994). Others are *Gradap* (Sprenger & Stokman, 1995),
Multinet (Richards, 1994), and *Structure* (Burt, 1991). All run on DOS-based microcomputers.
However, much network analysis can be done using standard general-purpose statistical
packages such as *SAS* and *SPSS* (Haythornthwaite & Wellman, 1996a; Wellman, 1992).

pate the social consequences of widespread involvement in computer-mediated communication (e.g., Stoll, 1995). Yet a good deal of research has demonstrated that in contemporary society, both dense, bounded groups and sparse, unbounded networks exist simultaneously at work and in communities. Indeed, the same persons may be involved in both, as they iterate between different work groups and communities, or as the work groups and communities themselves change in response to external situations and internal dynamics. Nevertheless, there are systematic ways in which involvement in dense, bounded groups of work and community are different from involvement in sparse, unbounded networks in which the active players shift frequently.

Dense, Bounded Groups

Work. Conceptualizations of how work is organized have developed since the preindustrial, Adam Smith-ian image of small groups of densely knit workers. With the coming of the Industrial Revolution, this image gave way to a notion of large masses of workers organized in compartmentalized bureaucratic structures whose reporting relationships resembled treelike hierarchies. Yet even in the most hierarchical organizations, small groups of solitary workers form mutual-aid structures within the bowels of the organization (Thompson, 1967). Shops, factories, and offices frequently contain dense, bounded groups in which a limited number of people are fully engaged with each other in doing a collective task, be they clusters of artisans, sets of assembly-line workers, or small software development firms. They may be a permanent feature of the organization, or they may be a temporary group set up within a large organization to solve specific work tasks, as when Data General created a team to develop a new minicomputer (Kidder, 1981). The work in these groups is physically typified by open office plans with coworkers having full visual, aural, and physical access to each other. Participants often describe their situation metaphorically as "working in a fishbowl." Almost all communication is inward, within the fishbowl. Such a group situation is typical of tiny computer start-up companies where each programmer is in a constant visual, aural, and computer network (Coupland, 1995). There is considerable cross-talk, both online and face-to-face (see also Haythornthwaite et al., 1995).

Community. Even more than the conceptualization of work, healthy communities have come to be viewed as densely knit, tightly bounded groups. Researchers have found that despite the traumatic changes of modernization, communities continue to flourish. People still neighbor, visit their relatives, and help each other. These are necessary refuges from outside pressures, sources of interpersonal aid in dealing with large bureaucracies, and useful means of keeping streets safe (Wellman, 1988a).

The celebration of dense, bounded village like groups of community and work pervades one strain of thought about computer-mediated communication. Many see it as a boon for the alienated and isolated who will no longer be huddled in front of their television screens. Rather, video screens have become magic communicators enabling people to use online discussion groups, bulletin board systems, virtual chat rooms, and the like to make meaningful contact around the world with newfound comrades (Rheingold, 1993; Wellman & Gulia, in press). For example, Phil Patton (1986) predicted that "computer-mediated communication ... will do by way of electronic pathways what cement roads were unable to do, namely connect us rather than atomize us, put us at the controls of a 'vehicle' and yet not detach us from the rest of the world" (p. 20). As the cofounder of the Electronic Frontier Foundation prophesied, "With the development of the Internet, and with the increasing pervasiveness of communication between networked computers, we are in the middle of the most transforming technological event since the capture of fire (Barlow, Birkets, Kelly, & Slouka, 1995, p. 36). He continued: "I want to be able to completely interact with the consciousness that's trying to communicate with mine.... We are now creating a space in which the people of the planet can have that kind of communication relationship" (Barlow et al., 1995, p. 40).

Sparse, Unbounded Networks

Work.   In practice, many people do not work in either alienating mass workplaces or small dense and bounded work groups, and many organizations are not heavily composed of compartmentalized groups structured into tree hierarchies. Such people often accomplish their work in such loosely coupled, open organizations through selective contacts with shifting sets of others (Kling & Jewett, 1994; Star, 1993; Weick, 1976). They are in work relationships that routinely cut across departmental boundaries, and they have multiple reporting relationships that are segmented by time and task. The relatively autonomous workers in such sparsely knit, unbounded networks switch frequently and routinely among the people with whom they are dealing throughout the day as they move from project to project or as they need different kinds of resources. This mode of work is often found among professionals who have to make multiple, often unexpected contacts with colleagues within and outside their own organizations. An archetypical situation is a "brokerage" where an intermediary links two strangers in a transaction, be it stocks, houses, or marriage (Abbott, 1988). It is also the nature of "scholarly communities" of far-flung academics sharing similar research interests (Star, 1993; Walsh & Bayama, 1996; Carley, 1990; Kaufer & Carley 1993). Yet not only professionals work this way. Similar forms of interaction occur among managers in some large organizations, blue-collar workers with a responsibility for a range of tasks, and socially independent workers such as truck drivers (Shrum 1990). Physically typified by closed (or home) offices, such workers often conduct individual contacts and much of their work in relative privacy. Coworkers who want to talk with them may have to knock on doors or hope that a telephone is answered. Rather than being a member of one all-encompassing group, such workers have limited interactions with many different members of their networks, either one-to-one or in small, frequently changing, sets (Burt, 1992).

Community. Just as loosely coupled network forms of cooperative work have become prevalent in the Western world, sparsely knit, unbounded communities also flourish. Although major changes in social, economic, and political organization have not destroyed community, they have profoundly affected the contexts within which daily lives operate (Fischer, 1984). Since the 1960s, sociologists have discovered that dense, bounded neighborhood and kinship ties are often only a portion of people's overall community networks because cars, planes, phones, and computer-mediated communication can maintain relationships over long distances. Just as cooperative work need no longer be defined in terms of colocated work groups, community need no longer be defined in terms of neighborhoods. There has been a paradigm shift away from definitions in terms of locality and solidarity and toward definitions in terms of social networks. Such communities are ramified to complex networks of kin, friends, and workmates who do not necessarily live in the same neighborhoods. Although the world is not a global village (McLuhan, 1962), one's "village" can span the globe (Wellman, 1988a, 1994).

Researchers have learned that such communities are: domestic, operating from a person's home rather than from relatively accessible public spaces such as pubs, cafes, and street corners; private, operated by each person rather than by a collectivity such as a kinship group or tribe; specialized, with different ties providing different types of resources; sparsely knit, so that most of the people in the network are not strongly connected with each other; fragmented, so that most people are members of a number of specialized multiple communities rather than being engulfed in a single all-embracing community (Wellman, 1994).

This form of community resembles how many social relationships are conducted over the Internet and other forms of computer-supported social networks. Sitting in the privacy of their homes, people connect online with fellow members of newsgroups and other, usually specialized forms of virtual communities (Danet, Wachenhauser, Bechar-Israeli, Cividalli, & Rosenbaum-Tamari, 1995). Such virtual communities inherently connect all directly with all—everyone can read all messages—but their size and fragmentation means that few members are strongly connected. Hence computer-supported social networks are not destroying community but are responding to, resonating with, and extending the types of community that have already become prevalent in the developed Western world (Wellman & Gulia, in press).

RELATING SOCIAL NETWORK CHARACTERISTICS TO COMPUTER-MEDIATED COMMUNICATION

Although the distinction between densely knit, bounded groups and sparsely knit, unbounded networks is a frequently made ideal-type, social networks can be described in more complex and multivariate ways. In this section, I discuss the implications of six characteristics of social networks for understanding online social relationships and social organization: density, boundedness, range, exclusivity, social control, and tie strength. As many of these characteristics are associated with each other, I organize the discussion in terms of how these characteristics are manifested in dense, bounded groups or sparse, unbounded networks (see also Mantei & Wellman, 1995).

Density

Social Networks.   Do all network members have contact with all others, or is each the center of a unique, sparsely knit social world? Dense, bounded groups have considerable communication among members.[5] Within the group, ease of access promotes connections among all members. Almost all contacts between all persons in the network are made and usually made frequently. A classic example is the densely knit networks of London kin described by Bott (1971) where the parents and siblings so controlled husbands and wives that they tended to lead independent lives.

By contrast, few members of sparse, unbounded networks communicate directly and frequently with each other. For example, our research group has found that the density of Torontonians' intimate personal communities

---

[5]*Network density* is a variable (ranging from 0.00 to 1.00) describing the proportion of all possible ties (between two network members) that actually exist. A very densely knit network, with a density of 1.00 or so, would have a line connecting every point to every other point. (In an interpersonal network, every person would be directly connected with every other.) In graph theory (and social network analysis), such a fully connected network is called a *clique*. In practice, only very small networks tend to be fully connected, so researchers usually study densely-knit networks in which most possible connections actually exist. There is no standard definition of where a network becomes densely knit (it is a continuum), but most researchers would apply this term to a network with a density of at least .67 (two thirds of all possible ties actually exist). Sparsely-knit networks are at the other end of the continuum where few ties connect network members. The basic way to measure network density is to create a matrix in which the members of the network are crossclassified by row and column. A "1" indicates the presence of a tie whereas a "0" indicates its absence. (For computational purposes, analysts often put a "1" in the main diagonal, indicating that a person is connected to herself. This facilitates additional manipulation of matrices to discover things such as indirect ties.) For further information about measuring density see Wasserman & Faust, 1993.

to be .33; that is, only one third of all possible intimate ties between the average person's socially close intimates actually do exist (Wellman, Carrington, & Hall, 1988). The resulting lack of communication among intimates means that a person must work harder to maintain each relationship separately. However, the structural holes in their networks also provide them with opportunities for maneuver (Burt, 1992).

Computer Networks. Computer-mediated communication supports both dense, bounded groups and sparse, unbounded networks. Dense groups are supported when all participants in computerized conferences read and respond to all communications and so are directly connected to each other online. Focused task groups, role-playing MUDs (multiuser dimensions), and some newsgroups resemble villagelike structures when they capture their participants' attention (Kollock & Smith, in press). Thus work groups using computer-mediated communication have a higher level of communication than those that do not (Bikson & Eveland, 1990), although a high level of online communication may reduce the use of face-to-face and telephone contact (Finholt & Sproull, 1990; Finholt, Sproull, & Kiesler, 1990). Moreover, the forward-and-copy features of most electronic mail (email) systems can increase network density. Forwarding communications to third parties provides indirect connections between previously disconnected people, as they become aware of each other's mutual interest. The ease of reply can transform an indirect tie to a direct tie.

Densely knit, online groups are also apt to be mutually supportive, with exchanges of help often forming a complex web of assistance among several group members. Motivations for providing assistance on a computer network are partially founded on norms of generalized reciprocity and group citizenship. People who have a strong attachment to the online group will be more likely to participate and assist others, even total strangers (Kollock & Smith, in press; Constant, Sproull, & Kiesler, chap. 13, this volume).

Computer networks are well configured to support participation in sparse, unbounded networks. People can quickly send private email to anyone whose address they know, they can belong to a number of computerized conferences, and they can easily send messages to separate personal distribution lists for different kinds of conversations and activities. Moreover, they can vary their involvement in different work groups and communities, participating actively in some and occasionally in others.

Boundedness

Social Networks. Boundedness refers to the proportion of network members' ties that stay within the boundaries of the social network (Laumann, Marsden, & Prensky, 1983). All networks are defined within a population, be it a workplace, a neighborhood, a set of organizations (networks can link organizations as well as people), or the world system.

Networks can be bounded groups or permeable ramifying networks in which people can reach out widely to connect with others. In tightly bounded networks (almost) all of the relationships remain within the population. Those that cross the population's boundaries are likely to be relationships maintained by a few gatekeepers, such as work group managers, who have routinized contact on behalf of the group with the rest of the organization, neighborhood, and so on. Tightly bounded groups have important implications for the flow of information, disease, and social resources. For example, the tight boundaries around the networks of those in the United States with AIDS have limited the spread of the disease to the general population (Laumann, Gagnon, Michael, & Michaels, 1994).

By contrast, the members of loosely bounded (or "unbounded") networks have many ties with people who are not members of this particular network. Their orientation to a network will not be as intense. Because so many ties go outside the network, it is likely that the network will be sparsely knit. For example, purchasing agents and salespeople often are on the organizational margins, developing strong bonds with people they buy from or sell to, at the cost of their loyalty to their own organization (Bristor, 1987; Dorsey, 1994).

Not only do networks link people, they link groups, for when ties connect two groups, they provide intergroup as well as interpersonal links (Breiger [1974] called this "the duality of persons and groups," p. 181). Moreover, networks are scalable as "networks of networks" (Craven & Wellman, 1973): interpersonal, intergroup, interorganizational, and international. Thus if two persons who are members of two different work groups or organizations are linked, their interpersonal tie is also an intergroup or interorganizational one. Thus the largest American corporations are linked in one densely knit network through the membership of their officers on each other's governing boards (Levine, 1986; Mintz & Schwartz, 1985). The logic and the analysis are quite similar to computer networks: Connectivity between local area networks creates an organizational network, whereras connections to the Internet support interorganizational computer networks.

Computer Networks.   Local and wide area computer networks can support dense, bounded groups, through computerized conferencing and distribution lists in which all can send and receive messages with all. Indeed, many organizations put tight boundaries around their computer networks to inhibit communication from leaving the organizational precincts and to forestall intrusion. Technical constraints may also reinforce tight boundaries. At present, multimedia systems such as Cavecat and its descendants, Telepresence and Corel Vision, only have the ability to support videoconferencing among a small set of participants who also have the necessary equipment. Participants are aware of who is available for interaction through slow-scan video snapshots and can then use computer commands to establish video links with another person or even a small group (Mantei et al., 1991; Buxton, 1991).

Many computer networks support unbounded social networks because both private email and computerized conferences makes it easy and inexpensive to maintain connections with distant acquaintances and form new ties with strangers. Such "weak ties" are usually better connected to other, more diverse social circles, and hence are more apt to be sources of new information (Granovetter, 1982). Information may come unsolicited through distribution lists, computerized conferences, forwarded messages from friends who "thought you might like to know about this," and direct email from strangers ("a mutual friend recommended that I contact you").

The lower social presence of email—as compared to inperson meetings or telephone conversations—makes it easier to contact strangers because there is less concern about rude intrusion or interpersonal risk (Stoll, 1995). The willingness of people to engage online contrasts with inperson situations where American bystanders have been reluctant to help strangers (Latané & Darley, 1976). Yet such bystanders are more apt to intervene when they are the only ones available to help or can withdraw easily in case of trouble. Analogously, online requests for aid are read by people alone at their screens. Even if the request is to a computerized conference and not by personal email, a recipient of requests may believe that she or he may be the only one who can provide aid. In computerized conferences, even when such support is a small act such as mailing get-well cards or "cyber chicken soup," such acts can cumulatively sustain a group. Each act is seen online by the entire group and perpetuates a norm of inclusionary mutual supportiveness in the organization or community (Rheingold, 1993).

Social processes can make loosely bounded networks develop tighter boundaries. Computer networks can integrate new workers into communication channels and culture and increase commitment (although an initial period of physical proximity may be necessary to build trust and consensus). Such networks have knit dispersed professionals, technicians, administrators, or sales personnel into "highly cohesive and highly cooperative ... groups, ... geographically dispersed yet coordinated" (Carley & Wendt, 1991, p. 407; see also Eveland & Bikson, 1988; Rice & Steinfield, 1994; Sproull & Kiesler, 1991; Steinfield, 1986; Walsh & Bayma, chap. 18, this volume). Researchers at different locations rarely coauthored papers before the advent of email (Galegher, Kraut, & Egido, 1990).

Computer networks often blur or shift the boundaries of work groups, organizations, and communities. They aid organizations to develop work teams that span unit boundaries, they facilitate interorganizational coordination of joint projects, and they easily link buyers and sellers in different organizations. They help people to maintain a stockpile of potentially useful contacts outside of their work group, organization, or community that can provide information, instrumental aid, and emotional support. For example, more than half of the email messages in one organization were from unknown people, different buildings, or people external to the work group or the chain of command (Finholt & Sproull, 1990; Sproull & Kiesler, 1991).

The Internet is an extreme example of an unbounded network. Its population boundary approaches infinity and is so in flux that it cannot be analyzed at any one time. Although it is inherently impossible to map all Internet relationships (or Web site hyperlinks), ego-centered analyses can trace the nature of the connections of a sample of Internet users. Another way to study the Internet (and other unbounded networks) is to trace flows of resources. For example, we are currently replicating Milgram's "small-world" study (1967) by asking randomly selected Internet users to try to contact a target person whom they may or may not know. If they do not know the person, they are asked to forward our message to someone in their social network and also copy the message to us. This is enabling us to trace the flow of messages through the Internet, seeing how close two nodes are to each other in terms of the links needed to connect them (Dantowitz & Wellman, 1996; see also Schwartz & Wood, 1993).

Range

Social Networks. The range of a network describes how large and diverse is the population within its boundaries.[6] With larger size comes the population basis for more heterogeneity in the social characteristics of network members (Wellman & Potter, 1996) and more complexity in the structural patterning of ties in networks. Dense, bounded networks almost always have a small range because a large network becomes unbounded relatively quickly. As the number of network members increases the population basis for more diversity within the network increases. Moreover, as the number of network members increases arithmetically, the number of connections required to sustain full connectivity increases geometrically.

Where dense, tight networks with small range are good for conserving existing resources, sparse, unbounded networks with a large range are good for obtaining additional resources. They provide the number of network members and the diversity for people to obtain a wide range of resources. Such large and heterogeneous networks tend to be structurally complex.

---

[6]*Range* is a combination of network size and heterogeneity that together indicate how many different kinds of people are in a network (Burt, 1983). Unlike network density, there is no standard definition of range. In a recent study (Wellman & Potter, in press), our research group measured it by first separately calculating network size (a simple count) and network heterogeneity. Network heterogeneity itself is a complex measure that we calculated by averaging standardized heterogeneity on both (a) continuous variables such as years of education that were measured by standard deviation, and (b) categorical variables, such as role type (kin, friend, etc.) which was measured by Schuessler's Index of Qualitative Variation (Mueller, Schuessler, & Costner, 1970). After factor analysis showed range to be a single factor encompassing both network size and network heterogeneity, we calculated a single combined measure from standardized size and heterogeneity.

Instead of a uniform distribution of relationships (as in densely knit networks), ties in networks with a large range tend to form clusters that only a few ties bridge (Granovetter, 1973). Hence, resources (such as information) tend to flow unevenly through these networks and the network members whose ties are bridges tend to accrue both power and suspicion as gatekeepers to other clusters. Espinoza's (in press) study of Santiago, Chile, barrios is a good example of the strengths and limits of networks with low range. The small, homogeneous networks of kin and neighbors are excellent in providing mutual aid but of little use in getting employment outside of the neighborhood.

Computer Networks. Computer networks increase the range of social networks, facilitating more relationships and a wider range of relationships. The asynchronous nature and distance-free cost structure of computer networks transcends spatial limits, thereby allowing people to communicate over different time zones and enabling more active contact in otherwise latent relationships. People can greatly extend the number and diversity of their social contacts when they become members of computerized conferences or broadcast information through distribution lists. Computer networks enable people to maintain a larger number of ties online than they probably could face-to-face. Computerized conferences and distribution lists provide permeable, shifting sets of members, with more intense relationships continued by private email. The resulting expansion of the size and proximity of one's online "communication audience" can increase the diversity of people encountered (Lea & Spears 1995). For example, four fifths of the email of one large, physically dispersed organization were from electronic groups and not individuals (Finholt & Sproull, 1990; Sproull & Kiesler, 1991). In another organization, an online work team formed more subcommittees than an offline team and was better able to involve its members in its activities (Bikson & Eveland, 1990).

The relative lack of social presence online fosters relationships with people who have more diverse social characteristics than might normally be encountered in person. It also gives participants more control over the timing and content of their self-disclosures (Walther, in press). Often, the only thing known about others are their signatures, which may provide minimal or misleading information (Slouka, 1995). This allows relationships to develop on the basis of shared interests rather than to be stunted at the onset by differences in social status (Hiltz & Turoff, 1993). In the absence of social and physical cues, people are able to get to know each online from their communication exchanges and decide later to broaden the relationship or expand it offline to the telephone or inperson meetings (King, 1994). It is possible that allegiance to computerized communities of shared interest may become more powerful than allegiance to one's physical neighborhood, for one study has found strong commitment to online groups that were perceived to be long-lasting (Walther, 1994).

Thus many computer-supported social networks are a continuation of the long-term shift to communities and work groups that are organized by mutual interests rather than by shared neighborhood or work site (Fischer, 1984; Wellman & Leighton, 1979). The lack of online cues about social status promotes socially heterogeneous connections across hierarchical or other forms of status barriers (Eveland & Bikson, 1988; Sproull & Kiesler, 1991). (However, it can also encourage the formation of networks that are culturally homogeneous because they are composed of people sharing similar concerns and values [Lea & Spears, 1992]). The relatively egalitarian nature of online contact can be empowering for those with disenfranchised social categories because there is little overt communication about one's gender, age, race, ethnicity, lifestyle, socioeconomic status, organizational position, or membership in cliques (Culnan & Markus, 1987; Hiltz & Turoff, 1993). However, participation online changes once people know the social characteristics of others (Weisband, Schneider, & Connolly, 1995). Consider the experience of "Amy" in Douglas Coupland's (1995) novel, *Microserfs*: "Reveal your gender on the Net, and you're toast" (p. 334; see also Herring, 1996; Shade, 1994).

Exclusivity[7]

Social Networks.   Do people interact primarily one-on-one or are their individual contacts available to a wider set of persons? The control that coworkers and community members have over access to each other can vary between little control/high access in dense, bounded groups to high control/low access in sparse, unbounded networks. In addition to variation in discretion over contact with network members, there can also be variation circumstances under which people can be interrupted (privacy) and or others can have access to their work (e.g., control over files).

Dense, bounded groups tend to be in situations where there is relatively little choice of network members, and little control over access and interactions. Common examples are kinship groups, isolated villages, and focused work teams where people are expected to work with whom they are assigned and to find community with their neighbours. Members of such groups share their activities with all others in the group, and many discussions and interactions are observed by all without any normative claims to privacy. One classic account is of the "bank wiring room workers" in a Western Electric plant who ensured that potential "ratebusters" did not work so hard as to drive up production norms (Roethlisberger & Dickson, 1939). By contrast, sparse, unbounded networks afford people more discretion in the persons, places, and times of their interactions. Such networks frequently have more physical barriers to access and interaction. Many

---

[7]I thank Marilyn Mantei for suggesting this term.

sparsely knit workers occupy private offices where entry is only by invitation, and it is rare for a North American to go bounding into another's home without a previous invitation and a knock on the door (Michelson, 1976). Because of the difficulty of coordinating sparse networks, interactions are more apt to be one-on-one, and much information tends to be privately held within a dyad or selectively shared with sparsely knit sets of similarly minded network members.

Computer Networks. Computer networks can be constructed to support either dense, bounded groups or sparse, unbounded social networks. For example, the Cavecat and Telepresence systems designed software that made sounds simulating knocking at a door when someone wanted to videoconference with another (Mantei et al., 1991; Buxton, 1991). At the other end, participants in this system could set their "door states" to allow a video connection to be made without knocking (door icon set to wide open), with knocking (door icon ajar), or not at all (door icon closed). It would have been even easier to design software in which no knocking was needed, thereby providing the immediate access that is common in dense, bounded groups. With respect to messages, many computer networks within organizations allow people to learn who has read the relevant messages whereas at least one software scheme also structures requests for responses and taking actions (Winograd, 1988). By contrast, although the Internet (like the telephone system) technically allows all to send messages to all, software filters (as well as human assistants) can screen out unwanted messages.

At a more macroscopic scale, the proliferation of computer-supported social networks both extends and counteracts the contemporary shift away from dense, bounded groups and to sparse, unbounded networks. To some extent, by confining people to their computer screens, computer-mediated communication has intensified privatized, exclusive relationships by turning people away from face-to-face relationships in public. Yet it is the highly privatized watching of television screens that is the modal leisure activity in the Western world. Hence computer-mediated communication may actually be enhancing community because computer networks support public computerized conferences as well as private email exchanges. Because all members of computerized conferences can read all messages—just as when a group talks in a café or an open office—groups of people can talk to each other casually and get to know the friends of their friends. "The keyboard is my café," said William Mitchell (1995, p. 7).

Social Control

Social Networks. How do external sources create, constrain, and manage a person's contacts and exchanges? At work, people may be embedded in flat, matrix, or tree-hierarchical organizations. Their community life may be subject to extensive social control by peers and influentials, or they may be able to maneuver among multiple, partial communities and keep their involvement in each community secret from the other networks in which they are involved. Controls for managing normative social behavior in dense, bounded groups are usually enforced by group pressure, work supervisors, and community influentials to ensure that participants work together for clearly defined collective goals.

There is less social control in sparse, unbounded networks because of their weak interconnectivity. The greater fragmentation of these networks means that people can avoid portions of the network where they are unwanted. No single supervisor or influential exists, and contact with higher status people is often weak and infrequent. Rather than being an externally disciplined corporate army, internalized norms and standardized organizational procedures control loosely coupled workers and community members (Abbott, 1988; Suttles, 1968). For example, in the "Blue" organization, the flow of communication through complex social networks creates discipline: organizing work processes and ensuring that tasks are completed (Wellman, Salaff, Dimitrova, Garton, & Haythornthwaite, 1994).

Computer Networks.   There is an inherent tension between management's desire to maintain control and those attributes of email that weaken network boundaries. Managers of sparse, bounded work units worry that they will lose control over information and work practices if they set up email systems, connect within-organization "intranets" to the outside world of the Internet, and allow workers to chat privately online. They fear that computer networks will threaten control as the networks accelerate the flow of (mis)information, including rumors, complaints, jokes, and subversive communications (Finholt & Sproull, 1990; Zuboff, 1984). Even when organizations explicitly encourage informal email, managers often view it with distrust. Hence system administrators may monitor online activities and read email and files. In one organization, network administrators promoted the "appropriate" use of the computer network and admonished those who used it for recreational or nonorganizational purposes (Orlikowski, Yates, Okamura, & Fujimoto, 1995). As such behavior can alienate workers who value their autonomy and have alternative job prospects, a tacit norm has developed that email is private unless access to online files is needed when a worker is seriously ill, out of communication, or suspected of illicit work behavior (Sipior & Ward, 1995).

Yet email itself can be used to extend managerial control, a practice revealed in its negation when some workers in an outlying branch never turned on a multimedia communication system that would have facilitated the central office's awareness of them (Wellman et al., 1994). However, Sproull and Kiesler (1991) suggested that attempts to use computer-supported social networks to strengthen central control may lead to organizational conflict. They forecasted that management practices may change to sparse, unbounded networks where "people work in multiple groups, when groups are composed of members who collaborate only electronically, and when soft structures emerge without management directive" (p. 160). Moreover, the limited social presence of computer-mediated communication is conducive to the kinds of uninhibited remarks, nonconforming behavior and diverse opinions that are characteristic of sparse, unbounded networks (Hiltz et al., 1978; Siegel, Dubrovsky, Kiesler, & McGuire, 1986; Sproull & Kiesler, 1991; Lea & Spears, 1992; Walther, Anderson, & Park, 1994).[8]

The sparse, unbounded nature of the Internet means that people unhappy with one interaction can maneuver between different computerized conferences and private e-relationships. They might maintain a dignified persona in several milieus and be a ferocious "flamer" (sending abusive email), "spammer" (sending junk email to many groups), or "cyberpunk" in others. When people belong to multiple social networks, no one network has exclusive control over them. The narrow focus of computerized conferences allows people to take risks in specialized relationships that may only exist in a single, partial, online social network. Some computer-supported social networks allow people to be anonymous or to use nicknames when they want to speak freely or try on different personas. The practice allows the maintenance of public communication networks while maintaining privacy (and protecting participants for retribution). It is more prevalent among virtual communities, although it also has some advantages for the free flow of ideas in work situations (Bechar-Israeli, 1995; Hiltz & Turoff, 1993).

Strength of Relationships

Social Networks.   The strength of relationships is a multidimensional construct encompassing the usually correlated variables of a relationship's social closeness, voluntariness, "multiplexity" (breadth), and to a lesser extent, frequency of contact (Granovetter, 1982; Wellman & Wortley, 1990).[9]

---

[8]These two paragraphs are based on a review by Laura Garton.

[9]The term *strong ties* was coined by Mark Granovetter (1973) in a classic essay comparing them to *weak ties* at the opposite end of the continuum. Granovetter thought that strong ties were some combination of intimacy (or socially close), voluntariness, multiplexity (interacting in a variety of contexts; i.e., multiple role relationships), and frequent contact. However, our group's studies of Torontonians' personal communities found that only intimacy, voluntariness, and multiplexity were so closely associated as to be usable in a combined *tie strength* measure (Wellman & Wortley, 1990). Frequency of contact was separate because people frequently saw neighbors or coworkers with whom they were not intimate and whom they would not voluntarily seek out. As yet, there is no standard measure of tie strength; analysts tend to use some combination of the variables discussed earlier.

Strong ties tend to provide more social support than weak ties: emotional aid, goods and services, companionship, and a sense of belonging. They also provide a wider variety of such social resources (Wellman, 1992). But weak ties are not useless. Their very weakness means that they tend to connect people who are more socially dissimilar than those connected through strong ties. Consequently, weak ties tend to link people to other social worlds, providing new sources of information and other resources (Granovetter, 1982, 1995).

In dense, bounded groups, relationships tend, somewhat paradoxically, to be both involuntary and socially close. Involuntary groups such as isolated villages and corporately formed work groups exist because the situation fosters the tie and not because people choose to be together. Yet the high frequency of contact in these groups and the wide range of activities that group members do together create socially close intimacy, whether the participants like it or not.

By contrast, relationships are more likely to be entered into voluntarily in sparse, unbounded networks whose participants have come together on the basis of a common interest or mutual advantage. Most friendship relationships are like this, but so too are work relationships when, for example, professionals have some discretion about whom they consult or managers are able to ask volunteers to join a work team. Such discretion has some costs because each tie must be maintained separately whereas the stronger social controls of dense, bounded groups do much of the work of maintaining ties. Because each tie operates separately, ties in sparse, unbounded networks tend to be more variable than those in dense, bounded networks in terms of what network members do together, how supportive they are, and how frequently they are in contact.

Computer Networks. Can the medium support the message? Research is showing that despite the more limited social presence of computer-mediated communication, online relationships are often strong with frequent, supportive, and companionable contact (Sproull & Kiesler, 1991). They are voluntary relationships in all virtual communities and many work situations. The ease and placelessness of email contact facilitates frequent and long-term contact, without the loss of the tie that so often accompanies geographical mobility.

If email were solely a means of information exchange, then online relationships would only be narrowly specialized rather than be broadly multiplex. Yet those who communicate online maintain a variety of links, encompassing information exchange, companionship, emotional aid, arranging services, and providing a sense of belonging (Hiltz, Johnson & Turoff, 1986; Walther, 1994). For example, although the majority of elderly users of "SeniorNet" reported joining the Net to gain access to information, nearly half had also joined to find companionship and the most popular activity was chatting with others (Furlong, 1989). Another online conference, "Systers," was originally designed for the exchange of information among female computer scientists but turned into a forum for networking and exchanging support (Sproull & Faraj, chap. 2, this volume). The members of a university computer science laboratory use email extensively for emotional support. As much of their time is spent online, it is natural for them to use email to communicate these problems to confidants. Moreover, when these confidants receive an online message of distress, it is easy for them to use the network for support (Haythornthwaite et al., 1995).

Although computer-supported social networks do sustain broadly multiplex relationships, they are particularly suited for fostering specialized relationships. The Internet encourages specialized relationships because it supports a market approach to finding social resources through online relationships. With more ease than in almost all situations, people can surf Internet email, newsgroups, and search the Web for resources within the safety and comfort of their homes or offices and with reduced search and travel time. Participants can browse through specialized conferences on the Internet and commercial services before deciding to join a discussion (Bechar-Israeli, 1995). Relationships in these conferences are often narrowly defined, although the inclusion of email addresses in most messages provides the basis for more multiplex relationships to develop.

Are such online relationships socially close enough to be strong ties? Some concerns about whether online communication can sustain strong ties are wrongly specified because both enthusiasts and critics tend to speak of relationships as functioning only online. Their technological fixation leads them to ignore the abundant accounts of community and work ties that operate offline as well as online, with email being just one of several ways to communicate. Much online contact is between people who see each other in person at work or in the community. As with the telephone and the fax, the lower social presence of email can maintain strong ties between persons who originally met face-to-face. Email exchanges intersect with inperson meetings, filling in gaps and making arrangements for future get-togethers. Conversations started on one medium may continue on others. In one organization, office employees communicate by email while they physically work side-by-side. This allows them to chat while giving the appearance of working at their computers (Eveland & Bikson, 1988; Finholt & Sproull, 1990; Garton, 1995; Haythornthwaite et al., 1995; Hiltz & Turoff, 1993).

Can relationships be strong if they are only sustained online? Some analysts have argued that the comparatively low social presence of computer-mediated communication cannot by itself sustain strong ties because of the lack of physical and social cues and immediate feedback. Others have contended that computer-mediated communication is rich enough to sustain intimacy (see the reviews in Garton & Wellman, 1995; Sproull & Kiesler, 1991). Indeed, there are many stories of high involvement in online relationships, at times to the sacrifice of real-life domestic relationships (Hiltz &

Turoff, 1993; Barlow, 1995; Rheingold, 1993; Kling, 1995). For example, some participants of a computerized conference came to feel that their closest friends were members of this online group, whom they seldom or never saw in person (Hiltz & Turoff, 1993).

Many online ties probably are "intimate secondary relationships": moderately strong, informal, frequent, and supportive ties that operate in only one specialized domain (Wireman, 1984). Over time, some of these relationships may become more personal and intimate. Perhaps the limited social presence and asynchronicity of computer-mediated communication only slows the development of strong ties, with online interactions eventually developing to be as sociable and intimate as in person ones (Walther, 1995).

COMPUTER-SUPPORTED SOCIAL NETWORKS: A RESEARCH SHOPPING LIST

There are more types of networks on the ether or earth than those who talk only of "groupware" have dreamed of. But does the computer-supported proliferation of unbounded, specialized networks portend the end of Western civilization as we know it? Many of those fearful that virtual community is not "real" community and that computer-supported cooperative work will create alienated workers are confusing the pastoralist myth of community and work for the present reality. Community ties are already geographically dispersed, sparsely knit, specialized in content, and connected heavily by telecommunications (phone and fax). Although virtual communities may carry these trends a bit further, they also sustain in person encounters between community members.

Work is also becoming less of a group activity and more of a network phenomenon, as the shift from manufacturing to information services lessens the importance of colocation. Many workers are involved in multiple work teams rather than solidary groups, and they are as apt to work with colleagues across the country as with those in the next seat. It is the computerized flow of information that drives their work and not the office clerk handing out the day's "snail mail."

It is clear that computer networks support sparse, unbounded networks as well—or sometimes better—than dense, bounded groups. Yet the early state of systematic research into computer-supported social networks has raised more questions than even first-approximation answers. There are too many arguments by assertion and anecdote in this literature, and too much research that ignores the social context in which online communication takes place. The subject is important: practically, scholarly, and politically. The answers have not yet been found. Indeed, the questions are just starting to be formulated. Here is a preliminary list of some basic questions to put on research agendas:

Modality

1. What are the modalities of using the Net? To what extent do people use private email, group email, distribution lists, or USENET newsgroups? How do these different modalities link together in people's practices? To what extent do they connect with uses of Web sites, such as personal home pages, hyperlinks to others, and accessible online documents?

2. To what extent are online relationships and virtual communities free-standing or integrated into other modes of communication, such as inperson get-togethers, telephone calls, or written communications?

Density

3. What is the structure of virtual communities and computer-supported cooperative work teams? How densely knit are they? Do cliques and clusters tend to form, and if so, on what principles?

Boundedness

4. Is there a natural history to online relationships? How do they get founded, maintained, transformed, or die?

5. How many people are using the Internet? (This is a question that is difficult to answer precisely because the Internet is actually a "network of networks," so that a two-tiered census would have to be taken of nodes and persons.) What are the social characteristics of participants?

6. How interconnected is the online world? How many online steps would it take to connect any two network members (an updating of the "small world" question originally asked by Milgram, 1967)? How many online steps would it take to connect the entire world (a question originally studied offline by Rapoport, 1957)?

Scale

7. What is the composition of people's personal networks online in terms of the similarity of their social characteristics?

8. To what extent are online relationships based on shared interests, similar social characteristics, or the sheer need for frequent communication (as between two neighbors or coworkers)?

9. Are people with socially disadvantaging characteristics (such as women, visible minorities, shut-ins, residents of the countryside, and the poorly educated) more or less empowered through online networks? What is the extent of their membership in computer-supported social networks? If they are members, what is the extent of their involvement?

Exclusivity

10. Can computer-supported social networks form the basis for political mobilization on a nonterritorial, shared interest basis? Can such networks supply empowering information and is it possible to build teledemocratic community forums online to sustain civic life? (See the discussions in Johnson-Lenz & Johnson-Lenz, 1993; Hiltz & Turoff, 1993; Ogden, 1994.) Will existing structures of power be open to such challenges?

11. Under what circumstances will private email exchanges at work and in the community become overshadowed by more public forums such as computerized conferences?

12. Will surveillance agencies develop easy means of monitoring online exchanges, automating them to overcome their presence reliance on labor-intensive procedures? If successful, will such surveillance engender movement away from online relationships for sensitive matters?

Social Control

13. How has the proliferation of computer-supported cooperative work changed the broader structure of organizations heavily involved with it?

14. What is the prevalence of deviant behavior online, such as harassment or hacking? What kinds are actually prevalent?

Strength of Ties

15. What is the composition of people's personal networks online in terms of the strength of their relationships?

16. How durable are online relationships? How much turnover is there in virtual communities? How does the distribution of involvement in virtual communities and computer-supported cooperative work teams compare with involvement offline?

17. How prevalent is active membership in multiple virtual communities and work teams? Do there tend to be some patterns in these memberships, such as maintaining a balance between instrumental and affective involvements?

18. What is the content of online relationships in terms of supplying companionship, information, and various types of instrumental and affective support?

ACKNOWLEDGMENTS

Laura Garton, Caroline Haythornthwaite, Sara Kiesler, and Marilyn Mantei gave me excellent substantive and editorial advice in the preparation of this chapter. I have also benefited from the stimulating ongoing comments of other members of our research group studying computer-supported social networks: Janet Salaff, Dimitrina Dimitrova, Milena Gulia, and Emmanuel Koku. Our research has been supported by the Social Science and Humanities Research Council of Canada, Bell Canada, and the Information Technology Research Centre. This chapter is dedicated to Philip J. Stone III, who first put me online in 1965.

REFERENCES

Abbott, A. (1988). *The system of professions: An essay on the division of expert labor.* Chicago: University of Chicago Press.

Barlow, J. P. (1995, March–April). Is there a there in cyberspace? *Utne Reader*, pp. 50–56.

Barlow, J. P., Birkets, S., Kelly, K., & Slouka, M. (1995, August). What are we doing on-line. *Harper's*, pp. 35–46.

Bechar-Israeli, H. (1995). From <Bonehead> to <cLonehEad>: Nicknames, play and identity on Internet relay chat. *Journal of Computer-Mediated Communication, 1*(2), On-line URL: http//www.usc.edu/dept/annenberg/vol1/issue2.

Berkowitz, S. D. (1982). *An introduction to structural analysis: The network approach to social research.* Toronto: Butterworth.

Bikson, T., & Eveland, J. D. (1990). The interplay of work group structures and computer support. In J. Galegher, R. Kraut, & C. Egido (Eds.), *Intellectual teamwork: social and technological foundations of cooperative work* (pp. 245–290). Hillsdale, NJ: Lawrence Erlbaum Associates.

Borgatti, S., Everett, M., & Freeman, L. (1994). *UCINet 4.* Columbia, SC: Analytic Technologies.

Bott, E. (1971). *Family and social network.* London: Tavistock.

Breiger, R. (1974). The duality of persons and groups. *Social Forces, 53,* 181–190.

Bristor, J. (1987). *Buying networks: A model of positional influence in organizational buying.* Unpublished doctoral dissertation, School of Business, University of Michigan, Ann Arbor.

Burt, R. (1991). *Structure 4.2.* New York: Columbia University, Center for the Social Sciences.

Burt, R. (1992). *Structural holes.* Chicago: University of Chicago Press.

Burt, R. (1983). Range. In R. Burt & M. Minor (Eds.), *Applied network analysis* (pp. 176–194). Beverly Hills, CA: Sage.

Buxton, B. (1991, October). *Telepresence: Integrating shared task and personal spaces.* Paper presented at the Groupware '91 Conference, Amsterdam.

Carley, K. (1990). Structural constraints on communication: The diffusion of the homophoric signal analysis technique through scientific fields. *Journal of Mathematical Sociology, 15*(3–4), 207–246.

Carley, K., & Wendt, K. (1991). Electronic mail and scientific communication. *Knowledge, 12*(4), 406–440.

Coupland, D. (1995). *Microserfs.* New York: Harper Collins.

Craven, P., & Wellman, B. (1973). The network city. *Sociological Inquiry, 43,* 57-88.

Culnan, M. J., & Markus, M. L. (1987). Information technologies. In F. Jablin, L. L. Putnam, K. Roberts, & L. Porter (Eds.), *Handbook of organizational communication* (pp. 420–443). Newbury Park, CA: Sage.

Danet, B., Wachenhauser, T., Bechar-Israeli, H., Cividalli, A., & Rosenbaum -Tamari, Y. (1995). Curtain Time 20:00 GMT: Experiments in Virtual Theater on Internet Relay Chat. *Journal of Computer Mediated Communication, 1*(2), On-line URL: http//www.usc.edu/dept/annenberg/vol1/issue2.

Dantowitz, A., & Wellman, B. (1996, June). *The small world of the Internet.* Paper presented at the meeting of the Canadian Sociology and Anthropology Association, St. Catherines, Ontario.

Dorsey, D. (1994). *The force.* New York: Ballantine.

Espinoza, V. (in press). Social networks among the urban poor: Inequality and integration in a Latin American city. In B. Wellman (Ed.), *Networks in the global village.* Boulder, CO: Westwood.

Eveland, J. D., & Bikson, T. (1988). Work group structures and computer support. *ACM Transactions on Office Information Systems, 6,* 354–379.

Finholt, T., & Sproull, L. S. (1990). Electronic groups at work. *Organization Science, 1*(1), 41–64.

Finholt, T., Sproull, L., & Kiesler, S. (1990). Communication and performance in ad hoc task groups. In J. Galegher, R. Kraut, & C. Egido (Eds.), *Intellectual teamwork: Social and technological foundations of cooperative work* (pp. 291–325). Hillsdale, NJ: Lawrence Erlbaum Associates.

Fischer, C. (1984). *The urban experience.* Orlando, FL: Harcourt Brace Jovanovich.

Furlong, M. S. (1989). An electronic community for older adults: The SeniorNet network. *Journal of Communication, 39*(3), 145–153.

Galegher, J., Kraut, R., & Egido, C. (Eds.). (1990). *Intellectual teamwork: Social and technological foundations of cooperative work.* Hillsdale, NJ: Lawrence Erlbaum Associates.

Garton, L. (1995). *An empirical analysis of desktop videoconferencing and other media in a spatially-distributed work group.* Laval, Quebec, Canada: Centre for Information Technology Innovation.

Garton, L., & Wellman, B. (1995). Social impacts of electronic mail in organizations: A review of the research literature. *Communication yearbook, 18,* 434–453.

Granovetter, M. (1973). The strength of weak ties. *American Journal of Sociology, 78,* 1360–1380.

Granovetter, M. (1982). The strength of weak ties: A network theory revisited. In P. Marsden & N. Lin (Eds.), *Social structure and network analysis* (pp. 105–130). Beverly Hills, CA: Sage.

Granovetter, M. (1995). *Getting a job: A study of contacts and careers.* Chicago: University of Chicago Press.

Haythornthwaite, C., & Wellman, B. (1996a). *Transforming ego-centered network data to whole network data.* Toronto: University of Toronto, Centre for Urban and Community Studies.

Haythornthwaite, C., & Wellman, B. (1996b). *Which kinds of network members communicate by email or face-to-face for what kinds of work?* Toronto: University of Toronto, Centre for Urban and Community Studies.

Haythornthwaite, C., Wellman, B., & Mantei, M. (1995). Work relationships and media use: A social network analysis. *Group Decision and Negotiation, 4*(3), 193–211.

Herring, S. (1996). Gender and democracy in computer-mediated communication. In R. Kling (Ed.), *Computerization and controversy* (2nd ed., pp. 476–489). San Diego: Academic Press.

Hiltz, S. R., Johnson, K., & Agle, G. (1978). *Replicating Bales problem solving experiments on a computerized conference: A pilot study* (Research Rep. No. 8). Computerized Conferencing and Communications Center, New Jersey Institute of Technology, Newark.

Hiltz, S. R., Johnson, K., & Turoff, M. (1986). Experiments in group decision making: Communication process and outcome in face-to-face versus computerized conferences. *Human Communication Research, 13*(2), 225–252.

Hiltz, S. R., & Turoff, M. (1993). *The network nation.* (2nd ed.). Cambridge, MA: MIT Press.

Johnson-Lenz, P., & Johnson-Lenz, T. (1993, December). Community brain–mind: groupware tools for healthy civic life. Paper presented at the Healthy Communities Networking Summit, San Francisco.

Kaufer, D., & Carley, K. (1993). *Communication at a distance: The influence of print on sociocultural organization and change.* Hillsdale, NJ: Lawrence Erlbaum Associates.

Kidder, T. (1981). *The soul of a new machine.* Boston: Little, Brown.

King, S. (1994). Analysis of electronic support groups for recovering addicts. *Interpersonal Computing and Technology, 2*(3), 47–56.

Kling, R. (1995). *Social relationships in electronic forums: Hangouts, salons, workplaces and communities.* Irvine: University of California, Department of Information and Computer Science and Public Policy Research Organization.

Kling, R., & Jewett, T. (1994). The social design of worklife with computers and networks: An open natural systems perspective. *Advances in Computers, 39,* 239–293.

Kollock, P., & Smith, M. A. (in press). Managing the virtual commons: Cooperation and conflict in computer communities. In S. Herring (Ed.), *Computer-mediated communication.* Amsterdam: John Benjamins.

Latané, B., & Darley, J. (1976). *Help in a crisis: Bystander response to an emergency.* Morristown, NJ: General Learning Press.

Laumann, E., Gagnon, J., Michael, R., & Michaels, S. (1994). *The social organization of sexuality: Sexual practices in the United States.* Chicago: University of Chicago Press.

Laumann, E., Marsden, P., & Prensky, D. (1983). The boundary specification problem in network analysis. In R. Burt & M. Minor (Eds.), *Applied network analysis* (pp. 18–34). Beverly Hills, CA: Sage.

Lea, M., & Spears, R. (1992). Paralanguage and social perception in computer-mediated communication. *Journal of Organizational Computing, 2*(3–4), 321–341.

Lea, M., & Spears, R. (1995). Love at first byte? Building personal relationships over computer networks. In J. T. Wood & S. Duck (Eds.), *Understudied relationships: Off the beaten track* (pp. 197–233). Thousand Oaks, CA: Sage.

Levine, J. (1986). *Levine's atlas of world corporate interlocks.* Hanover, NH: Worldnet.

Mantei, M., Baecker, R., Sellen, A., Buxton, W., Milligan, T., & Wellman, B. (1991, April–May). *Experiences in the Use of a Media Space.* Paper presented at the CHI '91 Conference, New Orleans.

Mantei, M., & Wellman, B. (1995). *From groupware to netware: Implications for CSCW design.* Toronto: University of Toronto, Departments of Computer Science and Sociology.

McLuhan, M. (1962). *The Gutenberg galaxy: The making of typographic man.* Toronto: University of Toronto Press.

Michelson, W. (1976). *Man and his urban environment.* (2nd ed.). Boston: Addison-Wesley.

Milgram, S. (1967). The small-world problem. *Psychology Today, 1,* 62–67.

Mintz, B., & Schwartz, M. (1985). *The power structure of american business.* Chicago: University of Chicago Press.

Mitchell, W. (1995). *City of bits: Space, time and the infobahn.* Cambridge, MA: MIT Press.

Mueller, J., Schuessler, K., & Costner, H. (1970). *Statistical Reasoning in Sociology.* Boston: Houghton Mifflin.

Nisbet, R. (1962). *Community and power.* New York: Oxford University Press.

Nohria, N., & Eccles, R. G. (Eds.), (1992). *Networks and organizations.* Boston: Harvard Business School Press.

Ogden, M. (1994). Politics in a parallel universe: Is there a future for cyberdemocracy? *Futures, 26*(7), 713–729.

Orlikowski, W. J., Yates, J., Okamura, K., & Fujimoto, M. (1995). Shaping electronic communication: The metastructuring of technology in the context of use. *Organization Science, 6*(4), 423–444.

Patton, P. (1986). *Open road.* New York: Simon & Schuster.

Rapoport, A. (1957). Contribution to the theory of random and biased net. *Bulletin of Mathematical Biology, 19,* 257–277.

Rheingold, H. (1993). *The virtual community: Homesteading on the electronic frontier.* Reading, MA: Addison-Wesley.

Rice, R., & Steinfeld, C. (1994). Experiences with new forms of organizational communication via electronic mail and voice messaging. In J. E. Andriessen & R. Roe (Eds.), *Telematics and work* (pp. 109–136). East Sussex, England: Lawrence Erlbaum Associates.

Richards, W. (1994). *Multinet*. Burnaby, BC, Canada: Simon Fraser University, Department of Communication Studies.

Roethlisberger, F., & Dickson, W. J. (1939). *Management and the worker*. Cambridge, MA: Harvard University Press.

Salaff, J., Fong, E., & Wong, S. L. (in press). Using social networks to exit Hong Kong. In B. Wellman (Ed.), *Networks in the Global Village*. Boulder, CO: Westview.

Schwartz, M., & Wood, D. C. M. (1993). Discovering shared interests among people using graph analysis of global electronic mail traffic. *Communications of the ACM, 36*, 76–89 .

Scott, J. (1991). *Social network analysis*. London: Sage.

Shade, L. R. (1994). Is sisterhood virtual? Women on the electronic frontier. *Transactions of the Royal Society Canada*, (Series VI), *5*, 131–142.

Shrum, W. (1990). Status incongruence among boundary spanners: Structure, exchange, and conflict. *American Sociological Review, 55*, 496–511.

Siegel, J., Dubrovsky, V., Kiesler, S., & McGuire, T. W. (1986). Group processes in computer-mediated communication. *Organizational Behaviour and Human Decision Processes, 37*, 157–187.

Sipior, J., & Ward, B. (1995). The ethical and legal quandary of email privacy. *Communications of the ACM, 38*(12), 48–54.

Slouka, M. (1995). *War of the worlds: Cyberspace and the high-tech assault on reality*. New York: Basic Books.

Sprenger, C. J. A., & Stokman, F. (1995). *Gradap 2*. Groningen, The Netherlands: ProGamma.

Sproull, L., & Kiesler, S. (1991). *Connections*. Cambridge, MA: MIT Press.

Star, S. L. (1993). Cooperation without consensus in scientific problem solving: Dynamics of closure in open systems. In S. Easterbrook (Ed.), *CSCW: Cooperation or conflict* (pp. 93–106). Berlin: Springer-Verlag.

Steinfield, C. (1986). Computer-mediated communication in an organizational setting: Explaining task-related and socio-emotional uses. *Communication Yearbook, 9*, 777–804.

Stoll, C. (1995). *Silicon snake oil: Second thoughts on the information highway*. New York: Doubleday.

Suttles, G. (1968). *The social order of the slum*. Chicago: University of Chicago Press.

Thompson, J. (1967). *Organizations in action*. New York: McGraw-Hill.

Tilly, C. (1984). *Big structures, large processes, huge comparisons*. New York: Russell Sage Foundation.

Walther, J. B. (1994). Anticipated ongoing interaction versus channel effects on relational communication in computer-mediated interaction. *Human Communication Research, 20*(4), 473–501.

Walther, J. B. (1995). Relational aspects of computer-mediated communication: Experimental observations over time. *Organization Science, 6*, 186–203.

Walther, J. B., Anderson, J. F., & Park, D. W. (1994). Interpersonal effects in computer-mediated interaction: A meta-analysis of social and antisocial communication. *Communication Research, 21*(4), 460–487.

Wasserman, S., & Faust, K. (1993). *Social network analysis: Methods and applications*. Cambridge, England: Cambridge University Press.

Weick, K. (1976). Educational organizations as loosely coupled systems. *Administrative Science Quarterly, 21*, 1–19.

Weisband, S. P., Schneider, S. K., & Connolly, T. (1995). Computer-mediated communication and social information: Status salience and status difference. *Academy of Management Journal, 38*(4), 1124–1151.

Wellman, B. (1988a). The community question re-evaluated. In M. P. Smith (Ed.), *Power, community and the city* (pp. 81–107). New Brunswick, NJ: Transaction Books.

Wellman, B. (1988b). Structural analysis: From method and metaphor to theory and substance. In B. Wellman & S. Berkowitz (Eds.), *Social structures: A network approach*, (pp. 19–61). Cambridge, England: Cambridge University Press.

Wellman, B. (1992). Which types of ties and networks give what kinds of social support? *Advances in Group Processes, 9*, 207–235.

Wellman, B. (1993). An egocentric network tale. *Social Networks, 17*(2), 423–436.

Wellman, B. (1994). I was a teenage network analyst: The route from the bronx to the information highway. *Connections, 17*(2), 28–45.

Wellman, B., Salaff, J., Dimitrova, D., Garton, L., Gulia, M., & Haythornthwaite, C. (1996). Computer networks as social networks: Collaborative work, telework, and virtual community. *Annual Review of Sociology, 22*, 213–238.

Wellman, B., Carrington, P., & Hall, A. (1988). In B. Wellman & S. D. Berkowitz (Eds.), *Social structures: A network approach*, (pp. 130–184). Cambridge, England: Cambridge University Press.

Wellman, B., & Gulia, M. (in press). Net surfers don't ride alone. In P. Kollock & M. Smith (Eds.), *Communities in Cyberspace*. Berkeley: University of California Press.

Wellman, B., & Leighton, B. (1979). Networks, neighborhoods and communities. *Urban Affairs Quarterly, 14*, 363–90.

Wellman, B., & Potter, S. (in press). The elements of personal communities. In B. Wellman (Ed.), *Networks in the global village*. Boulder, CO: Westview.

Wellman, B., Salaff, J., Dimitrova, D., Garton, L. & Haythornthwaite, C. (1994, August). *The virtual reality of virtual organizations*, Presented at the annual meeting of the American Sociological Association, Los Angeles.

Wellman, B., & Wortley, S. (1990). Different strokes from different folks: Community ties and social support. *American Journal of Sociology, 96*, 558–588.

Winograd, T. (1988). A language/action perspective on the design of cooperative work. *Human–Computer Interaction, 3*(1), 3–30.

Wireman, P. (1984). *Urban neighborhoods, networks, and families*. Lexington, MA: Lexington.

Zuboff, S. (1984). *In the age of the smart machine*. New York: Basic Books.

Part III

POWER AND INFLUENCE

Of all the possible effects of technology, none have fascinated researchers and the general public more than its potential effect on power and influence (e.g., Barley, 1986; Danziger, Dutton, Kling, & Kraemer, 1982; George & King, 1991; Laudon, 1986; Markus & Pfeffer, 1983; Yates, 1989; Zuboff, 1988). The appearance of nationally and internationally accessible electronic communication offers those officially in charge and those at the grassroots new ways of knowing about the environments in which they act, and new possibilities for organizing and directing their actions. Electronic communication offers new ways to form relationships with groups, to generate trust in consensual relationships—or mistrust because of relationships that one or more groups did not want.

Paramount among the potential effects of electronic communication are the strengthening of existing distributed interest groups and the creation of new such groups. In some cases, grassroots groups have become sufficiently powerful and influential to exert significant and concentrated pressure on established organizations and institutions. A coalition of antismoking groups, for example, has used the Internet to mobilize their previously disparate forces, and to publish internal documents from the tobacco firm, Brown and Williamson (http://www.library.ucsf.edu/tobacco). In a few instances, distributed interest groups have evolved features of size, hierarchy and operating norms common to organizations. Some researchers believe these are fundamentally new kinds of political organization, and show promise of exerting major social influence in the coming years.

The chapters in this section represent researchers' analyses of the effects of electronic communication on power and influence in group and individual relationships. Chapter 10 by Christopher Kedzie uses archival data to argue that countries that offer more access to telecommunications technology are, as a result, more democratic. Chapter 11, by Peter Carnevale and

Tahira Probst, draws on theory in social psychology to discuss why electronic communication might change social conflict, and they describe some of the current arguments over electronic communication from the perspective of conflict theory. A "box" by Rob Kling comments on "intranets," which are not just mechanisms of efficiency but also bear on people's power and influence.

REFERENCES

Barley, S. R. (1986). Technology as an occasion for structuring: Evidence from observations of CT scanners and the social order of radiology departments. *Administrative Science Quarterly, 31*, 78–108.

Danziger, J. N., Dutton, W. H., Kling, R., & Kraemer, K. L. (1982). *Computers and politics: High technology in American local governments.* New York: Columbia University Press.

George, J. F. & King, J. L. (1991). Examining the centralization debate. *Communications of the ACM, 34*, 62–73.

Markus, M. L., & Pfeffer, J. (1983). Power and the design and implementation of accounting and control systems. *Accounting Organizations and Society, 8*, 205–213.

Laudon, K. C. (1986). *Dossier society: Value choices in the design of national information systems.* New York: Columbia University Press.

Yates, J. (1989). *Control through communication: The rise of system in American management.* Baltimore: Johns Hopkins University Press.

Zuboff, S. (1988). *In the age of the smart machine.* New York: Basic Books.

10

A BRAVE NEW WORLD
OR A NEW WORLD ORDER?

Christopher R. Kedzie
Ford Foundation, Moscow

> *In the field of mass communication as in almost every other field of enterprise,*
> *technological progress has hurt the Little Man and helped the Big Man.*
> *—Aldous Huxley, 1958*

> *The newest techniques of communications, mass information and transport have*
> *made the world more visible and more tangible to everyone. International commu-*
> *nication is easier now than ever before. Nowadays, it is virtually impossible for*
> *any society to be "closed."*
> *—Mikhail Gorbachev, 1988*

Spectacular global events that marked the beginning of the final decade of the 20th
century seemed to smile on optimists. Coincident revolutions—the breakouts of
democracy worldwide and the breakthroughs in the communication and information
technologies—inspired the notion that the new technologies could promote a more
peaceful and democratic world. I examine evidence of the impact of electronic
communication on political regimes and explore the possibility that the new technolo-
gies can empower citizens relative to governments.

WHAT ALMOST WAS

For most of this century, an opposing, inimical relationship was postulated
between communication technologies and freedom. Hitler's Minister for
Armaments, Albert Speer, fueled the worst of these fears at his Nuremberg

trial. "Through technical devices like the radio and the loudspeaker, eighty million people were deprived of independent thought. It was thereby possible to subject them to the will of one man" (Huxley, 1958, p. 43). Later, in the 1960s, while the superpowers struggled for control of the globe and jousted with the technology that threatened to annihilate it, the means to collect and disseminate information were widely regarded as ill-boding implements that strengthened "Big Brother's" malevolent grip on society. From Vietnam to Watergate, evidence impugned technological progress which, arguably, governments had maliciously co-opted for weapon technologies and wiretaps. A man on the moon also meant a spy in the sky. A year before Neil Armstrong planted his famous footprint on the moon, Zbigniew Brzezinski (1971) predicted that "the capacity to assert social and political control over the individual will vastly increase. It will soon be possible to assert almost continuous surveillance over every citizen and to maintain up-to-date, complete files, containing even most personal information about the health or personal behavior of the citizen in addition to more customary data. These files will be subject to instantaneous retrieval by the authorities" (Brzezinski, 1971, p. 163).

Fortunately, 1983 did not bring *1984*. Instead it brought *glasnost*. It was not democratic dominoes that were tumbling by the end of the decade but the Berlin Wall, followed by statues of comrade Lenin. The demise of the Soviet Union is a particularly telling story in the play between information technologies and political regimes for two fundamental reasons. First, the USSR was the sinister synthesis of Orwellian and Huxleyan nightmares coming true simultaneously. In Huxley's (1958) own words, "The Soviet system combines elements of *1984* with elements that are prophetic of what went on among the higher castes in *Brave New World*" (p. 5). Second, leading democratic theorists were at a loss to explain what happened when the 1980s and the Soviet Empire both ended. Samuel Huntington of Harvard University had predicted in 1984 that "The substantial power of anti-democratic governments (particularly the Soviet Union) ... suggest[s] that, with few exceptions, the limits of democratic development in the world may well have been reached" (p. 218). Additionally, Seymour Martin Lipset, who had written the seminal work documenting the correlation between democracy and economic development in 1959, conceded in 1993 that "the emergence of multi-party electoral systems in Africa and the ex-Communist states of Eastern Europe and the Soviet Union in the late 1980s and early 1990s will sharply reduce the relationships [between democracy and economic development] reported here when research based on data from the 1990s is completed. Many extremely poor countries are now much freer than before" (Lipset, Seong, & Torres, 1993, p. 170).

The seed that grew to crack the foundation of the Soviet monolith blew in from a different wind. Politicians, analysts, and journalists pointed to information currents for having turned political weathervanes. In doing so, these people helped to validate the prognosis for "closed societies" that Gorbachev had proffered before the Assembly of the United Nations. The General Secretary of the Communist Party may have been more right than he could have wished or imagined. Six years later, Israel's Foreign Minister, Shimon Peres, would observe that "Communism fell without the participation of the Russian army, for or against; it fell without having a new political party against the Communists—if at all, it was done by the Communists; it fell without the intervention of the United States, Europe, China or anybody else.... Authoritarian government became weak the minute they could no longer blind their people or control information" (Peres, 1994). Concurring, RAND analysts Carl Builder and Steve Bankes (1990) postulated, "[T]he communist bloc failed, not primarily or even fundamentally because of its centrally controlled economic policies or its excessive military burdens, but because its closed societies were too long denied the fruits of the information revolution that was developing elsewhere over the last 40 years" (p. 15). The Moscow Bureau Chief for the *Baltimore Sun*, Scott Shane, provided substantial and specific evidence in his book *Dismantling Utopia: How Information Ended the Soviet Union*. Ultimately, Shane (1994) concluded that the August coup that catalyzed the ultimate dissolution of the USSR was:

> a revolution driven by information that the coup was designed to halt; information that had undermined ideology, exposed the bureaucracy, and shattered the Soviet family of nations. But it was also the liberating power of information that doomed the coup to failure—both the information that over five years had changed people's views of the world, and the information that now fueled the resistance with up to the minute reports. People were better informed than ever before about the past consequences of totalitarianism, helping them better understand now what was at stake. (p. 261)

Information revolution technologies armed those who would resist the coup and political oppression better than ever before in the seven decades of the Soviet reign. The president of Russia's first private electronic mail network, christened Relcom for "reliable communication," recalled the role of the new media throughout those ominous events, "When the putsch took place in August, over those three days we transmitted over the territory of the former Soviet Union about 46,000 pieces of news. We were in constant communication with Europe and America.... We were very much afraid at the time since all other channels were closed" (Soldatov, 1994). A foreign eyewitness effusively lauded electronic mail networks that "had proved worthy of the appellation, 'revolutionary tools.' During the crisis they had provided information around the world, but especially in the Soviet Union when all other forms of communication had been blocked." He gushed further, "I will not be surprised if the bronzed figure representing the proletariat will not be holding a rifle in his outstretched arm, but a printout, and a computer on his lap" (Valauskas, 1992, p. 47).

Detractors might argue that the weight of revolution was supported predominantly by the conventional media, not the new media. Unequivocally, conventional media were consequential. Shane (1994) described, at length, the positive influence of television and the printed media. The differing characteristics between the conventional and the new communication technologies and their implications on political regimes are addressed specifically later, but it is also important to recognize that the likely bias would be to underestimate the impact due to electronic networks for two reasons. First, state control over information must be airtight to be effective. It was Orwell's fear that "if all records told the same tale—then lies passed into history and became truth" (Orwell, 1949, p. 35). Of course, the whole balloon bursts from one small pinprick. The nondestroyed newspaper clipping that Orwell's protagonist, Winston Smith, discovered in *1984* could have been such a pin. Similarly the Soviet were unable to seal their borders from electronic pricks. The international flow of email messages strengthened the conventional media, which could no longer be deprived of outside sources for information. Second, the democratizing influence of electronic networks can extend beyond the countries in which they are prevalent. The demonstration effect can be a powerful impetus in international affairs. The political transformation of the Soviet Union, at least partially fueled by information revolution technologies, arguably emboldened lesser connected countries in other regions of the world, such as Africa, to experiment with more democratic rule.

Furthermore, the Russian story is not unique. Beyond the borders of the USSR, similar refrains of praise have been sung for electronic communication networks driving democratic change. "Back in '89, Czech students were trying to coordinate the uprising across the nation, and the technical students, including Martin, were running a telecom angle.... The Czech secret police were far too stupid and primitive to keep up with digital telecommunications, so the student-radical modem network was relatively secure from bugging and taps.... By mid-December, the Civic Forum was in power" (Sterling, 1995, p. 102). In China, "The students' ingenious uses of facsimile attracted the bulk of mass media attention, but perhaps more important, the Chinese uprising marked the first time in history that a computer network—the U.S. BITNET—was used extensively and for multiple purposes, by political dissidents" (Ganley, 1991, p. 10). From Mexico, anyone of the "30m people of the world can read instantaneously the communiqués issued from the jungles of Chiapas by Mexico's Zapatista rebels" ("Let the Digital Ages," 1995, p. 13).

WHAT THE EVIDENCE IS

As impressive as these national stories are, the global picture displays a worldwide trend that is even more compelling. Visual evidence of a positive relationship between democracy and information revolution technologies is provocative.

Figure 10.1 shows Freedom House democracy ratings for all the countries of the world. Darker shadings indicate higher levels of democracy. Figure 10.2 is a comparable projection of the prevalence of major worldwide email computer networks. The metric used in the second figure is "interconnectivity"[1] and darker shading indicates greater interconnectivity. The similarity of patterns between the two maps inspires more rigorous analyses.[2]

Electronic mail is the specific information revolution technology of interest for this inquiry because it enables people to communicate across national borders in ways that have not been possible since the time when borders were drawn around nation states. Internationally, email is also the most mature, most widespread, and most commonly used element of the "Net." The interconnectivity measure is a composite measure of the number of nodes per capita for the four globally dominant electronic mail networks—Internet, BITNET, UUCP, and FidoNet—as tracked and recorded by the Matrix Information Directory Service.

Univariate analyses show that Figs. 10.1 and 10.2 are indeed connected. A strong correlation does indeed exist between democracy and interconnectivity. The scatterplot and regression line in Fig. 10.3 display this relationship graphically and the correlation matrix in Table 10.1 numerically.

The correlation matrix includes a set of social indicators that are most often hypothesized as democracy's causal correlates. As the matrix indicates, the coefficient for interconnectivity is not only large, it is substantially larger than that of any other traditional predictors of democracy. Even the coefficient for economic development is smaller by .16.

Multiple linear regression analyses incorporating all the variables listed in Table 10.1 consistently show interconnectivity as the dominant predictor of democracy. With greater than 99.9% certainty, one can reject the null hypothesis that there is no relationship between democracy and interconnectivity.

Furthermore, the coefficient on interconnectivity is large. A single point increase on the interconnectivity scale corresponds to an increase of 5 points in democracy rating. The correlation of GDP (gross domestic product) with democracy is also statistically significant but the sign on the coefficient is negative. This result supports arguments of some scholars, as well as apologists for the Pinochet and Lee Kuan Yu economic development theories, that democracy is not costless.[3] All else being equal, e.g., interconnectivity and

---

[1]*Interconnectivity* is a term popularized by Larry Landweber for his measures of the proliferation of global email networks.

[2]A more thorough explanation and the details of the statistical analyses are presented in Kedzie (1995).

[3]For more discussion on the potentially negative economic consequences of democratization, see Shin (1994) or Rothstein (1991).

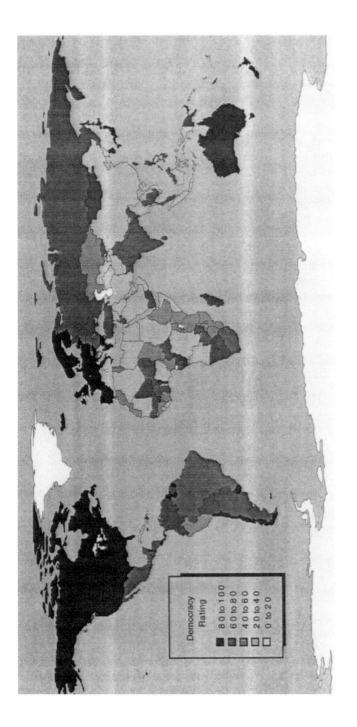

FIG. 10.1. Democracy rating. From Freedom House, "1994 Freedom Around the World."

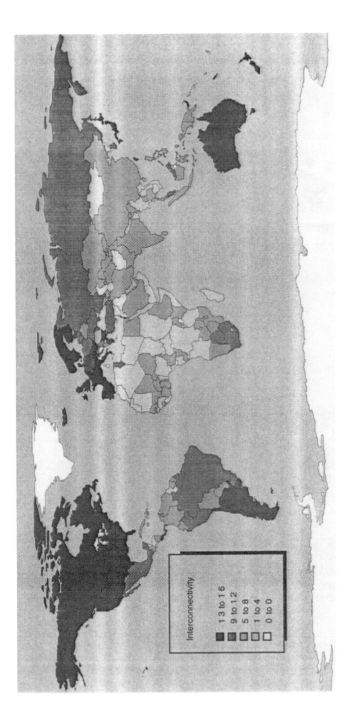

FIG. 10.2. Interconnectivity sources. From Matrix Information and Directory Services, Inc.

215

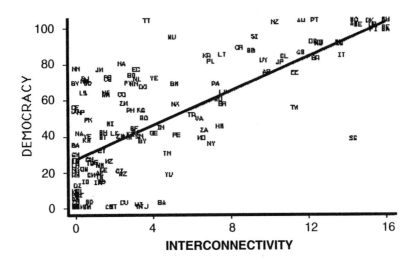

FIG. 10.3. Democracy versus interconnectivity.

TABLE 10.1

Correlation Matrix

Social Indicators	Social Indicators						
	Democracy	Interconn	Schooling	GDP	Life Expect	Ethnicity	Log(Pop)
Democracy	1.00						
Interconnectivity	0.73	1.00					
Schooling	0.67	0.82	1.00				
Per-Capita GDP	0.57	0.84	0.79	1.00			
Life Expectancy	0.53	0.71	0.87	0.71	1.00		
Ethnicity	0.27	0.26	0.35	0.23	0.42	1.00	
Log (Population)	-0.09	0.07	0.10	0.05	0.07	0.11	1.00

Note. Sources: Freedom House, "1994 Freedom Around the World" (Kaplan, 1994; Democracy) Matrix Information and Directory Services, Inc. (Interconnectivity), United Nations Development Program (Per-Capita GDP, Life Expectancy, Schooling), CIA World Fact Book (Ethnicity), World Telecommunication Development Report (Population).

population, greater economic development might be available only at the expense of democratization. The years of schooling and life expectancy also show some statistical significance. In the case of the latter, the negative sign is more difficult to explain although this is the weakest of the significant predictors. The coefficient on population is also significant, but the size of a country's population, largely inaccessible to foreign intervention, offers scarcely few policy recommendations (except perhaps to shine a glimmer of hope on the fractious states of Yugoslavia and the former Soviet Union that potentially may have a more democratic future than their larger predecessors).

Debates continue as to whether certain cultures or civilizations are more favorably disposed or fundamentally disinclined to embrace democratic principles of governance.[4] In either case, it is not difficult to appreciate a notion that cultural aspects influence the acceptance and use of information revolution technologies. For this reason, regional regressions were analyzed across six global regions: Asia, Africa, Eurasia, Latin America, the Middle East, and Western Europe. Graphical output is shown in Fig. 10.4.

In all six regions, the correlation between interconnectivity and democracy is positive. In half of the regions, the regression coefficient is both substantial and statistically significant. The correlation is most pronounced in those regions undergoing dramatic political transformation. This fact is important when considering causality. If the correlation were positive only in those regions where substantive democratization preceded the information revolution, one might be able to argue that the latter strengthened the former but certainly not that the latter caused the former. The evidence, however, is that the relationship is weakest in the regions characterized by established democracies and strongest in regions that are cultivating nascent democratic institutions, notably in Eurasia, the region that includes Russia and Eastern Europe.

It is tempting to infer causality from these impressive correlations and conclude that interconnectivity causes democratization. However, to do so might be premature. Causality could, in fact, flow in the opposite direction. Democracies rely on an informed public and uninhibited communication and may therefore seek interconnectivity. An alternative explanation could be that a third variable influences both simultaneously. The obvious candidate would be economic development. The same economic resources that can finance participation in the communications revolution could also conceivably fuel demands for personal rights and freedoms. Advanced regression techniques involving systems of simultaneous equations are employed to help unravel the tangled issues of mutual causality. In all viable models, interconnectivity proved to be a significant predictor of democracy and economic development, but never was the reverse true. The

---

[4]For characteristic arguments from both sides of the debate, see Huntington (1993) and Schifter (1994).

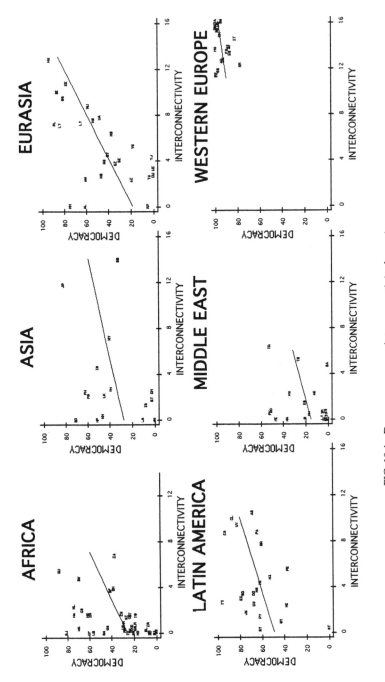

FIG. 10.4. Democracy versus interconnectivity by region.

consistent implication coincides with the anecdotal evidence; electronic interconnectivity contributes to democratization.

WHAT THE DIFFERENCES AMONG THE MEDIA ARE

The statistical evidence supports the statesman's realization, "that it is virtually impossible for any society to be 'closed.'" However, it does not necessarily contradict the futurist's contention of 30 years earlier. The communication technologies that were new in the 1950s differ from those available today in certain fundamental ways. Huxley's statement could have been true then and Gorbachev's could be true today. Alternatively, the effects of technology could be indeterminate. After having watched several of the newly independent states besmirch their newly won freedom with malicious nationalism and internecine violence, Shane (1994) concluded that, "Despite our wishful thinking, technology remains a maddeningly neutral tool, as it has been since man discovered that fire could preserve life or destroy it. The Soviet television tower at Ostankino could broadcast with equal efficiency the numbing speeches of Brezhnev or the electrifying iconoclasm of Vzglyad ['Glance,' a popular exposé television program]" (p. 282). Considering communication technologies in the aggregate, Shane may be correct. Specific technologies, however, are certainly easier for some political entities to use to their own relative advantage over others. "Vzglyad" and its cousin programs were able to broadcast only at the pleasure of the Brezhnev's government and that of his successors. This is pointedly clear from the anecdote of the Moscow kindergartner who replied, when asked to define the word *coup* a few days after the failed attempt, "That's when they show all the same thing at the same time on all channels" (Shane, 1994, p. 255).

The prevailing wisdom regarding communications technologies at the opening of this century was closer to Gorbachev's at the end of the century than to Huxley's in the middle. In the early 1900s, the innovative communications technology was the telephone. One of the important spokesmen of the day, General John J. Carty, also a key figure in the development of the American telephone and author of an anonymous column called "The Prophet's Corner" in the journal *Electrical Engineering*, envisioned a time when "we will build up a world telephone system making necessary to all peoples the use of a common language, or a common understanding of languages, which will join all the people of the earth into one brotherhood."[5]

In a broader historical context, advancements in the means of communication have profoundly affected the characteristics within and interac-

---

[5]Marion May Dilts, *The Telephone in a Changing World*, Longmans Green, New York, 1941, p. 38, as cited in Pool (1983a, p. 89).

tions between societies since the invention of language. Writing created permanence; the printing press widened distribution; the telegraph conquered distance; the telephone facilitated interactivity; and television mastered visual images. Now, asynchronous electronic telecommunication networks likewise, in this history of punctuated development, represent another fundamental, substantial, and discontinuous improvement in the ability to communicate. "If we look for historical precedents for this diffusion of power through information away from the elites, the Renaissance comes to mind" (Builder, 1993, p. 159).

"Soft technological-determinism" is the term that venerated communications scholar Ithiel de Sola Pool (1983b) used to understand and characterize the effects of centuries of changing communication technologies. "Freedom is fostered when the means of communication are dispersed, decentralized, and made easily available, as are printing presses or microcomputers. Central control is more likely when the means of communication are concentrated, monopolized and scarce, as are great networks" (p. 5).

The key is reciprocity. To the extent that the inherent characteristics of a communication technology enable others to respond readily and easily, via the same medium and to the same audience, that particular technology can facilitate the aspirations of those who would seek to bring about democratic change. To the extent that characteristics of a technology inhibit reciprocity, such aspirations can be more easily frustrated. Pool enumerated several dimensions in which the facilitating or inhibiting quality is apparent including economic, geographic, and system architecture.

Relative to these dimensions and to a few others, it is helpful to compare and distinguish the democratizing potential of the most common communication technologies.

Table 10.2 presents the results of these comparisons and illustrates revolutionary differences. The unit of analysis is a subjective measure of each technology's capacity to support an "ordinary" individual who would receive and respond to a specific message of interest originating in another country in a distant region of the world. Darker shading indicates greater capacity for reciprocity in each of the five major categories. The objective of the chart is contrast, not exactitude. Thus, although many of the particular cells may be vulnerable to quibbles and subjective assumptions and interpretations, email unequivocally stands apart from its predecessors as being more conducive to reciprocity in communication.

Mode.   Technological innovation in communication has historically improved the flow of information in one of two measures, distance and area. Telegraph and telephone stretched the distance across which individuals could exchange messages. Radio and television broadened the area of message transmission. The conquest over distance has improved the capability of discourse, the bidirectional communication intrinsic to functioning

TABLE 10.2

Comparison of Communications Media

Communications Media	Communications Mode			Message Content		Boundaries (Freedom From)		Cost (Low)		Speed (High)
	Uni-directional	Bi-directional	Multi-directional	Images	Data	State Institutions	Geography	Equipment	Transmission	Speed
Newspaper										
Postal Mail										
Telegraph										
Radio										
Telephone										
Television										
Facsimile										
E-mail										

free market operations and treaty negotiations between authorities of sovereign states. The conquest over area has improved the capacity for information dissemination, the unidirectional broadcast by which hierarchical institutions maintain control over rank-and-file members and societal leaders influence their constituencies.[6] Before the information revolution, the distinction between discourse and dissemination appeared to be inviolable. The telephone, for instance, has been largely as ineffective for disseminating information on a large scale as has the television for engaging in discourse.[7,8]

The pursuit of democracy summons the capabilities of both discourse and dissemination but also demands something qualitatively different. Conceptually, democratic processes rely on discourse for compromise, but closed one-to-one deal making can impair the confidence necessary for consensus building. A politically aware electorate requires mechanisms for information dissemination, but a limited number of "ones" controlling the one-to-many broadcasts undermines the free flow of information. Public debate, the multidirectional communication, is a democracy-enabling synergy of discourse and dissemination. The essence of multidirectional communication is that all people who receive information via a certain information channel can participate equally within the complete and identical context of the discussion. Indeed, the expressed goal for the Internet's predecessor, the ARPANET, was that "It should effectively allow the illusion that those in communication with one another are all within the same soundproofed room" (Baran, 1964, p. 1). Another term commonly used to describe multidirectional communication has been "many-to-many." However, this term can be misleading. The connotation of "many" in one-to-many can be the billion or so people around the globe who watch soccer's World Cup. Although the electronic newsletter *China News Digest* boasts of 35,000 subscribers (Tempest, 1995), many-to-many in the World Cup scale would be impossibly unwieldy. More important, quantifying the number of participants misses the most critical aspect of multidirectional communication. Independent of how many people are involved—even if there are

---

[6]For more thorough presentation of the means and efficiencies of markets, institutions, and networks, see Ronfeldt (1993).

[7]A "pleasure telephone" to be used as a mass media device providing news, music, and information was attempted in Budapest around the turn of the century and in Newark before the First World War. Both experiments proved unsuccessful primarily because the cost was too high and the medium did not lend itself to advertising (Pool, 1983a).

[8]"Interactive television" is not "discourse" in the usual sense of the term. Although information flows in two directions, the information content is greatly restricted to selecting predetermined menu items as opposed to free exchange of ideas. Nor do radio and television talk shows qualify as discourse. A limited number of host-selected participants address their one-shot on-the-air question or comment to the show hosts. The medium does not allow for continuing give-and-take among participants.

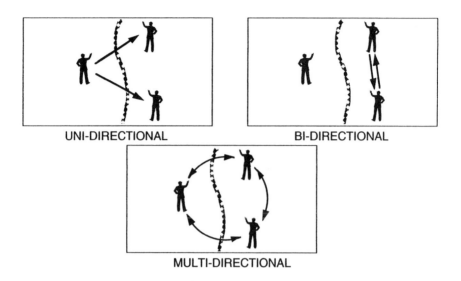

UNI-DIRECTIONAL   BI-DIRECTIONAL

MULTI-DIRECTIONAL

FIG. 10.5. Schematic modes of communication.

only three—email technology creates a different dynamic and thus can be expected to have differing social and political outcomes. The different modes of a single exchange are shown in Fig. 10.5 in a cross-border context.

It is interesting to note that the First Amendment to the U. S. Constitution specifically address each of these three modes as fundamental to the practice of democracy: *right to petition the government* pertains to the bidirectional nature of discourse, particularly between the citizen and the state; *freedom of the press* provides for unfettered unidirectional dissemination of information; the *right to assemble* preserves the multidirectional quality of public debate.

In successful public debate, each participant is able to hear and be heard. Democracy archetypes, the amphitheater of ancient Greece or the town meeting of colonial New England, offer appropriate metaphors. There is no comparable meeting place for democratizing nation states. Neither telephone discourse nor television dissemination provides adequate technological support. Computer networks alone successfully blend these capabilities into virtual town halls.[9]

Before computer networks had proliferated, Pool (1983b) foresaw that convergence of modes is blurring the lines between media, even between

---

[9]The store and forward capabilities of facsimile machines presaged the combination of discourse and dissemination in one device. However, there is no respond-to-all capability. Additionally, the reliance on images prohibits effective message manipulation and is likely to cause degradation in the integrity of the message with repeated sendings particularly in the developing world where the phone lines are very noisy.

point-to-point communications, such as the post, telephone, and telegraph, and mass communications, such as the press, radio, and television. A single physical means—be it wires, cables or airwaves—may carry services that in the past were provided in separate ways. Conversely, a service that was provided in the past by any one medium—be it broadcasting, the press, or telephony—can now be provided in several different physical ways. So the one-to-one relationship that used to exist between a medium and its use is eroding. (p. 23)

Pool's focus is on the media of transmission, that microwaves would be used for both telephone and radio, for instance. The empowering reality, however, may be a bit more subtle. Another important convergence is materializing within a terminal device. A computer can be used to achieve the ends of both a telephone and a television, thus achieving multidirectionality. The medium of transmission may be optical fiber, satellite link, coaxial cable, twisted copper wires, or more likely, some combination (completely transparent to participants). The closest approximation to multidirectional communication among the conventional technologies is a conference call with all its obvious timing, geographic, and size limitations. Historical examples might be short-wave and citizen's band radio, which never had staying power in the mainstream. Computer terminals are the first widely used telecommunications devices able to support multidirectional public debate to uphold democratic ideals, as was witnessed in Russia.

Some commentators pose the Ayatollah Khomeini's extensive use of audiocassettes in the nondemocratic revolution that overthrew the Shah of Iran in 1979 as the counterexample, proving that information revolution technologies can equally strengthen the dark forces (Goodman & Green, 1992). Khomeini's cassettes, however, did not allow for reciprocal exchange and are therefore more closely analogous to unidirectional radio than to multidirectional email networks. Networks are also precisely what Shane (1994) overlooked when he claimed that "information demonstrated an awesome capacity for destruction of the existing order—but no equivalent capacity for creation" (p. 280). His oversight is not uncommon. Theodore Roszak (1986) wrote, in *The Cult of Information*, "the computer lends itself all too conveniently to the subversion of democratic values.... A few of these [applications], like the networking capacity and educational possibilities of the microcomputer, have been seized upon by the hopeful democratic spirits like the guerrilla hackers; but such minimal and marginal uses of the computer are simply dwarfed into insignificance by its predominant applications" (p. 180). Roszak's book was published in 1986, when the exponential growth of networks was still not significant. Similarly, according to Peter Huber (1994) in *Orwell's Revenge: The 1984 Palimpsest*, missing the reciprocal capacity of networking in telescreen technology was "Orwell's biggest mistake" (p. 223).

The previous statistical analyses offer another interesting insight here. Population was a statistically significant indicator of democracy and the coefficient was negative. In small societies, networking, arguably, could be possible via traditional communication technologies. The most populous country that Freedom House labels as completely "free" became a democracy in 1776 when its population was only a fraction of its current size. At that time and at that size, printing presses and pamphlets were sufficient to support public debate.

Content. A dichotomy of communication technologies also seems to exist in message content: images versus structured data. The difference between the two can be conceived as the difference between a melody and a musical score, a graph and the underlying numbers, a speech and the text, an atomic particle trace and its mathematical model. Images (aural, visual, tactile, and olfactory) are the means by which human beings are traditionally comfortable communicating. In contrast, information, like a page of data or a bit stream, is opaque to an average observer. Yet, structured data is malleable and machine-readable; it can be retrieved, filtered, ordered, and altered and then retransmitted.

Alexander Graham Bell instigated the contentious images-versus-data debate a century ago hawking his vision of a widespread telephone system overseas in England. He claimed, "All other telegraph machines produce signals which require to be translated by experts, and such instruments are therefore extremely limited in their application, but the telephone actually speaks, and for this reason it can be utilized for nearly every purpose for which speech is employed" (Fagen, 1975, p. 21). Today's fans of the fax echo the telephone inventor's initial excitement now that visual images can also be transmitted across telephone lines.

Detractors, however, lament, "The fax is a step backward because it does not contain 'structured data,' but rather an image of text that is no more computer-readable than this page of *Wired* [a magazine] (unless you are reading it on America On-line [an email service]). Even though the fax was delivered as bits before it is rendered as an image on paper, those bits have no symbolic value" (Negroponte, 1994, p. 134). Confronted with exponentially increasing information flows, the ability to manipulate and filter messages becomes critical to produce order instead of overload.

However, in the context of electronic mail, the choice between image and structured data proves unecessary. This is another result of convergence. Whereas radio, telephone, and television can play the music, and postal mail, newspapers, and faxes can display the notes, computers can do both. "[A]s the world's information becomes digitized, those packets can carry every thing that humans can perceive and machines can process—voice, high fidelity sound, text, high resolution color graphics, computer programs, data, full motion video" (Rheingold, 1993, p. 74). Electronic messages can be both appreciated as images and manipulated as data.[10]

Arousing images have long been used to incite political change. During the Cold War, in the name of democracy, radio and television waves were modulated with America's message and consigned to breach the Iron Curtain. More recently, President Clinton (1994b) responded to criticism that he had betrayed the democratic movement in China with a proposal to "tell freedom's story to the people of China. We will launch Radio Free Asia, increase the Voice of America radio broadcasts to China and inaugurate a weekly VOA television program to report on developments" (p. B5). To these ends, information revolution technologies can be more effective, combining images with structured data, thus creating a multiplier effect. The democratic message becomes duplicable, adaptable, and redirectable, almost effortlessly. The medium also provides for accountability and permanence of messages. The messages themselves are tractable to analysis and verification. These are all capabilities that play away from a dictator's iron hand.

Boundaries.   Geography bounds conventional communications physically and state institutions functionally. Post office addresses and telephone numbers are specific to certain locations. Forwarding offers limited freedom, as do certain innovations such as cellular telephones, remotely accessible answering machines, voice mail, and beepers. Mass media, by design, can cover large swaths of the earth, but conventional publishing and broadcasting sites are hardly mobile. Transistor radios, videocams, VCRs, and portable satellite dishes have all shown significant improvements, but none compare to the geographic independence of seamless and global electronic computer networks. Discarding the need for geographic proximity, or even awareness of it, certain applications such as the World Wide Web and Gopher deliver information for which the country of origin may be completely transparent to the operator. Natural and human-designated boundaries dissolve.

Distinguishing itself from an ordinary postal mailbox, an email box can be accessible to its owner from anywhere on the earth via another networked computer. Such geographic independence is particularly liberating for itinerant individuals who cross borders often pursuing an international agenda. While circumnavigating the planet three times, writer Carl Malamud (1993), described continuous correspondences in his "technical trave-

---

[10]The union of images with information is the source of profound advancement in society according to some scholars. Paraphrasing Derek J. de Solla Price, Karl W. Deutsch (1963) wrote, "Western Science, and its offshoots, modern science, it has persuasively been argued, have derived from the marriage, in Hellenistic times, of the visual imagination of classical Greek science with the computational skills of the Babylonians; and the ever renewed union of new feats of visualization with computations that ever since has accompanied the development of mathematics, and of all the sciences" (p. 23).

logue." The author of this chapter accessed his own account in Tashkent, Uzbekistan, regularly from cities throughout Central Asia and other parts of the former Soviet Union. Erratic itineraries did not disrupt daily communications because worldwide colleagues could simply send messages to an email address while remaining blissfully oblivious to the tribulations of traveling in Eurasia.

Functional bottlenecks of traditional communication technologies allow powerful ruling elites of nation-states to exercise and reinforce central authority. "The only contact between self-contained national [telecommunication] systems was through the conjoint provision of international services arranged upon the basis of bilateral operation agreements between the PTTs [post, telephone, and telegraph]" (Genschel & Werle, 1993, p. 207). Such arrangements enabled the former Soviet Union, for instance, a country of nearly 300 million people, to restrict the number of international lines to dozens, never more than those on which the Soviet internal security agency could eavesdrop. Nazi Germany constricted international contact by levying high taxes (Pool, 1983a).

In contrast, electronic networks were designed as "distributed" and "adaptive." The underlying architecture of the ARPANET, precursor to the Internet, was conceived at RAND specifically to protect the integrity of military command and control structures in the case of an attack against the United States (Baran, 1964). Its architecture was such that it "would have no central authority. Furthermore, it would be designed from the beginning to operate while in tatters" (Sterling, 1993). Peter Lewis (1994), journalist for *The New York Times*, extolled the virtues of distributed communication to protect dissident writers. He wrote "because information travels in 'packets' of data that are typically scattered and reassembled at the receiving site, it is much harder to intercept or trace messages" (p. E18). Further, he quoted Gara LaMarche, associate director of the Human Rights Watch, "The notion of using the Internet to transcend international boundaries that have been used to suppress information is a visionary one" (p. E18).

In addition, not only are the new information technologies harder for authoritarian regimes to control, but even if they could control them, to do so would require such drastic measures that a regime might be forced to choose between political liberalization or severe economic consequences (Builder, 1993).

Costs. The information revolution is rightly described also as a devolution. Once the high-cost advanced technologies were accessible only to the political and media elite, precluding any glint of reciprocity. Decades of innovation and technological trickle-down eventually handed over Prometheus' torch from the governments to the people. Bearing the fire of information and communication, private individuals are now economically able to illuminate the workings of governments, enlighten fellow citizens, and brighten a path toward democracy.

Distributed networks have dispersed centers of control, and silicon chips, the raw material of which is sand, have shifted the marginal economics of information and communication. As if technology has switched allegiances, the dissemination, collection, and interpretation of information is no longer the exclusive prerogative of superrich governments. The satellite pictures of Chernobyl on the front pages of newspapers around the world that compelled the Soviet Union to recant its deceitful initial damage assessments were the work of a privately owned French satellite, SPOT (Wriston, 1988–1989). A private videotape of police brutality against Rodney King impugned state institutions in the United States. Integrated circuits and PCs locate as much computer-processing power on desks in private homes as had been in some government research labs. Although the fabrication facilities are still quite expensive, miniaturized marginal costs and economies of scale in the production of microchips and integrated circuits have made personal computers, personal copiers, personal fax machines, and even personal satellite reception dishes available to the general public at reasonable prices.

Both fixed and marginal costs of communication are plummeting. New-generation equipment prices are lower than that of their predecessors by several orders of magnitude. Satellite dishes, for example, decreased in price from $250,000 to $500 and video cassette recorders from $30,000 to $300 (Ganley, 1991). The capital expenditure for an individual to start sending messages overseas varies tremendously by medium. A PC and modem for email, which now cost in the hundreds of dollars—compared to thousands of dollars in the recent past—are somewhere in the vast middle, yet nearer to the cost of an airmail stamp than to a television studio.

Whereas the face value of postage stamps continues to rise, the per-message cost in some media has dropped dramatically in real terms. "In New York City 1896, phone service cost $20 a month, compared to the average worker's income of $38.50 a month" (Pool, 1983a, p. 22). International calls are still expensive relative to domestic calls. The standard tariff to Russia from the United States is $2.02 per minute, for instance, compared to $.14 for a coast-to-coast domestic call within the United States.[11] In the United States, as in much of the developed world, international calling is considered an "enhanced" service, the price of which is artificially high in order to subsidize the universalization of "basic" service on the local exchange. Competition in the international realm is likely to erode such pricing policies and the contrived barrier between domestic and international telephone connections (Bruce, Cunard, & Director, 1986).

For several decades now, the ability of anyone on the planet to communicate with anyone else was technically but not practically feasible. A real earth-shrinking breakthrough of computer networks is the reduction in per-message cost. The price of an electronic message entered into the

---

[11]Standard prices are quoted for Sprint, Inc.

network via a local phone call is independent of the destination (and often free to the user), whether across the street or across the ocean. Under these tariff systems, email compares in cost quite favorably to phone or fax for international communication. Yet, as already noted, these prices are distorted. The price of dialing internationally is inflated while the Internet is federally subsidized. This observation should not be overstated, however, for three reasons. First, the Internet subsidy is less than often assumed. Jeffrey MacKie-Mason and Hal Varian (1993) at the University of Michigan calculated the subsidy in the United States at less than $20 per year per host and less than $2 per year per user. That would pay for only a single 1-minute phone call to Moscow. Second, the marginal costs are vanishingly small. "If the network is not saturated the incremental cost of sending additional packets is essentially zero"[12] (MacKie-Mason & Varian, 1993, p. 5). Finally, these particular market distortions are not present in many developing countries where the marginal benefits of enhanced interconnectivity may be the largest. The asking price for a reliable phone connection to the United States from Uzbekistan, for instance, was $7 in the summer of 1993. An email message equivalent to one typed page cost $.15 via Relcom, a private Russian network service provider supported by only its own revenue. Furthermore, across "dirty" telephone lines common in developing countries, on which the need to shout to be heard is not exceptional, error correction protocols ensure the integrity of the email message. The comparative cost of a fax must often be doubled or tripled for repeat calls in order to obtain enough legible segments to constitute a complete document.

Total programmatic cost comparisons are also illuminating. In 1993, the National Science Foundation (NSF) was spending at a rate of $18.5 million per year for a clientele estimated at 10 million users (MacKie-Mason & Varian, 1993). In the same year, the Board for International Broadcasting granted more than 10 times that amount, $218 million, to Radio Free Europe/Radio Liberty (RFE/RL) (the model for Radio Free Asia) for private broadcasting activities.[13] In China, for the president's proposal to have a comparable effect per dollar of expenditure as has been demonstrated on the Internet, it would have to reach more than 100 million (1 in 10) Chinese citizens—and be interactive.

Time. Time, as well as distance, warps in the information revolution reality. As if a domestic version of Einstein's theory of relativity is being demonstrated in homes, schools, and offices, the definitive measure is no longer time or distance but light speed, the 186,000 miles per second at which electronic messages travel. The only technologies that surpass email

---

[12]MacKie-Mason and Varian (1993) argued that when the networks are not congested, the marginal costs of transporting additional packets along the medium are negligible. The primary costs that concern them are the delays during congestion at the bottleneck routers.

[13]The figures are available in the *United States Budget for Fiscal Year 1995*, p. 861.

as a versatile message carrier are perhaps post offices and courier services, and at least the former is infamous for anachronistic slowness. A posted letter to Russia may still spend 2 months or more en route—if it reaches its destination at all. Expensive express delivery services still ignore large patches of the populated planet. At the other end of the timeliness spectrum, radio and television commonly broadcast live. However, instantaneous does not imply spontaneous. If the intended audience is not notified in advance and tuned in at the right moment, the broadcast message may be lost into the cosmos. Telephones and facsimile machines operate in real time for a narrow bandwidth. Yet, even telephone messages are often delayed to obtain an available international line or for someone to be available to pick up the receiver in a distant time zone. Answering machines and programmable VCRs are limited ad hoc "store and forward" solutions. Email combines the speed of satellite links with the patience of delivery boys who wait by the door until the message is picked up. For the first time ever, any human being can engage in near-real-time communication with any other human being anywhere.[14]

WHAT COULD BE

The aggregate of the comparisons disclose the characteristics of one technology that almost without rival in any individual dimension, is relatively more spontaneous and instantaneous, low-cost and decentralized, versatile and multidirectional. These specific characteristics of electronic networks are fundamental to communicative reciprocity and as such engender revolutionary prospects for the spread of democracy. Not surprisingly, these findings concur with the results of the empirical analyses and the implications of the historic record.

Ultimately, a deep irony pervades these conclusions. During the chill of the Cold War, communications and computer technologies were closely guarded in the West for fear of their "dual-use" potential of conceivably aiding the harbingers of the brave new world. Now, it is revealed that information revolution technologies offer a new dual-use possibility, to foster global democracy, which resonates with hopes for creating a new world order.

REFERENCES

Baran, P. (1964). Summary overview. *On distributed communications: XI* (Tech. Rep. No. RM-3767-PR). Santa Monica, CA: RAND.

---

[14]The author is indebted to RAND colleague Jeff Rothenberg for observing that real-time communication between human beings anywhere may only be a temporary historical anomaly. Once humans begin to venture off the planet, vast distances measured in light-minutes or light-hours will again introduce technologically unavoidable transmission delays. The capability for instantaneous and spontaneous communication may exist only for a century or two.

Bruce, R. R., Cunard J. P., & Director, M. D. (1986). *From telecommunications to electronic services: A global spectrum of definitions, boundary lines and structures.* Boston: Butterworth Legal Publishers.

Brzezinski, Z. (1971). Moving into a technetronic society. In A. F. Westin (Ed.), *Information technology in a democracy* (pp. 161–167) Cambridge, MA: Harvard University Press.

Builder, C. H., & Bankes, S. C. (1990). *The etiology of European change.* (Tech. Rep. No. 7693) Santa Monica, CA: RAND.

Builder, C. H. (1993, March). Is it a transition or a revolution? *Futures*, pp. 155–167.

Builder, C. H., & Bankes, S. C. (1991). *Artificial societies: A concept for basic research on the societal impacts of information technology* (Tech. Rep. No. P-7740) Santa Monica, CA: RAND.

Clinton, W. J. (1994a, January 14). [Remarks in live telecast]. Moscow, Russia: Ostankino TV Station.

Clinton, W. J., (1994b, May 31). Clinton: Isolating China wouldn't improve human rights. *Los Angeles Times*, p. B5.

Deutsch, K. W. (1963). *The nerves of government.* London: The Free Press.

Fagen, M. D. (Ed.). (1975). *A history of engineering and science in the Bell system.* New York: Bell Laboratories.

Ganley, G. D. (1991, Spring). Power to the people via personal electronic media. *The Washington Quarterly*, pp. 5–22.

Genschel, P., & Werle, R. (1993 From national hierarchies to international standardization: Modal changes in the governance of telecommunications, *Journal of Public Policy, 13*(3), 203–225.

Goodman, S., & Green, J. (1992). Computing in the Middle East. *Communications of the ACM, 35*(8), 21–25.

Gorbachev, M. (1988, December 7). (Novosti Press Agency Publishing House, Trans.) Speech presented at the United Nations, New York.

Huber, P. (1994). *Orwell's revenge: The 1984 palimpsest.* New York: The Free Press.

Huntington, S. P. (1984). Will more countries become democratic? *Political Science Quarterly, 99*(2), 193–218.

Huntington, S. P. (1993, Summer). The clash of cultures. *Foreign Affairs*, 22–49.

Huxley, A. (1958). *Brave new world revisited.* New York: Harper & Row.

International Telecommunications Union. (1994). *World telecommunication development report.* Geneva Switzerland: Author.

Kaplan, R. (Ed.). (1994, January). *Freedom Review, 25*(1).

Kedzie, C. R. (1995). International implications for global democratization. In R. A. Anderson et al. (Eds.), *Universal access to e-mail: Feasibility and societal implications* (Tech. Rep. No. MR-650-MF). (pp. 151–168). Santa Monica, CA: RAND.

Let the digital age bloom. (1995, February 25). *The Economist*, pp. 13–14.

Lewis, P. H. (1994, June 5). On the Internet, dissident's shots heard 'round the world. *New York Times*, p. A18.

Lipset, S. M., Seong, K.-R., & Torres, J. C. (1993). A comparative analysis of the social requisites of democracy. *International Social Science Journal, 45*, 155–175.

MacKie-Mason, J. K., & Varian, H. (1993, May). *Pricing the Internet.* Paper presented at the conference Public Access to the Internet, Cambridge, MA.

Malamud, C. (1993). *Exploring the Internet.* Englewood Cliffs, NJ: Prentice Hall.

Negroponte, N. (1994, April). The fax of life: Playing a bit part. *Wired*, p. 134.

Orwell, G. (1949). *1984.* New York: Harcourt Brace.

Peres, S. (1994, September 11). Address at Foreign Ministry seminar marking the First Anniversary of the signing of the Declaration of Principles, Israel.

Pool, I. de Sola. (1983a). *Forecasting the telephone: A retrospective technology assessment.* Norwood, NJ: Ablex.

Pool, I. de Sola. (1983b). *Technologies of freedom.* Cambridge, MA: The Belknap Press of Harvard University Press.

Quarterman, J. S. (1993, October). [Unpublished data]. Austin, TX: Matrix Information and Directory Services, Inc.

Rheingold, H. (1993). *The virtual community.* Reading, MA: Addison-Wesley.

Ronfeldt, D. (1993). *Institutions, markets and networks: A framework about the evolution of societies* (Tech. Rep. No. DRU-590-FF). Santa Monica, CA: RAND.

Roszak, T. (1986). *The cult of information.* New York: Pantheon Books.

Rothstein, R. L. (1991, Spring). Democracy, conflict, and development in the Third World. *The Washington Quarterly,* pp. 43–63.

Schifter, R. (1994, Summer). Is there a democracy gene? *The Washington Quarterly,* pp. 121–127.

Shane, S. (1994). *Dismantling utopia: How information ended the Soviet Union.* Chicago: Ivan R. Dee, Inc.

Shin, D.C. (1994). On the third wave on democratization: A synthesis and evaluation of recent thepry and research. *World Politics 47* (October) 135–170.

Soldatov, A. (1994, July 29). Paper presented at the New Media for a New World Conference in Moscow, Russia.

Sterling, B. (1993, February 1993). A short history of the Internet, *The Magazine of Fantasy and Science Fiction.*

Sterling, B. (1995, January). Triumph of the plastic people. *Wired,* pp. 101–158.

Tempest, R. (1995, April 25). The Internet scales Great Wall of communication with China. *Los Angeles Times,* p. H/2.

United Nations Development Programme. (1993). *Human development report.* New York: Oxford University Press.

Valauskas, E. J. (1992, January). On the nets and on then streets: A first-person report of the Soviet coup. *Online,* pp. 41–47.

Wriston, W. B. (1988–1989). Technology and sovereignty. *Foreign Affairs, 67*(2), 63–75.

11

CONFLICT ON THE INTERNET

Peter J. Carnevale
Tahira M. Probst
University of Illinois at Urbana–Champaign

Humans have always tried to use technology in the service of resolving and winning social conflicts—stones, arrows, guns, computer-assisted "smart bombs." Sometimes technology changes the amount of conflict. For example, people with weapons are more likely to fight rather than flee from an attack. Sometimes technology transforms social conflict, and changes its very nature. The invention of the stirrup and its migration to Europe led to the greater efficacy, and use of, horses in war. The popularity of horses in conflict increased nobility's need for land, and its seizure or purchase from the Church, which in turn led to the domination of the feudal system, to the culture of chivalry, and to the practice of shock combat (White, 1964). The computer probably has had just as revolutionary an effect on society as the stirrup did. Of all computer-based technologies, one of the most socially powerful is electronic communication, the exchange of communication and information by people across computer networks.

The purpose of this chapter is to detail the forms and impact of electronic communication on the manner in which social conflicts are manifest and resolved. Most of the examples in this chapter refer to the Internet and World Wide Web, but there are many other networks where conflict occurs, including military networks, private networks, and inhouse company networks.

There are two parts to this chapter. The first part is a primer on the behavioral literature on social conflict and negotiation, with a focus on classes of procedures for resolving conflicts, negotiation strategies, and the theory of negotiation and conflict. This sets the stage for a discussion of some of the characteristics of electronic communication that relate to social conflict. The second part is a discussion of the processes, due to electronic communication, that transform, exacerbate, and mollify social conflict, as well as features of conflicts that arise over the technology itself.

SOCIAL CONFLICT AND NEGOTIATION

Social conflict entails the perception of divergent interests, which means that the parties believe that they have incompatible preferences among a set of available options (Carnevale & Pruitt, 1992; Coombs, 1987; Raiffa, 1982). The parties (also called "disputants") may be individuals, groups, organizations, or political units such as nations. Sometimes both parties want different things, but must settle for the same thing. For example, husband and wife differ on where to spend their vacation; labor and management differ on the plan for medical benefits; the new member of the start-up company wants 10% ownership, but the current owners offer only a salary. At other times, both parties want the same thing, but must settle for different things. For example, one nation wants the land, and so does another nation; two managers both want the nice corner office, but only one can have it. Divergent interests can be found in all social arenas, from relations between children on the playground to international relations.

Procedures for Resolving Social Conflict

Three broad classes of procedures for resolving conflicts can be distinguished: (a) working together to find a solution, (b) taking the conflict to a third-party decision maker, and (c) taking independent action. Table 11.1 presents an outline of the different responses (and subresponses) to conflict:

TABLE 11.1

Classes of Procedures for Resolving Social Conflicts

I. Joint decision making
    A. Negotiation
        1. Concession making
        2. Contending
        3. Problem solving
        4. Inaction
        5. Withdrawal
    B. Mediation (assisted negotiation)
II. Third-party decision making
    A. Adjudication
    B. Arbitration
    C. Agreement by authority
III. Separate action
    A. Retreat
    B. Struggle
    C. Tacit coordination

1. The first class is *joint decision making*, which includes negotiation and mediation. Negotiation is a conversation that has the apparent aim of resolving a divergence of interest and thus resolving social conflict. Mediation is a form of negotiation in which a third party helps the disputants reach agreement.

2. *Third-party decision making*, which includes adjudication (going to court), arbitration, and decision making by legitimate authorities, is the second class.

3. The third class, *separate action*, in which the parties make independent decisions, includes (a) retreat, in which one party yields to the other's requirements, (b) struggle, which can take the form of physical combat (military battles, strikes), wars of words (shouting matches, accusations to the press), political contests (vying for allies), or taking unilateral advantage (e.g., theft), and (c) tacit coordination (also called "tacit bargaining"), in which the parties accommodate each other without a discussion (Schelling, 1960). An example of tacit coordination is the pattern of alternation that often develops when two lines of cars are entering the same single lane. Tacit coordination often follows a period of struggle. For instance, two movie-goers seated side-by-side may elbow each other for a period of time before settling down to a nonverbal agreement in which one uses the front and the other the back of the armrest between them.

Decisions among the conflict procedures involve a weighing of pros and cons. The joint decision procedures—negotiation and mediation—have a number of advantages over third-party decision making and separate action. Third-party decision making can be quite expensive: Going to court costs money, bosses usually do not like to be troubled by disagreements between their employees, and so forth. Furthermore, third-party decision makers often do not understand the parties' interests well enough to locate mutually beneficial, "win–win" agreements, and may not regard such agreements as their aim. In addition, joint decision making is usually less costly and dangerous than struggle, the most common form of separate action. Struggle often requires great expenditure of resources (e.g., bombs, loss of customers in a strike, frayed nerves) and endangers the relationship between the parties. Negotiation and mediation tend to be much more benign.

Despite these points about the benefits of joint decision making, third-party decision making and separate action, particularly struggle, are popular. Sometimes direct communication is difficult, because the parties cannot meet or do not understand each other when they do. Trust may be so low that they dare not enter into an explicit agreement with each other. One party may be too proud to concede or too hostile to agree to anything that favors the other's welfare. Both parties may be so angry at each other that their discussion degenerates into arguments and name calling (Deutsch, 1973); or their values may be so different that information exchange between them may lead to a sense of shock and outrage (Druckman & Zechmeister, 1973; Rubin, 1980).

Moreover, it is common for the parties to believe that they can achieve more through struggle or third-party decision than through joint decision. One's power may seem greater than that of the other party, encouraging an effort to exploit the other. One's case may seem stronger than that of the other party, encouraging appeal to an arbitrator or judge. This is especially the case if there is no continuing relationship to worry about. Another disadvantage of negotiation and mediation is that it is usually necessary for *both* parties to agree to enter into them. By contrast, the other party can often be forced to submit to third-party decision making, and struggle is always the default option.

Some of the preceding points help to explain why negotiation or mediation often follow a period of struggle. People fight and then work out their differences. Unions go on strike and then talk it over. Nations threaten each other and then negotiate. What usually happens is that struggle seems initially advantageous to one or both parties, but its costs become more apparent over time. The costs of struggle often increase to the point where they become prohibitive. Experience shows that the other party cannot be exploited or pushed around; or the other concedes for a while and then becomes resistant to further pressure. The parties enter into what Touval and Zartman (1985) called a "hurting stalemate." As struggle loses its allure, other forms of separate action may be considered, although they too have their problems. For example, tacit coordination often cannot produce the kind of fine-tuned agreement that is needed to permanently end the controversy. Therefore, eventually the parties turn to negotiation or mediation.

Negotiation Strategies

It is possible to distinguish five broad strategies that can be used in negotiation, each with a parallel among the broad conflict procedures identified earlier. A negotiation strategy is a plan of action, specifying broad objectives and the general approach that should be taken to achieve these objectives. Some of these strategies must be translated into more specific tactics in order to be used. The negotiation strategies are:

1. *Concession making* involves reducing one's goals, demands, or offers. Unilateral concession making in negotiation has the same effect as retreat.
2. *Contending* is the process of trying to persuade the other party to concede or trying to resist similar efforts by the other party. There are many tactics that can be used to implement this strategy, including threats (messages indicating that one will punish the other party if the other fails to conform) and positional commitments (messages indicating that one will not move from a particular position). Contending in negotiation is analogous to struggle.

3. *Problem solving* means trying to locate and adopt options that satisfy both parties' goals. There are a host of problem-solving tactics, including active listening and providing information about one's own priorities among the issues under discussion. A key requirement for successful problem solving is information exchange pertaining to preferences and other aspects of the issues (Pruitt & Carnevale, 1993; Walton & McKersie, 1965). Problem solving can be thought of as a verbal form of tacit coordination.
4. *Inaction* involves doing nothing or as little as possible, for example, avoiding contact, putting off meetings, talking around the issues, and so on.
5. *Withdrawal* is dropping out of the negotiation.

The first three strategies in this list can be thought of as "coping strategies," because they are alternative ways of moving toward agreement. The latter two indicate a preference for the status quo.

The General Negotiation Paradigm

Much of the behavioral research on negotiation has been guided by a general paradigm that posits that the conditions that prevail at the time of negotiation have an impact on psychological states, such as motives, perceptions, and cognitions. The conditions that prevail at the time of negotiation include factors such as time pressure, and social context variables such as the presence or absence of constituents. Psychological states include motives such as the desire to beat the other, to achieve a fairness principle such as equal outcomes, or to establish or improve a positive relationship with the other. Psychological states also include negotiator cognition, beliefs about the issues, whether outcomes are framed as gains or losses, and how information is processed. The study of negotiator cognition has mainly concerned the application of information processing and decision models to negotiation. Finally, the paradigm posits that the psychological states, motives, and cognitions, in turn, have either a direct impact on outcomes, or an indirect impact that is mediated by the strategies and tactics chosen by the parties (Pruitt & Carnevale, 1993).

A general proposition that has received much empirical support is that conditions that reduce the likelihood of using one of the coping strategies (concession making, problem solving, or contending) increase the likelihood of using the remaining two. If two of the coping strategies are problematic, the third will be given larger consideration. Consider two people, engaged in negotiation, who expect to work together in the future and believe that a positive relationship is important. In this case, they are less likely to use contending, and more likely to use concession making and problem solving. The evidence suggests that people regard contending as likely to offend the other and disrupt the relationship (Pruitt & Carnevale, 1993).

Another aspect of social conflict is escalation. Through a vicious circle of action and reaction, conflicts can escalate from light contentious tactics (e.g., the use of persuasive arguments) to heavy tactics (e.g., a threat to initiate air strikes). The issues can change from small to large, as more people become involved and as increasingly large amounts of available resources are devoted to the conflict. Initially, few people may be involved, but this number can increase, especially via coalition building. Issues can move from matters of specific focus and incident, to general principle. Motives can progress from breaking even, to winning, to hurting the other.

Conflict can produce changes in the parties, the groups, or the communities in which they belong (Pruitt & Rubin, 1986). At the level of the individual, there are psychological changes, which include increased rigid thinking and the development of a "win–lose" mentality. At the group level, changes pertaining to group structure often occur, for example, the development of militant leadership that serves to perpetuate the conflict. Finally, community changes can result, such as polarization, where various subgroups take sides in the conflict.

ELECTRONIC COMMUNICATION

Network technology evolved in the manner it did primarily because it was initially designed by the U.S. Department of Defense to protect communications in the event of attack and to enable researchers to connect with remote computers. The designers of the network did not sit down and discuss how the network might directly contribute to social welfare, and they certainly did not talk about whether it would increase or decrease conflict in society. Although the specific ways in which people connect to Web sites, send and receive messages, and interact in newsgroups do not intentionally or directly bear on conflict, one should keep in mind that the technology people use for communication usually bears on social conflict somehow. The relevant question is, What is it about electronic communication that can affect the development of conflict and the manner in which it is resolved? Nine characteristics of electronic communication are particularly relevant:

1. The first is *specific architecture of the network and email software, for example, perceived anonymity.* In network email, because senders typically are identified as well as receivers (unlike via telephone), "caller ID" is not needed to know the identity of the sender (or at least her email address). This technical nonanonymity of email probably has reduced the incidence of harassment and misrepresentation in networks. However, because communication is by text, and often lacks information about the location or role of the sender, the sender and receiver's sense of anonymity is often heightened. Therefore, electronic interactions themselves are probably affected

just as anonymous interactions are in other domains, with their attendant effects on social facilitation, deindividuation, and so forth.

2. *Speed* is key. Electronic communication speeds up interaction at long distance and across time zones. Because people who live at a distance also tend to differ in other ways (e.g., nationality, ethnicity, culture), electronic communication can speed up communication across social groups. In addition, it can lessen the time in which information is communicated up and down hierarchies and within dispersed groups.

3. *Access* is also important. Electronic communication increases access to others who might have been more difficult to reach in the past. Access to "broadcast rights" is a major change. People can post on electronic newsgroups or on the Web and in that way communicate their ideas to thousands of others without the need for a broadcast license. Within work organizations, access also changes. People have greater access to superiors, just as superiors have greater access to subordinates.

4. The fourth characteristic is the *ability to create groups*. Electronic communication through newsgroups, listservers, distribution lists, MUDs, MOOs, Web pages, and search engines helps people to find others who have similar interests, to join groups, or even to create groups if the ones available do not strike their fancy. If you have a beef about speed traps, you might not find anyone who shares your passion in your neighborhood or at work, but on the Net you can publish a Web page and suddenly have a group (see http://www.speedtrap.com/speedtrap/). The Internet has many such groups composed of people with similar yet highly specialized interests.

5. Fifth is *text communication*. Most electronic communication today is done by text. The exchange of text is a relatively difficult mode of communication and increases information-processing load over telephone or face-to-face communication (Hinds, 1995). In addition, text communication is thought to be less "rich" than other forms of communication, making it more difficult to interact on complex topics.

6. The *absence of social context cues* is also relevant. Social context cues, and nonverbal behavior, act as signals of norms and of people's intentions, and hence they regulate social behavior. The use of text in most electronic communication thus far means that regulation has had to be accomplished through text alone. As more pictures come online, the context will be better defined (e.g., the difference between formal and informal meetings). But until we have audio communication in real time as well, dynamic cues and simultaneous or concurrent feedback will be missing. And the ability to look each other in the eye is not yet readily available.

7. Another key characteristic is the *ability to edit, forward, and store others' and one's own communications*. The fact that messages and pictures are in digital form gives individuals a great deal of power to manipulate the content and source of messages. Individuals can copy, change, or forward others' "intellectual" property (perhaps to have an effect greater than if they

wrote the same message), pass along one message a million times over, and so on.

8. Next is the *difficulty of judging the size of one's audience*. Electronic groups interact often with no idea as to how many other people will read their messages. Because people interact differently in small versus large groups and in crowds, the inability to know the size of one's group might be important to the interplay of conflict.

9. It is a *new technology*. Electronic communication is a new enough technology that people's expectations, norms, rules of politeness, laws, and policies are not fully worked out. In addition, the fact that the technology itself is changing so rapidly makes it hard to develop standards that can accommodate or anticipate future directions.

ELECTRONIC COMMUNICATION AND CONFLICT

Electronic communication exists within social systems and the conflicts therein. But electronic communication also creates new value, and new social systems, and thus also creates the opportunity for new conflicts. The technology can affect qualitative changes in the nature of existing social conflict, and can create new conflict. It can affect how people think about conflict and the way in which conflict is engaged. It can affect who the audience is and the definition of the issues. And it can serve as a mechanism for participation in political processes, and even achieving democratic ideals to the extent that it is accessible at all levels of society.

One effect of the Internet and other forms of electronic communication is to give people greater access to conflicts. This greater access may be to people interested in resolving the conflict, or to people who inadvertently or intentionally expand the conflict.

We distinguish between two broad ways in which electronic communication can influence social conflict:

1. Electronic communication can cause the dispute to undergo a transformation as a direct result of the technology. This transformation can result in changes in both the beginning phases of conflict (conflict escalation, struggle, and contending) and ending phases of conflict (de-escalation, involvement of third parties, coordination, and problem solving).

2. Conflicts can arise that pertain to the technology itself. These include primarily the following: value-added conflict, conflict over procedures, rules and norms of appropriate content and behavior, and conflict over privacy and control.

Electronic Transformations of Disputes

Electronic transformations of disputes pertain to the changes over time in the nature and scope of the conflict. Sometimes the transformations initiate conflict or exacerbate escalation of an existing conflict, and promote the use of struggle and contending tactics. One example of electronic escalation is "cross-roasting," passing an inflammatory message to a group that is known to have a hostile, opposite view of the message. It is "the act of following up a message posted to a Usenet newsgroup by adding one or more additional newsgroups to the response in an effort to bring the original post to the attention of those likely to flame it. For example, in a follow-up to a particularly over-the-top feminist rant, a cross-roaster might add the post to alt.mens-rights and soc.men" (Branwyn, 1996, p. 56).

In other cases, the transformations contribute to de-escalation of the conflict and encourage coordination, problem solving, and third-party intervention.

Mobilization for Struggle and Contending. The Internet can mobilize participation and group formation in conflicts and social movements, and can be used as a vehicle to enhance struggle and contending in conflict. Because the Internet provides fast and efficient communication and enhances information exchange among potential participants, it can provide an easy basis for people to share information and learn about a conflict, determine if they are affected and therefore interested, and learn about others who are involved and what tactics are useful in the struggle (Neumann, 1996). The examples are numerous; here are 10:

1. The Internet was used in the organization of a nationwide campaign on university campuses in a campus protest over the "Contract With America," the basis of the legislative agenda of House Republicans. Organizing was easy and quick, and evidently discussion was facilitated by the Internet (Herszenhorn, 1995).

2. A nationwide campus protest against California's antiimmigration measure, Proposition 187, was organized over the Internet, which resulted in protestors on 20 campuses and a protest march in San Francisco of 2,000 people (Eng, 1995).

3. A group within the Sierra Club sent messages over the club's computerized mail system disapproving the club's leadership approving an administration bill to open land in Montana for logging and other development (Cushman, 1994).

4. The AFL-CIO's home page, "LaborWeb" (http://www.ilr.cornell.edu/vlib/Index/LaborUnions/CIO-AFL), contains policy statements, press releases, issue papers, and the List of National Boycotts sanctioned by the AFL-CIO. Also included are updates on current labor conflict, for example, Caterpillar UAW employees in Peoria, Illinois, bus drivers in Mexico City, and New York City janitors. Their page has links to many other related domains, including LaborNet, the Internet home for AFSCME, Teamsters, Sheet Metal Workers, United Electrical Workers, and

others, for purposes of "information-sharing and collaboration to support the human rights and economic justice of workers" (http://www.igc.org/igc/labornet/index.html). It also contains an "Action Alert Section," with, for example, "urgent appeals" for support and request to sign a petition on behalf of the Jute and Textile workers in Bangladesh who went on strike February 13, 1995, and who suffered violence.

5. "GripeNet" was an IBM network of employees voicing dissatisfaction (Emmett, 1981). Zuboff (1988) gave examples of how computer communication makes ties stronger and challenge existing power structures, as in feminist computer networks. Political pressure groups such as GreenNet, PeaceNet, EcoNet, and WomensNet also show how computer communication can aid in collective action (Perry, 1992) (cf. ConflictNet).

6. The social movement in southern Mexico, in the state of Chiapas, that concerns human rights, welfare, property, and dignity of indigenous people, can be seen vividly at the home page of the Zapatista National Liberation Army, containing statements of history, philosophy, and press releases at this writing, http://www.peak.org./~justin/ezln/about.html. The EZLN leader, known as Subcommander Marcos, reportedly posted communications to outsiders, and communicated with his followers, via the Internet (Dillon, 1995). A photo of Subcommander Marcos, with mask on, carrying AR-15 rifle, and smoking a pipe, is at http://www.peak.org/~justin/ezln/MARCOS.html (see Fig. 11.1).

FIG. 11.1. Subcommander Marcos (http://www.peak.org/~justin/ezln/MARCOS.html).

7. The Association for Progressive Communications has been active in organizing international human rights networks (Whittaker, 1993). Their electronic communication facilitates grassroots movements and political organizing, where new communities of individuals with common interests can link from remote locations, achieving their goals through telephone, fax, computers.

8. The USENET newsgroups served a similar function during the Tienamen Square confrontation in June 1989. The newsgroup soc.culture.china was used as a highly interactive forum for communication and decision making, and sharing information for Chinese students in the United States and Europe for how to respond to the crisis. It was also a vehicle for organization and mobilization from remote locations.

9. Sinn Fein, the political organization of the Irish Republican Army, has a home page (http://www.irlnet.com/sinnfein.index.html) with links to speeches that include the September 27, 1995 Belfast speech by party President Gerry Adams, which accused the British of not having a "peace strategy." This speech presaged a resumption of violence.

10. The home page of the "Association of Flaming Ford Owners" (http://www.flamingfords.com/) detailed the history of the dispute between owners of Ford, Lincoln, and Mercury automobiles, and the manufacturer. Some of these cars apparently contained an ignition switch that caused vehicle fires in the steering column area. At the home page, one can enter the model and year of a car, and get feedback on whether that car is likely to contain the faulty switch. Ford announced a recall of 23 million cars with a promise to replace the switches, evidently due in part to the Internet discussion.

Escalation and Expansion of Conflict. One mechanism for transforming disputes is through expansion and escalation, often driven by the presence of new participants and a new audience. The role of an audience in expanding a dispute and the role of communication in defining the audience can be seen in a dispute in Iowa in the mid-1960s (Mather & Yngvesson, 1981). The conflict was between a small group of Old Order Amish families and the local government of Buchanan County, Iowa. This group of Amish wanted the school board to pay for the required state certified teachers in their schools. But the school board refused to pay for the certified teachers. This led the Amish to fire the certified teachers, which resulted in the school board concluding that the Amish schools were substandard. At the local level, the conflict was defined in part by the economic matter: who would pay for the certified teachers. But the dispute changed dramatically when the school board and sheriffs, with reporters, went to one of the schools and attempted to remove the children by force. A dramatic photograph that appeared in the national press, showing the Amish children running away from the sheriffs, generated huge public concern and sympathy for the Amish. As a result, the conflict was redefined as government persecution of a religious minority, this despite the fact that other groups of Amish in the area were content paying for certified teachers in their schools.

It is interesting to note that the mass electronic communication effect, that is, the news media effect identified by Mather and Yngvesson (1981), can have parallel effects in mass personal electronic communication, as with the Internet.

De-Escalation of Conflict and Involvement by Third Parties. Electronic communication can also provide a basis for third parties to enter the dispute. In the Amish conflict described previously, the publicity and wider audience brought the ACLU and increased financial and legal aid to the conflict. Eventually the Amish won the right in state court to set their own school standards. In addition, the conflict produced a nationally organized lobbying group and a victory before the U.S. Supreme Court in *Wisconsin v. Yoder* (1972), which modified the legal framework for conflicts between religious groups and state educational policy (Mather & Yngvesson, 1981).

In other words, electronic communication, with its speed and access to others, can increase the opportunity for mediators and other third-parties to enter the fray and attempt to resolve the conflict. Conflict will tend to de-escalate in a variety of circumstances as, for example, when there are third party forums such as arbitral services (e.g., courts) and mediation services.

Another important mechanism for controlling escalation and fostering de-escalation is social bonds, such as common group membership, perceived similarity, cross-cutting relationships, and contact. Cross-cutting linkages provide bonds of perceived similarity and common group identity—and provide an impetus to others to mediate. Cross-cutting relationships entail individuals who belong to multiple groups and thus have overlapping group membership with many others (Coleman, 1957). Therefore, the opportunities for positive contact with others and information exchange that may dispel group prejudices and biases are enhanced. Nelson (1989), for example, found that organizations characterized as having a higher number of intergroup ties were less likely to have conflict. Network technology can be used to establish contacts between parties with common interests on both sides of a conflict.

There is evidence that intergroup contact has less of a positive effect on intergroup cooperation if there are status differences between the groups (Hewstone & Brown, 1986). This suggests a particularly useful aspect of computer-mediated interaction: a reduction in social context information and an inhibition of status-based cues and effects (Kiesler, Siegal, & McGuire, 1984). The implication is that the Internet may be a positive vehicle for intergroup contact (cf. Spears & Lea, 1994).

Electronic communication can be used to establish trust. It can allow people to talk when direct talk is unlikely, as when there is distance, animosity, or distrust. It can facilitate the formation of coalitions that cut across group boundaries and that are required to form a basis for agreement (Pruitt & Carnevale, 1993).

Another feature of electronic communication is that the parties do not necessarily see one another. Text-based communication eliminates nonverbal and paraverbal elements of messages, and this may affect the likelihood of conflict escalation. There is a danger with text communication in that emotional signals can be miscommunicated. For example, it sometimes is difficult to tell the difference between sarcasm and genuine irritation. Text-based electronic communication is less "rich" in information than video or face-to-face communication. Therefore, many of the social context cues are lacking in electronic communication. One can only judge the implications of the message from the text itself; there are no body gestures or tone of voice to provide crucial context information. Because of this, miscommunication can occur and conflict can arise, often unintentionally. To help avoid misinterpretation of messages and to compensate for the dearth of context cues, many users employ emotion symbols, for example joy :-), sadness :-(, YELLING, and so forth.

However, several studies have shown that removing nonverbal behaviors, when the context is hostile, can reduce contending in negotiation (Carnevale, Pruitt, & Seilheimer, 1981; S. A. Lewis & Fry, 1977). As a result, cooperative behavior such as concession making and problem solving are more often found when nonverbal cues are removed. This reliable effect is probably due to two nonverbal elements of contending, staring at the other party and moving into the other's territory, both of which are more likely in hostile contexts (S. A. Lewis & Fry, 1977). With electronic communication without video, people cannot see their opponents doing these things and hence are less defensive.

Electronic Interdependence.   Electronic communication can also amplify the speed and urgency of conflict and foster greater interdependence among contemporaneous conflicts. For example, within a few hours of its announcement, Haitian generals learned of the U.S. decision to withdraw troops from Somalia. They too faced an impending invasion of U.S. forces. This led them to quickly organize a protest on the docks of Port-au-Prince as a U.S. warship entered the harbor, with demonstrators shouting "Somalia, Somalia," in front of CNN reporters. There is little doubt that CNN has increased the pace with which international events occur (Rosenstiel, 1994), and the Internet can have the same effect. The distinction between mass electronic communication and personal electronic communication is becoming less clear.

The access of news media to real-time events requires some degree of cooperation between news media and military planners. A case in point was the Haitian conflict of September 1994 with U.S. troops poised to invade Haiti. The U.S. Department of Defense asked, and CNN agreed, not to report live certain events, such as which beach the troops would land on, and when airplanes departed. CNN Executive Vice President Ed Turner (1994) defended the agreement citing the potential negative consequences " ... of showing the planes taking off live and thus enabling Haiti's General Raoul Cedras and his staff in Port-au-Prince to calculate when those planes would arrive and permit them to take specific steps" (p. A23).

Electronic Coordination of Negotiation Information.   Another manner in which computers can be used is to provide easy access to large amounts of information about the exchange of goods and services. The growth of commercial enterprises on the Internet reflects this. For example, some insurance companies have a common Web site, which allows consumers to access the site and easily compare services without having to contact each company separately (P. H. Lewis, 1995). Eckhouse (1988) described the "Fish Exchange," a San Francisco-based computer network for buying and selling fish. Subscribers to the service search for good buys, list fish for sale, and so on, at a level of efficiency that they otherwise could not achieve. A coupon exchange group on the Web allows individuals to put their money-saving coupons up "for sale" and barter them among themselves. For example, one childless individual in San Francisco holding a rare coupon offering a discount on diapers can negotiate an exchange with a woman in Buffalo for her Betty Crocker points plus a discount coupon for movie rentals at Blockbuster. Indeed, any industry that provides information-based products can be structured this way. Presumably, access to service providers and relevant information will produce greater efficiency in market pricing.

Malone, Yates, and Benjamin (1987) made this point in arguing that a main benefit of information technology is a reduction in the costs of coordination. They predicted a general increase in economic activity organized by markets due to electronic technology. This has been borne out by the results of an Office of Technology Assessment Report compiled in 1994. It was concluded that businesses are using information networks in a vast and increasing manner to reduce administrative overhead, reduce costs, speed production, enhance product quality, achieve greater flexibility and responsiveness, and generally reduce the cost of gathering, exchanging, and using information (Office of Technology Assessment Report, 1994).

Another aspect of coordination is the use of computer networks to enhance the work of existing groups and organizations. More than 200 physicists on three continents, many of whom have never met, participate with one another via a network in large high-energy physics experiments at the Fermi National Accelerator Laboratory in Batavia, Illinois. They can share data generated by the accelerator.

Another example is the use of the Internet for collecting data and research collaborations on international conflict (Singer, 1995). There are a variety of academic email bulletin boards that contain information and discussions about the science of social conflict. One such example is the CMDnet listserv, for conflict researchers who associate with the Conflict Management Division of the Academy of Management. The newsletter of this organization is: http://vancouver.wsu.edu/fac/tripp/cmd/cmdhp.html.

Yet another example is the use of the Internet to learn about methods of and access to those in the business of conflict resolution and conflict education. Via the ConflictNet home page, for example, one can learn what universities offer degree programs in conflict resolution. One can access the American Arbitration Association home page, its list of members, and the section entitled "What's new in Alternative Dispute Resolution."

Programs for Problem Solving. Computer systems have been designed to aid problem-solving processes in negotiation. The aim of the software is to develop integrative, efficient agreements. Computers can do human intellectual work, and can be a resource for problem solving. Computer technology can compensate for limited human information processes in negotiation and therefore facilitate problem solving (Shell, 1995; Wheeler, 1995). For example, computers can store and retrieve information and can simulate aspects of complex environments to aid in the understanding of complex scenarios about the future.

Software can assist one negotiator, or two simultaneously and thus serve as an electronic mediator. Therefore, computer programs can also be used to provide some of the problem-solving features of mediation (Carnevale, 1986). For example, Kolodner and Simpson (1989) developed a program called MEDIATOR, which uses case-based reasoning for different tasks in problem solving, where previous solutions to problems are remembered and adapted to fit new cases.

Other efforts by Poole, Holmes, and DeSanctis (1991) and Nyhart and Samarasan (1989) on negotiation support systems extend concepts from group decision making to negotiation. Nyhart (1988) and Nyhart & Samarasan described efforts that place computer software in the hands of both negotiators and third-party facilitators. The software functions to simulate the problem and build models, calculate risk and uncertainty, select decision procedures, introduce integrative bargaining and joint problem solving, and thus optimize settlements. The software is perhaps most relevant to complex negotiations that require sophisticated, deep understanding of technical knowledge of the sort that was required, for example, in the multilateral, international negotiations over deep-ocean mining. One feature of this modeling is to facilitate coalition formation in the service of agreement and suggest potential agreements among subgroups (Nyhart & Samarasan, 1989). The general assumption is that joint modeling can aid information and problem-solving processes in negotiation and foster the development of win–win integrative agreements.

In addition, software assists in negotiation by structuring the interaction and leading negotiators to focus on matters that they might not otherwise. For example, a program that requires negotiators to specify their priority ordering of a subset of issues and then compare their priority ordering with the opposing negotiator, in essence, forces the negotiators to consider the issues simultaneously, as opposed to sequentially. Research shows that simultaneous consideration of the issues improves the likelihood of integrative agreements (Froman & Cohen, 1970).

To the extent that the parties believe computer modeling will aid in providing acceptable outcomes, the implementation of the these systems should increase the likelihood of joint decision making, such as negotiation, and a problem-solving strategy in the negotiation. The use of the these systems should lessen the likelihood that disputants will adopt a contentious strategy in negotiation, choose separate action such as struggle, or opt for third-party decision making.

However, if competitive motives are strong, the parties may be inclined to use the technology to bolster a contentious strategy or to use it deceptively as a vehicle for gaining the advantage in negotiation. One example of this is the use of strategic misrepresentation in the elicitation phase for preferences (Lax & Sebenius, 1986; Raiffa, 1982). Regardless, the implementation of problem-solving and conflict resolution software on the Internet, and its accessibility to disputants, represents an area that has intriguing potential.

Conflicts About Electronic Communication

Conflicts also arise over the technology itself. For example, much has been said about computers being more available to the rich than to the poor, which may exacerbate divisions already fomented, for example, between haves and have nots (Toffler & Toffler, 1993). Negroponte (1995) provided numerous examples of conflicts created over new and developing technologies, including those with vested interests in fiber optics cable versus those who want copper cable; the "Bit Police," the Federal Communications Commission; issues of competition versus monopoly, protection and freedom, cross-ownership of information media, and so on, including issues of censorship (see http://www.yahoo.com/Government/Politics/Censorship/Censorship_and_the_Net/). There are several distinct classes of conflicts over technology. The primary issues that have been raised in connection with electronic communication include: value-added conflict, conflict over procedures, rules and norms, and conflict over privacy and control.

Value-Added Conflict.   Advances in technology create new value, and conflicts over control of that value. Lyall (1994), for example, wrote about the control and pricing issues regarding electronic rights to books online and on CD-ROM, and noted the difficulty in establishing contracts that are flexible enough to anticipate developments in as-of-yet discovered distribution media.

Another example is conflict over copyrights on the Internet. Current legislation targets "cyberjackers," individuals who post copyrighted material on the Internet, with one important question pertaining to the liability of the service providers (Rupley, 1995). Computerization creates conflict between institutions and the public over issues such as ownership and control of new data, collected by computers, on people.

Procedures, Rules, and Norms. Conflicts about technology also concern the procedures, rules, and norms that will guide use and access to the technology. The Internet provides new forms of, and forums for, human interaction. One can play duplicate bridge in real time with people from other continents. The MUD (multiuser dungeon) is a real-time bulletin board that offers the opportunity to socialize anonymously, to create alternative selves and worlds. In LambdaMOO, debate on the network surfaced over governance, whether to make it more like a representative government (i.e., efficient) or more like a committee of the whole (more democratic) (see Hafner, 1994).

The Internet has an evolving set of norms about what is appropriate communication. There is increasing interest in "netiquette" (abbreviation of net etiquette), guidelines and rules for appropriate behavior (see http://www.fau.edu/rinaldi/net/elec.html). Many people consider advertising improper on the Internet, and treat those who post advertisements with disdain. Some have gone so far as replying to advertisements with hostile messages, even writing programs such as the "cancelbot" that tracks down and erases offending messages. Many people also consider it inappropriate to post messages to (unmoderated) newsgroups that have nothing to do with the realm of interest to the newsgroup. Such messages tend to elicit flaming. Many networks are moderated, and many have software programs that screen obscenities and business solicitations and bounce them back to senders. P. H. Lewis (1994a) reported the case of a lawyer who advertised his services over the Internet and that caused a torrent of protests and expulsion from the network.

Electronic shouting matches are not uncommon. One example reported in *The New York Times* (December 13, 1992) was the Prodigy Money Talk bulletin board on November 22, 1992. William Donoghue, publisher of the widely read *Donoghue MoneyLetter*, wrote several erroneous statements about variable annuities sold by Vanguard mutual funds. A series of rather pointed criticisms led Donoghue to admit his error on the November 30 bulletin board.

Another example of Internet conflict concerns how to control congestion (MacKie-Mason & Varian, 1994). Each packet sent imposes a cost on other users because the resources that one user takes are not available to others. The cost can come in the form of delays or even lost data. The structure is that of the classic "tragedy of the commons" (Hardin, 1968). Congestion can be a problem, in particular if there is no incentive to economize. This is particularly a problem with the growing demand for multimedia services.

Solutions to the problem include charging a usage price, reliance on voluntary efforts to control congestion, and peer pressure. MacKie-Mason and Varian (1994) offered a case that makes the point: "Recently a single user started broadcasting a 350–450 Kbps audio–video test pattern to hosts around the world, blocking the network's ability to handle a scheduled audio broadcast from a Finnish University. A leading network engineer sent a strongly worded email message to the user's site administrator, and the offending workstation was disconnected from the network" (pp. 85–86). They noted, however, that peer pressure is inefficient because it occurs *after* the disruption, and that there is an ever-increasing number of unsophisticated users who tend to be unaware of the impact of their behavior. Recently an undergraduate student sent email requesting readers to forward his message and to send a reply message saying "hi"—ostensibly as a research project demonstrating the far-reaching span of the Internet. The student did not realize that receiving thousands of email messages from those respondents would effectively bring the university server to its knees.

Privacy and Control. Computer networks can also cause conflict over invasion of privacy and control. For example, there is potential for abuse of corporate and government databases, medical records, and logs of consumer buying habits. P. H. Lewis (1994b) wrote about the great concern for security in commercial transactions over the Internet, and the quest for secure systems. MacKie-Mason and Varian (1994) noted the requirements for electronic commerce over the Internet. One issue is anonymity so that buying and selling habits cannot be sold to marketing agencies or otherwise used surreptitiously. Another issue is whether governments should provide data network services as public goods. The Clinton administration has established a policy that all published government documents be available to anyone, free, in electronic form.

Another issue of concern is the potential use of electronic communication for criminal activity, and the steps that should be taken to curtail this activity. This includes fraudulent buying and selling, fraudulent transfer of assets, creation and promulgation of viruses, and other destructive activity. Antisocial, criminal groups are able to pursue their objectives with increased efficiency. A case in point is the neo-Nazi "Thule Network" in Europe (Bajak, 1994). The network consists of more than a dozen bulletin boards where extreme rightists exchange information about rallies and how to create hate media. It raises issues of freedom and rights, judgments about what is offensive, and matters of social responsibility and collective welfare.

CONCLUSIONS

This chapter examined a few ways in which electronic communication and technology can influence the course of social conflict. Electronic communication and conflict interact in two fundamentally different ways. First, technology can result in a transformation of the dispute. Electronic transformations occur at any stage or level of the conflict: initiation, escalation, or expansion of conflict, enhanced mobilization of supporters, increased use of problem-solving tactics, or introduction of third parties to the dispute. In addition, the existence of new technology can engender conflict. Disputes occur over regulation of the technology, operating procedures, rules, and norms, and issues of privacy and control.

With the advent of electronic communication, the concept of conflict has expanded beyond the local location of personal face-to-face contact, and the concepts of time and distance in conflict are also altered (Macduff, 1994). The historian Paul Schroeder (1994) commented on the speed in which the Gulf War coalition was put together and, further, added that communication technology requires a modification of the Old Testament saying that "The sins of the fathers are visited upon the children to the third and fourth generation." This saying had been amply documented in the history of international affairs: " ... [O]nly in 1919 and 1945 did the full consequences of Bismarck's founding of the Second Reich in 1871 become clear" (Schroeder, 1994, p. 40). But no longer is this the case, according to Schroeder: "In the New World Order, with history accelerated and the speed of communication enormously increased, it is no longer unreasonable to expect children to see and repudiate the sins of their fathers while the fathers are still around" (p. 41).

Cohen (1992) wrote about the effect of electronic communication on the legitimacy and power of nation states, commenting on the collapse of communism: "Galloping technologies have weakened the ability of the state to control information flowing to its citizens. The two revolutionaries of our era may turn out to be not Marx and Lenin but the Bell Labs and the Boeing Corporation—the inventors of the transistor and the wide-bodied jet—which between them have enabled ideas and people to move cheaply, and sometimes instantly, over and through the iron and bamboo curtains."

New problems in social conflict will emerge with the introduction of new technology. Uneven development of technology, for example, where the parties to a conflict differ in their level of technological sophistication, poses unique problems that may affect conflict. Superior technology is not always a benefit. The U.S. military learned how difficult it was to capture the Somalian leader, Aidid, in part because he was so low-tech—he wisely avoided use of the telephone, and the search was done using high-tech devices.

In addition to serving as a mobilizing force, electronic communication can also tempt strategic ploys and gamesmanship, forms of struggle and contending. Schelling (1960) gave a colorful analysis of technology-driven strategic communication games: Two people parachute into an area, get separated, but each has a map of the terrain. Each is ignorant of where the other has dropped and they cannot communicate. But they must get together to be rescued. Schelling argued that people in this situation can coordinate if they develop convergent expectations about what they each might do ("I bet she will go to the bridge, she will think that I will too, so I'll go to the bridge"). The expectations are driven by a focal point that attracts attention (there is only one bridge, and it is in the center of the map).

Expectations have an effect even when there is conflict of interest. For example, suppose the parachutists dislike walking. If they could communicate, they might negotiate where to meet, and attempt to convince the other to do the walking. But there is an interesting paradox here, identified by Schelling (1960), that gives an advantage to the person who is not able to communicate. One parachutist sends the message: "Come to location G7 and, by the way, I am unable to receive email; I'll wait for you here at G7." The other has no choice but to walk. Her counteroffer could not be effective because it could not be received. The paradox is that an apparent disadvantage—not being able to communicate—provides an advantage in the strategic game.

One interesting feature of conflicts on and about the Internet is that they tend to generate quite a bit of material, which then becomes available, online, to others interested in learning more about the conflict. For example, the dispute involving the Church of Scientology and the Internet/USENET community over issues of privacy, copyright, and control has a Web site containing extensive links to first-person accounts, legal papers, and newspaper and magazine articles on the dispute (see http://www.cybercom.net/~rnewman/scientology/home.html). One beneficial effect of the online storage of conflict material is that it can facilitate analysis and study by conflict researchers.

The conflicts that arise over new forms of electronic communication are unique in that electronic communication itself may affect the transformation of these conflicts and their eventual resolution. To understand the relationship between electronic communication and conflict may be integral in the effort to move forward and employ this technology in a productive, beneficial manner.

ACKNOWLEDGMENTS

The authors are grateful to Sara Kiesler, Andrea Hollingshead, and Chris Elford for the very helpful comments and suggestions on this chapter. This material is based in part on work supported by the National Science Foundation under Grant SBR-9210536.

REFERENCES

Bajak, F. (1994, February 2). Computer network adds bytes to neo-Nazi barks. *Pittsburgh Post-Gazette*, p. A-5.

Branwyn, G. (1996, January). Jargon watch. *Wired*, p. 56.

Carnevale, P. J. (1986). Strategic choice in mediation. *Negotiation Journal, 2*, 41–56.

Carnevale, P. J., & Pruitt, D. G. (1992). Negotiation and mediation. *Annual Review of Psychology, 43*, 531–582.

Carnevale, P. J., Pruitt, D. G., & Seilheimer, S. (1981). Looking and competing: Accountability and visual access in integrative bargaining. *Journal of Personality and Social Psychology, 40*, 111–120.

Cohen, S. P. (1992). U. S. security in a separatist season. *The Bulletin of the Atomic Scientists, 48* (6), 29–32.

Coleman, J. S. (1957). *Community conflict*. New York: The Free Press.

Coombs, C. H. (1987). The structure of conflict. *American Psychologist, 42*, 355–363.

Cushman, J. H., Jr. (1994, May 1). Environmental group divided by Federal logging proposal. *The New York Times*, p. A17.

Deutsch, M. (1973). *The resolution of conflict*. New Haven, CT: Yale University Press.

Dillon, S. (1995, October 2). Mexican rebel denounces his foes, and melts away. *The New York Times*, p. A4.

Druckman, D., & Zechmeister, K. (1973). Conflict of interest and value dissensus: Propositions in the sociology of conflict. *Human Relations, 26*, 449–466.

Eckhouse, J. (1988, March 9). Fishing industry gets a hot line. *San Francisco Chronicle*, p. D18.

Emmett, R. (1981, November). Vnet or gripenet. *Datamation*, pp. 48–58.

Eng, L. (1995, January 22). Internet is becoming a very useful tool for campus radicals. *The Journal Star*, p. A8.

Froman, L. A., & Cohen, M. D. (1970). Compromise and logroll: Comparing the efficiency of two bargaining processes. *Behavioral Science, 15*, 180–183.

Hafner, K. (1994, November 7). Get in the MOOd. *Newsweek*, pp. 58–65.

Hardin, G. (1968). The tragedy of the commons. *Science, 162*, 1243–1248.

Herszenhorn, D. M. (1995, March 29). Students turn to Internet for nationwide protest planning. *The New York Times*, p. B8.

Hewstone, M. R., & Brown, R. J. (1986). Contact is not enough: An intergroup perspective on the contact hypothesis. In M.R. Hewstone & R.J. Brown (Eds.), *Conflict and contact in intergroup encounters*: 181–198. Oxford, England: Blackwell.

Hinds, P. (1995). *Workload and the fundamental attribution error in email*. Unpublished manuscript, Carnegie Mellon University, Pittsburgh.

Kiesler, S., Siegal, J., & McGuire, T. W. (1984). Social psychological aspects of computer-mediated communication. *American Psychologist, 39*, 1123–1134.

Kolodner, J. L., & Simpson, R. L. (1989). The MEDIATOR: Analysis of an early case-based problem solver. *Cognitive Science, 13*, 507–49.

Lax, D. A., & Sebenius, J. K. (1986). *The manager as negotiator*. New York: The Free Press.

Lewis, P. H. (1994a, April 19). An ad (gasp!) in cyberspace. *The New York Times*, pp. D1.

Lewis, P. H. (1994b, August 12). Attention shoppers: Internet is open. *The New York Times*, pp. C1–C2.

Lewis, P. H. (1995, October 24). Insurers join common Web site, allowing consumers to compare. *The New York Times*, p. C21.

Lewis, S. A., & Fry, W. R. (1977). Effects of visual access and orientation
on the discovery of integrative bargaining alternatives. *Organizational Behavior and Human Performance, 20,* 75–92.

Lyall, S. (1994, March 28). Publishing: To avoid future shocks, publishers and authors are fighting for the electronic rights to books. *The New York Times,* p. C6.

Macduff, I. (1994). Flames on the wire: Mediating from an electronic cottage. *Negotiation Journal, 10,* 5–15.

MacKie-Mason, J. K., & Varian, H. (1994). Economic FAQs about the Internet. *Journal of Economic Perspectives, 8,* 75–96.

Malone, T. W., Yates, J., & Benjamin, R. I. (1987). Electronic markets and electronic hierarchies. *Communications of the ACM, 30,* 484–487.

Mather, L., & Yngvesson, B. (1981). Language, audience, and the transformation of disputes. *Law and Society Review, 15,* 755.

Negroponte, N. (1995). *Being digital.* New York: Knopf.

Nelson, R. E. (1989). The strength of strong ties: Social networks and intergroup conflict in organizations. *Academy of Management Journal, 32,* 377–401.

Neumann, A. L. (1996, January). The resistance network. *Wired,* pp. 108–114.

Nyhart, J. D. (1988, April). Computer modeling in dispute resolution—An overview. *Dispute Resolution Forum, 3,* pp. 11–14.

Nyhart, J. D., & Samarasan, D. K. (1989). The elements of negotiation management: Using computers to help resolve conflict. *Negotiation Journal, 5,* 43–62.

Office of Technology Assessment (1994). U. S. Congress, Electronic Enterprises: Looking to the future (OTA-TCT-548). Washington, DC: U.S. Government Printing Office.

Perry, T. S. (1992, October). E-mail at work. Electronic Mail. *IEEE Spectrum,* pp. 24–48.

Poole, M. S., Holmes, M., & DeSanctis, G. (1991). Conflict management in a computer-supported meeting environment. *Management Science, 37,* 926–953.

Pruitt, D. G., & Carnevale, P. J. (1993). *Negotiation in social conflict.* Pacific Grove, CA: Brooks/Cole.

Pruitt, D. G. & Rubin, J. Z. (1986). *Social conflict: Escalation, stalemate, and resolution.* New York: Random House.

Raiffa, H. (1982). *The art and science of negotiation.* Cambridge, MA: Harvard University Press.

Rosenstiel, T. (1994, August 22 & 29). The myth of CNN. *The New Republic,* pp. 27–33.

Rubin, J. Z. (1980). Experimental research on third-party intervention in conflict: Toward some generalizations. *Psychological Bulletin, 87,* 379–91.

Rupley, S. (1995). Judge rules on electronic copyrights. *PC Magazine, 14,* 30.

Schelling, T. (1960). *The strategy of conflict.* Cambridge, MA: Harvard University Press.

Schroeder, P. W. (1994). The new world order: A historical perspective. *The Washington Quarterly, 17,* 25–43.

Shell, G. R. (1995). Computer-assisted negotiation and mediation: Where we are and where we are going. *Negotiation Journal, 11,* 117–121.

Singer, D. (1995, June). *The Internet and computer data in conflict research: What use? What future?* Paper presented at the symposium conducted at the Annual Conference of the International Association for Conflict Management, LO-Skolen, Elsinore, Denmark.

Spears, R., & Lea, M. (1994). Panacea or panoptica? The hidden power in computer-mediated communication. *Communication Research, 21,* 427–459.

Toffler, A., & Toffler, H. (1993). *War and anti-war.* Boston; Little, Brown.

Touval, S., & Zartman, I. W. (1985). *International mediation in theory and practice.* Boulder, CO: Westview.

Turner, E. (1994, September 28). In Haiti reporting, CNN acted responsibly. *The New York Times,* p. A23.

Walton, R., & McKersie, R. (1965). *A behavioral theory of labor negotiations: An analysis of a social interaction system*. New York: McGraw-Hill.

Wheeler, M. (1995). Computers and negotiation: Backing into the future. *Negotiation Journal, 11*, 169–175.

White, L., Jr. (1964). *Medieval technology and social change*. Oxford, England: Oxford University Press.

Whittaker, G. (1993). MacHumanRights: New technologies are changing the nature of grassroots activism. *Index on Censorship, 2*, 14–15.

Wisconsin v. Yoder (1972). 405 U. S. 205.

Zuboff, S. (1988). *In the age of the smart machine: The future of work and power*. New York: Basic Books.

Coordination, Control, and Intranets

Rob Kling
Indiana University

In the early 1990s, excitement about the Internet as a medium for coordinating work led to the development of "intranets" in organizations. Intranets refer to computer networks that serve internal organizational functions but use the Internet packet-switched communication protocol TCP/IP. To build intranets, companies can use Internet services such as Web servers (today's hot item) and various Internet software for file transfer and email. Despite the enthusiasm of technologists, managers, and journalists, intranets often are adopted slowly and with difficulty, and they have not yet been shown to dramatically improve flexibility, collaboration and cooperation in workplaces. Perhaps Internet-related computer technology is too new to have a major effect on how work is done in the modern corporation. Another possibility is that the technology has real consequences, some of them undesirable. Technology often is introduced in organizations without a clear analysis of how work processes must change for the technology to work, who needs to support these changes, and, in the process, who will gain and who will lose. For example, if an intranet helps people share data, how do routines for data flow need to change? Who needs to support these changes in routines? How will the new system for sharing data (technology and work process) affect people's relationships and roles?

Some research has directly examined these processes in workplaces. For example, Wanda Orlikowski (1993) examined the use of Lotus Notes at a major consulting firm in the months it was being installed. Notes' use was related to the reward structure at the consulting firm. The staff and partners who had significant job security were most willing to learn Lotus Notes and share professional information. By contrast, the numerous associates were preoccupied with their careers and the risk of being fired if they did not produce lots of billable services for their immediate clients. They were reluctant to learn Notes or to share their special expertise with each other. Why should people whose promotions depend upon being seen as having unique expertise be willing to give it away to others, just because a slick computer system facilitates it (Thorn & Connolly, 1987; see also Grudin, 1989)?

A key to understanding the adoption and usage of intranet applications lies in our observing that it is hard to change cooperation and collaboration without affecting control too. Cooperation and control often depend on one another. To take an extreme case, prisoners in chain gangs often cooperate with their guards. Workplaces are much less coercive than chain gangs, but they do not lack control of "cooperative" behaviors through the exertion of authority, expertise, and rules. Likewise control would probably be impossible without people who are cooperative and who develop social roles and relationships with those who exert formal control. Computer systems that change patterns of cooperation usually portend a change in control too.

System developers chart work and information flows in organizations when they develop and introduce new systems. Developers need to chart social relationships when they develop intranet systems. They need to ask, "How will people's differing goals be supported by this system?" If we study the rich multivalent social relationships in workplaces—simultaneously cooperative, conflicting, collaborative, controlling, convivial, and competitive—we will understand intranets better too. For discussions of many social aspects of the Internet in workplaces see Kling, 1996.

REFERENCES

Grudin, J. (1989). Why groupware applications fail: Problems in design and evaluation. *Office: Technology and People, 4,* 245–264.

Kling, R. (1996). *Computerization and controversy: Value conflicts and social choices.* (2nd ed.). San Diego: Academic Press.

Orlikowski, W. J. (1993). Learning from Notes: Organizational issues in groupware implementation. *The Information Society , 9,* 237–250.

Thorn, B. K., & Connolly, T. (1987). Discretionary data bases: A theory and some experimental findings, *Communication Research, 14,* 512–528.

Part IV

COMPUTER-SUPPORTED
COOPERATIVE WORK

The idea of computer-supported cooperative work has garnered an enthusiastic following of researchers and developers, many of whom meet at a biennial Association of Computing Machinery conference called "CSCW." Those who started CSCW thought applications developers, information systems professionals, and behavioral scientists had put too much emphasis on the creation of systems for one person working independently. Since most people work with collaborators and in groups, committees, teams, and task forces, we need systems that support collaborative and group work (Galegher, Kraut, & Egido, 1990; Licklider & Vezza, 1978). For those interested in CSCW, electronic communication is the key infrastructure. Email, the World Wide Web, Lotus Notes, project management software, electronic calendars for groups, and electronic bulletin boards running on networks all are CSCW applications.

Despite the idea's popularity, CSCW is still mysterious. What attributes of electronic communication sustain or create cooperation? What attributes of electronic communication pull people apart? Some theoretical work suggests that electronic communication can reduce the coordination costs of joint work and of commerce (Malone, 1987). Also it has been argued that electronic communication can reduce the individual and organizational costs of learning from others (Lederberg, 1978; Levin & Cohen, 1985) and increase commitment to the organization (Huff, Sproull, & Kiesler, 1989) and productivity of peripheral workers (Hesse, Sproull, Kiesler, & Walsh, 1993). Others have pointed out that cooperation depends on trust and the development of routines for communicating and doing work, both of which are most likely to develop when people work together in specific local settings (e.g., Allen, 1977; Suchman, 1988). A body of theory, in fact, suggests that distributed groups having invisible members tend to engender free riding and defection (e. g., Thorn & Connolly, 1987).

The chapters in this section illustrate recent work on the social aspects of computer supported cooperative work. Chapter 12 represents a fairly large literature of "meeting room" or group decision support CSCW technologies. Meeting room technology typically consists of multiple computers or terminals in one meeting room, networked together. A computer program allows people in the room to display messages so everyone in the group can see them; also they can vote on everyone's ideas, rank order or rate the contributions, and edit them to make a group report. Terry Connolly's chapter discusses the most successful application of group decision support systems—for group brainstorming. He describes research showing when these systems improve productivity and when they don't, and he shows how electronic brainstorming raises intriguing questions for theory in social psychology.

Email is indisputably the most successful and popular CSCW application. But when people can send messages easily to "anyone, anywhere," even more people will be receiving messages from anyone, anywhere. Chapter 13, by Steve Whittaker and Candy Sidner, represents one of the first systematic studies of one resulting social irony, "email overload." The authors ask why people keep the hundreds or thousands of email messages they have received, including "junk" messages from distribution lists that they have never even read. The authors, based on their interviews, propose some answers and a redesign of email applications to help people better cope with their email. This chapter also suggests a more general problem. That is, as technology unleashes our ability to communicate across the constraints of time and distance, how will we allocate our own limited attention resources to all this communication and information? A "box" points readers to Warren Thorngate's fascinating analyses of "attentional economics."

REFERENCES

Allen, T. J. (1977). *Managing the flow of technology*. Cambridge, MA: MIT Press.

Galegher, J., Kraut, R. E., & Egido, C. (Eds.). (1990). *Intellectual teamwork: Social and technological foundations of cooperative work*. Hillsdale, NJ: Lawrence Erlbaum Associates.

Hesse, B. W., Sproull, L., Kiesler, S., & Walsh, J. P. (1993). Returns to science: Networks and scientific research in oceanography. *Communications of the ACM, 36*, 90–101.

Huff, C., Sproull, L., & Kiesler, S. (1989). Computer communication and organizational commitment: Tracing the relationship in a city government. *Journal of Applied Social Psychology, 19*, 1371–1391.

Lederberg, J. (1978). Digital communications and the conduct of science: The new literacy. *IEEE Proceedings, 66*, 1314–1319.

Levin, J. A., & Cohen, M. (1985). The world as an international science laboratory: Electronic networks for science instruction and problem solving. *Journal of Computers in Mathematics and Science Teaching, 4*, 33–35.

Licklider, J. C. R., & Vezza, A. (1978). Applications of information networks. *IEEE Proceedings*, *66*, 1330–1346.

Malone, T. (1987). Modeling coordination in organizations and markets. *Management Science*, *33*, 1317–1332.

Suchman, L. A. (1988). *Plans and situated actions*. Norwood, NJ: Ablex.

Thorn, B. K., & Connolly, T. (1987). Discretionary databases: A theory and some experimental findings. *Communication Research*, *14*, 512–528.

12

ELECTRONIC BRAINSTORMING: SCIENCE MEETS TECHNOLOGY IN THE GROUP MEETING ROOM

Terry Connolly
University of Arizona

Social psychologists have long been interested in understanding group processes; software engineers have more recently become interested in changing them. There is a real, two-way relationship between the two enterprises, but it is not simple or straightforward. The author explores the relationship using as an example work on group brainstorming, both face-to-face and on electronic networks. He notes, among other points, the importance of mismatches in time constants, the looseness of the coupling between science and technology, and the special sorts of research designs and theory building that are appropriate for technology development efforts. He concludes that the enterprise of connecting behavioral research and network technology, though tricky, is worth the effort.

A student learning a well-developed technology, such as the design of airframes, steam turbines, or buildings, is generally first taught the relevant theory or science (aerodynamics, thermodynamics, theory of structures), and then goes on to the application of this knowledge in practice. Because technologists typically learn little of the history of their professions, students probably assume that the sequence of teaching mirrors the sequence of discovery—that the development of aerodynamics preceded and led to the development of workable planes, or that knowledge of thermodynamics drove the design of steam engines. Such an assumption is, in fact, quite wrong for these two technologies, and probably for many others. Successful practice and successful theory intertwine and stimulate one another in complex ways. With young technologies, in particular, it is common for the practice to outrun, or even to run counter to, the existing theory. Learned predictions of the impossibility of heavier-than-air flight, for example, suggest the possible gaps between theory and practice.

This chapter examines the development of one modest technology, electronic brainstorming (EBS), with particular emphasis on the interplay of theory and practice. I first review the development of nonelectronic brainstorming research over a period of 20 years or so immediately preceding early EBS technology. I then sample some of the newer research examining the effectiveness of the new technology, and the sorts of methodological as well as substantive issues this research raises. Mostly I use examples from projects in which the author has been involved at the University of Arizona, where colleagues have been developing and commercializing group support systems (GSS) for electronic meetings, including EBS. Finally, I offer some thoughts on the interplay between research and technology in this area.

NONELECTRONIC BRAINSTORMING

In 1953, Alex Osborn, an advertising executive, published a book entitled *Applied Imagination*. It was not a scholarly work but a how-to-do-it book for a managerial audience. In it, Osborn emphasized the importance to advertising of creative, new, original ideas, and advocated a technique by which such originality could be stimulated: group brainstorming. The heart of the technique was straightforward: Groups of diverse individuals with an interest in the topic were to be assembled. They were to interact uninhibitedly, aiming to generate as many ideas as possible, without regard to quality, and the wilder the better. Members were encouraged to improve, combine, and "piggyback" off the contributions of others. No criticism was allowed.

Osborn's claim was that groups using his brainstorming technique would generate more, and more original, ideas than would those using other, more conventional techniques. Behavioral researchers, starting with Taylor, Berry and Block (1958), quickly focused on this claim, generally interpreting the appropriate baseline for comparison to be the ideas generated by the same number of individuals working alone: the equivalent "nominal group." Osborn was read, not unfairly, as advocating a particular form of group session designed to stimulate the idea generation of individual members. The nominal group was to provide a measure of what the individuals were capable of on their own. The group's output above this baseline was then to provide a measure of the stimulation provided by the group, and would serve to guide the fine-tuning of such matters as optimal group size, composition, and schedule.

It soon became apparent ("soon," in this context, meaning "within a decade or two") that the nominal-group baseline was not the floor but the ceiling: Interacting groups consistently *under*performed the nominal-group baseline, over a wide range of tasks, group sizes, interaction patterns, and instruction sets. A typical study of this period (Lewis, Sadosky, & Connolly, 1975) pitted interacting groups of size two, four, and six, working in various sequences of group and individual work, against nominal groups of similar individuals working alone under brainstorming instructions. The problem was a real-world problem in industrial engineering (methods for shifting bulk sugar in a soft-drink plant), and the subjects were student and professional industrial engineers. The results:

> support and extend a number of previous studies which suggest that group brainstorming is no more productive of ideas, and may be less productive, than combining the results of individual brainstorming efforts. Previous research has generally supported this finding for four-man student groups working for brief periods on laboratory puzzles. The present study found similar results for a "real-world" problem, for group sizes of 2, 4 and 6, for time periods of 50 and 90 minutes, and for various mixtures of group and individual work. (Lewis et al., 1975, p. 123).

By 1980 or so, then, it was clear that Osborn's (1953) technique, and modest variants on it, did not pass the simple-minded test of outperforming equivalent nominal groups in laboratory conditions. Whatever assets brainstorming groups might enjoy, they seemed to be outweighed by their liabilities. McGrath (1984) gave a succinct summary:

"The evidence speaks loud and clear: *Individuals working separately generate many more*, and *more creative* (as ranked by judges), *ideas than do groups*, even when the redundancies among member ideas are deleted, and, of course, without the stimulation of hearing and piggybacking on the ideas of others. The difference is large, robust, and general" (p. 131; emphasis in original).

Despite the consistent empirical evidence of the technique's ineffectiveness, both theoreticians and practitioners maintained an interest in group brainstorming. The technique appears to have enjoyed a steady popularity in managerial practice and management textbooks (e.g. Gibson, Ivancevich, & Donnelly, 1991; Northcraft & Neale, 1990). Researchers in group processes continued to study the technique, presumably more to advance general understanding of the social psychology of groups than in hope of developing an effective idea-generating technique. By 1987 Diehl and Stroebe were able to propose a rather detailed theoretical analysis of the problems facing brainstorming groups, and to assess the evidence bearing on this theory. They identified three major liabilities that had been proposed as accounting, in whole or in part, for the shortcomings of these groups:

1. *The first is evaluation apprehension.* Participants in interacting groups offer their ideas in a public setting, potentially open to the scorn or negative evaluations of others. Anticipating such negative evaluations (even if no

explicit criticism was voiced) might well inhibit some members from offering unusual, risky, or potentially silly ideas. (This possibility, presumably, motivated Osborne's (1953) "no criticism" rule.) Nominal group members, in contrast, work alone, and are thus presumably less inhibited about proposing all their ideas, wild or not.

2. *Next is social loafing/free riding.* This second possibility turns on the diffusion of rewards for effort in a group, as compared to individual work. On this account nominal group members working alone work harder, and produce more ideas, because all the reward for each additional idea generated accrues to them. Members of a group of N individuals, in contrast, anticipate receiving only $1/N$th of the marginal reward per idea, and thus feel a weaker incentive to contribute effort. (Because few of the studies include monetary reward per idea, the notion is, presumably, more broadly construed here to include the experimenter's gratitude and approval and other intangibles.)

3. *Finally, there is production blocking.* In a group of size N, only one member can talk (i.e., contribute ideas) at a given instant. The other $(N-1)$ members are, at best, listening or thinking, waiting their turn to speak. It is possible that, during this delay, ideas are forgotten, counterarguments occur to the waiting member, attention wanders, and so on, with the result that ideas are lost to the group. Working alone, in contrast, the nominal group member can (ideally) produce ideas as they occur.

Diehl and Stroebe (1987), after an impressive marshalling of their own and others' evidence, concluded that the first two candidate mechanisms accounted for little if any of the groups' productivity loss. The major—perhaps the only—villain was production blocking. Mullen, Johnson, and Salas (1991), using meta-analysis, reached somewhat different conclusions.

In the 30 or so years following Osborn's (1953) book, then, brainstorming flourished in management practice. Careful behavioral research, however, seemed to show pretty conclusively that it did not work as claimed, and had arrived at some theoretical maturity in explaining why not. This is the background against which a new technology of group interaction started to emerge: the electronic meeting.

ELECTRONIC BRAINSTORMING

During the 1980s, continuing efforts were made in a number of groups to harness the power of networked microcomputers to improving the productivity of the group meeting. A variety of combinations of face-to-face discussion, individual computer-supported work, and shared communication technologies were explored. The University of Arizona group emphasized designs involving essentially no face-to-face interaction, relying instead on networked, computer-mediated interaction and public screens for shared display. A variety of software tools, supported by a human facilitator, provided structured group interaction for generating, evaluating, and selecting among ideas. (Nunamaker, Dennis, Valacich, Vogel, & George, 1991, gave an overview of this process.)

It seems unlikely that the software engineers who designed these systems spent much time reviewing the discouraging brainstorming research noted earlier. They simply saw the opportunities the technology offered and went ahead with a system that seemed to make practical sense (possibly informed by the popularity of brainstorming in managerial practice). The procedure they devised for idea generation was straightforward. Each participant sits at a terminal, which displays a brief statement of the topic on which ideas are sought. The remainder of the screen is divided horizontally into two "windows," both initially blank. The participant types a comment of a line or two, which appears in the lower window, and "sends" the file by a function key to a common pool. The initial file is immediately replaced by another drawn randomly from the pool, showing another participant's first comment in the upper window. On adding a second comment and "sending" the file, the participant receives another, with two comments now in the upper window. The files thus grow longer and longer as the session proceeds, with strings of earlier comments in the upper window offering stimulation for idea generation on each round. A noncomputerized analog would be for the members to share a pool of note pads, seizing one pad from the pool, adding a comment on it, throwing the pad back into the pool, taking another for the next comments, and so on. The session is generally brought to an end by the facilitator when idea generation flags. The procedure is known as electronic brainstorming (EBS).

EBS is popular among participants in electronic meetings, and it certainly leads to the generation of a lot of ideas. (Indeed, coping with the flood of material generated in these sessions has stimulated interest in automatic computer classification of the text generated: See, e.g., Chen, Hsu, Orwig, Hoopes, & Nunamaker, 1994.) However, the first direct comparison between EBS and nominal groups was reported rather late in the developmental sequence, in Valacich, Dennis, and Connolly (1994). These authors reported three experiments pitting EBS groups of various sizes (3, 9, and 18 in Experiment 1; 4, 8, and 12 in Experiment 2; 6 and 12 in Experiment 3) against appropriate nominal groups. In all three experiments, the largest EBS groups generated significantly more ideas than did the equivalent nominal groups, with no differences in idea quality. No difference in productivity between EBS and nominal groups was found for the smallest groups (see Fig. 12.1). These experiments are, as far as we know, the first careful demonstration of a productivity gain for EBS groups (and then only for the largest groups). A subsequent study by Dennis and Valacich (1993) confirmed the result for 6- and 12-person groups: Only the 12-person groups significantly outperformed the nominal-group baseline.

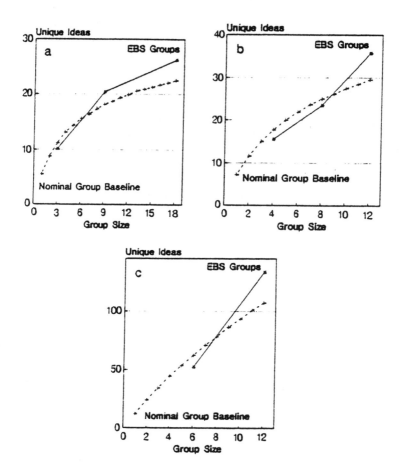

FIG. 12.1. Mean numbers of unique ideas generated by actual EBS groups compared to their nominal group baselines plotted against group size. From Valacich, Dennis, and Connolly (1994). Copyright 1994 by Academic Press, Inc. Reprinted by permission.

Osborn's (1953) claim for the superiority of brainstorming groups thus finally gains some support, with two provisos: The groups must interact electronically, and they must be relatively large. Electronic interaction overcomes production blocking, the primary liability of the interacting group. All members can effectively type at once, whereas all talking at once is ineffective. It remains unclear, however, why large groups are necessary to generate the advantage. The basic puzzle can be seen at the level of the individual. In both "nominal group" and interacting conditions, the individual works alone at a computer, typing in ideas that appear in the lower half of the screen, and browsing a string of previously generated ideas in the upper half of the screen when inspiration lags. The data suggest that this browsing is of value when the ideas browsed come from a large number of others, but not when they were produced by a few others, or by oneself.

One possible explanation is that the browsable strings are especially stimulating when they contain many unusual ideas—ideas that are, on statistical grounds alone, more likely to be generated by large groups. In a direct test of this hypothesis Connolly, Routhieaux, and Schneider (1993) had students generate ideas on a focal problem, and then selected the rarest and the commonest ideas. Subjects in a second phase were given ideas from one or the other list, interleaved with their own ideas. No difference in idea generation was found between the two groups, so the "rarity stimulates" hypothesis received no support. Dennis and Valacich (1993) attributed the gain to the groups' synergy and avoidance of redundant ideas, though they did not explain why these should be found only in large groups.

If the mechanism of operation remains unclear, so does the persistent popularity of brainstorming, both electronic and conventional. One possible hint emerges from an earlier study (Connolly et al., 1990), which explored the effects of anonymity and evaluative tone on the output of four-person EBS groups. In half of the groups comments were labeled with the author's name, whereas in the others no identifying labels were attached. In each group a confederate posing as a group member provided no substantive ideas, but simply typed from a prepared script a string of encouraging or critical comments as the files passed. The intent was to probe the evaluation apprehension account of group inhibition: We predicted inhibition only when evaluation was harsh, facilitation when evaluations were supportive, with both effects larger when subjects were identified than when they were anonymous.

The results did not fit this pattern. We found two simple main effects: Anonymous groups outperformed identified, and critical groups outperformed supportive (Fig. 12.2). (We still have no fully satisfactory account of this result, though it offers a hint here that norms of pleasant interpersonal manner may not be universally desirable in interactions such as this—a little blunt criticism appears to have had a stimulating effect.) Ratings of process satisfaction showed a precisely opposite pattern, with members whose comments were identified enjoying the process more than those whose comments were anonymous, and those in supportive groups enjoying themselves more than those in critical groups. The interesting incidental finding was that, when asked to rate their groups as to idea-generating effectiveness, subjects' ratings tracked the satisfaction rather than the productivity measure. Mean self-rated effectiveness was, in fact, significantly and negatively correlated ($r = -.37$) with actual number of ideas generated by a group. Thus, in addition to the forces leading to a general "illusion of productivity" for brainstorming groups (Stroebe, Diehl, & Abakoumkin, 1992; Paulus, Dzindolet, Poletes, & Camacho, 1993), participants may also misperceive their own effectiveness, confounding their satisfaction with the process (which they can observe) with their effectiveness compared to other

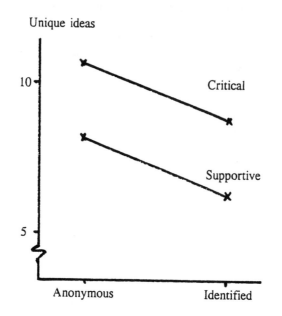

FIG. 12.2. Mean numbers of unique ideas generated by EBS groups as a function of
anonymity and evaluative tone. From Connolly, Jessup, and Valacich (1990). Copyright
1990 by the Society for Personality and Social Psychology, Inc. Adapted by permission.

groups (which they cannot). Such mechanisms seem adequate to account
for the otherwise perplexing popularity of brainstorming, both electronic
and conventional, despite evidence of its ineffectiveness.

The independent variables in Connolly et al.'s (1990) study were selected
primarily because they lend themselves reasonably easily to change in the
design of an EBS session. Whether or not comments are labeled with their
author's name is a simple software switch; and moving the evaluative tone
toward criticism or support could be achieved fairly easily by training and
injunction. There was some modest theoretical guidance in the earlier
research on evaluation apprehension, but the motivating spirit of the study
was plainly engineering: Here are two variables that (a) we can manipulate
reasonably easily and that (b) we have grounds for thinking may influence
performance. Let us assess their impact.[1]

Much the same spirit guided a later study (Dennis, Valacich, Connolly,
& Wynne, 1996). This study was designed to address another practical

---

[1]Note that a careful social psychologist would include a face-to-face condition in such
studies, as well as the variant EBS conditions we explored. To the engineer the face-to-face
brainstorming group is a failed technology; the reasons for its failure are of less interest than
the refinement of the successful EBS technology.

question: How best to structure the focal problem for an EBS group? Again, the spirit is engineering refinement rather than broad theory building. If one wants to generate ideas on a given topic, and to be efficient with respect to the participants' time, is it more effective to present the problem in aggregate form for a single EBS session or to disaggregate it into components and run miniature EBS sessions on each? As before there is some connection to existing theories of creativity, such as the importance of remote associations (which would appear to argue for aggregate presentation), or the importance of cognitive focus (arguing for decomposition), but nothing that one would consider as a serious theory of the matter. There is a straightforward engineering issue (what level of decomposition to use?), and reason to believe that it will make a difference.

As it turns out, level of decomposition does appear to make a substantial difference. Dennis et al. (1996) reported two experiments. In the first, members of a local Chamber of Commerce brainstormed electronically on the issue of what might be done by business leaders, elected officials, and the general public to resolve some current crisis. Some groups brainstormed on the problem as stated for 30 minutes; others ran in three 10-minute sessions, addressing each part of the question sequentially. In the second experiment, students attempted to identify data elements of input, storage and output for an information system, either in a single 45-minute session or in three 15-minute sessions. In both experiments groups working on the decomposed version of the problem generated 60% more ideas than did those working on the intact problem—a very large difference by the standards of EBS experiments and, presumably, large enough to be of managerial significance.

A NOTE ON EXPERIMENTATION

Because some readers of this chapter may come from nonexperimental traditions, a brief aside here on why and how we conduct experiments may be of value. The "why" is straightforward: We experiment because we know of no other method for disentangling the complex causal chains of human behavior. Suppose, for example, that we were to observe a large number of EBS groups, and noticed that members of highly productive groups tended to be more critical of one another, whereas less productive groups were more supportive. The observation would be consistent with the inference made by Connolly et al. (1990) that a critical tone enhances idea generation. It is, however, equally consistent with other mechanisms: For example, some groups happened to include lots of sociable people, who spent their time supporting one another rather than generating ideas. Perhaps sociable people are simply less creative. Perhaps the mental strains of highly productive groups led to shortened tempers and predominantly critical comments. Observational studies, however careful, leave such issues of causal direction unresolved. Only experiments, in which the supposed causal element is controlled by the investigator, offer the potential to resolve causal direction, and thus of purposive intervention.

If the "why" of experimentation is straightforward, the "how" is more complex. It is an intriguing mixture of mundane labor and craft skill. Compared to textbook descriptions of standard psychological experiments, our EBS work is easier in some respects, harder in others. Recruiting and motivating subjects is generally little problem. We often use student subjects, because they are cheap and readily available, and use professionals when opportunity offers. Both students and professionals are eager to try out the equipment and, given a problem they find interesting, work energetically for 30 or 40 minutes. (Our campus subjects were happy to share their thoughts on the campus parking problem, our Chamber of Commerce subjects on the city's leadership crisis!) Keeping track of their output is also easy: The software produces an electronic and printed record of every exchange. Content coding, on the other hand, can be a huge chore. The investigator must pore through page after page of printed output, marking off apparently discrete "comments" and assigning each into a category from the evolving coding scheme. Careful cross-checking with other coders working independently is essential. Panels of experts can sometimes be assembled to rate the quality of the ideas. For example, a group of campus parking officials were kind enough to evaluate the many proposals offered for improved parking. Statistical procedures and analyses are, in contrast, generally routine.

The crucial question, of course, is: To what extent can these experimental results be extrapolated to the "real world" (generally meaning "a real work setting")? As usual, no definitive answer can be given, but the EBS context offers some grounds for optimism. The standard critique raises issues about the generalizability of results from experiments using inexpert college students working unfamiliar tasks for brief periods and with little incentive to perform well. In the EBS experiments, however, we chose tasks (like campus parking) on which students are both informed and motivated. The EBS technology, if novel to many students, is at least equally novel to most managers and professionals (and appears to be stimulating for both). Where we have checked the effects of offering monetary incentives for good performance, the same patterns of results were found as with unpaid subjects. We are thus not surprised when studies such as Dennis et al. (1996) find similar results for students and professionals.

Generalizing from one task, subject pool, and setting to another is, as always, to be done cautiously, but seems a somewhat better bet in the EBS context than in many behavioral domains. Retesting on the task, participants, and setting of interest remains essential for confidence. Extrapolated results should always be treated as working hypotheses for the new context, not guaranteed predictions. One might speculate that patterns will change as participants become familiar with the technology, and as its use is extended to issues of large significance in the participants' lives—would, for example, an assurance of anonymity ensure candor if the topic were criticism of an autocratic boss? Threats to generalization, then, are to be considered one by one, and checked out when their plausible impact seems large. So far, we have been encouraged by the robustness of our results across various tasks, populations, and settings.

DISCUSSION

This chapter has had two purposes. The first was to review several studies in a program of behavioral research into the effects of computer support for meetings. The second was to offer some reflections of possibly greater generality on how and when such programs may best be formulated. Some tentative generalizations emerge:

1. *Time constants matter.* Operating technology, whether in the form of a managerial technique for running meetings, or an electronic analog such as EBS, moves quickly. New techniques are conceived and implemented in a time frame of weeks or months. Behavioral research, in contrast, operates on a time frame of months or years. Formulating questions, designing experiments, learning techniques, devising measures, spotting pitfalls and avoiding errors seem inherently slow. As noted, some 10 or 20 years passed between Osborn's (1953) book advocating group brainstorming and the emergence of a strong consensus in the research community that it didn't work. In the commercial software world where new versions of successful software may ship annually, it is hard to imagine that the successive refinements are based to any large extent on careful behavioral research. If we wish to contribute to these designs and redesigns, we need to think hard about speed of response.

2. *Linkage between network technology and behavioral research is weak.* In the EBS example, as noted, virtually no behavioral researcher who knew the group brainstorming literature would, in 1980, have advised building an electronic version of the technique. The failure of the manual technique was an essentially settled matter. The software engineers, either in defiance or ignorance of these findings, did build the electronic version, apparently guided by common sense and technological availability. Later research found that the EBS tool, by overcoming the production-blocking problem, allowed adequate performance for small groups, and superior performance for large ones. We still lack an adequate explanation of why these large groups perform so well, so we are unable to advise on how the process can be further improved. If consulted, the 1980s behavioral researcher would have misadvised the technologist on two counts: Group brainstorming seemed deleterious overall, and especially for large groups.

3. *Successful technologies may be "tricky mix" problems, and require special research methodologies.* A "tricky mix" problem is one in which effective operation requires that all of a number of variables be present simultaneously before anything useful happens. Breadmaking is a simple example: If any of the key ingredients—flour, water, leaven, oven temperature, and so on—is wrong, the effort fails entirely. It seems likely that such technologies as EBS share this property. To be at all effective, one requires something close to the right mix of people, process, problem, motivation, timing, and technology. If any one of these is missing, virtually no work gets done at all.

Problems of this sort require special research designs. A conventional factorial design will be enormously wasteful, in that all but one cell in the 2 x 2 x 2 and so on design will yield only messes: product unrecognizable as bread, meetings at which nothing gets done. What might be called "subtraction designs" will be hugely more efficient. They start with one instance of successful practice and then modify the conditions one variable at a time to attempt to identify which variables are, in fact, critical. The starting point requires respectful attention to what has been achieved by working empiricists already, building outward from good practice rather than inward from grand theory.

4. *Theory matters, but should probably be of a locally grounded sort.* As suggested by the Connolly et al. (1990) study of anonymity and evaluative tone, some attention to earlier findings and theory may be of value in devising the close-to-practice experiments, selecting variables to modify, and so on. This should not be confused with grand theory building. For example, it seems clear that the effectiveness of an EBS group is jointly influenced by aspects of the individuals involved, the task they are working on, the group process imposed, and the technology of interaction. A dozen plausible variables can be readily identified under each heading—say, 50 variables in all. Even if it turns out that each influences effectiveness in the simplest possible way (independently and linearly), the average impact of each cannot be more than 2% of total variance. Tracking down these effects would be a tedious and frustrating enterprise, far too slow and expensive to guide technology in real time. A more plausible goal is to develop modest local theory grounded in effective practice, and specifying the effects of variables significant to that practice.

5. *Beware the grateful testimonial and technological imperatives.* As long as participants have an enjoyable time in a process, they will generally give that process positive reviews. The popularity of conventional brainstorming seems to follow this rule: Participants enjoy the process, and see that a lot of ideas get generated, so they believe it to be an effective way of generating ideas. Within EBS, the findings of Connolly et al. (1990), that self-rated productivity was associated with member satisfaction, not with group productivity—in fact, was negatively correlated with group produc-

tivity—suggests that postsession questionnaires may be unreliable guides to process improvement.

In the absence of (or even in defiance of) other guidelines, technologists understandably delight in the newest technology. Improving the technology may not improve the process. For example, there is evidence that idea generation is facilitated by anonymity, even in student groups, and it is easy to suppose the effect will be larger in real-world settings where participants risk offending powerful superiors by their suggestions. However, new generations of the EBS technology are moving to incorporate names, photographs, and brief biographies of other participants on-screen, and real-time video images with sound are not far in the future. It will require a firm facilitator to "degrade" such state-of-the-art technology to take advantage of the disinhibiting effects of anonymity.

6. *Science is not technology.* There clearly is a connection between the relevant science (here, primarily, the social psychology of group behavior) and technology (here, computer technology for group meetings), but it is not especially close in this case. Simply to point out the obvious, the technology of an electronic meeting room is, by academic standards, expensive. Most such rooms have been heavily underwritten by computer companies, who are interested in developing salable products in a realistic time frame. This interest is ill-matched to the slow-moving, theory-focused, contentious world of conventional social psychology.

All this is to argue for caution, not for pessimism. My experience as a behavioral researcher in the EBS context has been largely positive. It is fun to work with sophisticated, reliable technologies instead of the usual laboratory improvisations. It is fun to see practical application of one's work. We clearly have a level of methodological sophistication in the design and conduct of behavioral experiments that greatly surpasses that of the average software designer. And we have a body of potentially relevant theory to draw on to suggest variables worth considering in design experiments. There is, in short, a modest path between behavioral research and network technology in this area, and it runs in both directions. The note of caution is simply to remind travelers that the path is not short, nor is it free from traps. It is, however, worth traveling.

REFERENCES

Chen, H., Hsu, P., Orwig, R., Hoopes, L., & Nunamaker, J. F. (1994). Automatic concept classification of text from electronic meetings. *Communications of the ACM, 37*, 56–73.

Connolly, T., Jessup, L. M., & Valacich, J. S. (1990). Effects of anonymity and evaluative tone on idea generation in computer-mediated groups. *Management Science, 36*, 689–703.

Connolly, T., Routhieaux, R. L., & Schneider, S. K. (1993). On the effectiveness of group brainstorming: Test of one underlying cognitive mechanism. *Small Group Research, 24*, 490–503.

Dennis, A. R., & Valacich, J. S. (1993). Computer brainstorms: More heads are better than one. *Journal of Applied Psychology, 78*, 531–537.

Dennis, A. R., Valacich, J. S., Connolly, T., & Wynne, B. E. (1996). Process structuring in electronic brainstorming. *Information Systems Research, 7*, 268–275.

Diehl, M., & Stroebe, W. (1987). Productivity loss in brainstorming groups: Toward the solution of a riddle. *Journal of personality and social psychology, 53*, 497–509.

Gibson, J. L., Ivancevich, J. M., & Donnelly, J. H. (1991). *Organizations: Behavior, structure, processes* (7th ed.). Homewood, IL: Irwin.

Lewis, A. C., Sadosky, T. L., & Connolly, T. (1975). The effectiveness of group brainstorming in engineering problem solving. *IEEE Transactions on Engineering Management, EM-22*, 119–124.

Mullen, B., Johnson, C., & Salas, E. (1991). Productivity loss in brainstorming groups: A meta-analytic integration. *Basic and Applied Social Psychology, 12*, 3–23.

Northcraft, G. B., & Neale, M. A. (1990). *Organizational behavior: A management challenge.* Chicago: Dryden.

Nunamaker, J. F., Dennis, A. R., Valacich, J. S., Vogel, D. R., & George, J. F. (1991). Electronic meeting systems to support group work. *Communications of the ACM, 34*, 40–61.

Osborn, A. F. (1953). *Applied imagination.* New York: Scribner's.

McGrath, J. E. (1984). *Groups: Interaction and performance.* Englewood Cliffs, NJ: Prentice-Hall.

Paulus, P. B., Dzindolet, M. T., Poletes, G., & Camacho, L. M. (1993). Perception of performance in group brainstorming: The illusion of group productivity. *Personality and Social Psychology Bulletin, 19*, 78–89.

Stroebe, W., Diehl, M., & Abakoumkin, G. (1992). The illusion of group effectivity. *Personality and Social Psychology Bulletin, 18*, 643–650.

Taylor, D. W., Berry, P. C., & Block, C. H. (1958). Does group participation when using brainstorming facilitate or inhibit creative thinking? *Administrative Science Quarterly, 3*, 23–47.

Valacich, J. S., Dennis, A. R., & Connolly, T. (1994). Idea generation in computer-based groups: A new ending to an old story. *Organizational Behavior and Human Decision Processes, 57*, 448–467.

13

EMAIL OVERLOAD: EXPLORING PERSONAL INFORMATION MANAGEMENT OF EMAIL

Steve Whittaker
Candace Sidner
Lotus Development Corporation

Email is one of the most successful computer applications yet devised. Our empirical data show, however, that although email was originally designed as a communications application, it is now being used for additional functions that it was not designed for, such as task management and personal archiving. We call this email overload. We demonstrate that email overload creates problems for personal information management: Users often have cluttered inboxes containing hundreds of messages, including outstanding tasks, partially read documents, and conversational threads. Furthermore, user attempts to rationalize their inboxes by filing are often unsuccessful, with the consequence that important messages get overlooked, or "lost" in archives. We explain how email overloading arises and propose technical solutions to the problem.

WHY STUDY EMAIL?

Email is one of the most successful computer applications yet devised. There are millions of email users worldwide who often spend significant proportions of their work time using email. Research suggests that email has contributed to the growth of distributed organizations, by allowing people in different geographical areas to communicate across time and space. It has also led to the emergence of online communities by supporting asynchronous communication (Sproull & Kiesler, 1991). Email has been the subject of many studies, including pioneering early work that focussed on the social and communicative aspects of email, comparing its usage with face-to-face communication (Sproull & Kiesler, 1991). Nevertheless, there is little systematic data on its usage and utility as a workplace technology. Furthermore, the success and popularity of email has led to high daily volumes of email being sent and received. Research has not yet addressed how people organize and manage large amounts of information. This study therefore presents a quantitative analysis of the mailboxes of 20 users, along with 34 hours of interviews to address these new questions.

Email applications were originally designed for asynchronous communication, but as our analysis shows, email has evolved to a point where it is now used for multiple purposes: document delivery and archiving, work task delegation, and task tracking. It is also used for storing personal names and addresses, sending reminders, asking for assistance, scheduling appointments, and handling technical support queries. We use the term *email overload* to describe the use of email for functions that it was not designed for. We discuss three main email functions: task management, personal archiving, and asynchronous communications. The central question is how well a single tool can support all these functions. Subsidiary questions must also be asked in each category.

Task management requires users to ensure that information relating to current tasks is readily available. This both preserves task context and allows users to determine the progress of ongoing tasks. Task management also involves reminding oneself about when particular tasks or actions have to be executed (Barreau & Nardi, in press; Kidd, 1994; Lansdale, 1988; Malone, 1983). How do people do this in email?

Personal archiving or filing addresses how people organize and categorize longer term information, so that it can later be retrieved. Archives are not of immediate relevance to current tasks, but are constructed for reference or anticipated future use. Research shows that users experience major problems in generating appropriate folder labels when filing longer term information for later retrieval, and in reconstructing these labels when they engage in later retrieval (Barreau & Nardi, 1995; Kidd, 1994; Lansdale, 1988; Malone, 1983). To what extent do these problems occur in email?

Asynchronous communication is concerned with interaction in a permanent medium across space and time. Research has characterized face-to-face workplace communications as consisting of repeated brief communications (Kraut, Fish, Root, & Chalfonte, 1992; Whittaker, Frolich, & Daly-Jones, 1994). Such interactions are seldom one-shot, and workers often engage in multiple intermittent interactions in order to complete a task. Workers are also usually engaged in several independent, but concurrent ongoing conversations, with the requirements of tracking separate conversational threads and switching contexts between conversations (Whittaker et al.,

1994). Does email communication have these characteristics, and how are asynchronous communications conducted?

To provide preliminary answers to these questions, this study presents qualitative and quantitative information about the use of email for task management, personal archiving, and asynchronous communication. We describe the problems people experience with each of these functions, and the strategies they invoke to address the problems. Finally we suggest potential technical solutions.

SYSTEM AND METHOD

We studied users of NotesMail, the email component of Lotus Notes. This client–server system has a graphical user interface (GUI) with a number of standard features, including the ability to compose, reply to, copy (cc), and blind copy (bcc) messages to other users. Incoming unread messages are delivered into the inbox (called "uncategorized" in Notes), where they appear in a different color from messages the user has "opened" and read. Once opened, they appear in the standard color. The system provides users with the ability to file information: They do so by creating categories (equivalent to folders in other email systems), so that related messages can be stored and accessed together, by category label. There is no conversational threading of messages: Although responses generated using the reply option appear with *re* in the subject line, the system does not allow the user to automatically view messages from a given thread together. It is, however, possible for users to view messages in terms of various other properties. One can view by sender, date, size, or category. The system also has a text search capability: email databases can be full text indexed, so that keyword or Boolean queries are possible. There is no formal support, or policy for, archiving.

The 20 study participants were office workers representing four major job types: 4 high-level managers, that is, people who had other managers reporting to them, 5 first-level managers, 9 professional workers with no management responsibility, and 2 administrative assistants. All participants were experienced users with between 2 and 15 years experience of email. They had all used NotesMail for more than 1 year. All participants were employees of Lotus Development Corporation, a software development firm. We chose our subjects because we wanted to investigate email use in multiple job types, with different responsibilities. Our participants were drawn from marketing, consultancy, software development, support, and research groups. We chose the organization both because of its pervasive use of email and ready access to subjects. Given these choices, we studied NotesMail because it was the most frequently used system in the Lotus organization.

We collected quantitative data about the mailbox of 18 users: (a) total number, age, and size of messages in their mailbox, (b) number of messages in each archival folder, (c) conversational threads. Due to technical difficulties, we were unable to collect quantitative data for the final two users. Ideally we would have wished to collect longitudinal data over an extended time period, to look at changes in mailbox size and structure, but the logistics of repeated access to personal data prevented this. We were, however, able to collect a "snapshot" of each mailbox at a given point, from which we drew important inferences, which we report later.

We also interviewed all 20 participants for 1–2 hours using semistructured questions. We asked them to describe: (a) the volume of email they sent and received, (b) their prioritization, reading, and reply strategies, (c) their correspondence management, for example, when they used reply, cc, and bcc features, and how they managed conversational threads, (d) their filing behaviors. We also discussed: (e) the main problems they were experiencing with email, and (f) their reactions to certain technical solutions addressing these problems. Interviews were carried out in people's offices and participants were encouraged to demonstrate their statements and strategies with reference to their actual systems.

We analyzed our interviews by collecting user comments about each issue just described. We present representative quotes from participants about these, and where there was substantial disagreement or inconsistency between participants' opinions, then we present quotes representing alternative points of view.

EMAIL OVERLOAD: THE PROBLEM

Participants were generally highly positive about email as a communication tool. They stressed how it enabled them to collaborate with others across time and distance (Sproull & Kiesler, 1991). They also pointed out its advantages over other technologies such as the telephone, and even face-to-face interaction. Nevertheless, certain individuals experienced major problems in reading and replying to email in a timely manner, with backlogs of unanswered email, and in finding information in email systems. The inability to effectively manage communication means lost information, and reduced responsiveness. These have clear negative outcomes for both individual and corporate productivity.

> Waiting to hear back from another ... employee can mean delays in accomplishing a particular task, which can ... have significant impact on our overall operations. Depending on the situation, it can either be critical or just frustrating.

> One of my pet peeves is when someone does not get back to me, but I am one of the worst offenders. I get so many emails [average 30-40/day] and phone messages (15-20) that I cannot keep up and also do my real job....

Given the sheer volume of stuff that passes through here. I mean I couldn't even give you a percentage of how much is missed. I mean - — not necessarily missed but certainly recorded but never followed up on.

I dedicate somewhere between minimally 2 hours at the outlying range, up to 10 hours on any given day trying to stay on top of email.

So why do these problems arise? A simple one-touch model of email might assume incoming messages that are informational—that is, those not requiring a response—are read, and then either deleted or filed, depending on their relevance. Incoming messages that form part of a correspondence (i.e., requiring a response) are answered, and then either deleted or filed. According to the one-touch model, information can therefore be in two possible states: unread and filed. The user's inbox at any point should solely consist of a small number of unread incoming messages, and the rest of their mailbox consist of filed items.

Our quantitative data show the one-touch model is patently incorrect. The mean number of inbox items is 2,482, and the mean number of filed items (858) is small compared with the number of inbox items, so that the inbox constitutes on average 53% of people's mail files. It is implausible that users receive 2,482 new items each day, so what is happening and why is the inbox so full? It turns out that there are two related reasons for this: (a) the inbox operates as a task manager, where people are reminded of current tasks, and where people can keep information relevant to those tasks accessible, and (b) people find it hard to file information to remove it from their inbox, both because filing into folders is difficult and there may also be few benefits to creating folders.

EXPLAINING THE FULL INBOX: MANAGING WORKING INFORMATION

Our users received a large number of messages each day (mean 49). One reason for the large volume of incoming messages is that email is now the source of many different office tasks, serving as the place in which work is received and delegated: "It's where things come into your life in a way. It's the place where ... people hand things off to you, it's the electronic office."

Email can be an important determinant of how people spend their working day, again suggesting that it is a place that users receive and hand off tasks:

I check it before I leave the house just in case there's anything I didn't get the night before. I read it as soon as I get into the office.... It does change what I do throughout the day, like what — I may come in thinking I was going to do one thing, but get mail that sort of diverts me into doing something else.... If I haven't checked my mail it makes me uncomfortable. And there's invariably a piece of something I was supposed to do, that's time sensitive.

Both the volume of incoming mail and the fact that mail is being used for task management lead to a breakdown in the one-touch model. Although there is evidence that users try and process information at once, there are a number of reasons why immediate responses are sometimes not possible or not appropriate, so that incoming messages remain undischarged in the inbox.

One general reason relates to the amount of time users have currently available. If the message requires more than a certain amount of time or effort to process, then users delay dealing with it and proceed to other potentially more urgent or manageable messages in the inbox. There are also specific types of messages that are often not discharged immediately:

1. There are the "to dos," those messages that require the user to execute some action. In some cases, the message may require the user to engage in further complex activities that might take days to achieve. The user does not usually suspend the process of reading email to discharge these activities. These "to dos" are commonly kept in the inbox as reminders of unfinished tasks.

2. Alternatively, there are the "to reads," messages that are long documents. Although these are often informational and do not require a reply, they still take time and effort to read, and users often delay reading them, so that the inbox may contain unread or partially read documents. The quantitative data support this. We found that on average 21% of the inbox (i.e., an average of 334 messages) were long, when a long message was defined as more than 10Kbytes (~5 screensfull).

3. Third are messages of indeterminate status. One issue with informational messages is that users are often unsure of the significance of an incoming message when it first arrives. Rather than investing valuable time in reading it at once, they register its arrival, but delay dealing with it until some later point when they are more certain of its importance. What makes immediate decisions difficult is that the value of a given message may depend on events that occur after the message has been received: A flurry of subsequent messages on the topic may reveal its importance, or else it may turn out to be a "dead-end" with no follow-up being necessary. Rather than delete it immediately, users often conservatively retain it just in case it turns out to be important. This user describes keeping such documents in her inbox:

> I've gotten messages, I haven't dealt with them, haven't known what to do about them. And starting this new position, ... I got a lot of mail messages, but I didn't have the knowledge to know what on earth they were about.... You know, people were talking about servers and infrastructure.... I just realized some day I would understand it, and I saved a lot of that stuff, and actually had to make a presentation where it all came in handy — where I went, I've been sitting with this information all this time and I didn't know it ... so you're conservative about keeping stuff, and ... at some point in the future it may come in useful.

People also explained how retaining such unread messages was useful for unplanned contingencies, for example, when they received surprise phone calls about them. They were able to read the documents in the course of the call, while pretending to have already read them:

> [Email] is the best that's ever happened for covering your ass ... because while the guy's on the phone, he says, well, I sent that to you a week and a half ago, and you think, shit, I never saw that. But you say, 'really? Yeah, oh yeah, I remember reading that,' as you're reading it.

4. Finally, there is ongoing correspondence. The inbox is sometimes used for ongoing, but incomplete, threads of asynchronous conversations. The user may delay responding to a question from another person because a careful reply is necessary that takes more time than is currently available. Alternatively, users may be unable to reply immediately, because they currently do not have the answer, and they await further information from other people.

For more complex interactions involving multiple exchanges over an extended time period, users may also track and sometimes save their own and other people's contributions to the conversation. An issue may take several email exchanges to be resolved, or users may require the responses of multiple individuals in order to collate opinion, or reach consensus. A major problem with email correspondence is that there are no agreed upon conventions about whether to include the context or history of prior messages as the conversation proceeds. Often this context is important, because it is necessary for interpreting what each subsequent message means. One user describes this problem with one of his coworkers:

> X is unbelievable in that he never puts the context in which, of what he's replying to. He always comes up with these one-line responses, and I have no idea what it is that he's talking about, you know, it's like, "Re: the Internet." ... And, in many cases, he's replying to something that somebody else sent, but I wasn't on the original distribution list, but he thinks that I'd be interested.... So I get this totally out-of-context great idea.

For multiple interchanges extending over periods of days or weeks, it is easy to forget who said what and to whom. For legal purposes, it can also be important on occasion to record exactly what was said by whom. For these reasons, for certain critical interactions, users sometimes save both the originating message, as well as subsequent interactions:

> The people that I consider some of the best problem solvers in my organization are fanatical about the history. And you get the whole thing. Yeah, the audit trail of what happens. We do that, have to do that a lot in support ... because you could be dealing with an extended customer issue that bounced around ... especially the people that are right on the front lines, it's almost like second nature to them .... It's not only everything that's being said.... It's every person that has been involved.

This conversational record serves multiple functions: an archive of what has been discussed, a reminder to the user that the conversation is in progress, and a record of the status of the conversation, and whether one "owes" or is "owed" a response. The importance of conversational tracking, as well as the absence of conventions about whether others will include history, can mean that each exchange of a lengthy conversation will appear as a separate message in the inbox. Not only does this increase the number of messages in the inbox, it is often difficult to gather together the related threads of a conversation, because conversational exchanges are often interleaved with other unrelated information: "That reply with the history of previous stuff .... When some people do that and some don't and the fact that it's all interspersed with all other kinds of crap in my email, and then I just can't pick up an email and find out what else it belongs with."

The quantitative data indicate the pervasiveness of inbox conversational threads. We examined the subject line of each message and counted the number of instances in which it contained "re," signaling it was a reply to an original message. By this metric[1], we found that inboxes contain a mean of 209 such messages, and that these constitute 12% of the total inbox messages.

To summarize, multiple types of items linger in users' inboxes: actions the user has yet to do, documents that are partially read or unread, and correspondence that is still in progress. What unifies these is that they are all incomplete, and the usual strategy is to leave them in the inbox to serve as reminders that some further action is required. They are not normally filed away, because filing would mean that they are no longer visible whenever new email is read or the inbox searched:

> The reason that I don't categorize things but leave them in here [the inbox] is that I realize ... there are a certain number of things that I keep in my mind, and I will go back for.... And others, I do have to count on tripping over them. And as long as there is that mess that I know I have to do the multiple passes of reading over.... I'm kind of depending on that serendipitous tripping over it again as a way to remind me.

The importance of this visual reminding function is evidenced by the fact that five users had experimented with a strategy of filing undischarged information in an "action," or "to do," folder. In all but one of these cases, this action folder was abandoned, because users had to explicitly remember to go to it, open it, and view its contents, rather than being reminded of

---

[1]This measures the number of messages that are part of extended conversations, rather than the total number of conversational threads. It underestimates the proliferation of threaded messages, because it does not detect the message that originated the thread. It also occasionally overestimates: People report taking the last message by another person and simply replying, to avoid having to regenerate another user's mailing address, and on rare occasions forgetting to modify the subject line when they do this.

these unintentionally, by the mere fact of being in the inbox reading new email:[2] "I used to have an 'unread' folder. Which was messages I'd opened up, but I had never finished reading. Like those big ones that ... I didn't get through right away. I didn't go back to it [the unread folder] often enough though." The single person who was successfully using "to do" folders had reconfigured her mailbox user interface (UI), so as to be reminded about this folder. Her "to do" folder appeared immediately above the first new unread item in her inbox, so that she would automatically see the "to do" folder whenever she read new email.

A second reason for leaving information in the inbox concerns its availability. In the case of extended interactions, users often keep conversational history in the inbox, because they believe it to be more accessible there: "You may not want to file it. Because it might be something you need to refer to.... I don't want to file that yet, because it's active ... there are things that are happening as a result of that. It's easier for me to find it. So I want to keep in my 'in' box, keep it current."

GETTING INFORMATION OUT OF THE INBOX: THE PROBLEM OF FILING

We have seen that incomplete tasks being "kept around" can lead the inbox to be full. A second complementary reason is that users find it difficult to move messages out of the inbox by filing them into folders containing collections of related messages. Why is this? First generating and maintaining these folder collections requires considerable effort. Second, and more important, the resulting collections may be of little use in message retrieval.

Filing is a cognitively difficult task (Kidd, 1994; Lansdale, 1988). Successful filing is highly dependent on being able to imagine future retrieval requirements. It is hard to decide which existing folder is appropriate, or, if a new folder is needed, how to give it a memorable name: "Any piece of information longer than five lines has at least several axes along which you might want to look it up and it really depends how you're coming at it and what you're thinking about at the time. [Filing] isn't reliable."

Users also may not file messages because they are concerned about failure to remember where information has been filed. Failure can have severe consequences especially if the message requires action: "I don't know where to put it. And ... by making a wrong decision, I could really forget about it...." Another reason for not filing is that users want to

---

[2]An exception occurs when users create a folder for an ongoing conversational thread, for which there is a large number of daily incoming messages. There seem to be two reasons for this: The first is the pressing need to remove the multiple interactions "cluttering up" the inbox, and the second is that the frequency of these messages means that the user will be reminded of the fact that the conversation is still in progress.

postpone their judgment in order to determine the value of information. Users do not want to create archives containing information that later turn out to be useless or irrelevant. The strategy here is to wait and see the extent to which subsequent events indicate a message is valuable: "I'm reluctant to archive junk.... I know that the consequence of archiving junk is to make it that much harder to find the good stuff ... in the archive.... Especially if information seems like it eventually will be overcome by events, I'd be very loath to move it into a [folder]. I'd be more likely to kind of hold it in my 'in' box."

Folders also may not be useful after they are constructed. One problem is that users may not be able to remember folder labels, especially after a time has elapsed: "If it's sort of older stuff, the category names are not going to mean anything to me anymore." Users experienced special problems when they had large numbers of folders. They had to remember the definition of each when filing and to be careful not to introduce duplication by creating new folders that were synonymous with preexisting ones. Duplication detracts from their use in retrieval.

In addition, folders can be too small to be useful. A major aim of filing is to reduce the huge number of undifferentiated inbox items into a relatively small set of folders each containing multiple related messages. Filing is clearly not successful if the number of messages in a given folder is small: If a folder contains only one or two items, then its existence has not significantly reduced the complexity of the inbox, nor gathered together significant amounts of related material. However our data show that filing often fails: On average 35% of users' folders contain only one or two items. Furthermore, not only do these tiny "failed folders" not significantly reduce the complexity of the inbox, the user has the dual overheads of (a) creating them in the first place, and (b) remembering multiple definitions every time there is a decision about filing an new inbox item.

The quantitative data reflect the problem of trying to remember multiple folder definitions. The larger the number of folders a user has, the more likely that person is to generate failed folders containing only one or two items [$r(16) = .75, p < .001$]. User statements bear this out: "I wish I viewed creating a category as a lightweight activity. And for some reason I don't ... it seems like, you know the more of them I create, the harder it is to find any of them that are there."

Folders can also fail because they are too big. When there are too many messages in a folder, it becomes unwieldy. It is difficult to find the relevant message in a large folder. The relationships between different messages in the folder become tenuous, so that one benefit of keeping them together is much reduced: "So what happened was the size of the chunks associated with the categories got large. So now one key stroke would get me to a hundred things. So I really was no better off [filing information]."

To conclude, we have seen that users experience difficulties in creating folders. In addition, the returns for this effort may not be great: folders can be too large, too small, or they may be too numerous for people to remember their individual definitions. As a consequence, folders may be of little use either for retrieval or for viewing related messages together. There is also a third problem: Filing information means that it is less available to remind users about that topic. Some users therefore to finesse this problem: Instead of filing incoming information, they simply leave it all in their inbox and use full-text search to find individual messages. We now examine users' strategies with respect to the problems of organizing the inbox, so that it can be an effective method for managing ongoing tasks and conversations.

STRATEGIES FOR HANDLING EMAIL OVERLOAD

Given the dual problems of managing ongoing conversations and tasks, combined with the issue of filing, we identify three different user strategies, based on two criteria: (a) whether or not users currently use folders, and (b) whether they "clean up" their inbox on a daily basis. This yields three strategies: nonfilers (no use of folders), frequent filers (folder users who try and clean up their inbox daily), and spring cleaners (folder users who clean up their inbox only periodically). The data associated with each are shown in Table 13.1.

Nonfilers made no current use of folders (mean 11.33), but relied on full-text search to find information. Their folders were historic remnants from when two of the no-filers still filed. As a consequence of not filing, their inboxes were huge (3,093.5 items, making up 95% of all their email). Their inboxes were overloaded: They included a large numbers of conversational threads (mean 288). More significantly, over half of their inbox was old information that arrived more than 3 months ago. Their strategy for reducing the size of the overloaded inbox was periodic purges in which they deleted large numbers of old items or copied them to a separate independent archive. Four of the six nonfilers were managers.

Frequent filers made strenuous attempts to minimize the numbers of inbox messages. They made daily passes through their inbox filing or deleting its contents. Their inboxes were relatively small, containing only 43.4 items, which was a very small percentage (5%) of the total number of mailbox messages. In addition, the inbox consisted almost exclusively of new items (90% were less than a month old, and only 5% were older than 3 months), and it was almost devoid of conversational threads (mean 3.6). They made frequent use of folders, and were relatively successful in their use of these, with only 21% being failed folders. The five frequent filers included both the administrative assistants, but only one manager.

Spring cleaners dealt with the overloaded nature of their inboxes by intermittent clean-ups—normally every 1–3 months. They made extensive use of folders, even though this was often unsuccessful, as evidenced by the fact that over half of their folders failed. They also had large overloaded

TABLE 13.1

The Three Strategies for Managing Email

Strategy	N	# Inbox Items	Total # Items	Inbox as % total mailbox	Old Inbox Items (% inbox > 3 month old)	New Inbox Items (% inbox < 1 month old)	# Inbox Conversation threads	# Folders	Failed folders (# folders with < 3 items)	Daily messages received
Nonfilers	6	3,093.5	3,271.1	95.25	51.58	11.78	287.5	11.33	4.5	58
Spring Cleaners	7	1,492.29	2,818.71	51.02	40.15	24.22	257.86	61.43	30.85	45.71
Frequent Filers	5	43.4	1,062.2	4.96	4.75	90.34	3.6	70.6	16.6	42

inboxes (mean 1,492.3), containing large numbers of conversational threads (mean 258). Over 40% of their inbox message were more than 3 months old. Four of the seven spring cleaners were managers.

IMPACT, OVERHEAD, AND CHOICE OF STRATEGIES

All quantitative results are summarized in Table 13.1. In the remainder of the section, these data are used to explore the impact of strategy choice. We discuss the trade-offs between strategies, and look at why users choose different strategies by examining the relationship between (a) strategy choice, and (b) factors such as job function and incoming message volume.

The three strategies differ in terms of their benefits and maintenance costs. A major advantage of the frequent filing strategy is that the inbox can function as a genuine "to do" list containing a small number of outstanding messages relating to key current tasks, rather than having these items interspersed with huge numbers of conversational threads or unfiled old messages. It is also noteworthy that the average number of items in a frequent filer's inbox (43) can fit in two screens, and frequent filers report that it is important for them to be able to see items in this way. They are able to capitalize on the fact that when they view incoming unread email, they should be reminded of the majority of their outstanding tasks, because these should be visible or immediately accessible in the inbox.

> I don't have any other system, that keeps track of an email message that needs a response ... usually the next day, hopefully it's still sort of near the bottom of the [inbox], ... I will see it when I look at new mail messages, so it won't get scrolled off the screen.

> But I live in the inbox. And that is kind of my "to do" list. I'll keep things in there ... there's probably about 20 or 30 in there now of things that I want to keep like in my frontal lobes, that I have to deal with.

Frequent filers are effective in their use of folders, experiencing fewer failed folders. This may be because of frequency with which they file enables them to remember the label definition and contents of each folder. However, despite the benefits of the clean "to do" list, opportunistic reminding, and the availability of current projects, there are major costs to this strategy. It requires significant maintenance: Users have to make frequent passes through the inbox, filing and removing discharged items: "After I read the new day's mail ... I go back to the whole 'in' box, right back. And there's almost like a sifting that keeps happening, where the less pressing ones start ageing. And it gets to the point where I say, 'I'm either not going to do something about this.' ... And I just delete them."

It may be that frequent filing is only possible for lower volumes of incoming email, and for job specifications that do not require users to be away from their desk for long periods of time. Workers such as managers receiving higher volumes with less time to process email may not be in a position to exploit frequent filing.

The nonfiling strategy stands in direct contrast to frequent filing. Here users make few attempts to reduce the complexity of their inbox. When possible they answer messages as they receive them, but they seldom review the inbox for outstanding undischarged messages. The fact that their inbox is cluttered with threads, as well as partially read and unread messages, means that outstanding tasks are not easily visible and are quickly displaced and scroll out of sight. Opportunistic reminding and task tracking are therefore unlikely to occur.[3] Users of this strategy admit that the clutter in their inboxes results in important tasks sometimes being overlooked:

> When you're dodging all this other stuff it's hard to pull out what could potentially be pretty important ... like anyone else who may have that volume ... after a couple of days you're not going five screens up anymore. You're just looking at your current screen or maybe one more. Who knows what you've missed. I was on vacation for 2 weeks. Who knows what ... passed through ... email during that time.... I saw a lot of it but I ... let a lot go by. I find that the most aggravating thing is when the inbox starts to grow and I don't know what to do with it necessarily.

When high volume of incoming email is accompanied by large amounts of time away from their desks, this may reduce the likelihood of no-filers constructing elaborate filing systems or engaging in extensive periodic clean-ups. The following no-filer described why he had abandoned any attempt to manage his inbox: "Because what I used to do was use [spring cleaning] as a way as organizing and reviewing and catching anything that was falling off the end of the earth. I've given up on it ... where am I going to get that time? If I wake up at three A.M., and I've got nothing else to do, that's when I'm going to do it."

The spring cleaners are intermediate to the two other strategists. As with nonfilers, as their inbox gets large, its size and complexity makes it ineffective as a "to do" list. The fact that it is usually cluttered with threads and unread messages means it is poor for task management, so opportunistic reminding is unlikely to occur. Furthermore, the inbox was perceived to be of little archival use: "It might as well be deleted as buried in this pile of junk.... Email may have value, but I will never avail myself in its current form, in this mail file. And so, it might as well be gone as sitting there, because either way I don't have it. It's not at my disposal and not usable."

Spring cleaners have very strong feelings about the disorder of their inboxes: They use terms like "disgust" to describe their reactions to their inbox and are motivated by "seizures" to clean up. However, the fact that

---

[3]One reason for the lack of task tracking may derive from no filers' organizational status: Because they are usually managers, they tend to delegate tasks. They expect their employees to carry out the task, and report when it is done.

they do occasionally go through the inbox means that outstanding unprocessed messages are detected and can be replied to, even if these are sometimes late: "So what I started to do was, either weekly, ... then monthly, I would go back to my mail, partly to categorize it and actually truthfully to catch things that I had just dropped the ball on."

This group seems to be less successful at creating useful folders than frequent filers. One possibility is that spring cleaners create folders infrequently, so that they forget folder definitions. Hence they may create duplicates of already existing folders. In terms of maintenance this strategy stands between the others: It does not require the daily efforts of frequent filing, but occasional clean-ups are required. This strategy choice may be explained by the inputs and workload of spring cleaners: They receive fewer messages and are less likely to be managers than are nonfilers, giving them more time to devote to managing their email. We then tested these observations statistically. Because of our small subject pool, we were forced to combine data from both spring cleaners and nonfilers in order to make comparisons. The analysis shows that frequent filers differ from the other strategies in a number of respects: They have smaller mailboxes [$t(16)$ = 2.35, $p < .05$], and smaller inboxes [$t(16)$ = 3.94, $p < .005$]. Frequent filers' inboxes contain fewer inbox threads [$t(16)$ = 3.99, $p < .005$], and also tend to consist of newer items [$t(16)$ = 2.41, $p < .05$]. Furthermore, there is a suggestion that they are more successful filers, with fewer failed folders [$t(16)$ = 2.06, $p = .058$].

Finally, we looked at the impact on strategy choice, of factors such as organizational role and incoming volume of messages. We found only partial statistical evidence for the effects of role and volume. Managers were more likely to receive greater volumes of email [$t(16)$ = 3.06, $p < .005$]. We then looked at whether managers were less likely to be frequent filers, given their higher volume of received email and greater time spent in meetings. Although only one frequent filer was a manager, there was no strong evidence of a direct relationship between strategy and status [chi square (*df* = 1) = 2.49, $p < .05$].

REDESIGNING EMAIL TO FIT ITS FUNCTIONS

There are both design and theoretical implications to these results. Although email was originally designed for asynchronous communication, the application is actually being used for multiple functions. Email therefore needs to be redesigned to support filing and task management as well as asynchronous communication. Our analysis of different users' strategies shows that both nonfilers and spring cleaners experience problems with both filing and task management. These problems lead to backlogs of unanswered messages and "lost" information in archives. Furthermore, the group who experienced fewest problems, namely frequent filers, may only be able to operate successfully because of strenuous efforts to trim their inboxes. It is therefore important that we address overload. As email volumes continue to increase, even those users who are currently frequent filers may end up spending much of their energy in reading and responding to messages, leaving them with little time to maintain their inboxes, and folders. As a result, they may be forced to behave more like spring cleaners or even nonfilers.

We now discuss possible techniques to support the three functions. We have shown that the inbox is often used as a place for incomplete tasks, unfiled information, and ongoing conversations. In all these cases, users preserve working information in the inbox both to keep it available and as a reminder that further actions are required. We have also seen, however, that opportunistic reminding is compromised when the number of inbox messages is too large, because messages scroll off the screen and remain unseen. A key technical requirement is therefore to reduce inbox clutter to allow visual reminding, but without compromising the availability of working information. We now present technical solutions for each email function addressing different ways of presenting and viewing the inbox to support both availability and reminding for working information.

Although email was originally designed for asynchronous communication, the current system has limitations in supporting this function. The key requirements for asynchronous communication are: (a) threading to support context regeneration and the management of conversational history, and (b) the ability to track the status of a conversation. Users want to avoid: scrolling back through large numbers of heterogeneous inbox messages to find all previous elements of a conversational thread, lost context when someone omits message history, and forgetting who has the next turn in the conversational sequence.

How can we address these asynchronous communication problems? One solution to the problem of communication management automatically marks email messages from the same conversation using a common thread ID, allowing the user to collect related messages together, and trace back through conversations. The user would subsequently be able to view by thread. Viewing by thread allows a user to select any message, use that message to access all messages from that conversation, and hence view any message in its conversational context. This functionality is equivalent to having a single message containing the forwarded history of an entire conversation. Unlike a single message, viewing by conversation is not beset by the navigational problem of trying to follow a conversation that is many layers deep, where information may be buried within a single message. Viewing by thread provides several additional benefits. It helps determine conversational status: By looking at the last message in a thread, the user should be able see whether they owe or are owed a response. Furthermore, it should be possible to file an entire thread, but leave a representative message from that thread in the inbox. This serves the purpose of reducing inbox clutter, even when users choose to copy themselves on every re-sponse. As we have seen with frequent filing, a representative message in an uncluttered inbox can remind the user that a conversation is in progress. When the conversation is concluded, the entire thread can also be archived or deleted as the user wishes.

What about filing? Given users' uncertainty about the value of much incoming information, they often end up with large numbers of incoming informational messages in their inbox. These documents are in a "holding pattern" while users attempt to determine their relevance and importance. In addition, our data show that filing may not be crucial for retrieval, because it may ultimately be superceded by full-text search. Nevertheless, users may want to cluster and view semantically related messages together, for example, while they learn about a new topic.

How might we support this temporary buffering of incoming informa-tion? Information retrieval techniques could be used to cluster semantically related documents automatically, and the presentation of these clustered documents might be analogous with conversational threads. Users might therefore reduce the clutter of their inboxes, by leaving one semantic category exemplar in their inbox as a reminder and filing the rest. As with threads, each incoming message could be viewed in the context of other (in this case semantically) related information. This may partly address the problem of failed folders, and it might also help users to decide the useful-ness of an arriving message. Two provisos are necessary here. First, incom-ing documents should not be "filed" before the user has seen them. User comments and their experience with email filters clearly indicated that "automatic filing" was not desirable: Users wanted to be made aware of the arrival of incoming documents, otherwise they would be ignorant of their existence. Furthermore, users were concerned that automatic filing would mean they wouldn't know the folder in which a given message had been filed.[4] Second, this semantic classification needs to be dynamic, given that the status of a document can be changed by the arrival of subsequent ones.

Finally, when we consider task management, it is clear that conversa-tional threading and semantic clustering should reduce the amount of inbox clutter by having each conversation or folder represented by one inbox message. The consequent reduction of the number of visible items in the inbox should help users to more easily see their outstanding tasks, and hence support reminding and tracking. Keeping important things "in view" could also be helped by having the inbox temporally sequenced and having threads and folders gradually "decay" by scrolling off the screen if they have not shown recent activity. Two further requirements seem to be crucial for task management. The first is the ability to mark particular inbox items

---

[4]The observation that users do not want "automatic filing" has important implications for work advocating automatic filtering techniques (Maes, 1994).

as requiring action. This marker should be highly visible, and it should be possible to view only the "action items" in the absence of threads or folders. Note that this is different from creating an action folder: The action items are not filed away, but remain visible in the inbox, to serve their reminding function. The second requirement is the ability to program reminders. A critical problem occurs with action items that either can't be done immediately or don't need to be done at once. Here it would be useful to program these items so they would reappear as an action item, as the deadline approaches.

Turning to outstanding research issues, we need to test the generality of these results. Although NotesMail is representative of current technology, we must see how the findings extend to both different email systems and a broader user population. It would be of particular interest to investigate systems lacking some of the features in NotesMail, for example, text search, and also systems that have sophisticated filtering mechanisms, which NotesMail does not possess. To what extent do different features affect handling strategies? Our results about the effects of email volume and job specification on email- processing strategies also need to be replicated with larger numbers of subjects.

Last, this work supports the findings of recent theoretical studies pointing to the interactive nature of cognition, and the fact that people use external environmental sources or artifacts to mediate cognition (Norman, 1988; Walker, 1996; Whittaker et al., 1994; Whittaker & Schwarz, 1995). We saw that email folders function as an external archival memory store. More important, people frequently access the email inbox, which means that properly organized it can operate as a visual device for attention manipulation and reminding, and as a way of extending working memory and maintaining the context of ongoing activities in an interrupt-driven environment. The importance of visual reminding and need to manage working information are reinforced by recent research on the organization of physical and electronic desktops (Barreau & Nardi, in press; Kidd, 1994; Malone, 1983). Past work has focussed almost exclusively on long-term storage (Kraut et al., 1992). Future theoretical work should address these new issues of attention and the management of ephemeral and working information.

ACKNOWLEDGMENTS

Thanks to the users for participating, to Sal Mazzotta for writing the analysis macros, also to Marilyn Walker, John Patterson, Irene Grief, Sara Kiesler, and the members of Egrpsem for comments. This chapter is reprinted, with slight changes, from a conference paper, Whittaker, S. & Sidner, C. (1996). Email overload: Exploring perosonal infomration management of e-mail. In *Proceedings of the CHI '96 Human Factors in Computing Systems* (pp. 276–283). New York: ACM Press. By permission.

REFERENCES

Barreau, D., & Nardi, B. (1995). Finding and retrieving information: File organization from the desktop. *SIGCHI Bulletin, 27*, 43–49.

Kidd, A. (1994). The marks are on the knowledge worker. In *Proceedings of CHI'94 Human Factors in Computing Systems* (pp. 186–191). New York: ACM Press.

Kraut, R., Fish, R., Root, B., & Chalfonte, B. (1992). Informal communication in organizations. In R. Baecker (Ed.), *Groupware and computer supported cooperative work* (pp. 287–314). San Mateo, CA: Morgan Kaufman.

Lansdale, M. (1988). The psychology of personal information management. *Applied Ergonomics, 19*, 55–66.

Maes, P. (1994). Agents that reduce work and information overload. *Communications of the ACM, 37*, 31–40.

Malone, T. (1983). How do people organize their desktops? Implications for the design of office information systems. *ACM Transactions on Office Information Systems, 1*, 99–112.

Norman, D. (1988). *The psychology of everyday things.* New York: Basic Books.

Sproull, L., & Kiesler, S. (1991). *Connections.* Cambridge, MA: MIT Press.

Walker, M. (1996). Limited attention and discourse structure. *Computational Linguistics, 22*, 255–265.

Whittaker, S., Frohlich., D., & Daly-Jones, O. (1994). Informal workplace communication: what is it like and how might we support it? In *Proceedings of CHI'94 Human Factors in Computing Systems* (pp. 130–137). New York: ACM Press.

Whittaker, S., & Schwarz, H. (1995). Back to the future: Pen and paper technology supports complex group co-ordination. In *Proceedings of CHI'95 Human Factors in Computing Systems* (pp. 495–502). New York: ACM Press.

More That We Can Know:
The Attentional Economics
of Internet Use

Warren Thorngate
Carleton University

Last summer, after teaching for 5 weeks in Iran, I returned to face my accumulated mail. In addition to the mail brought to me by post, fax, and phone, I found 347 new email messages. It took me about 2 weeks doing nothing else to clear the backlog and another 4 days to clear the backlog from these 2 weeks. Such was the price of my hiatus.

Later I learned that I am not alone. Most of my colleagues face an equivalent volume of email and other correspondence. Alas, the increasing volume of the former has not reduced the volume of the latter. Each of us now spends an average of about 2 hours each day simply tending our Internet gardens. To find the time we sleep less, work longer and ignore each other more.

I think this shift in our time budget indicates a fundamental error in discussions of the information economy. All economies are based on some form of scarcity, but there is no scarcity of information in the world. Instead, there is a scarcity of time to "spend" and attention to "pay" for the information available. Life typically gives each of us about 29,220 days (80 years) of time. We spend about 10,000 days of this time sleeping, about 1,200 days eating, about 240 eliminating bodily wastes. The time remaining, like the 14 days I spent catching up on my correspondence, is a finite and nonrenewable resource. It is the scarce commodity that defines an economy of attention governing the relationship between information produced and information consumed.

Enter the Internet. Its low cost, ease of use, high speed, and reliability make the Internet almost perfectly suited to those of us who spend so much of our time producing and consuming information. Therein lies the fundamental dilemma of an attentional economy. Because the Internet is such a good way to distribute and exchange information, we are increasingly using it for these purposes. Information thus proliferates at an increasing rate. Yet our time remains constant. As a result, the limits of our time force us to pay less attention to more information. By distributing more information more widely, quickly and cheaply, the Internet intensifies an already fierce competition for our limited resource.

Where will the competition end? Optimists argue that as information proliferates on the Internet, a buyer' market will assure that the good stuff will drive out the bad. Pessimists argue the opposite. Central to their arguments are questions of how Internet users choose to spend their attention while there. Why do we spend our time on the Internet? When do we choose to burrow or to browse? What governs our decisions to spend time producing new information for the Internet or to spend time consuming the old? Under what conditions do we try to avoid paying attention to unwanted information (an error of inclusion) though we necessarily increase our chances of overlooking desired information (an error of exclusion)? Under what conditions do we try to avoid the reverse? Indeed, to what extent do we agree what is desirable information and what is dross? Whom can we trust to tell us? Where can we find the time to judge for ourselves? What are the consequences for human communication of developing a medium that allows everyone to pay attention to different information, thus reducing the possibility of shared meanings and common discourse?

These and related questions arise from examining the Internet as an information marketplace governed by principles of attentional economics. About 10 years ago, I began to publish articles about attentional economics, but no one paid attention so I stopped. Much to my surprise, the editor of this volume found my work and thought it relevant to the theme of this book. My work mainly concerns the economics of attention and the growth of psychology, but the principles apply to those areas now using new information technologies to distribute more of their information as widely as they can.

The principles of attentional economics in the papers referenced here are not yet fully developed. Some of their fragments seem similar to classical economics. But attention is not money, and where they differ, their economics diverge. Perhaps some day, economists will fully develop attentional economic principles. Until then, the fragments still seem useful for understanding the dilemmas of Internet use.

For more about attentional economics, see Thorngate, 1988, 1990.

REFERENCES

Thorngate, W. (1988). On paying attention. In W. Baker, L. Mos, H. Van Rappard, & H. Stam (Eds.), *Recent trends in theoretical psychology* (pp. 247–264). New York: Springer-Verlag.
Thorngate, W. (1990). The economy of attention and the development of psychology. *Canadian Psychology/Psychologie Canadienne, 31,* 262–271.

Part V

NETWORKED ORGANIZATIONS

Organizations throughout this century have experienced an enormous economic and social transition that promises to continue into the next. Among the changes is the increasing dependence on computers by all organizational participants—owners, managers, employees, stockholders, bankers, suppliers, and customers. The widespread diffusion of computers in organizations has provided an unprecedented opportunity for social scientists to examine theories of technological innovation and its effects within organizations.

The earliest literature on computers in organizations was speculative; there were few information systems to study until the 1960s and electronic communication did not become widespread until the 1980s. In the 1980s researchers began observing the computerization of firms and government agencies, and the introduction of electronic communication. Much of this work touched on intra-site issues such as how management implemented technological change, monitoring of employees, and whether computers changed performance. There is a considerable published literature on these and other questions about computers, information systems, and electronic communication in organizations (e.g., Kling, 1987; Kraut, 1987; Sproull & Kiesler, 1991). Many journals of organization science now regularly publish papers on these topics.

The focus of organization research changed during the last 5 years as organizations increasingly used computer networks to reorganize and distribute work and workers across departments, regions, and projects, to connect sites or even different organizations (e.g., through Internet connections), and to expand markets globally. Many researchers hypothesized that transformative social effects would occur from these changes. For example, if work groups were less permanent and widely distributed geographically, the traditional command hierarchy and culture of organizations might be shaken. Employees could work at home, perhaps with dire effects on management's ability to control the work process. Organizations would become "flatter" with fewer managers supervising more people. Greater participation in communications by peripheral employees such as junior workers or employees in distant branches of a firm might increase their knowledge of the organization, their commitment, or even their influence. Easy communication of employees with those in other organizations through the Internet and other international resources might speed up innovation, turnover, mobilization for change.

Here we introduce a small sample of this new literature. Chapter 14, by David Constant, Lee Sproull, and Sara Kiesler, continues the computer-supported collaborative work theme from the previous section. The authors, using some of the social network concepts described in chapter 9 by Barry Wellman, studied electronic information sharing among employees in a high technology global firm. Chapter 15, by Robert Kraut and Paul Attewell, also is a study of a global firm (but in the banking industry). The authors study the effects of electronic communication on employees' knowledge and influence.

Understanding how and to what effect organizations introduce technology is an important topic of industrial organization (Cohen & Levinthal, 1990; Tushman & Anderson, 1986). The next two chapters in this section examine the introduction of electronic communication in two kinds of "service" organizations, libraries and schools. In chapter 16, Lisa Covi and Rob Kling describe some changes facing university libraries as they attempt to become major resources for digital information. Especially, they address the question of how different groups will define "the library." In chapter 17, Janet Schofield, Ann Davidson, Janet Stocks, and Gail Futoran describe teachers' responses to the introduction of electronic communication in the Pittsburgh school system. This chapter, in particular, documents the high hopes that people attach to electronic communication. However, lest readers conclude "real" businesses are immune to these emotional and symbolic aspects of technological change, there is ample evidence of their prevalence in industry also (National Research Council, 1986, 1989).

REFERENCES

Cohen, W., & Levinthal, D. A. (1990). Absorptive capacity: A new perspective on learning and innovation. *Administrative Science Quarterly, 35*, 128–152.

Kling, R. (1987). Defining the boundaries of computing across complex organizations. In R. Boland & R. Hirschheim (Eds.), *Critical issues in information systems* (pp. 307–362). New York: Wiley.

Kraut, R. E. (Ed.). (1987). *Technology and the transformation of white-collar work.* Hillsdale, NJ: Lawrence Erlbaum Associates.

National Research Council, Committee on the Effective Implementation of Advanced Manufacturing Technology, Manufacturing Studies Board, Commission on Engineering and

Technical Systems. (1986). *Human resource practices for implementing advanced manufacturing technology*. Washington, DC: National Academy Press.

National Research Council, Panel on Information Technology and the Conduct of Research, Committee on Science, Engineering, and Public Policy. (1989). *Information technology and the conduct of research: The user's view*. Washington, DC: National Academy Press.

Sproull, L., & Kiesler, S. (1991). *Connections: New ways of working in the networked organization*. Cambridge, MA: MIT Press.

Tushman, M. L., & Anderson, P. (1986). Technological discontinuities and organizational environments. *Administrative Science Quarterly, 31*, 439–465.

14

THE KINDNESS OF STRANGERS: ON THE USEFULNESS OF ELECTRONIC WEAK TIES FOR TECHNICAL ADVICE

David Constant
Carnegie Mellon University

Lee Sproull
Boston University

Sara Kiesler
Carnegie Mellon University

People use weak ties—relationships with acquaintances and strangers—to seek help unavailable from friends or colleagues, but help through weak ties may have doubtful value. We studied how employees of a global computer manufacturer used weak ties to obtain technical advice, what motivated people to provide advice, and what influenced seekers' receiving more or less useful advice. Theories of weak ties suggest that the usefulness of advice may depend on the number of weak ties, the diversity of ties, or the resources of help providers. We predicted that providers' firm-specific resources and organizational motivations would predict the usefulness of advice. The data supported this hypothesis and provided some support for resource and diversity explanations of weak tie influence. We discuss how the organization's culture sustained useful information exchange through weak ties.

In geographically dispersed organizations, employees cannot always get useful advice from their local colleagues. If expertise is not available locally, simply finding out who has it may be difficult. Inducing those who have it to share it may be even more difficult. People in organizations usually prefer to exchange help through strong collegial ties, which develop with physical proximity (e.g., Allen, 1977; Kraut, Galegher, & Egido, 1988; Finholt, 1993), group membership (Zurcher, 1965), a history of prior relationships (Krackhardt, 1992, 1994), and demographic similarity (Zenger & Lawrence, 1989). Depending on unknown employees at distant locations for technical advice requires depending on the kindness of strangers.

Computer networks, which are being used by growing numbers of organizations, make it relatively easy and inexpensive to ask distant acquaintances for advice via email. They also make it possible to ask strangers for advice. A person can post a query of the form, "Does anybody know …?" to a large electronic distribution list, electronic conference, or computer bulletin board without knowing who might read it. People who read the query can reply without having to know the person who posted it. Computer networks can link people in the absence of acquaintance, physical proximity, group membership, a history of prior relationships, and demographic similarity. This chapter explores the process of giving and receiving technical advice over an organizational computer network. We draw on theories of weak ties and prosocial motivation to suggest how this process can lead to useful advice and use data from one multinational firm to illustrate the process.

THEORETICAL FRAMEWORK AND PREDICTIONS

A theory of "the strength of weak ties" proposed by Granovetter (1973, 1982) suggests that relative strangers could offer an advantage over friends and colleagues in obtaining useful information. Granovetter argued that strong-tie relationships occur among people who are similar in many respects; similar people may not have dissimilar information. When information is unavailable through strong ties, people may obtain it through weak ties—relationships characterized by absent or infrequent contact, lack of emotional closeness, and no history of reciprocal services. Weak ties serve as information bridges across cliques of strong ties and can offer people access to resources that are not found in their strong-tie relationships (e.g., Stevenson & Gilly, 1991).

Weak-tie theorists have proposed three arguments for why weak ties are useful. One argument is simply that weak ties comprise more numerous potential helpers than strong ties do (Friedkin, 1982). If an employee broadcasts a request for technical information on a computer network, many people will see the request. Numerous replies increase the probability of finding one correct answer. This argument leads to our first hypothesis: *Advice from more people will be more useful than advice from fewer people.*

Numerous weak ties might not result in more useful advice, however. A bigger sample of weak ties is likely to increase bad advice as well as good advice. Perhaps it is not the number of people giving advice, per se, that makes weak ties useful but the range or diversity of those ties (Burt, 1983). A diverse range of ties increases the probability of finding a useful answer if expertise is heterogeneously distributed across groups. Group diversity also could increase alternative solutions or provide pieces to a multipart solution. This argument leads to our second hypothesis: *Advice from more diverse ties will be more useful than advice from less diverse ties.*

Useful weak ties might draw on not merely diverse resources, but superior resources. Lin, Ensel, and Vaughn (1981) argued that those using weak ties will solicit help from people having desirable resources—wealth, status, prestige, power, or access to others (see also DiMaggio & Mohr, 1985; Marsden & Hurlbert, 1988). Investigations evaluating this idea have been concerned primarily with job mobility. Useful weak-tie contacts tend to have resources that are superior to those of job seekers. In the context of technical advice, superior resources are ones that increase the probability of a contact's offering correct or otherwise useful advice. A contact's personal and social resources derived from his or her organizational position, department, or location might be differentially helpful (e.g., Krackhardt, 1992). The more technical expertise and experience a contact has, the more likely that contact will provide useful technical advice. Physical proximity to other experts also is important for the exchange of technical information. Thus proximity to the technical center of the organization can be viewed as a useful resource. Finally, an organizational cliché is that people whose technical knowledge is outdated are promoted into management. Alternatively, even though managers may no longer have useful technical information themselves, they may know who does have it. In this case, a contact's hierarchical status would be positively related to useful technical knowledge.

We posed the following general resource hypothesis: *Advice from people with more resources will be more useful than advice from people with fewer resources.*

The Problem of Motivation

The usefulness of computer network help from strangers is problematic. The seeker has no direct way of assessing the provider's reliability, expertise, possible strategic motives for misinformation, or knowledge about the seeker's situation. The seeker also has no control over the provider's incentives. The provider has little information about the seeker and therefore may misunderstand the request for help or advice, use inappropriate assumptions in generating a response, or formulate that response using language or concepts not shared by the seeker. These difficulties should increase with the weakness of the tie, that is, with the physical and social distance of the information provider from the seeker.

Even when weak ties are potentially helpful, the motivation of strangers to help may be poor. People provide help to people they know, people they like, people who are similar, and people who have helped them (see Dovidio, 1984; Heimer, 1992; Krackhardt, 1992). In personal relationships, benefactors themselves benefit from providing help, either through increasing the beneficiary's obligation to reciprocate or through receiving the beneficiary's esteem or both. Some theorists suggest that if help is offered in the absence of direct reciprocity, it may not be very useful (e.g., Thorn & Connolly, 1987). In this view strangers who could offer high-quality help will find it too costly do so. Only those who have "nothing better to do" may offer assistance, which is likely to be of poor quality.

Generalized requests for help over a computer network do not meet the requirements of personal connection. Why would someone respond to a request for help from a stranger when the likelihood of direct personal benefit is low? Friendship and similarity are unlikely explanations. Personal friendships are uncommon across the geographic distances spanned by computer networks (Feldman, 1987). Computer networks offer few cues to make demographic similarity salient to a potential benefactor (Sproull & Kiesler, 1986). Also, computer networks do not provide a very rich medium for proffering esteem and gratitude (Daft & Lengel, 1986).

Theories of prosocial motivation suggest two alternative processes that could lead people to provide useful technical help to strangers, even when this help is personally costly. First, some theorists have posited that people are not only pragmatic but also expressive of feelings, values, and self-identities (Schlenker, 1985). If technical expertise is important in self-identity, experts can gain personal benefits from helping strangers on a computer network with technical problems. Helping others can increase self-esteem, personal identification with the organization, self-respect, respect from others, and feelings of commitment (e.g., Orr, 1989). However, the usefulness of advice from experts motivated by personal benefit is questionable because such advice may be provided idiosyncratically or without close attention to the requirements of information seekers.

A second theoretical argument is that instead of direct personal benefit, help on a computer network is founded on organizational citizenship (e.g., Bateman & Organ, 1983) and norms of generalized reciprocity (Mauss 1925/1967; Berkowitz & Daniels, 1964; Titmuss, 1971). Those who are organizationally motivated are concerned with such things as how much they are needed, how they can be useful to others, and how their advice might solve organizational problems. People who have a strong organizational orientation are likely to be sensitive to the needs of help seekers and to adjust their advice to the requirements of those asking for help. Accordingly, we offer a fourth hypothesis: *Advice from people who are more organiza-*

tionally motivated will be more useful than advice from people who are less organizationally motivated.

Generalized reciprocity emerges when people have positive regard for the social system in which requests for help are embedded and show respect for it through offering help. Their regard may have an indirect basis in personal experience. For instance, they may have been helped by others on the computer network in the past or they may expect that someone on the network would help them in the future. Alternatively, their regard might stem from a more abstract view of the computer network as an organizational resource and worthy institution. In either case offering help is unrelated to direct reciprocity and more related to maintaining the social institution of the network as an organizational resource. Hence, in opposition to the prediction developed from an economic rational theory of exchange (e.g., Thorn & Connolly, 1987), we offer a fifth hypothesis: *On average, information providers will represent a pool of people whose resources for helping are at least as good as and perhaps better than those of information seekers.*

METHOD

Previous research on weak ties has been conducted mainly through studies of people's retrospective accounts of their search for a successful outcome. These studies usually do not provide information on all the weak ties that seekers of help tried, and do not include ties that proved useless. Further, retrospective accounts often produce "good stories." By collecting data from information seekers and each of their subsequent information providers, our study provides a way to estimate the overall value of search.

Research Setting

The study was conducted at Tandem Computers Incorporated, a Fortune 500 computer manufacturer whose headquarters and main technical organization are located in Silicon Valley. Virtually all employees use a corporate computer network, which allows employees to send and receive mail messages from computer terminals on their desks. The system is used extensively: Employees from all levels of the company and from all locations feel free to (and in fact do) send messages to the president, to managers not in their direct chain of command, or to people outside their subunits; tens of thousands of messages are sent and received each day.

The email system at Tandem organizes messages into first-class, second-class, and third-class mail. First-class mail is for person-to-person messages and for work-related distribution lists (e.g., All_Sales_Reps). Second-class mail is for work-related broadcast messages that go to the entire organization, including announcements from headquarters, industry news, and requests for information. Third-class mail is for extracurricular broadcast messages such as restaurant reviews or "want ads." The focus of this research is broadcast requests for information appearing on second-class mail. About 30% of the second-class messages on the network contained such requests. An example of a query and responses found in second-class mail is given in Fig. 14.1.

Study Design and Data Collection

The study used an event-driven survey methodology, whose triggering event was a request for information broadcast in second-class mail. During the 6- week research period, 82 employees broadcast one or more questions and announced they would make the replies available in public reply files on the network. When each question appeared, we sent survey question-naires electronically to the information seeker who broadcast the question and to the information providers who replied to the question.[1] Information seekers received two surveys: The first asked them about themselves and requested that they keep all replies to their question; the second survey, sent 1 week later, asked them to evaluate each reply they had received. The survey sent to information providers asked them for information about themselves and about why they replied to the information seeker. We also captured the text of each question and all replies that had been placed in public reply files. We used Tandem's online organizational database to gather data on respondents' geographic location, job type, and hierarchical level.

For purposes of comparison we also collected data from an additional 67 employees who broadcast requests for information but did not create public reply files. We captured the text of their questions and sent them both surveys but we did not collect data from their providers because their providers' replies had not been made public.

Independent and Dependent Variables

Strength of Ties and Relationship Variables.   We   measured   the strength of ties by asking information providers how well they knew the information seeker on a Likert scale (1 = "don't know at all" and 10 = "know very well"). We measured network history by asking how many questions they had posed and replies they had given in the past year on second-class

---

[1]In the case of 17 people who broadcast more than one question during the research period, we asked only about the first question. In the case of people who replied to more than one question, we sent a separate survey about each reply they sent up to three.

THE QUESTION

FROM: BOULANGER_NADIA *Information Seeker*
TO: DL.ALL_TANDEM @SLC
SUBJECT: 2:?? 2311 at 7 but still too dim ??
Hi all,

I am sure I'm not the first to ask this question but I can find no help in Quest [on-line database of previous public questions and replies] so I'm copying the world to see if I can get any answers.

I have a number of 2311's [computer terminals] (50+) installed at ABC Co. and many of them are starting to get too dim even at the max brightness setting. Is there any way to increase the brightness on these monitors or is the solution a replacement.

Any info would be greatly appreciated.

Replies if any at \SLC.$CE.DIM2311.REPLYS [location of public replies file].

Regards, Nadia

THE REPLIES

1. FROM: REICH_STEVE @AUSTIN
How long have these 2311s been installed? What is the duty power-on cycle (5days/10hrs, 7days/24hrs, etc.)? Are they/were they using screen-saver? If so, what was the value?
Value to Information Seeker = $5.00

2. FROM: GLASS_PHIL @AUSTIN
Hi, Try tweaking the potentiometer inside the monitor. I've had to do the same with the terminals and Agelbars (no comments please) when I worked in the private sector. I've never taken a 2311 apart, so I can't tell you the location of the pot, but you should see something on or near it to indicate that it controls brightness. My only word of warning is to be damn careful when you stick a screwdriver in there. You may want to cover the shaft in a layer of electrical tape. Good luck.
Regards, Phil Glass
Value to Information Seeker = $5.00

3. FROM: SCHOENBERG_ARNIE @BELGIUM
Hallo Nadia,
No problem. With two screws you can easily remove the top cover of the 2311. Under the cover you will find the monitorboard and on that board the two potmeters for brightness and contrast.
Greetings, Arnie
Value to Information Seeker = $25.00

4. FROM: CAGE_JOHN @PRUNE
Nadia,
We had a few of 'em that we took apart and tweaked up a pot labeled "brite" or "brightness" or some such. They're still working! jc
Value to Information Seeker = $20.00

FIG. 14.1. Broadcast question and replies on the computer network. (This example is verbatim from our sample, except that the proper names of employees and products have been changed. The values of each reply are the actual rating "Nadia" made of the usefulness of her replies.)

5. FROM: PENTLAND_BARBARA @ORCA
THE COST TO MAINTAIN THESE UNITS WOULD GREATLY EXCEED THE PRICE IN
WHICH WE BOUGHT THEM FOR.   THE BEST SOLUTION IS TO THROW THESE UNITS
OUT AND PURCHASE NEW ONES.   BESIDES THAT REPLACEMENT PARTS ARE SLIM
TO NONE..

Value to Information Seeker = none given

6. FROM: SCHAEFFER_MURRAY @EASY
Nadia,
There is probably an adjustment inside the monitor. You should ask
your CE [customer engineer] about adjusting the range with the internal
pot.

Murray
Value to Information Seeker = $5.00

7. FROM: THEBERGE_PAUL @PITT
HI THERE,
THERE IS AN INTERNAL BRIGHTNESS POT THAT CAN BE ACCESSED BY OPENING
UP THE MONITOR.   I HAVE ADJUSTED QUITE A FEW TERMINALS THIS WAY. I
DON'T KNOW IF THIS IS THE PRESCRIBED METHOD BUT IT WORKS! HOPE THIS
HELPS!
                              PAUL THEBERGE
Value to Information Seeker = $20.00

8. FROM: LEVERKUHN_ADRIAN @OMAHA
Nadia, I had a couple of the Beta units and that was one of the
problems, only it occurred after a week. I tried getting inside and
adjusting, just as I have done with 2316s with about the same results.
You can crank up the brightness a bit but then you start to lose your
contrast and get complaints of "fuzzy"characters. We have found that
the units, being FRUs [field-replaceable units] in-toto are not worth
the effort.   Adrian

Value to Information Seeker = $15.00

Fig. 14.1. Continued

mail. We evaluated the demographic similarity of seekers to providers
based on whether both were at headquarters, both were managers, and the
difference in their hierarchical level and firm and industry experience
(Zenger & Lawrence, 1989).

Resources.   We used years of firm experience and years of experience
in the computer industry as measures of resources for both seekers and
providers. We estimated the expertise of information providers by asking
them on a 10-point scale: "How informed are you on the subject matter of
this question?" (1 = novice and 10 = expert). We also used three measures
of resources associated with a person's organizational position: (a) location
at headquarters—the site of most engineering and product development,

(b) whether or not the person held a managerial position, and (c) hierarchical level, the number of levels to the CEO. Because the organization had field offices all over the world, we operationalized diversity for each information seeker's providers as the number of different countries where information providers were based. We also operationalized diversity as the number of different hierarchical levels of information providers.

Provider Motivation. We measured providers' motivations by asking them to allocate 100 points among several reasons that they might have had for replying to the information seeker. We listed four reasons associated with personal benefits and four reasons associated with organizational motivation.

Usefulness of Aid. To measure the usefulness of advice, we asked information seekers to "please -award' $0 to $25 to each answer based on how helpful it was to you." We asked information providers to award themselves $0 to $25 according to how useful they thought their reply was to the information seeker. We also asked information seekers to impose a "fine" of as much as $25 on any answer that wasted their time. And we asked information seekers an open-ended question, "What have you done or what do you intend to do as a result of each reply?" We coded the responses to indicate whether one or more of the replies solved the seeker's problem (solved problem = 1; did not solve problem = 0).

Analyses

The data were grouped, with each group consisting of data about: (a) an information seeker, (b) the question broadcast by the seeker, (c) the information providers who responded to that information seeker, and (d) the replies given by the information providers. We tested hypotheses involving individual characteristics, such as the resources of information providers, at the individual level controlling statistically for group (i.e., information seeker). This procedure controls for dependence among providers and replies to the same question. We tested hypotheses involving group characteristics, such as diversity of contact resources, at the group level.

RESULTS

Response Rates and Sample Characteristics

We collected 100% of the 82 question texts and sent two questionnaires sequentially to the 82 information seekers who posted them, 55 of whom completed both (67% response rate). These information seekers reported receiving 429 replies to their broadcast questions, an average of 7.8 replies per question. They gave us the names of 365 repliers to whom we sent surveys. We received 295 completed surveys from the repliers (80% response rate) and obtained the text of 263 replies. We obtained online organizational employee data for 92% of information seekers and providers.

For analyses combining data from different sources (seeker and provider characteristics, and question and reply characteristics), we used a core sample of information exchanges with no missing categories of data. These exchanges include the seeker's question, two completed questionnaires from the information seeker, a text file of public replies to the question, and completed questionnaires from the repliers. Full data were available for 48 of the 82 questions broadcasted, leaving an effective response rate of 58%—48 information seekers, their 48 questions, their 263 information providers, and the 263 public replies they gave.

Our research sample was similar to the population of employees who use second-class mail. Sample employees were predominantly male professionals, proportionally the same as those who used second-class mail generally and the same as in the company as a whole. However, significantly more of our sample and of second-class email users were in sales and field support positions than in the company as a whole, and more were located in smaller sites, in offices more distant from headquarters, and outside the United States.

Questions Asked and Information Received

Information seekers asked primarily technical questions that averaged nearly half a page (mean = 12.1 lines of text, SD = 8.7). They did not pose their questions lightly: 91% of information seekers reported querying at least one other information source before broadcasting their question. Information providers, on average, estimated they spent 9 minutes (SD = 4.1) on their replies. Replies averaged about three fourths of a page (mean = 19.1 lines, SD = 81.3). Fifty-four percent of the answers contained technical information, and 53% contained a referral to another source of information, such as a specific person or computer file.

Information seekers valued the usefulness of the average reply they received at $11.30 (SD = $8.70; min. = $0, max. = $25). (For instance, see Fig. 14.1.) The value of the best reply was highly correlated with the value of the mean reply ($r = .79$). This correlation suggests either a "halo" effect of good replies or that reply values are additive. Information seekers used fines so infrequently (8.4% of the time) that we did not use fines in the analysis. On average, information providers valued their own replies at $13.20 (SD = $8.00; min. = $0, max. = $25).

Half of the information seekers (49%) said that the replies they received solved their problem. The mean usefulness of information seekers' replies was positively but not significantly correlated with whether or not information seekers said their problem was solved (r = .18). The value of the best reply also was not significantly correlated with whether or not the problem was solved (r = .20).

Strength of Ties and Basis of Relationship

As we had expected, people did not have a personal connection to the person they helped. Information providers did not know their seekers; 81% of the providers said they did not know the seekers at all; an additional 10% said they were barely acquainted. Acquaintanceship was uncorrelated with the number of replies (r = −.11), with the usefulness of replies (r = .07), or with the solution of the seekers' problems (r = .05). A history of posting or answering questions on second-class email was uncorrelated with acquaintanceship (rs = 0) nor did this history predict the number of replies (rs = 0) or their usefulness (r = .06, r = .03, respectively) or whether or not seekers' problems were solved (r = −.07, r = .03). Providers did not help based on the friendliness, social content, or tone of the questions they saw. We used three "sociability" measures: whether the question included a greeting, a closing, or named the company. The presence of a personal opening or closing or both in the question was negatively correlated with the number of replies, r[48] = −.30, p < .05. The social content of questions did not predict the usefulness of replies or whether or not the problem was solved.

Information providers generally did not help based on their similarity to the person needing help. On only one measure of similarity, whether both or neither person worked at a headquarters location, were information providers more similar to their "own" information seeker than they were to the mean of all the information seekers. There was no similarity effect for managerial status, hierarchical level, firm experience, and industry experience. Adding similarity variables to a regression of usefulness on information provider did not improve the model (R^2 without similarity variables = .34; with similarity variables = .37, change F = 1.64, n.s.). The similarity of information providers to their information seeker also was uncorrelated with whether or not the seeker's problem was solved; none of the individual correlations was significant and a logistic regression of problem solution on information provider and similarity variables was not significant.

In sum, the data do not describe a system of direct social exchange whereby people give useful help to those with whom they have a personal relationship, to those who are similar, and to those who have helped them. Neither acquaintanceship, a history of reciprocity using the network to exchange advice, nor similarity was very important in predicting the incidence or usefulness of replies.

The Usefulness of Information

We examined three hypotheses about the usefulness of weak-tie information: The number of replies will predict the usefulness of replies, the range
or diversity of groups from which providers come will predict the usefulness of replies, the resources of information providers will predict the
usefulness of replies. In each analysis we used hierarchical regression to
estimate the contribution of separate groups of variables to the overall
model. At the individual level we could test hypotheses about how the
number of replies and the resources of information providers predict usefulness. At the group level we could test hypotheses about how the number
of replies, resources, and diversity predict problem solutions as well as
usefulness.

Number of Replies. We regressed the usefulness of replies on the
number of replies controlling for information providers' resources. This
regression was significant at $p < .01$ and the coefficient for the number of
replies was negative. This result does not support the hypothesis that the
number of weak ties statistically increases the likelihood of obtaining good
advice.

We explored this relationship further by investigating if the number of
replies was positively related to the most useful reply, reasoning that more
replies might offer more opportunity to find one truly useful answer.
Regressions of the most useful reply on the number of replies were carried
out at the group level, because each information seeker can have only one
best reply (or several replies receiving a tie score for most usefulness). The
coefficients were positive but not statistically significant, with and without
controls for resources (bivariate $r = .22, p < .14$). The number of replies was
more strongly related to the least useful reply (bivariate $r = -.30, p < .04$).
This relatively big drop in the usefulness of the worst reply when there were
more replies could explain why mean usefulness declined with more
replies. The same result was obtained in analyses using information providers' own assessments of the usefulness of their replies which, unlike seekers'
assessments, are not affected by their evaluations of other replies.

The number of replies also did not predict whether or not information
seekers' problems were solved. In sum, for these information seekers, more
replies did not improve the net benefit of weak ties.

Information Provider Resources. On average, information providers
had more resources than information seekers did (see Table 14.1). Resources
of information providers also were positively related to seekers' usefulness
ratings. At the individual level, controlling for the number of replies, there
were significant coefficients at the .05 level for the resources of being a
manager, hierarchical level, and expertise. In a similar analysis controlling
for information seeker instead of number of replies, the only significant

TABLE 14.1

Mean Resources of Information Seekers and Information Providers

Resources	Information Seekers (n = 48)	Information Providers (n = 281)	t statistic
HQ location (yes = 1, no = 0)	14%	31%	2.88**
Manager (yes = 1, no = 0)	2 %	12%	3.23**
Hierarchical level[a]	6.0 (.8)	5.6 (1.0)	2.50*
Firm experience (years)	4.0 (2.7)	4.3 (3.0)	.71
Industry experience (years)	12.2 (6.2)	13.8 (6.8)	1.52

[a]The fewer the levels to the CEO, the higher the position.
*p < .05, **p < .01

coefficient was the resource of expertise. These analyses generally support our hypothesis that weak ties for technical advice in an organization are useful to the degree they tap people with superior resources.

At the group level we used mean usefulness of replies as the dependent variable and tested effects of groups of replies rather than of individual replies. A model with resources, controlling for number of replies, was significant at the .06 level. The model contained significant coefficients at the .10 level for the resource of being a manager and at the .05 level for the resource of firm experience.

Diversity. In the group-level analysis described in the previous section, we used the number of different countries and the number of different hierarchical levels represented in a group of replies as proxies for diversity. We regressed mean usefulness on number of replies, resources, and diversity. Diversity contributed slightly to the prediction of usefulness but in a direction opposite to the hypothesis. In the combined model, at the .05 level or better, the resources of being a manager and firm experience, but fewer levels of the hierarchy represented in replies, contributed to usefulness. Adding diversity to a model containing number of replies and resources increased the R^2 by .09 ($p < .10$). This analysis suggests that advice from a less hierarchically diverse (rather than more diverse) set of ties increased usefulness.

Solving the Problem

A group-level model regressing solving the problem on resources, controlling for number of replies, was significant ($\chi^2 = 17.25, p = .02$). Within this model the coefficient for working at the technical center of the organization was significant at the .05 level. In contrast to the findings for mean usefulness, the diversity of ties contributed positively to the model when problem solution was the dependent variable. Generally, the coefficients were positive in this analysis. In the full model, the resources of working at the technical center ($p < .01$) and being an expert ($p < .10$), but not being a manager ($p < .05$), and having more countries represented in the replies (p < .10) predict solving the problem. Diversity alone, controlling for number of replies, does not predict problem solution. The full model with resources and diversity, controlling for number of replies, was an improvement over a model without diversity ($\chi^2 = 4.85$, $p < .10$).

Effects of Motivation

When asked, "Why did you answer this question?" information providers gave reasons of personal benefit as well as reasons related to general organizational benefit, but they gave more of the latter than the former (paired-t [262] = 8.75, $p < .01$). That is, they favored the reasons, "The problem is important to the company," "I expect others to help me, so it's only fair to help them," "it's part of my job," and "answering questions like this is part of being a good company citizen" over personal benefits: "I enjoy helping others," "I enjoy solving problems," "I enjoy earning respect," and "the company rewards information sharing." We found no correlational evidence that providers' personal history of giving or receiving help over the network or their acquaintanceship with information seekers predicted the reasons they gave for helping.

We next carried out individual-level analyses regressing usefulness of advice on personal benefits and organizational motivations for answering questions. The regressions were conducted with and without controls for resources (not shown in a table). The personal benefit of earning respect ($p < .05$), and the organizational motivations of "it's part of my job to help" ($p < .05$) and "it's only fair to help" ($p < .10$), predicted the usefulness of replies. Change statistics indicated that adding personal benefits to the model did not improve the model, but adding organizational motivation to the model did improve it ($p < .05$). Adding provider's resources to the model strengthened results in the same direction.

These results support our hypothesis that organizational motivations of information providers and "earning others' respect" predicted how seekers rated the usefulness of replies. Self-reports of motivation may be suspect, particularly when they emphasize socially desirable traits. However, there is no reason to believe that providers' ratings of their motivation should have affected seekers' usefulness ratings. Hence we have cause to take providers' self-reported motivations at face value.

If information providers help simply because they have nothing better to do, their resources and the quality of their help is likely to be inferior. If, instead, information providers are motivated by a communal orientation to the needs of others and to the problems of the organization, they may represent a pool of helpers whose resources are as good or superior to those of information seekers. The data we presented in Table 14.1 suggest this is the case.

DISCUSSION

In this study, weak ties established through a computer network offered information seekers technical information or referrals. Information providers gave useful advice and solved the problems of information seekers despite their lacking a personal connection with the seekers. Table 14.2 gives a summary of our findings from the regression analyses. Generally this shows that weak ties to superior resources provided more useful informa-

TABLE 14.2.

**Summary of Regression Analyses of the Usefulness of Advice
and Whether Replies Solved the Information Seeker's Problem.**

Independent Variables	Usefulness of the Single Reply	Usefulness of All an Information Seeker's Replies	Whether the Replies Solved the Problem
Number of replies	–	0	0
Resources of repliers:			
At headquarters	0	0	+
Manager	+	+	–
Higher level	+	0	0
Expertise	+	0	+
Firm experience	+	+	0
Industry exper.	0	0	0
Diversity of replies:			
Diverse countries	n.a.	0	+
Diverse levels	n.a.	–	0
Replier motivation:			
Helping others	0	n.a.	n.a.
Solve problems	0	n.a.	n.a.
Earn respect	+	n.a.	n.a.
Company rewards	0	n.a.	n.a.
Good citizen	0	n.a.	n.a.
Impt to company	0	n.a.	n.a.
Part of my job	+	n.a.	n.a.
Only fair to help	+	n.a.	n.a.

Note. n.a. means the variable could not be tested in this case. + = a positive effect. – = a negative effect. 0 = no effect. Complete tables are reported in Constant et al. (1996).

tion. Controlling for those resources, the number of replies was not positively related to the average usefulness of replies, to the most useful advice, or to the solution of problems. The diversity of ties as well as the resources of information providers contributed to whether or not seekers' problems were solved.

In this study, expertise contributed both to the usefulness of advice and to problem solving. But replies could be deemed useful without actually solving problems. Information seekers obtained advice they considered very useful (but that did not necessarily solve the problem) from ties with managers and from those having more firm experience. By contrast, information seekers' problems were solved through diverse ties from different countries and from lower levels and by those having more ties at the technical center. Apparently, information providers who gave very useful advice and those who solved people's problems were somewhat different groups. Perhaps repliers who gave especially useful advice gave broader firm-specific knowledge (which managers and people with longer firm experience would have) whereas those who solved the seeker's problem gave site-specific technical answers (which would be tapped more easily at the technical center as well as through more diverse ties).

Our results are consistent with the theory that weak ties' usefulness is due to their bridging capacity as Granovetter (1982) and Burt (1983) hypothesized, rather than to their sheer number, as was suggested by Friedkin (1982). The computer network used to draw on weak ties linked people across distance, time, country, and hierarchical level and organizational subunit. Consistent with the resource arguments of Lin and his colleagues (1981), these links were useful to the degree they put people in touch with those offering superior resources; they were not useful nor did they have a greater likelihood of solving the information seeker's problem when they were simply greater in number. People who received more replies did get replies of high quality; they also received replies of very low quality. Perhaps many replies caused confusion or uncertainty, which detracted from potentially beneficial information.

Ours is a case study of weak-tie sharing within one geographically dispersed organization. The firm we studied views the computer network as a critical corporate resource, encourages employees to use it, and rewards them for devising software that improves communication. We have no data on employees who did not help—the baseline statistics on the motivations or expertise of employees in general—so our inferences must be cautious. Yet it seems unlikely that, in the absence of a culture that supports information sharing and considers the network to be an organizational resource, the kinds of information exchanges among weak ties we observed could be sustained for long. The form of exchange we observed had been established more than 6 years before the data were collected, evidence of considerable stability. Technology alone will not impel this kind of weak-tie sharing over time; an organizational culture that fosters it also is necessary. In this organization strangers incur the costs of "kindness" because they can perform as experts and meet important needs of others. Norms of generalized reciprocity sustain kindness as a social institution and lead people who can provide useful help to do so.

Given a corporate culture that promotes information sharing, we suggest three probable scope conditions for our findings related to kind of information, degree of slack in employee time, and intensity of usage. Technical information is relatively more likely to be exchanged in a computer network weak-tie environment than are other kinds of information such as strategic, political, or personal information. For example, we never saw any broadcast questions of the form, "Does anybody know who will be named as the next engineering vice president?" or "Does anybody know what X is like as a boss?" Undoubtedly people used the computer network to search for nontechnical information, but they probably did so within their strong-tie relationships rather than through weak ties. Although answering questions had relatively low costs, it was not costless; information providers had to have enough slack in their work day so that the 9 minutes (on average) they reported it took them to produce a reply was not viewed as excessive. By contrast, in professional organizations that require employees to account for their time to the 10th of an hour for billing purposes, 9 minutes of "free" help could be viewed as costly to the provider. The number of questions asked per day must be governed by self-limiting processes. We saw about 7 questions a day; if there had been 700 or 7,000 the system would have been swamped and, presumably, would not have continued to yield useful answers.

Broadcasting requests for help over a computer network can be viewed as a public goods problem in which it is in no one's best interest to respond and in which people rich in resources will be particularly disinclined to respond (Thorn & Connolly, 1987). Others have noted that a small "critical mass" can overcome this problem (e.g., Marwell, Oliver, & Prahl, 1988). The models generally assume a situation where free riders cannot be excluded but neither increase the net cost to providers nor decrease the net benefit to recipients. These characteristics are true of the situation we studied, because neither information providers nor information seekers would notice free riders who read the public reply files. A remaining problem, however, is that a person's contribution may be inconsequential or redundant. Our data do not show that inconsequentiality was a problem. Information providers with more expertise tended to believe fewer others replied (r [205] = $-.21$, $p < .01$). However, 73% of the information providers could give us the name of at least one other person who could answer the question. And the average provider estimated that 15.4 other people replied to the question to which they replied. It seems that providers, including experts, replied in spite of their apparent inconsequentiality.

Macy (1990) argued that group members can learn to contribute despite their marginal value when they observe others contributing and see rewards to the public good. Once a critical mass of contributors is achieved, the legitimacy and value of contributing can be self-reinforcing. Computer networks with public reply files and other facilities for public information exchange, like those at the company we studied, may contribute to the creation of a critical mass by increasing the visibility of prosocial behavior (Cialdini, Reno, & Kallgren, 1990). Computer networks make it physically easy to reach large numbers of people and make weak-tie contacts, and they also make it relatively easy to respond to information requests. They also offer more opportunities to see others contributing than would be available in face-to-face interactions. By facilitating social observation of technical information exchange, computer networks may encourage people to contribute for personal benefits such as pride, and they may reinforce norms of contribution within a culture that values it. Hence computer networks can provide a means for leveraging the "kindness of strangers."

ACKNOWLEDGMENTS

This chapter is an abridged version of Constant, D., Sproull, L., & Kiesler, S. (1996). The kindness of strangers: The usefulness of electronic weak ties for technical advice. *Organization Science, 7*, 119–135. We thank Terry Connolly, Tom Finholt, Robyn Dawes, David Krackhardt, and anonymous reviewers for their helpful comments. This research was supported by a National Research Council of Canada fellowship to David Constant, a System Development Foundation grant to Lee Sproull, and an NIMH Research Scientist Development award MH 00933 to Sara Kiesler.

REFERENCES

Allen, T. J. (1977). *Managing the flow of technology.* Cambridge, MA: MIT Press.

Bateman, T. S., & Organ, D. W. (1983). Job satisfaction and the good soldier: The relationship between affect and employee "citizenship." *Academy of Management Journal, 26*, 587–595.

Berkowitz, L., & Daniels, L. R. (1964). Affecting the salience of the social responsibility norm: Effects of past help on the response to dependency relationships, *Journal of Abnormal and Social Psychology, 68*, 275–281.

Burt, R. S. (1983). Range. In R. S. Burt & M.J. Minor (Eds.), *Applied network analysis* (pp. 176–194). Beverly Hills, CA: Sage.

Cialdini, R. B., Reno, R. R., & Kallgren, C. A. (1990). A focus theory of normative conduct: Recycling the concept of norms to reduce littering in public places. *Journal of Personality and Social Psychology, 58*, 1015–1026.

Daft, R., & Lengel, R. (1986). Organizational information requirements, media richness and structural design. *Management Science*, 32, 554–571.

DiMaggio, P., & Mohr, J. (1985). Cultural capital, educational attainment, and marital selection. *American Journal of Sociology*, 90, 1231–1261.

Dovidio, J. F. (1984). Helping and altruism: An empirical and conceptual overview. In L. Berkowitz (Ed.), *Advances in experimental social psychology* (Vol. 17, pp.). New York: Academic Press.

Feldman, M. S. (1987). Electronic mail and weak ties in organizations. *Office: Technology and People*, 3, 83–101.

Finholt, T. (1993). *Outsiders on the inside*. Unpublished doctoral dissertation, Carnegie Mellon University, Pittsburgh.

Friedkin, N. (1982). Information flow through strong and weak ties in intraorganizational social networks. *Social Networks*, 3, 273–285.

Granovetter, M. (1973). The strength of weak ties. *American Journal of Sociology*, 78, 1360–1380.

Granovetter, M. (1982). The strength of weak ties: A network theory revisited. In P. Marsden & N. Lin (Eds.), *Social structure and network analysis* (pp. 105–130). New York: Wiley.

Heimer, C. (1992). Doing your job and helping your friends: Universalistic norms about obligations to particular others in networks. In N. Nohria & R. G. Eccles (Eds.), *Networks and organizations: Structure, form, and action* (pp. 143–164). Boston: Harvard Business School Press.

Krackhardt, D. (1992). The strength of strong ties: The importance of philos in organizations. In N. Nohria & R. Eccles (Eds.), *Organizations and networks: Structure, form, and action* (pp. 216–239). Boston: Harvard Business School Press.

Krackhardt, D. (1994). Constraints on the interactive organization as an ideal type. In C. Heckscher & A. Donnelan (Eds.), *The post-bureaucratic organization* (pp. 211–222). Beverly Hills, CA: Sage.

Kraut, R. E., Galegher, J., & Egido, C. (1988). Relationships and tasks in scientific collaboration. *Human–Computer Interaction*, 3, 31–58.

Lin, N., Ensel, W. M., & Vaughn, J. C. (1981). Social resources and strength of ties: Structural factors in occupational status attainment. *American Sociological Review*, 46, 393–405.

Macy, M. (1990). Learning theory and the logic of critical mass. *American Sociological Review*, 55, 809–826.

Marsden, P. V., & Hurlbert, J. S. (1988). Social resources and mobility outcomes: A replication and extension. *Social Forces*, 66, 1038–1059.

Marwell, G., Oliver, P., & Prahl, R. (1988). Social networks and collective actions: A theory of critical mass III. *American Journal of Sociology*, 94, 502–532.

Mauss, M. (1967). *The gift*. New York: Norton. (Original work published in 1925).

Orr, J. E. (1989). Sharing knowledge, celebrating identity: War stories and community memory among service technicians. In D. S. Middleton & D. Edwards (Eds.), *Collective remembering: Memory in society*. Beverly Hills, CA: Sage.

Schlenker, B. R. (1985). Identity and self-identification. In B. R. Schlenker (Ed.), *The self and social life*. New York: McGraw-Hill.

Sproull, L., & Kiesler, S. (1986). Reducing social context cues: Electronic mail in organizational communication. *Management Science*, 32, 1492–1512.

Stevenson, W. B., & Gilly, M. C. (1991). Information processing and problem solving: The migration of problems through formal positions and networks of ties. *Academy of Management Journal*, 34, 918–928.

Thorn, B. K., & Connolly, T. (1987). Discretionary data bases: A theory and some experimental findings. *Communication Research*, 14, 512–528.

Titmuss, R. M. (1971). *The gift relationship: From human blood to social policy*. New York: Pantheon Books.

Zenger, T. R., & Lawrence, B. S. (1989). Organizational demography: The differential effects of age and tenure distributions on technical communication. *Academy of Management Journal*, 32, 353–376.

Zurcher, L. A. (1965). The sailor aboard ship: A study of role behavior in a total institution. *Social Forces*, 43, 389–400.

15

MEDIA USE
IN A GLOBAL CORPORATION:
ELECTRONIC MAIL
AND ORGANIZATIONAL
KNOWLEDGE

Robert E. Kraut
Carnegie Mellon University

Paul Attewell
Graduate Center of the City University of New York

How has the proliferation of communications media changed the volume of communication and the distribution of information in large organizations? There is reason to think that the availability of more communication media increases the amount of communication employees receive, with positive effects on their organizational knowledge and commitment, but negative effects on their perception of being overloaded. Prior research suggests that electronic mail may differ from other media by more effectively spreading organizational information to peripheral employees, and doing so while interrupting them less than other styles of communication. This chapter uses survey data from a large U.S.-based multinational corporation to examine the effects of communication by electronic mail and other media. Results are that employees who used electronic mail extensively, net of their communication over other media, were better informed about their company and more committed to its management's goals. One reason for their superior organizational knowledge seems to be that electronic mail promotes "information spillover" from a focal recipient of a message to others who are less directly interested in a message, but does so without subjecting the marginal parties to the burdens of interruption and information overload.

Over the last 15 years there has been a proliferation of communications media available to employees in large corporations. Facsimile (fax), electronic mail, and videoconferencing now supplement traditional media such as face-to-face meetings, postal mail, and the telephone. What are the effects of this rich mix of communication media? Although organizations generally introduce new information technology to improve effectiveness or productivity, the results are not always straightforward or beneficial at the individual or organizational levels (Attewell, 1994; Landauer, 1995; Sproull & Kiesler, 1991).

Does the rich mix of communication media available in many organizations result in more communication, with the result that organizational participants are better informed, or do they simply experience more interruption and information overload? Are far-flung parts of multinational organizations better integrated into the firm because of the new media, or does the communication enhance local communication and benefit primarily those who already at the center of the organization?

Although our interests in this chapter are to understand the impact of the new media, in order to do so we must also confront questions of media choice, if only for methodological reasons. To examine the effects of new media, one must control for their use by different people with different organizational roles and their use in different situations to accomplish different tasks .

These issues are addressed below through an analysis of survey data from a large U.S.-based multinational corporation that has one of the largest and oldest firm-wide electronic mail networks, as well as the full complement of other communications media (phone, fax, mail, videoconferencing). We begin with a review of preexisting theories about media use and effects that inform the design of our own study.

Media Effects: Overload and Peripherality

There are many potential effects of the new mix of communications media. In this study, we focus on two that are of particular salience in corporate settings—the extent to which new communication media change the volume of communication in an organization and the extent to which they change the distribution of information.

Overload. A potential consequence of today's media-rich environment is that it increases the volume of communication within an organization to initiate and receive. There is substantial evidence that the demand for communication is elastic. If one reduces the monetary costs of communication, by reducing its tariff, or the behavioral costs, by making it easier to accomplish, the amount of communication typically increases (Mayer, 1977; Zipf, 1949).

introduction.

Although for many purposes this increased volume is desirable, a potential negative outcome is that it might disrupt users' work lives. In general, communication is a resource-consuming process. It takes effort and attention to initiate and receive communication. As a result, one would expect that as the volume of communication increases, so will the problems of feeling rushed and overloaded. One reason that some employees work at home is that work at the office is often too hard to accomplish, at least in part because the volume of communication in the office is too intense and too interrupting (Gerson & Kraut, 1988).

Analytically one may distinguish two disruptive impacts of heavy communication: information overload (an increase in information received and/or requests for information) and communication intrusion (an increase in interruption of work by communications). Although all communications media may increase information overload, some communications media are clearly more intrusive than others. Synchronous media, such as telephones and face-to-face meetings, take place in real time—all parties have to be available at the same time. In contrast, with asynchronous media, such as fax, electronic mail, and postal mail, communication takes place through staggered rounds and can be scheduled by both sender and recipient at times convenient to them. The asynchronous communication, as a result, is nowhere near as disruptive as a synchronous medium like the phone, where one has to stop what one is doing to answer it.

Because many of the new corporate communications media, like electronic mail, are asynchronous, we hypothesize that they can add information without adding commensurate intrusion. Yet is likely that the total volume of communication, irrespective of medium, will be associated with information overload.

A second and neglected issue concerning media disruption involves looking at individuals' separate roles as senders and receivers of messages. These differences in role also have implications for the degree to which communication media are disruptive. Generally, a communication episode involves one party who initiated it and another who is a recipient of it. These two roles are different in terms of goals, costs, and benefits. The initiator has a reason in mind for starting the communication and schedules it at a time that is convenient to him or herself. The recipient, on the other hand, may be thought of as a more or less willing victim of the initiator's designs. From the recipient's perspective the communication is likely to arrive at a random time, often interrupting ongoing work. The communication is often a request for information or aid that will benefit the initiator, not the recipient. Thus initiators and recipients of communications are likely to experience the same communication very differently.

Our research examines the perceived value and costs of communication for each role, and documents the extent to which role differences vary by medium. We hypothesize that role differences would be reduced in asynchronous media such as electronic mail, fax, and voice mail, which enable receivers to schedule their receipt of messages.

Peripherality. The new communication media have the potential not just to increase the total volume of communication within an organization, but to increase it most for people who are at its periphery and thus relatively communication deprived. Several authors have argued that electronic mail in particular has the capacity to increase the level of knowledge and degree of emotional involvement of people at the periphery of an organization—from night-shift workers to geographically distant branches to low-status employees who might otherwise hesitate to speak up (Feldman, 1987; Hesse, Sproull, Kiesler, & Walsh, 1993.) To understand why such outcomes are expected requires a brief overview of studies of space, knowledge, and organizational communication.

In large corporations, members learn much of the core technical knowledge they need to do their jobs and a substantial amount of incidental information by bumping into interesting people or situations, through incidental communication (Kusterer, 1978). Employees use unplanned encounters both to keep up with information about customers, technical developments, or company politics and to learn the often-unwritten rules of performance, such as the degree to which customer service is valued or the extent to which fudging is tolerated in expense vouchers.

Physical and geographical proximity of organizational members increase both informal communication and more official interactions (T. Allen, 1977; Conrath, 1973; Monge, Rothman, Eisenberg, Miller, & Kirste, 1985). Zipf (1949), Festinger, Schachter, and Back, (1950), and Allen (1977) all documented that communication between individuals declines rapidly with distance. The volume of this communication is important, because much coordination, on-the-job training, socialization, and development of organizational culture occur through informal communication.

A company headquarters often is the political and operational center of an organization. Compared to those who have offices at headquarters, employees who are geographically distant have fewer opportunities for communication with colleagues, for influencing and being influenced by them, and for observing them at work. Peripheral organizational members are therefore disadvantaged in knowing about their firm and its work environment (Hesse et al., 1993.) In national and international companies, with very large distances between sites, the difficulties of spontaneous contact for periphery employees are compounded by time-zone differences and transportation difficulties that make even intentional contact and attendance at headquarters' meetings difficult.

Although being peripheral within an organization is partly a matter of geography, there are other more sociological dimensions of peripherality as well. Seniority, occupational status, placement in organizational networks, and even gender may affect peripherality, and hence may influence both communication and organizational knowledge.

Feldman (1987) and Hesse et al. (1993) argued that electronic mail is particularly well suited to reducing peripherality disadvantages in organizations. First, electronic mail has features like distribution lists and electronic bulletin boards that increase the number of people who will receive any particular communication. These mechanisms enable electronic mail users to bump into information and other organizational members serendipitously, just as physical proximity functions elsewhere. Second, Kiesler and Sproull (1986) argued that compared with other media, electronic mail reduces social context cues, so that one is less sensitive to the sender as a social presence. They argued that this reduces the peripherality deficits associated with low status or seniority, gender, and other personal attributes. Thus, they hypothesized that heavy use of electronic media, especially electronic mail, should compensate for both geographic and social peripherality in organizations.

However, there is an alternative view. Distance-reducing technologies are often used to supplement prior face-to-face communications. In addition, although these technologies are relatively insensitive to distance, people mostly use them to communicate with people who are geographically close by. (See Eveland & Bickson, 1987, for electronic mail and Mayer, 1977, for telephone.) The implications of these latter findings are that electronic media may not reduce differences between centrally located versus peripherally located individuals but may even exacerbate preexisting inequalities in communication and knowledge within an organization.

A major goal of our research is to examine the extent to which differential use of various media is associated with improvement in organizational knowledge and the extent to which the peripherality deficit is reduced, and to identify the characteristics of media that are associated with differences in organizational knowledge.

The Ecology of Organizational Communication

To answer questions about the effects of new media, one must also control for their differential use across people and tasks. That is, in order to assess whether the new media mix causes information overload or whether the use of electronic mail makes people at the periphery of an organization better informed, one must examine and control for the reasons people differ in the amount they communicate and the media with which they choose to do so. We briefly discuss some important attributes of jobs, of communication media, and of their interaction that might influence the amount that people communicate and the effects of that communication.

Some work by its nature is interdependent and requires contact with customers or coordination with coworkers, and thus more communication. Management, for example, is primarily a coordination job, and Mintzberg

(1973) noted over 20 years ago that communication is the central activity in managerial work. If indeed jobs vary in their communication intensity, then one would expect that people in communication-intensive jobs would heavily use all of the media available to them.

Jobs differ not just in the amount of communication they require, but the type of communication as well. Moreover, communication media may differ in the types of tasks for which they are most appropriate. *Media richness* (Daft & Lengel, 1984, 1986) and *social presence* (Short, Christie, & Williams, 1976) are two related theories that emphasize the fit between job characteristic and the amount and kinds of information that can be carried by different media, that is, their *carrying capacity*. Both hypothesize that people will choose to use richer media—that is, media that are more like face-to-face communication—when they are faced with greater uncertainty, when they have more complex information to communicate, when they must persuade, or when the social dynamics of their communication are important. Thus, people whose jobs are more social, ambiguous, or complex should habitually use richer media, that is, media that are more interactive and expressive.

The implication of media richness theory is that people will specialize in a type of communication. Mintzberg (1973), for example, argued that because managers have to deal with uncertainty continually, they have a strong preference for face-to-face communication. If there is competition among media, then one might expect people who send a lot of electronic mail to do less faxing, or that heavy telephone users would communicate less through face-to-face conversations. This specialization hypothesis can be contrasted with a synergy hypothesis, that heavy use of one medium would lead to heavy use of others. According to this thesis, media are to a degree interchangeable and may even supplement each other. For example, one might use the fax to distribute documents before a face-to-face meeting, and then follow up the discussion with both telephone calls and electronic mail exchanges.

In testing for the effects of electronic mail and other communications media on employees' organizational knowledge, their perceptions of overload, and amount they are interrupted, we attempt to control for job and media attributes that media richness theory and the synergy hypothesis implicate as important in media choice.

METHODS

Overview.   We conducted a survey of both high- and low-volume electronic mail users in the United States and international locations of a large commercial bank in 1992. We selected this organization for study because it was a multinational corporation, which made problems of peripherality likely, and it had one of the oldest and largest corporate electronic mail networks in the world. At the time of the study, the company had about 100,000 employees in over 83 countries on five continents. At that time, its electronic mail network was almost 10 years old and was used by over 26,000 employees spread across North America, Europe, Latin America, and Asia. The corporation spent approximately $14 million per year in running and maintaining its electronic mail network.

The proprietary electronic mail package used by over 90% of employees who used any electronic mail system allowed them to send to and receive messages from other users of the company-sponsored network, but did not support gateways to external networks. That is, they could communicate only with people who had accounts on the corporate system. The electronic mail software provided a corporate-wide directory, commands for sending messages to individuals and locally created mailing lists, and a rudimentary news and clipping service. The system also had commands for looking up name, title, and location of individuals on the system, for saving messages to external files, and for uploading formatted documents previously written on personal computers. Only system administrators were allowed to send messages to corporate-wide distribution lists (i.e., to everyone). They typically did so as agents for senior executives. The user interface to the electronic mail system consisted of typed commands and a cumbersome line-oriented editor for composing and modifying messages. Users accessed the system by dialing in to the corporate telephone network.

Sample. Using lists provided by the bank, we drew a sample of 2,733 employees. Of these, 928 were a control sample of employees in the United States selected randomly from the corporate phone book, independently of whether they used electronic mail. The remainder was a stratified random sample of employees who had used an electronic mail account in 1991. Stratification was used to ensure that respondents varied by geographic location and also varied in their heaviness of use of electronic mail. Of the stratified sample, 1,097 individuals were located at corporate headquarters, 261 were located in other parts of the United States, 254 were located in London, and 261 were located in Hong Kong. Among these employees approximately half were selected to be clustered around the 25th percentile and half around the 75th percentile of frequency of electronic mail usage (i.e., we sampled heavy and light users, but not the far extremes).

Of the questionnaires mailed out, 403 were returned as undeliverable. After sending a reminder postcard and a follow-up questionnaire, we received 973 completed questionnaires, which is an effective response rate of 42 %.

Questionnaire and Analyses: In order to examine media use, we constructed a multipage questionnaire that probed employees' job attributes, demographic control variables, organizational knowledge, information overload, and media use. Most Cronbach alpha measures for multi-item scales were between .60 and .80, showing lower reliability than we would have liked, but sufficient for exploratory research.

Several job attributes related to communication intensity or that previous researchers had demonstrated to be associated with media choice were measured. To measure the uncertainty and equivocality associated with a job we adapted Van der Ven, Delbecq, and Koenig's (1976) measure of procedural work (the degree to which a job consisted of routine tasks) and Cammann, Fichman, Jenkins, and Flesh's (1983) measure of work challenge (the degree to which job tapped a variety of skills). We also included more detailed measures of work process relevant to needs for richness and social presence in communication media, adapted from Bikson (1986) and Markus et al. (1992). Managerial work (the extent to which respondents managed people or handled emotional situations) and sales work (the extent to which a job required sales or persuasion) are equivocal and socially demanding, whereas text work (the extent to which respondents read and wrote) and quantitative work (the extent to which respondents worked with numbers and charts) are less so.

To measure the interdependence associated with a job, we adapted Van der Ven et al.'s (1976) measure of work interdependence (the extent to which a job required coordination among multiple parties). We also measured the interdependence of jobs in more detail: the number of employees supervised, working on task forces (the extent to which employees worked with temporary groups), and working with outsiders (the extent to which employees worked with people who were organizationally or geographically remote).

As control variables, we included the demographic variables of age (which was highly correlated with job seniority) and gender. We also included organizational level (from staff member to vice president) and several material conditions of work, such as working outside normal location or hours and having a secretary.

As outcome measures we were interested in respondents' organizational knowledge, their organizational commitment, and their experience of being overloaded. Our organizational knowledge scale consists of an eight-item multiple-choice test of facts about the company (e.g., Whom did the corporation recently name as a vice chairman? How many employees is the corporation expecting to cut in 1991 and 1992? Cronbach's Alpha = .76) . The facts were taken from national newspaper articles in the 6 months prior to the distribution of the survey. The organizational commitment scale came from a survey that the company had conducted 12 months prior to our research, as part of its regular assessment of corporate morale. The latter focused on respondents' evaluation and agreement with senior management's strategic direction (e.g., I agree with the corporation's strategic direction and goals. Cronbach's Alpha = .80). From Cammann et al. (1983) we derived a measure of overload (e.g., I frequently receive more information during the day than I can use; My work is frequently interrupted. Cronbach's Alpha = .76).

Our primary measure of peripherality was geographic, the distance between an employee's work location and corporate headquarters, coded in three steps (at corporate headquarters, in other areas of the United States, or abroad). Demographic and job characteristics such as age, gender, and organizational level provided sociological measures of organizational peripherality.

The questionnaire probed each user's experience with several communication media, including face-to-face communication, telephone conversations, electronic mail, fax, voice mail, and overnight mail services. The questions included both aggregate and episode-specific items. In the aggregate items, respondents averaged their descriptions or estimates over many experiences. For example, they estimated the number of conversations or meetings they had per day and the number of electronic mail, voice mail, facsimile, voice mail, overnight mail, and telephone calls they sent and received during a typical week. Because these estimates were not normally distributed (there was a long tail of very high volume communicators), they were converted to a log scale in the analyses that follow. To derive a measure of total communication, we converted these estimates to z scores and summed them. As a measure of media penetration, respondents also estimated what percentage of the people with whom they needed to communicate for work could be reached through each medium.

Although we asked questions about a variety of media, we focus our analyses on face-to-face, telephone, electronic mail, and facsimile communication. Empirically, these four represent the most frequently used communication modes in the bank. Theoretically, they vary in interactivity and expressiveness, the two dimensions of media richness (Kraut, Galegher, Fish, & Chalfonte, 1992). Face-to-face and phone communication are more interactive than fax and electronic mail. Face-to-face and fax communication are more expressive respectively than phone and electronic mail communication. Face-to-face communication provides physical context and facial expression missing in phone conversations; fax allows graphics, letterheads, formatting, and signatures missing in the ASCII electronic mail available in this corporation.

Episode-specific questions asked respondents about their most recent communication episode in each of the four communication modalities. They indicated who initiated the episode and, on 3-point Likert scales, the extent to which the communication interrupted work, whether they kept a record of the communication, and the usefulness of the communication along three dimensions derived from McGrath (1984): (a) product: getting work done, (b) interpersonal: developing or sustaining a work relationship, and (c) organizational maintenance: keeping up with organizational news, politics, or people. Even though each respondent described multiple communication events (one for each modality), in the analyses that follow we randomly selected one event for each respondent to control for the inflation in degrees of freedom.

Analyses using the episode-specific questions treated the media as differing on two dimensions: interactivity and expressiveness. Interactivity contrasts highly interactive media (face-to-face and phone communication) with minimally interactive ones (fax and electronic mail communication). Expressiveness contrasts media that transmit more information with media that transmit less. We examined expressiveness within interactivity, through two single degree of freedom contrasts. The first contrast compared face-to-face communication with phone communication (both high interactivity, but the former being more expressive) and the second contrasted fax communication with electronic mail (both low interactivity, the former being more expressive).

RESULTS

Media Use

Respondents reported having a large volume of communication. Over all media, respondents reported having a median of 265 conversations or messages per day, or more than one communication every 11 minutes. They estimated they spent 39% of their workday communicating. Although Panko (1992) argued that self-report estimates are only moderately accurate, he noted that they tend to underestimate the total amount of communication, because respondents frequently discount brief or routine communication episodes. Regression analyses, not reported here in detail, show that people who do sales and persuasion work, whose work is interdependent with others, who work in task forces, who have challenging work, and who work outside of normal hours and location are all heavy communicators. Surprisingly, neither respondents' managerial level nor the number of employees they supervise predict the amount they communicate.

We found that at the aggregate level, people who communicate heavily in one modality tend to communicate heavily in others as well. That is, people do not seem to specialize in certain media at the expense of others. Table 15.1 shows the intercorrelations among measures of use of each medium. Although the average correlation is weak, all are positive, and summing the amount of communication across the six modalities produces a communication intensity scale with a Cronbach's alpha of .51. These data contradict the media specialization hypothesis and are consistent with the media-synergy hypothesis discussed earlier.

Because we found that communication across media is intercorrelated, when creating regression models for electronic mail usage and various

TABLE 15.1

Correlations Among Use of Different Communications Media

	Electronic Mail	Facsimile	Voice Mail	Overnight Mail	Phone Calls
Facsimile	.177	1.000			
Voice mail	.006	.164	1.000		
Overnight mail	.120	.488	.103	1.000	
Phone calls	.195	.340	.218	.211	1.000
Face-to-face	.064	.067	.037	.113	.079

Note. Ns range from 757 to 794. Correlations were based on the log of the number of communications per week in each media. Correlations greater than .064 are significant at least at the .05 level.

dependent variables in the analyses that follow, we hold constant the use of other media, by constructing a scale for the combined frequency of use of all other communication media.

Total communication volume is partially explainable by job function and work characteristics. People whose work is interdependent or involves selling, working on task forces, working outside the conventional business schedule and location (and therefore having greater coordination needs), and those who have more challenging work—all report higher rates of total communication.

Consequences of Media Use

Our hypotheses about the consequences of media use were that people who were peripheral to an organization would be disadvantaged in keeping up with relevant organizational information, and that they would feel less committed to the organization. However, because electronic mail has attributes that can help to overcome these deficits, those peripheral employees who were heavy users of electronic mail would be more informed and committed. Electronic mail, along with other noninteractive media, might provide this information without substantially increasing overload.

Tables 15.2 through 15.4 show regressions predicting scores on the organizational knowledge scale, the organizational commitment scale, and the overload scale. For each dependent variable, we conducted three analyses: (a) a basic analysis in which the predictors are geographic peripherality and control variables measuring demographics, jobs, and total communication volume, (b) an analysis that added electronic mail use to this equation, and (c) an analysis that also added electronic mail by peripherality interactions. The entries are standardized beta coefficients for those variables significant at least the .05 level.

TABLE 15.2

Predicting Organizational Knowledge From Electronic Mail Use and Control Variables

Variable	Control Variables	Control + Electronic Mail	Control + Electronic Mail + Interactions
Gender (Male)	.15	.15	.15
Management level	.20	.19	.19
Have a secretary	.10	NS	.10
Do managerial work	−.08	−.09	−.09
Do text/analysis work	NS	NS	NS
Do quantitative/graphics work	.08	.10	.10
Work interdependence	NS	NS	NS
Work with customers & distant others	.08	.08	.08
Work outside normal hours & location	NS	NS	NS
Work is procedural	NS	NS	NS
Work is challenging	NS	NS	NS
Geographic peripherality	−.15	−.17	−.16
Use of other communication media	NS	NS	NS
Use of electronic mail		.14	.13
Electronic mail × peripherality			NS
Adjusted R squared	.137	.150	.150

Note. Entries are standardized beta weights significant at least at the .05 level. $N = 683$.

Organizational Knowledge. The data are consistent with the thesis that peripheral employees are less informed about their company than non-peripheral members. The first column of Table 15.2 shows that women know less than men, those at lower managerial levels know less than those at higher managerial levels, and those who work in Asia, Europe, or nonheadquarters sites in the United States know less than those located at corporate headquarters.

The data also show that heavier users of electronic mail know more about the organization than lighter electronic mail users, holding other variables constant (see Table 15.2, col. 2). Moreover, extensive use of other communication media was not associated with increased organizational knowledge. As previous researchers have suggested, there does seem to be something distinctive about electronic mail in facilitating organizational knowledge.

Finally, we tested the prediction that the use of electronic mail would especially alleviate the deficits in knowledge associated with geographic and other peripherality. Statistically this was done by including a peripherality by electronic mail interaction term in the regression for which organizational knowledge was the dependent variable. The last column of Table 15.2 reports the interaction for geographical peripherality. Other analyses not reported here show similar results for social peripherality. In all cases, the interactions were not statistically significant. In this corporation, electronic mail does not differentially advantage peripheral employees, in terms of organizational knowledge.

One mechanism through which heavy use of electronic mail could enhance organizational knowledge is a communication spill-over effect. In using electronic mail, it is easy to add additional readers through a copy or "cc" command and to electronically copy and forward documents or messages. This means that information addressed to one person is often routed to others who were marginal to the original conversation or who had expressed no direct interest in being party to it. Routine audits of the electronic mail traffic at this corporation show that a typical electronic mail message has three or four recipients. Examining the ratio of messages received to messages sent in our sample suggests that people receive considerably more messages by electronic mail than they send out: a ratio of 2.7 incoming electronic mail messages for every outgoing one. This contrasts with the use of other media, where the ratio of messages received to sent is closer to 1:1. (For fax the received to sent ratio is 1.2:1, and for telephone calls it is 1:1.) This distinctive characteristic of electronic mail means that through electronic mail people can bump into information that they had not intended to see, much as physical proximity can put them into unintended face-to-face contact with other people.

The use of electronic bulletin boards or clipping services would be a more direct mechanism for electronic communication to lead to organizational knowledge. However, it does not seem to explain the link at this corporation. Although typically people who use electronic mail are also likely to subscribe to corporate electronic bulletin board services, in this corporation these services were used infrequently. In the 6 months prior to the survey, only 26% of the sample had used them, and these respondents used the services less than once per month. Thus, the use of bulletin board services is unlikely to account for the observed association of electronic mail use with organizational knowledge.

Organizational Commitment. Contrary to our expectations, geographic and social peripherality did not affect levels of organizational commitment, defined as approval of the company's strategic direction and trust in its leadership. Both people who had routine work and those who had challenging jobs in this firm were more committed to senior managers' plans, whereas those who worked alone were less committed. (See Table 15.3).

However, heavier use of electronic mail, controlling for other factors, was associated with higher levels of organizational commitment. This was not

TABLE 15.3

Predicting Organizational Commitment
From Electronic Mail Use and Control Variables

	Control Variables	Control + Electronic Mail	Control + Electronic Mail + Interactions
Gender (Male)	.08	.08	.08
Management level	NS	NS	NS
Do managerial work	NS	NS	NS
Have a secretary	.08	NS	NS
Do text/analysis work	NS	−.08	−.07
Do quantitative/graphics work	NS	NS	NS
Work interdependence	.10	.09	.09
Work with customers & distant others	NS	NS	NS
Work outside normal hours & location	NS	NS	−NS
Work is procedural	.20	.21	.21
Work is challenging	.14	.14	.14
Geographic peripherality	NS	NS	NS
Use of other communication media	NS	NS	−.08
Use of electronic mail		.10	.10
Electronic mail × peripherality			NS
Adjusted R squared	.081	.089	.087

Note. Entries are standardized beta weights significant at least at the .05 level. $N = 748$.

true of other media: Those who had heavy communication volume through other media were less committed. Thus, in addition to increasing employees' knowledge of the firm, electronic mail appears to increase employee commitment to top management's strategic direction, holding other pertinent variables (such as level in the firm) constant.

Again, none of the peripherality by electronic mail use interactions approached significance. Electronic mail did not affect peripheral members' sense of commitment any differently than that of nonperipheral employees.

Overload and Interruptions. Employees who communicated more (across all media combined) indicated greater problems with information overload, interruptions, and feeling rushed. High volumes of communication do exact a cost. However, consistent with our expectations, even though electronic mail increased the amount of information employees receive, it did not increase their psychological experience of being over-loaded, rushed, and interrupted, over and above their volume of communication by other media. (See Table 15.4)

We anticipated that electronic mail would be relatively nonintrusive because it is asynchronous, and therefore doesn't interrupt normal work flow. One can read and respond to electronic mail at one's own convenience. We confirmed this explanation in the part of our questionnaire that asked respondents to rate their most recent communications for each medium. Figure 15.1 plots responses to the question, "How much did this communication interrupt your work?" by medium and communication role (initiators or recipient). A communicator role X interactivity X expressiveness analyses of variance shows that synchronous media are substantially more intrusive than asynchronous media [$F(1, 824) = 83.8$; $p < .001$], and that

TABLE 15.4

Predicting Overload From Electronic Mail Use and Control Variables

Variable	Control Variables	Control + Electronic Mail	Control + Electronic Mail + Interactions
Gender (Male)	NS	NS	NS
Management level	NS	NS	NS
Do managerial work	.14	.14	.14
Have a secretary	NS	NS	NS
Do text/analysis work	.17	.16	.16
Do quantitative/graphics work	NS	NS	NS
Work interdependence	NS	NS	NS
Work with customers & distant others	NS	NS	NS
Work outside normal hours & location	NS	NS	NS
Work with task forces	NS	NS	NS
Work is procedural	–.07	–.07	–.07
Work is challenging	.16	.16	.16
Geographic peripherality	NS	NS	NS
Use of other communication media	.16	.16	.16
Use of electronic mail		NS	NS
Electronic mail × peripherality			NS
Adjusted R squared	.195	.196	.197

Note. Entries are standardized beta weights significant at least at the .05 level. $N = 759$.

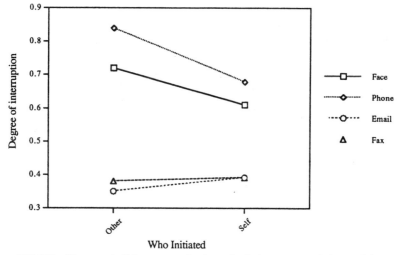

FIG. 15.1. How much did a communication episode interrupt work, by modality and communication role?

recipients of communication are interrupted more than initiators [F (1,824) = 6.62; $p < .01$]. The significant interactivity X role interaction shows that the difference between recipients and initiators occurred only for the two synchronous media. Among the synchronous media, telephone and face-to-face communication were not significantly different in terms of work disruption, and among the asynchronous media, electronic mail and fax did not differ.

Communications Value. We earlier found that people received more messages by electronic mail than they sent. Our evidence also shows that compared to other media, electronic mail messages were perceived to be especially valuable for keeping up with organizational information (as opposed to getting focal tasks done or maintaining personal relationships). Respondents evaluated a recent communication episode on three dimensions: getting work done, maintaining a work relationship, and keeping up with corporate information. Figure 15.2 plots these results.

Analysis of variance shows that for accomplishing work and for maintaining relationships, initiators perceived the communications to be more valuable than did recipients, and that for all three dependent variables synchronous communication was perceived as more valuable than asynchronous media. However, electronic mail was judged to be especially useful for keeping up with company news, personalities, and gossip. For this purpose, electronic mail was rated as positively as face-to-face communication and significantly better than fax [F (1,810) = 7.35, $p < .01$].

Recording Communication. Finally, the communication episode data show that people were more likely to keep records of asynchronous communication (about 63% of messages) than synchronous communication (about 38% of conversations), presumably because electronic mail and fax were already in a recorded form [F (1,813) = 29.7, p < .001]. Although respondents reported to be slightly more likely to keep records of fax communication (70%) than of electronic mail (64%) this difference was not statistically reliable [F (1,813) = .13; p > .50]. In field work in the corporation we were struck by the extent to which both electronic mail and fax had been absorbed into normal bureaucratic record keeping. Many employees printed and filed copies of all electronic messages they received. Others archived messages selectively on disk.

DISCUSSION

This research was intended to explore the consequences of a rich multimedia environment typical in today's corporations.

Our first finding was that even though individuals do choose between media for specific messages, they don't specialize in terms of their communication in the aggregate. People whose jobs require substantial communication communicate heavily across all the media available to them. They do not seem to favor one channel over another, such as being a phone user rather than an electronic mail user. In this firm, the heaviest communicators tended to be people in temporary teams or in work groups, and people whose work involves persuasion or sales. In theoretical terms, the multiple

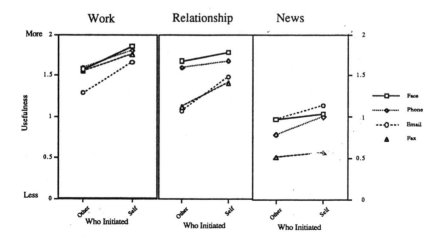

FIG. 15.2. How valuable was a communication episode for different activities, by modality and communication role? Activities include getting work accomplished, maintaining work relationships, and keeping up with company information.

communications media in this organization appear to be in a synergistic or additive relationship rather than being competitive.

We found that electronic mail was distinctive in several respects. Employees who used electronic mail extensively, net of their use of other media, were better informed about their company and were more committed to management's goals. This finding remained significant after factoring out potential confounding issues such as users' status within the firm, kind of work, and so on.

One reason for electronic mail users' superior organizational knowledge may be that electronic mail promotes information spillover from a focal or intended recipient to other parties not directly involved in a message. Electronic mail, compared to other media, requires little effort to add multiple recipients to a message, to send messages to distribution lists, or to capture electronic messages for resending. Our data suggest that electronic mail is the only medium in which the ratio of messages received to messages sent is so large. This suggests that the spillover effect is stronger for electronic mail than for other media.

This spillover phenomenon has been dramatically illustrated in several recent episodes in large corporations in which privileged information spread throughout the corporation via electronic mail. Our findings suggest that electronic mail doesn't just broadcast organizational gossip; it also informs large numbers of employees about important company events, and that this informative function is associated with greater commitment and understanding of company strategy. Given the centrifugal tendencies in any large organization, this aspect of electronic mail is likely to be welcomed.

Several researchers have reported that electronic mail is particularly advantageous for peripheral members of an organization, that it can help night-shift workers feel more involved or increase the effectiveness of low-status individuals. Although we found that peripheral employees were indeed less knowledgeable than others, and that electronic mail increases knowledge, we did not find evidence that peripheral employees are especially aided by electronic mail use or by other communications media. The use of electronic mail benefits central and peripheral employees equally. We were unable to support the peripherality thesis.

Finally, we studied the disruptive effects of communications media, including both information overload and interruptions from media. Respondents' reports of disruption of work are associated with heavier communications levels. However, the problem appears more severe with face-to-face and telephone communications than with the newer asynchronous media. Electronic mail and fax are less likely to disrupt work because the receiver has more control over answering and replying. Thus the proliferation of these newer asynchronous media is unlikely to provide the straw that breaks the camel's back.

REFERENCES

Allen, T. (1977). *Managing the flow of technology.* Cambridge, MA: MIT Press.

Attewell, P. (1994). Information technology and the productivity paradox. In D. H. Harris (Ed.), *Organizational linkages: Understanding the productivity paradox.* Washington, DC: National Academy Press.

Bikson, T. (1986). Understanding the implementation of office technology. In R. E. Kraut (Ed.), *Technology and the transformation of white-collar work.* (pp. 155–176). Hillsdale, NJ: Lawrence Erlbaum Associates.

Cammann, C., Fichman, M., Jenkins, D., Jr., & Flesh, J. R. (1983). Assessing the attitudes and perceptions of organizational members. In S. E. Seashore, E. Lawler, P. H. Mirvis, & C. Cammann (Eds.), *Assessing organizational change.* (pp. 71–138). New York: Wiley.

Conrath, D. W. (1973). Communication environment and its relationship to organizational structure. *Management Science, 20,* 586–603.

Daft, R. L., & Lengel, R. H. (1984). Information richness: A new approach to managerial behavior and organization design. In B. Staw & L. L. Cummings (Eds.), *Research in organizational behavior, 6.* Greenwich, CT: JAI.

Daft, R. L., & Lengel, R. H. (1986). Organizational information requirements, media richness, and structural design. *Management Science, 32,* 554–571.

Eveland, J., & Bikson, T. (1987). Evolving electronic communication networks: An empirical assessment. *Office: Technology and People, 3,* 103–128.

Feldman, M. S. (1987). Electronic mail and weak ties in organizations. *Office: Technology and People, 3,* 83–101.

Festinger, L., Schachter, S., & Back, K. (1950). *Social pressures in informal groups: A study of human factors in housing.* Palo Alto, CA: Stanford University Press.

Gerson, J., & Kraut, R. G. (1988). Clerical work at home or in the office: The difference it makes. In K. E. Christensen (Ed.), *The new era of home-based work* (pp. 49–64). Boulder, CO: Westview.

Hesse, B., Sproull, L., Kiesler, S., & Walsh, J. (1993). Returns to science: Computer networks in oceanography. *Communications of the ACM, 36,* (8), 90–101.

Huff, C., Sproull, L., & Kiesler, S. (1989). Computer communication and organizational commitment: Tracing the relationship in a city government. *Journal of Applied Social Psychology, 19,* 1371–1391.

Kiesler, S. B., & Sproull, L. S. (1986). Reducing social context cues: Electronic mail in organizational communication. *Management Science, 32,* 1492–1512.

Kraut, R. E., Galegher, J., Fish, R. S., & Chalfonte, B. (1993). Task requirements and media choice in collaborative writing. *Human–Computer Interaction, 7* (4), 375–408.

Kusterer, K. C. (1978). *Know-how on the job: The important working knowledge of unskilled workers.* Boulder, CO: Westview.

Landauer, T. (1995). *The trouble with computers.* Cambridge, MA: MIT Press.

Markus, M. L., Bikson, T. K., El-Shinnaway, M., & Soe, L. (1992). Fragments of your communication: Email, Vmail, and Fax. *The Information Society, 8,* 207–226.

Mayer, M. (1977). The telephone and the uses of time. In I. de Sola Pool (Ed.), *The social impact of the telephone* (pp. 225–245). Cambridge, MA: MIT Press.

McGrath, J. E. (1984). *Groups: Interaction and performance.* Englewood Cliffs, NJ: Prentice-Hall.

Mintzberg, H. (1973). *The nature of managerial work.* New York: Harper & Row.

Monge, P. R., Rothman, L. W., Eisenberg, E. M., Miller, K. L., & Kirste, K. K. (1985). The dynamics of organizational proximity. *Management Science,31,* 1129–1141.

Panko, R. R. (1992). Managerial communication patterns. *Journal of Organizational Computing, 2,* 95–122.

Short, J., Williams, E., & Christie, B. (1976). *The social psychology of telecommunications.* New York: Wiley.

Sproull, L., & Kiesler, S. (1991). *Connections: New ways of working in the networked organization.* Cambridge, MA: MIT Press.

Van der Ven, A. H., Delbecq, A. L., & Koenig, R., Jr. (1976). Determinants of coordination modes within organizations. *American Sociological Review, 41,* 322–338.

Zipf, G. K. (1949). *Human behavior and the principle of least effort.* Cambridge, MA: Addison-Wesley.

16

ORGANIZATIONAL DIMENSIONS OF EFFECTIVE DIGITAL LIBRARY USE: CLOSED RATIONAL AND OPEN NATURAL SYSTEMS MODEL

Lisa Covi
University of Michigan

Rob Kling
Indiana University

Behind the expectations that digital libraries will provide access to any document at any time to anyone in any place are questions about whether digital collection, storage, and transmission are useful to people who depend on library materials. This study focuses on digital library use for research activities in PhD-granting institutions. Instead of studying digital library use solely from the perspective of providers—librarians and researchers with electronic materials, resource streams, computer equipment, and know-how, we also studied use from the point of view of faculty researchers who produce and make use of scholarly materials. We contrast findings from two disciplines (molecular biology and literary theory) in two universities, with two systems models—closed rational systems and open natural systems. The latter model in particular provides a theoretical framework for understanding digital library use in different social worlds.

The terms *digital library, library of the future,* and *electronic library* conjure images of networked collections of historical, cultural, and knowledge-related artifacts in various electronic formats (Kling & Lamb, 1996). The organizations and individuals who promote the importance of digital libraries emphasize comprehensive collections that are universally accessible to people who need them. Despite the growing body of literature about digital libraries, and even multimillion dollar grants to develop them, there is no consensus about precisely which kinds of collections of digital materials should be encouraged or developed and which should not.

Digital libraries would be of little value or interest if people did not use them routinely or effectively. However, researchers have not yet produced behavioral theories for understanding how materials are produced and selected for digital libraries, and how diverse people actually choose and use the materials that they find in them. This study provides one empirical anchor for such theories. Although we focus on digital library use in the academic research setting, we would expect our findings to resonate with other types of specialized knowledge work in organizations.

There are ongoing research programs that examine social aspects of computerization in a way that transcends the technological particulars of specific technologies (Kling, 1980; Markus & Keil, 1994; Walsham, 1993; see also chap. 18 of this volume). Instead of focusing on mechanisms that change over time and making predictions based on the conceptualizations of current technologies, these studies identify enduring conditions that shape information systems' use. Our study builds on this research by examining some of the conditions that facilitate effective use of digital libraries.

We used a broad working definition of digital libraries that would be meaningful to people who participated in our study. We define digital libraries as collections of electronic documents, images, messages, artifacts, indices, and associated services for creating, searching, reading, and disseminating materials in a variety of formats.[1] Digital libraries include personal, distributed, and centralized collections such as on-line public access catalogs and bibliographic databases; distributed databases (including gopher and World Wide Web [WWW]); scholarly and professional discussion lists; and electronic journals, other online databases, forums, and bulletin boards. This expansive definition differs from some others, because it does not require that a digitized collection provide full text of materials, that it be accessible through the Internet, or that it be indexed, searchable, or browsable in a consistent manner.

The increasing availability of academic materials across computer networks in a wide variety of formats confounds definition of the digital library and may change how fields communicate and work. Direct communication between scholars via electronic mail may bridge geographic barriers but it also increases the frequency of communication and adds another task that requires attention. People use electronic mail to exchange and request digital documents, but also to request delivery of books and articles

---

[1]This definition resembles one of two definitions that emerged from a National Science Foundation workshop on social aspects of digital libraries. A preliminary report is available at http://www.gslis.ucla.edu/DL/dl_handout.html.

in paper form. Researchers use word processing to prepare manuscripts and may simultaneously check electronic dictionaries, citation records, and databases of research results. Some academics view the diffusion of distributed databases such as gopher and World Wide Web and new publishing formats such as electronic journals as forums for results or ideas not embraced by extant print channels, less costly and more effect storage replacements for their critical sources, or threats to status quo arrangements for determining quality work.

Because our focus is on the human activities that make digital libraries useful, we interviewed a sample of faculty, computer resource providers, and librarians who depend on these resources to create knowledge via university research. Although our primary focus is on researchers, teachers and students also are relevant to the ecology of faculty research. Seminars help researchers focus on particular scholarly themes, classes provide an opportunity for faculty to familiarize themselves with new materials or subject matter, and students participate as research assistants, technicians, programmers, and coauthors. Although research activities are frequently separate from and compete for time with teaching activities, we found synergy between them in the ways researchers conceptualize and use materials.

We interviewed respondents using several key questions:

1. What is the organizational environment that shapes faculty conceptions of effective use of digital libraries for research and teaching?
2. How do digital library service providers compare with faculty in their conceptions of research and professional activities?
3. How do patterns of digital library use vary across fields and universities?
4. What is the relationship between digital libraries and faculty patterns of production and communication of scholarly research?
5. And more generally, what are the needs of the faculty for digital libraries?

Most studies in library assessment focus on measuring circulation and quantifiable service measures such as the number of requests, percentage of requests filled, user ratings of satisfaction, and so on (Van House, 1989; McClure & Lopata, 1996). Online resources passively compile statistics on number of commands issued, usage of databases, and system load. Instead, our study describes the ways that faculty and providers assess the value of different kinds of digital libraries. We expected that faculty in the two fields we looked at, molecular biology and literary theory, would use digital libraries differently, but we also asked how librarians accounted for these differences and how computer centers supported them.

We find sociological theory of organizations helpful for shedding light on these beliefs and practices (Scott, 1992). The participants in human activity systems are members of organizations, so we would expect theories about their work and other activity to be relevant to digital library users and providers. Our study contrasts two broad analytical models of organizational behavior: closed rational systems models and open natural systems models. We portray these models with simplified schemas based on themes that emerged from our interviews. Comparisons between the two sets of organizational models helps us understand disparities and commonalities in how people characterize effective digital library use.

ORGANIZATIONAL THEORY: CLOSED RATIONAL AND OPEN NATURAL SYSTEMS MODELS

When people think about what constitutes effective digital library use, they draw upon conceptions of what defines effective organizations. A digital library might be viewed as relatively effective or ineffective depending on "internal" criteria such as the costs of transactions or the amount of material available. The same digital library also might be evaluated by "external" criteria such as the extent that it requires specialized software, must be accessed in special locations, or includes resources that nonusers see as important and legitimate. The second set of criteria are external in that they take into account people, social relationships, and activities outside of the digital library, such as where people live and work or software used for work other than searching the digital library. Models of digital library use are less narrow to the degree they account for external criteria of performance.

In social theory, systems are organized groups of elements that strongly interact with one another and have a relation to an external environment.[2] How a system, such a digital library, is conceived relative to its environment defines whether a systems model is closed or open. In closed systems models, a core system has little influence from its external environment whereas in open systems models a core system is extremely responsive to external influences. A closed systems model of digital library use would circumscribe the analysis to include "proximate elements" such as technologies, budgets, and staff support. It would exclude potential influences such as national library funding, the organization of teaching and research programs, and people's work styles. In contrast, open systems models of digital library use could readily take account of this second set of influences.

For instance, U.S. Vice President Al Gore employs the image of a small girl in rural Tennessee accessing the wealth of knowledge collected by the Library of Congress as a model for the use of digital libraries. His closed systems model circumscribes digital libraries and their users to include

---

[2]This empirical criterion (strong mutual interaction) is different from administrative criteria (e.g., report to a common manager), geographical criteria (e.g., are housed in the same building), or technical criteria (e.g., share common technologies or information flows).

people of all ages, in any geographical area who interact with computer equipment in their homes via a computer network. He might also tacitly include human skills or regulatory arrangements that would make this network available. Gore suggests that access by rural children is a condition for the effective use of digital libraries such as the Library of Congress.

The open systems model includes influences upon "the user" and alternative ways of valuing and finding materials. An open systems model would identify different systems in which to understand effective digital library use. For instance, an open systems model could highlight the ways rural children might benefit from stronger local libraries in which they can find equipment and help to find electronic or paper books, as well as in accessing diverse digital libraries. An open systems model might also examine the roles of bookstores and direct mail with vivid color catalogs in supporting children's reading. Similarly, the nature of local schooling can influence the extent to which children seek books of different kinds. If enhancing children's reading is a key value, then the use of digital libraries would have to be understood within a larger open systems model. This contrast between open and closed systems models plays a key role in our analysis.

Closed Rational Systems Models
of Digital Library Use

Rational systems models describe organizational behavior as purposeful moving toward defined goals with formalized processes. They often take into account elements that constrain action such as costs, coordination efficiency, and performance measures. For example, rational analysts may focus exclusively on digital library use from the point of view of service provision. This model would ask how digital libraries may reduce the cost of book preservation, create efficiencies by providing new data on digital library use patterns for evaluating services, or make expensive scientific data more available and affordable.

If the answers to these questions focus on influences contained by the focal system of action, the model is also considered to be a closed system. For example, to illustrate how digital libraries create more efficient services, a closed rational analysis would focus on the labor and materials costs, the time of completion of requests, and the new capabilities that users gain from using the supplied digital libraries. An open rational analysis of service provision would include constraints outside the system, such as the justification for public funding of digital libraries, the conditions necessary for assuring user satisfaction, and the conditions affecting production costs of digital library materials.

Closed rational systems models do not help us understand why organizations do not meet their goals or behave in ways inconsistent with the purposes they espouse. They also do not explain why systems may embrace or reject values or ambiguities. Closed rational models of digital library use do not explain why faculty, librarians, and computer specialists hold ambiguous conceptions of digital libraries and how they are used. The kinds of problems that arise when researchers start to use digital libraries may have rational explanations that are not workable with disparate goals and incentives.

We have found that closed rational models of digital library use are commonplace in discussions of digital libraries. Ann Okerson's (1991) speculations about the future of electronic journal publishing focused on the ways these digital libraries will reduce access costs (particularly of paper delivery) and drive changes in copyright arrangements. She thus drew a tight boundary around the communities of readers, authors, and publishers in her argument. She asserted that participation and ownership of electronic journals by librarians and scholars will transform writing and publishing into this more cost-effective, quicker, and more easily searchable medium. Her conception of readers focuses upon the direct costs of acquiring an article on one's workstation, and ignores other aspects of readers' work styles, such as where they prefer to read intensively.

This portrayal of scholar-centered journal publishing describes much of the enthusiastic reasoning our informants expressed for digital libraries. However, it sharply contrasts with complaints by faculty about the reduced clerical support for production of articles, grant proposals, and other necessary documents. The closed rational systems model does not explain faculty values about the work that they prefer or external influences such as the different conditions and skills necessary to be an author or a publisher (Kling & Covi, 1995). We next examine the open natural systems model.

Open Natural Systems Models
of Digital Library Use

Natural systems models view organizations to some extent like organisms who struggle to survive. Organizational participants in natural systems models develop informal arrangements with their other elements to shape goals that perpetuate their values and their existence. For example, natural systems analysts would focus on clusters of participants who share the same values and social practices surrounding digital libraries. We found that reference librarians who need ready access to a wide variety of information-seeking tools conceptualize and utilize digital libraries differently than departmental programmers mounting a World Wide Web home page for graduate admissions.

Closed natural systems models focus exclusively on human activity within the circumscribed organization. These explanations are not very useful to us unless we are only concerned with the internal mechanisms of perpetuating group values. Even so, the influences of values outside the group—the basis on which the group survives—are difficult to separate analytically. Open natural systems models provide a more holistic representation of organizational behavior that suits a wide variety of large complex organizations.

Open natural systems models help us understand the role of external conditions in shaping action and response by the model's elements. They also examine the consequences of survival struggles on formal behavior and structure. These systems models explain ambiguity in decisions and strategy, resource flow patterns, and the creation of shared experiences over time. However, they are more complex and less deterministic than rational systems models.

Steve Harnad's (1990) analysis of "scholarly skywriting" is a rare example of using open natural systems models of digital library use. He said that faculty who read electronic publications are primarily concerned with the legitimacy (quality) of the materials and with preserving the viability of the peer review process. Harnad proposed a scheme to retain the hierarchy of the peer review process in electronic publishing. His analysis draws upon open system models because he recognized the importance of extended social relationships beyond the direct connection between authors and readers. Furthermore, his analysis draws upon natural systems models because he is concerned with maintaining the long-term viability of scholarly publications.[3]

Closed rational systems models remain powerful models for understanding some aspects of digital library use. Practical discussions within organizations about developing and adopting digital libraries are heavily influenced by circumscribed conceptions of rational elements such as tasks, equipment capabilities, users, and costs. For example, our collection developers justified the choice of networked bibliographic databases by evidence that they can serve more users more efficiently with electronic indexes than the expansive and often out-of-date print indexes. In contrast, open natural systems models elucidate complex activities that shape digital library use, such as work habits, patterns of legitimation in a social group, and organizational politics. They also allow us to focus on more enduring explanations than those based on changing technology. Open natural systems models encourage us to examine the behavior of the organizations themselves as systems with rich political orders where important practices and structures may be institutionalized and inflexible.

---

[3]Even though Harnad (1990) relied on open natural systems models, they are not automatically valid. His proposals have been the subject of considerable interest and controversy (Okerson & O'Donnell, 1995; Fuller, 1995a, 1995b).

We now summarize findings from interviews with faculty, librarians, and computer professionals in molecular biology and literary theory in two different universities (Covi & Kling, 1996).

DIGITAL LIBRARY USE
AS CLOSED RATIONAL SYSTEMS MODELS

Faculty.   We first model our results on faculty digital library use as a closed rational system. This is a self-contained system of formal processes to ensure effective use of its elements (Covi, 1996). Our model simplifies scholarly communication rather than providing an exact description of the communication systems our informants regularly use. For studies of the latter, see Garvey (1979; also, chap. 18, this volume).

The publication-centered schema (Fig. 16.1) illustrates certain conceptions of digital library use that we found in many of our interviews. It depicts one way of integrating digital libraries into faculty work life. Our faculty informants described their world in terms of their publication process. Biologists described how their source of publishable ideas was anchored in laboratory work and systematic data analysis, whereas literary theorists emphasized their close reading of texts as key sources. Their movement from ideas to making them accessible via publication involves peer review, editors, publishers, vendors, and librarians. They conceptualized each participant in this cycle as filtering and adding value to the

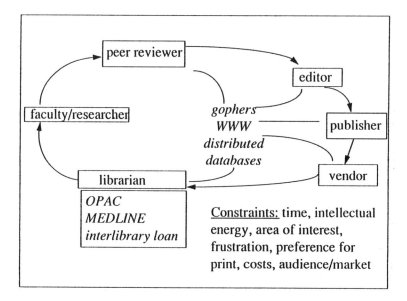

FIG. 16.1.   Publication-centered schema of digital library use as a closed rational system.

knowledge provided: The peer reviewer edits and checks for plausibility, accuracy, and research significance; the editor solicits, collects, and coordinates contributions; the publisher attends to the details of printing, binding, and advertising; the vendor provides distribution channels; and the librarian chooses which offerings to collect and provides materials to the researcher for creating new scholarship.

A closed rational systems model examines this bounded group of relationships and defines effective digital library use as a means to improve efficiency within the constraints of these relationships. This schema shows how distributed databases can bypass some steps in producing and disseminating paper publications. Our informants expect that the increasing use of electronic communication to transmit their work to other participants in this process will shrink the time required to make it available to other researchers. As more researchers make materials available on media like the WWW, our informants whose views are publication-centered should judge the effectiveness of digital libraries according to efficiencies or inefficiencies of the steps portrayed in Fig. 16.1. One interview segment with a biologist illustrates: "I would like to have as much flexibility as possible. I have a program that I use called Pro-Cite, just to keep track of my reprint collection … and that lets me search any field with any key and I wish I could do that on MEDLINE."

Librarians. Professional librarians and computer specialists have different roles, skills, and missions within a university, and each group held distinctive conceptions of digital libraries. The librarian-centered schema illustrates the ways that some librarians characterized digital library use as enhancing organizational efficiencies by speeding up processes, lowering costs, and increasing access to materials. These informants viewed librarians as central to effective use of materials, as curators of cultural knowledge, and as concerned about the viability of accessible collections. Librarians reported selecting the collection of digital library resources and services that best serve the faculty and other clients. Librarians add value to digital resources by selecting helpful classifications and searching mechanisms for their users to locate materials, even if they are not held within the libraries' walls. The focus of collections, in this schema, is on selection criteria controlled by the librarians and blurs differences between formats, such as print, microfiche, or electronic (i.e., physical formats are interconnected with electronic resources and services). Librarians portray themselves as gatekeepers who contain, preserve, and make available what researchers need to do their work. Librarians ensure this function under the constraints imposed by university budgets and other resources. As one librarian put it: "[The role of the librarian is] to get to the people that need the information, the information that they need. It doesn't matter what format that's in."

Figure 16.2 depicts a closed rational systems model that places librarians at the center of a matrix of relationships with their clients (faculty) and

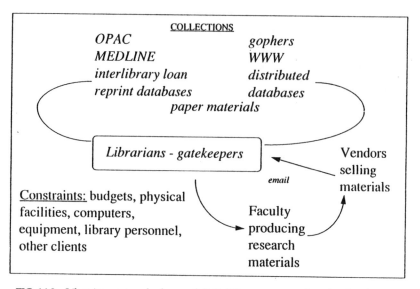

FIG. 16.2.   Librarian-centered schema of digital library use as a closed rational system.

suppliers (vendors). It is a closed model because the librarian informants discussed these groups primarily (and sometimes exclusively) in relationship to their particular collections. Librarians tacitly refer to this schema when they emphasize the ways that digital libraries will help speed up acquisitions, lower the costs of research collections, and maximize their availability and viability. Figure 16.2 depicts librarians in the central role of mediating between research collections, their clients (faculty), and suppliers (vendors). It reflects the beliefs of those librarians who see their major role as maintaining responsibility for the viability, authenticity, and content of the collections.

This schema reflects the beliefs of those librarians who portray themselves in a central role in proving research materials for faculty. However, Fig. 16.2 does not include the diverse disciplinary and career demands that lead faculty to prefer or ignore various digital library resources and services. It also does not help us understand why librarians do not archive (either in print or digital media) electronic materials, preferring instead to maintain pointers to electronic storage outside their universities.

Computer Specialists.   In contrast to librarians, computer specialists conceive of digital library resources and services as an open collection available to all. Our informants characterized digital library collections as disparate materials that are freely shared on computer networks. They characterized the effective use of digital libraries by how much people utilize them; they see "more use" as "better use." Some computer specialists describe digital library resources and services as "toys" or "tools." They believe that digital library resource use parallels the faculty research process but it should be fun and engaging.

The information technology resource-centered schema (Fig. 16.3) depicts a closed rational systems model of digital library use. It is information technology resource centered because it focuses on the technological elements of digital library use. It is a closed rational model because it ignores or rejects the factors that influence the abilities of researchers to contribute materials to the digital libraries because of the availability of equipment, skill, time, and the social rewards that they accrue (or lose). Instead, it focuses on the importance of knowing which information technology resources are available, and utilizing them in ways that create new contributions in the form of digital documents, tools, or collections. A common complaint by computer specialists is that the faculty do not take steps to use materials effectively: "The [faculty] never pay attention whenever they are getting something to learn unless they're having to use it."

The information technology resource-centered schema privileges contribution through creating digital materials and often ignores the scholarly arrangements to add intellectual value that faculty emphasize in a publication-centered schema (Fig. 16.1). It also directly conflicts with the tight control of the librarian-centered schema (Fig. 16.2). The closed rational models of both librarians and computer specialists place these support staff in mediating roles between faculty research (which is diverse and decentralized) and resources that they administer. Their schemas of effective digital library use highlight the importance of librarians and computer specialists—professionals that faculty often take for granted and sometimes

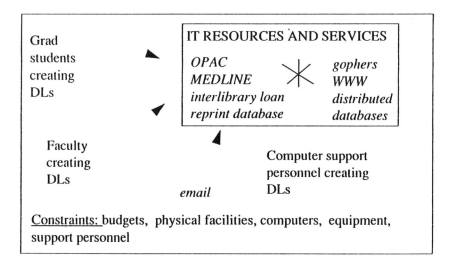

FIG. 16.3.   Information technology resource-centered schema of digital library use as a closed rational systems model.

stigmatize. Unfortunately, their closed rational system models do not help us understand why faculty do not take the time to make effective use of digital libraries. Moreover, just as libraries and computer support organizations have differing goals and formalized processes in the closed rational model, the open natural systems models reveal different professional values and different organizational identity issues.

OPEN NATURAL SYSTEMS MODELS

Faculty. The next schema (Fig. 16.4) models faculty digital library use based on the concept of scholarly communication with invisible colleges. An invisible college is an organization of researchers in a particular field or subspecialty into an "ingroup" that routinely communicates via conferences and circulation of preprints and who controls personal prestige and the fate of new scientific ideas and strategy (Price, 1963, 1965). We show how processes to ensure the legitimacy of the invisible college meet the gaps not explained by the closed rational systems model.

The scholarly communication schema of digital library use shows how new knowledge is produced through a spiraling series of activities that are subject to approval by colleagues. Digital library use in this context connects elements internal to this process, for example, a molecular biologist, her word-processing equipment, MEDLINE, and email to support peer review

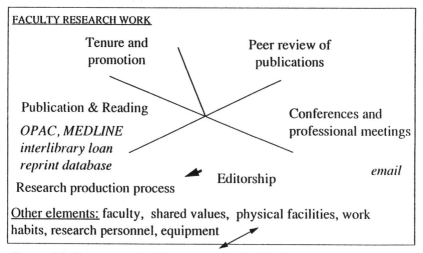

External influences: research programs, family demands, teaching, administrative meetings

FIG. 16.4. Scholarly communication schema of digital library use
as an open natural systems model.

of her colleagues' research publications. Researchers are not wholly autonomous agents; their practices and products are subject to reviews that are permeated with the norms of their invisible colleges. Influential elements that lie outside of the processes through which scholars communicate particular studies include research programs, the family demands of individual academics, and nonresearch responsibilities such as teaching and administration.

This schema also illustrates informant perceptions of legitimacy in one discipline or subspecialty. Our faculty informants described their activities as subject to norms of several invisible colleges, for example, a particular research area, a mainstream group within a discipline, or the invisible college of the majority of members of a department. The open natural systems model explains patterns of faculty digital library use by examining value-laden choice criteria. Because the invisible colleges determine the character of quality research, analytical models that include this source of values help us better understand how faculty judge effective digital library use. Contrasting these first two schemas of faculty conceptions of digital library use help us to identify contradictions and limitations of closed rational systems models. We found that faculty use digital libraries to supplement but not to supplant research activities that preserve their invisible college's values. A biologist who had recently done some collaborative work put it this way: "Just because we're in a very competitive field and in order to keep up, it's hard to do it all yourself because other labs can do it faster.... You sort of have to decide whom to align yourself with. It's tricky. I try to keep on pretty good terms with all my competitors [via email] just so everybody knows what's happening."

In the closed rational systems model, intellectual value is incrementally added in the creation of digital libraries. In contrast, the open natural systems model conceptualizes intellectual value as being shaped by communication with powerful academic peers.

Librarians. University libraries serve broader missions than the research mission that is the focus of this study. They provide study space for students, subsidize access to expensive resources in great demand (e.g., access to the Internet and course reserves), and support elaborate back room operations for acquisition, upgrades, preservation, and keeping track of voluminous material and equipment. Libraries as organizations are committed to proving reliable and consistent service to their clients. Open natural systems models highlight trade-offs and dilemmas in digital library service provision exacerbated in meeting the preferences of diverse researchers. These models also help us understand how libraries cope with external influences and act to preserve the integrity of their values.

Librarians organize their services in order to preserve the viability of their values in providing service to the university. There is a trade-off between providing the best services to the public and supporting the underlying processes that make the public services good. For instance, in order for libraries to provide good reference to distributed networked databases, they need some level of corresponding access to the physical equipment and computer services that the library users have. Libraries are not computer centers, however. They assume a broader role to provide more holistic research assistance to achieve effective faculty digital library use.

The library-centered schema (Fig. 16.5) depicts the conceptions of librarians who view effective digital library use in the context of preserving their library's organization and values. Adding electronic formats to the collection entails many of the same functions of other materials (right side of triangle). Consequently, effective digital library use would preserve traditional organizational structures, functions, and roles. To the extent that digital library services help libraries provide better service and support their professional practices, librarians will adopt, promote, and utilize digital library resources. This schema presents a pyramid of service layers and associated functions, values, and artifacts to the right. The upper functions such as reference and training are more visible to a library's clients than are the functions toward the base of the triangle. Faculty email and personal databases of references are rarely administered by academic libraries even though faculty use them to supplement their library use.

The schema in Fig. 16.5 represents the major functions that libraries have developed to manage their archival resources. These arrangements are familiar to faculty researchers who depend on them in their conception of

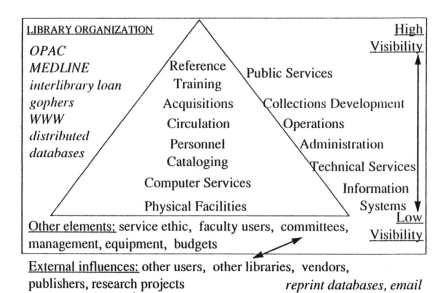

FIG. 16.5.   Library-centered schema of digital library use as an open natural systems model.

effective use of digital libraries. However, as digital library resources and services are being created outside the domains and influence of academic libraries, it becomes increasingly difficult for them to easily adopt them into their professional arrangements. External to this pyramid, but acting upon it are the influences of nonacademic library users, other libraries, vendors, publishers, research project demands, or even individual librarians. Librarians with a more open systems view are more amenable to these changes. As one interviewee said, "I think that's really exciting, to be able to provide access to information, information within your own four walls in a much more efficient, easier, transparent to the user, a way that's much less labor-intensive, and then, ... is the ability to go outside the walls of this library into libraries all over the world, literally."

Whereas the closed rational systems schema depicts efficiencies for gatekeeping librarians as the major driver for effective digital library use, the open natural systems schema uses the library organization of service functions as the central criterion.

Computer Specialists.   Even though our computer specialist informants face similar challenges to librarians in providing digital library support, they conceptualize faculty digital library use differently. The information technology development schema (Fig. 16.6) focuses on a portrait of effective digital library use as a continuous spiral of activity that privileges the development of shared digital library resources while it makes current research tasks more effective. Academic computing centers (ACCs) sustain themselves, in this schema, on their ability to create and sustain a common infrastructure for a whole campus. One computer specialist put it this way: "It's a very delicate balance between providing as much support as you can and not pursuing suicidal tendencies." Similar to the libraries, ACCs must simultaneously balance the maintenance of current services, access, and usability by continually developing information technology resources and services.

The information technology development schema is an open natural systems model because the segments of information technology development reinforce the computer specialists' priorities of continuously creating better information technology. The tasks in each step are repeated as new digital library resources and services become available. Disciplinary norms, departmental budgets and librarian involvement all influence the degree to which computer specialists can support information technology development.

The information technology development schema in Fig. 16.6 resembles the scholarly communication schema (Fig. 16.4), which is also a spiral of repeated tasks. Whereas librarians can use their service organizational structure to manage their operational responsibilities, computer specialists manage use by encouraging information technology development. Computer specialists do not organize in one visible physical location or have a

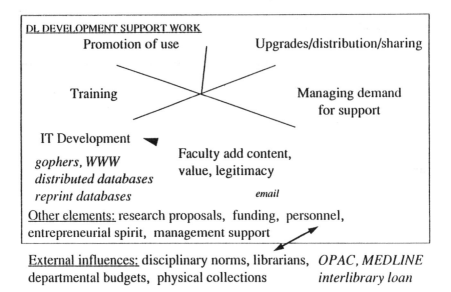

FIG. 16.6.   Information technology development schema of digital library use

well-known long tradition of professionalized training to preserve their role within the university. In fact, computing support has become increasingly decentralized, although universities still require centralized coordination of network facilities.

CONCLUSION

We have described six kinds of schemas of effective digital library use. In the main, faculty are still anchored in the world of print publication and face-to-face scholarly communication. Otherwise, faculty and librarians share a view of infrastructure that is more alike than that of faculty and computer specialists. However, faculty do share with computer specialists ideas about new digital library resources and services. The librarians and computing specialists share a service orientation subject to faculty input, but they have evolved separate norms and task structures to fulfill their stated and unstated missions. The librarian schemas, more than the computer specialist schemas, respect controlled development of digital library resources and services that are tied into operational arrangements to access both paper and digital materials.

Our contrast between the narrower closed systems models and the open systems models provides a helpful distinction to understand differing conceptions of effective digital library use. Rational systems models use functional arguments to explain differential use, and focus on efficiency. Natural systems models use arguments about professional values and social practices, and focus on people's relationships and work arrangements. We believe that although open systems schemas are not the dominant model for discussing digital libraries thus far, a focus on open natural systems models will help us frame alternative conceptions of digital libraries and provide a basis from which to better plan effective digital libraries of the future. For example, closed rational systems models suggest that librarians and computer specialists will soon be replaced by fast, reliable, and easy-to-use electronic resources. Faculty will produce more new research in less time and at reduced cost. Students and industry will reap the benefits of instantaneous learning and communication of new ideas. Such arguments are painfully familiar, and have always proved to miss important features of real situations. They do not help us understand the important role of interpersonal referral, human assistance, and relevant discrimination skills in research work practices.

Closed rational systems analyses do not even help us understand current efficiency losses. They do not explain faculty members' inattention to digital library resources and services, and faculty choices of subsets of services. They also do not help us understand why librarians have trouble adapting digital documents and distributed databases to their collections. Closed rational systems models do not explain why computer specialists are frustrated by failed incentives for faculty to contribute directly to information technology development.

It is hard to generalize broadly about digital library infrastructural arrangements by comparing only two fields at two universities. However, our findings serve as a basis for exploring in the future how providers' attitudes and administrative decision making influence how digital library resources are used on their campuses. In a subsequent study we will examine how budgetary structures and the degree of library decentralization influence the kinds of materials that are available in faculty offices. Although some of our informants in this study attributed differences in digital library resources to leadership in high administration or in the libraries, we think people's conceptions of what a digital library is, based on their organizational alignments and work practices, will play an important role.

ACKNOWLEDGMENTS

A full description of this research may be found in L. M. Covi and R. Kling (1996). Kling's work was funded in part by the U.S. Department of Education through Grant R 197D40030 and the University of California Faculty Mentor Program. The authors wish to acknowledge the helpful contributions of Aya Betensky, Jaap A. Jasperse, anonymous reviewers, colleagues, and librarians, especially Terry Winograd, and Julia Gelfand. Special thanks to Mary Froehlig for early assistance in setting up the project.

REFERENCES

Covi, L. M. (1996). Social worlds of knowledge work: How researchers appropriate digital libraries for scholarly communication. In *ASIS Mid-Year Meeting* (pp. 84–100). Washington, DC: American Society for Information Science.

Covi, L. M., & Kling, R. (1996). Organizational dimensions of effective digital library use: Closed rational and open natural systems models. *Journal of the American Society for Information Science, 47*, 672–689.

Fuller, S. (1995a). Cybermaterialism, or Why there is no free lunch in cyberspace. *The Information Society, 11*, 325–332.

Fuller, S. (1995b). CyberPlatonism: An inadequate constitution for the republic of science. *The Information Society, 11*, 293–303.

Garvey, W. D. (1979). *Communication: The essence of science*. New York: Pergamon.

Harnad, S. (1990). Scholarly skywriting and the prepublication continuum of scientific inquiry. *Psychological Science, 1*, 342–343.

Kling, R. (1980). Social analyses of computing: Theoretical perspectives in recent empirical research. *Computing Surveys, 12*, 61–110.

Kling, R., & Covi, L. (1995). Electronic journals and legitimate media in systems of scholarly communication. *The Information Society, 11*, 261–271.

Kling, R., & Lamb, R. (1996). Analyzing visions of electronic publishing and digital libraries. In R. P. Peek, G. Newby, L. Lunin (Eds.), *Scholarly publishing: The electronic frontier* (pp. 17–54). Cambridge, MA: MIT Press.

Markus, M. L., & Keil, M. (1994). If we build it, they will come: Designing information systems that users want to use. *Sloan Management Review, 35*, 11–25.

McClure, C. R., & Lopata, C. L. (1996). *Assessing the academic networked environment: Strategies and options*. Washington, DC: Coalition for Networked Information.

Okerson, A. (1991). The electronic journal: What whence and when? *The Public Access Computer Systems Review, 2*, 5–24.

Okerson, A., & O'Donnell, J. (Eds.). (1995). *Scholarly journals at the crossroads: A subversive proposal for electronic publishing*. Washington, DC: Association of Research Libraries.

Price, D. J. de S. (1963). *Little science, big science*. New York: Columbia University Press.

Price, D. J. de S. (1965). Networks of scientific papers. *Science, 149*, 510–515.

Scott, W. R. (1992). *Organizations: Rational natural and open systems*. Englewood Cliffs, NJ: Prentice-Hall.

Van House, N. A. (1989). Output measures in libraries. *Library Trends, 38*, 268–279.

Walsham, G. (1993). *Interpreting information systems in organizations*. Chichester, England: Wiley.

17

THE INTERNET IN SCHOOL: A CASE STUDY OF EDUCATOR DEMAND AND ITS PRECURSORS

Janet W. Schofield
Ann Davidson
Janet E. Stocks
Gail Futoran
University of Pittsburgh

This qualitative study of K–12 educators' reactions to a project designed to stimulate Internet use in instructional activities concludes that, despite earlier research suggesting that teachers often resist using computers, a large number of them wish to use the Internet in their classrooms. Evidence of this included (a) the very strong response to a competition held to select projects for support, (b) educators' expenditure of substantial amounts of personal time and money to facilitate Internet activities, (c) a high demand for training even when it was unpaid, and (d) initiative on the part of many not gaining access through the competition to get it in other ways. Factors contributing to this high level of demand included the existing dearth of modern computer equipment in the school district, teachers' interest in the Internet for personal purposes, and teachers' belief that the Internet use would help students. Also contributing very importantly to demand was the grassroots approach taken by the project that welcomed and supported novice computer users, let teachers design Internet uses consistent with their own goals, and emphasized site-level change agents and expertise. Although it contributed to demand in important ways, this approach also had some drawbacks, which are discussed.

In recent years there have been many calls to connect teachers and students in our nation's schools to the Internet (Carlitz, 1991; Hunter, 1992; Newman,

1992). Advocates of wide-area networking (WAN) for schools argue that access is vital because of its potentially transformative effects. Scholars envision, for example, "new kinds of virtual communities to facilitate the restructuring and reform process" (Hunter, 1992, p. 25) as well as a national network that "has the potential to become the foundation on which all educational programs and materials are developed and distributed" (Carlitz, 1991, p. 26). Among the benefits predicted are increased collaboration among teachers, schools, and outside institutions, increased ability for students to access data and tools, and more equitable social interactions among individuals from different kinds of backgrounds.

A chorus of cautionary voices, however, remind enthusiasts of the plethora of failed school reform efforts (Cohen, 1987; Cuban, 1984, 1986; Hodas, 1993; Sarason, 1990). Despite abundant suggestions for curricular and pedagogical reform, for example, there have been only modest changes in classroom organization, teacher–student relationships, and instructional methods during the 20th century (Cuban, 1984). Massachusetts Institute of Technology professor Jerold Zacharias concluded, "It is easier to put a man on the moon than to reform public schools" (quoted in Cuban, 1986, p. 1). Computers, too, may fail to live up to the promise many feel they hold for improving education. A major recent government report on teachers and technology has approximately the same number of pages in its first chapter addressing the barriers to computer use in schools as it has on the potential uses of computers (U.S. Congress, Office of Technology Assessment, 1995). Teacher reluctance to embrace new technologies is posited to relate to factors such as school and classroom cultures, availability of equipment, quality and availability of training, and school decision-making structures (Cuban, 1986; Hodas, 1993).

Without teachers' interest in using networking, efforts to link schools to the "information superhighway" are likely to be futile. This chapter explores a "bottom–up" or "grassroots" approach to technology implementation and teachers' demand for Internet access and training. We draw on literature that links the change models typically employed in school districts, which frequently fail to elicit the input and insights of teachers, to teachers' lack of enthusiasm for change and reform. Enthusiasm for reforms has come typically from school boards and educational administrators; in the worst-case scenario teachers view reforms as imperatives imposed on them by administrators or university personnel out of touch with or unsupportive of the daily rigors of the classroom (cf. Cuban, 1986; Grant, 1988; Hodas, 1993). Yet studies show that teacher satisfaction and engagement are connected to their opportunities to participate in decisions concerning the organization and realization of their work (cf. Bacharach, Bauer, & Conley, 1986; Corcoran, 1990; Dawson, 1985). Drawing on data collected in our study of Common Knowledge: Pittsburgh (CK:P), a project that emphasizes school-level definition and control of wide-area networking-based curriculum projects, we contend that CK:P's grassroots approach to introducing technology has played an important role in supporting and encouraging teacher interest in network curricular projects. In addition, the chapter addresses important and problematic issues that can emerge when one takes a grassroots approach to technology implementation.

COMMON KNOWLEDGE: PITTSBURGH: HISTORICAL CONTEXT AND APPROACH

Common Knowledge: Pittsburgh is an ongoing collaboration between the Pittsburgh Public Schools, the University of Pittsburgh, and the Pittsburgh Supercomputing Center, which provides supercomputing and technical resources to scientists and researchers throughout the country. The project is one of four large-scale wide-area networking projects, or "testbeds," funded in the United States by the National Science Foundation. These projects are designed to explore the potential and the problems of using wide-area networking in elementary, junior high, and high schools.[1] Technical aspects of the project's implementation are the responsibility of computing staff, whereas education functions such as training and working with teachers are handled by CK:P's educational staff, all of whom had worked in the school system.[2]

Although CK:P as a funded project began in January 1993, its roots go back much earlier. In the 1980s a physics professor at the University of Pittsburgh, Robert Carlitz, became interested in the potential of networks to enhance the K–12 curricula through providing teachers with electronic access to resources outside the school walls. Several teachers in the Pittsburgh Public Schools shared this vision and were given guest accounts on the Internet via the University of Pittsburgh at Carlitz's request. These teachers explored the Internet primarily by dialing in on modems from their home computers.

When the National Science Foundation circulated a request for proposals for network testbeds, Carlitz and four coinvestigators submitted a proposal strongly influenced by his experiences with these teachers. Although a high-level administrator from the Pittsburgh Public Schools was associated with the proposal as a principal investigator, the major impetus for the school district's involvement sprang from the enthusiasm of classroom teachers. Consistent with the project's history, after funding, the CK:P educational staff continued to promote a grassroots approach to the implementation of school-based wide-area networking. Project staff advocated recruiting teacher "pioneers" to lead initial CK:P efforts. The project also

---

[2]For additional details on testbed sites, see Hunter (1994), Newman (1994), and Pea (1994).

[3]The authors are members of the CK:P assessment staff, which is responsible for tracking the factors that shape the implementation of wide-area networking in the schools.

emphasized school-level expertise and commitment. Thus, the educational staff explicitly discouraged participation by those who were reluctant or not personally motivated. Further, although interested neophytes were welcomed by CK:P project members, there was a strong expectation that after an initial period of relatively intensive training and support, the projects at various schools would become reasonably self-sufficient. For example, the CK:P model sees teachers as taking on roles such as system administrator for the file servers at their sites.

Thus, with the exception of the project's first year, when four schools with interested teachers were simply selected by CK:P staff to receive Internet connections,[3] CK:P schools have not been awarded Internet access by project staff. Rather, schools have had to apply for access through a competitive process, with interested groups of educators submitting proposals detailing how the Internet would be used in service of curricular and educational goals. In turn, a committee made up of parents, school board members, teachers, district personnel, and CK:P staff has chosen among these proposals to award access to a limited number of schools. Although the projects at each school vary significantly, they are similar in the sense that they were designed and developed primarily by teachers and school librarians.

Also consistent with a grassroots philosophy, project participants must develop their own curriculum ideas rather than implement "prepackaged" ideas proposed by the educational staff or others. The educational staff has attempted to provide teachers with resources, both physical and intellectual, that they hope teachers will use in innovative and flexible ways to accomplish educational goals. However, the educational staff does not go the next step and try to work out the details of how these resources can or should be used. The underlying assumption is that teachers and others will more likely be willing to invest time and energy in making their own ideas work in the classroom.

Given this grassroots approach, it is not surprising that school-level projects vary widely. (See Table 17.1 for examples). Some were planned to involve the entire school, whereas others were intended for very specific and limited purposes. Some projects focus very intensely on a particular discipline, whereas others were intended to support interdisciplinary curriculum units. Although most projects were designed to give students electronic access to a wealth of individuals and resources, some were intended to involve students with other individuals using the Internet. For example, the original grant proposal included a project in which students place online a collection of art owned by the school district along with information written by students about the art and the artist.

---

[3]Three of these sites were given access in order to implement curriculum projects using the Internet, and the fourth to serve as a center for orientation, training, and resource exploration for teachers and other staff in the district.

Table 17.1

Internet Use in Common Knowledge Schools

Third Grade	Pairs of students are learning how to navigate online MOO (Multiuser Object-Oriented) environments. The MOOs are virtual environments that, among other things, are populated by characters who "tell" children's stories. The students simultaneously read and respond electronically to these stories. Some have posted their own stories as well.
Fourth and Fifth Grades	Students are designing and developing projects appropriate for posting to the school newsgroup. For example, the fourth-graders posted a survey. Other classes in the building then responded to the questions. The students will train other students in the school to read and post information to their school newsgroup.
Fourth and Fifth Grades	Students locate math problems that are posted on the Common Knowledge gopher. After figuring out the solutions, they send them to a math teacher outside their school who reads and questions them about their solutions.
Seventh and Eighth Grades	Students are using email as a vehicle to exchange and discuss current news stories with classes in Singapore, Sweden, and England.
High School	Students in foreign language classes are corresponding by email with pen pals in other countries who are native speakers of the language they are learning.
High School	Students working on the school newspaper staff are publishing the newspaper on the school's World Wide Web server as well as in the regular newsprint version.
Junior and Senior High School	Students are paired to work on a research project together. The students work together to find online resources. Students publish their finished research products on the Internet.

The school-level context of these projects is also extremely varied. The first-year sites were an elementary school and two high schools; in subsequent years, five elementary schools were added to the project, as were four middle schools and one high school. Some of the sites have quite heterogeneous student bodies, whereas others are markedly more homogeneous in terms of race and social class. The groups proposing and implementing the projects, called the "network teams," also differ in size, composition, internal dynamics, and the extent of members' initial familiarity with a computer network.

RESEARCH METHODS

The major methods of data gathering utilized in the study of CK:P have included qualitative observations, semistructured interviews, the collection of archival material, and the collection of quantitative information through such methods as on- and offline surveys and monitoring of network use. We paid careful attention to developing a role in the school district's social system that caused as little disturbance as possible, presenting ourselves as researchers who were interested in learning about the factors that shape the implementation of wide-area networking in the schools and highlighting the fact that the information we gathered would be treated confidentially.

Extended and repeated observations were conducted in a wide variety of settings ranging from training sessions to network team meetings to classrooms in which wide-area networking was being used. Trained observers used the "full field note" method of data collection (Olson, 1976), which involves taking extensive handwritten notes during the events being observed. Care was taken to make the field notes as factual and as concretely descriptive as possible. All field notes were audiotaped and transcribed. Transcribed field notes and interviews were coded for themes that emerged as important to the implementation and educational impact issues central to our effort.

Because interviews can be so useful for providing participants' perspectives on events, both formal and informal interviews were used extensively. In constructing and conducting these interviews, strong efforts were made to procure valid and unbiased data. For example, questions were posed in a balanced manner so that leading questions were avoided, individuals were assured that no one other than members of the research team would have access to their interview transcripts, and the like. By the end of the second year of the project, 78 interviews had been conducted with 54 educators in the school district. In addition, 42 interviews were conducted with CK:P staff and Pittsburgh Public Schools administrators. These formal and informal interviews have been supplemented with surveys. For example, surveys were used to tap the attitudes of network team members before and after the formal training sessions, and a later survey was sent electronically to over 1,000 individuals who had Internet accounts through CK:P.

We also collected usage data, in the form of login statistics, to measure growth of Internet usage. Weekly summaries of login data, including the number of unique users per week, average login time per user, time of day of Internet access, and related information, allowed us to track data such as the growth of the number of people using the Internet, the amount of time users spent online, and patterns of usage by time of day and time of year.[4]

Archival materials are another important source of information used in this research. Materials such as proposals submitted by individual schools in response to the districts' Request for Proposals, curriculum plans, monthly technical status reports, meeting agendas, and email from individuals reporting problems to the technical staff were systematically collected. Again, care was taken to procure data that were as representative and valid as possible and to be cognizant of unavoidable biases. For example, with participants' permission the research team's email address was added to virtually all group mailing lists connected with the project

---

[4]These usage data can be found on the World Wide Web at <http://info.pps.pgh.pa.us/assessment/month_rpt.html>.

(e.g., network teams, educational staff, principal investigators' group) so that we could monitor most normal email correspondence between members of these groups rather than just getting the material that individuals specifically decided to forward to us. Although this resulted in a huge volume of material to winnow, much of which was of relatively little value for our purposes, it also provided a more representative view of the issues that arose and of individuals' attitudes than we would have had we depended on a subset of materials that individuals chose to forward to us.

TEACHERS WANT TO EXPLORE THE INTERNET: EVIDENCE OF DEMAND FOR ACCESS AND TRAINING

Our evidence suggests that teachers' demand for Internet access is substantial, at least when network implementation is approached as it was by CK:P. Further, demand is not just for hardware and software per se, though, as discussed later in this chapter, this motivation does play a role. Teachers who want access to the Internet also seek training and appear eager to explore Internet resources. Finally, though it is too early to say whether the current positive attitudes will translate into sustained classroom use, teachers express substantial interest in using network to support instruction.

Teachers' Response to the Request for Proposals

The first piece of evidence indicating that a great many teachers want access to the Internet is the enthusiastic response to CK:P's request for proposals. Because of insufficient resources to accomodate everyone, CK:P put out a request for proposals from teachers in schools. Although no more than half a dozen or so new projects could be supported in the first year, 33 separate proposals were submitted from 250 school-site educators, of whom approximately 170 were teachers.[5] This response is all the more impressive because there was no district-wide policy facilitating the preparation of proposals through practices such as release time from classroom responsibilities.

This pattern was repeated during the second proposal year despite the fact that these proposals required more information from the schools. For example, in addition to the proposal text (about 10 pages), each network team member was required to write a letter expressing his or her commitment to the project, and teams were also encouraged to include letters of support from other individuals such as administrators, parents, and com-

---

[5]Proposal members also included administrators and personnel involved in special programs. In addition to school-site educators, more than 20 parents/community members and several district personnel were members of network teams submitting proposals during 1993–1994.

munity organization members. In order to avoid disappointing too high a proportion of the applicants and to even out the representation of age groups in the project, the 1994–1995 competition was limited to schools with middle school-aged children. Of the 19 eligible comprehensive and specialty schools in the district, 10 applied to become one of three CK:P third-year sites.[6] Over 120 middle school educators signed on as members of the 10 proposed network teams participating in the RFP process during its second year.

Personal Teacher Effort

A second indicator of teachers' interest in network activities was the large number of teachers who invested money and time to facilitate their network activities. Many teachers purchased computer equipment for their homes, with their own money, during the first 2 years of CK:P. A survey of all individuals with CK:P-sponsored accounts conducted in spring of 1995 found that 74 % of respondents reported having spent at least some of their own money to purchase new equipment to connect to the Internet since receiving access through CK:P. The most commonly reported amount spent was about the cost of a modem (between $100 and $250). Also, 30 % of the respondents reported spending $1,000 or more, nearly the cost of a home computer.[7] In all, individuals who responded to the survey reported spending a total of over $440,000 on equipment that would enable use of the Internet since the project's beginning.

In addition to expenditure of personal funds, teachers who bought new equipment invested time at home learning to use their equipment and to navigate the Internet. The number of individual teachers and librarians in the district logging on to the computer that served as the main file server during the first 2 years of the project rose from about 3 per week just before the first training sessions in June 1993 to between 274 and 278 per week in the closing months of the spring term 2 years later. On average, teachers spent more time online during nonworking hours than they did during school hours; further, the total nonschool login time for teachers increased steadily over the first year of the project. Teachers used this time to find ways in which they could use the network for professional, as well as personal purposes. For example, teachers reported exploring the Internet

---

[6]These included three "specialty schools" as well as 7 of the 13 comprehensive middle schools in the district without Internet access (1 middle school was awarded access during the 1993–1994 competition).

[7]These figures must be interpreted with caution. First, the response rate was just over 40 %. Second, because no control group completed the survey, it is not possible to estimate how much participation in the project itself increased computer purchases over some base-line level that would have occurred without CK:P.

and finding resources relevant to realizing their curricular goals, saying things about their home use such as: "It's been very exciting. It's inspiring to get on the Relay Chat and be able to communicate with people in France in French. It can be very motivational.... And if it's motivational for me, it's going to be motivational for my students as well. So I think that's been very, very exciting."

Demand for Access From Non-CK:P Schools and Teachers

Each year many more schools were turned down than were accepted as CK:P sites. Teachers and administrators at a number of these rejected schools continued to look for ways to fund Internet connectivity.[8] Some schools held bake sales or T-shirt sales to raise money for the equipment they would need. Others investigated alternative sources of grant support for network access. At least one school informally allocated money from the school budget for computer equipment, at the risk of incurring later criticism for inappropriate use of funds.

Frequently, the educational staff of CK:P received calls from teachers and administrators asking if they or their students could be given an account that would allow access to the Internet from a home or school machine, even if their school was not formally one of the Common Knowledge sites. The number of accounts rose from about 200 in early 1993 at the very beginning of the project to just over 2,000 by October 1995. Of these accounts, approximately 31 % were held by teachers, librarians, and administrators from non-CK:P schools. Indeed, the demand for accounts from persons outside the CK:P network was a frequent concern for project staff, who did not want to disappoint or alienate interested individuals but who were concerned about setting a precedent they could not maintain by giving an account to everyone who requested one.

Demand for Training

During the first 2 years of the project, the educational staff provided a variety of training opportunities, including not only visits to CK:P sites, but also open houses and workshops at their training facility. The workshops ranged in length from a series of several meetings covering a broad range of topics to highly targeted training opportunities on topics such as ad-

---

[8]Many queries came through telephone calls and email from outside the district. Also, the World Wide Web site set up by CK:P staff to disseminate information about the project attracted attention. Shortly after it was set up, the number of accesses to it in a week was about 260, divided roughly into 70 % local and 30 % remote accessors. The most recent information available at the time of the writing of this chapter suggests a rather dramatic increase to between 2,600 and 3,600 accesses a week, with roughly 55 % of these accesses from remote sources.

vanced email, using gopher, using World Wide Web, using FTP, and Unix commands. Workshops and similar training opportunities were consistently oversubscribed to the point where waiting lists were set up. Behaving in a way that was reportedly quite unusual in the school district, some teachers pressed to be allowed to attend an already overflowing multiday summer training workshop as unpaid observers. (Others were being paid $500 for their time.) A later multipart training experience developed by the educational staff that required a total of 18 hours either Mondays after school hours or on four successive Saturdays was oversubscribed, even though no attendees received pay for their time. The only recompense aside from the knowledge gained was the fact that, in some cases, attendance counted toward credits that could eventually lead to a minor pay increase.

Broad Demand From Novice and Expert Computer Users

Generally speaking, the teachers expressing interest in using the Internet in their classrooms tended to share a common trait: a marked lack of prior experience with either computers or networks. In a survey of teachers participating in a multisession training course during the project's second year, almost 40% of respondents ($N = 69$) did not at the time of their training own home computers. Further, a small number of those who reported owning computers said that they personally did not use them. Both findings suggest a relatively low level of exposure to computing, because many of these respondents had no computers in their classrooms either. Nearly 90% of the respondents indicated that they had had little or no experience with the Internet before participating in the proposal process.

In addition to lacking experience, many network team members reported anxiety about computers prior to their involvement in CK:P. Phrases such as "computer phobia" and "fear of computers" were used repeatedly by project teachers and other school staff without embarrassment to describe their reactions to computing. As one elementary school teacher put it during an interview: "Well, before I went through the Common Knowledge training, I would consider myself computer illiterate. I was scared to death of computers.... Using the Internet is not difficult and I'm a person who never used a computer [before]."

CREATING DEMAND
FOR SCHOOL-BASED NETWORKING:
CONTRIBUTING FACTORS

Given the substantial demand for WAN access and training documented earlier, and given existing literature suggesting that teachers are, generally speaking, unlikely to be enthusiastic about using new technology in their classrooms, the question arises why so many educators went out of their way to become involved in the CK:P project. In this section of the chapter we examine six factors that our work suggests played an important role in stimulating demand. In general, no single factor in isolation appears to account fully for the expressed desire on the part of educators to attempt to use networking in their schools for curricular purposes. Rather, these factors combined in different ways in different individuals and within different network teams to foster interest, as is often the case with complex social phenomena.

We begin this section of the chapter by discussing some of the more obvious explanations for teachers' high demand, including the dearth of technology in the district, personal interest, and a belief that Internet access will benefit students. We follow this with a discussion of three factors that emanate from CK:P's grassroots change model that also served to encourage and stimulate teacher demand. These include teachers' ability to define Internet use in relation to diverse and valued classroom goals, an emphasis on site-level change and expertise, and a pro-novice orientation.

The Existing Dearth
of Modern Computer Equipment in the District

The dearth of up-to-date computers in the majority of district schools was one obvious factor stimulating demand. Schools had outdated equipment and reported difficulty getting approval for even minor technical upgrades, such as a new telephone line. In most cases, the desire for equipment appeared to be coupled with a sincere interest in networking. However, there were also cases of a phenomenon that we call false demand, that is, cases in which apparent interest in using the Internet was primarily a disguised desire for new computer equipment for other purposes. One member of the educational staff reported at a meeting that a teacher told him, "The only reason I did the proposal was to get more [computer] hardware." This same staff member complained at another point that one of the schools submitting a proposal seemed to view the project as a "cash cow" and said that he reminded teachers there that the project was not designed to supply schools with computer labs. When it was apparent that the desire for computer hardware for purposes unrelated to network use was the moving force behind a proposal, it was not funded, because CK:P was supposed to explore the uses of networks in the schools.

Interest in Network Access for Personal Purposes

Considering the extraordinarily rapid growth of the Internet, the pronounced attention it has received during the last few years in widely circulating magazines, and the heated controversies that have swirled around proposals to regulate its content, it is not surprising that many educators appeared interested in participating in CK:P, at least partly because they were curious about the Internet or because they hoped that they or their family members could make personal use of it. For example, educators reported exploring the Internet in order to find information relating to a variety of personal hobbies and interests and wishing to use email to communicate with friends and relatives. In other cases, teachers wanted to learn about the Internet so that they could teach their children, whom they believed might benefit from its use.

That individuals start with personal motives for using the Internet does not preclude their coming to use it professionally. A previous study of the use of personal computers in schools suggests that a potentially effective long-term strategy for encouraging instructional use of computers is to introduce computing to teachers in a somewhat more personal context—one in which teachers first learn to use computers to simplify some of the clerical and administrative work they perform (Schofield, 1995). A CK:P network team leader and teacher argued similarly:

> I think most people initially get involved for personal reasons.... You're doing your own email and you're getting to explore for these things, and you can—I know like Darcy does a lot of research for her papers that she does and so on ... but I think that's how you have to get people involved. You can't say "We're going to do this for the children," because that's too big a step ... it has to be buy into it for yourself, and then you start seeing how it's beneficial, and you start picking up on things. "Oh, I could do this with the kids!".... And then it spills over into what you're doing with the children.

Belief That Network Access Benefits Students

As a project, CK:P stressed the importance of using networking in the service of the curriculum. Consistent with this, teachers predicted that a variety of cognitive benefits and skills would result from network access. For example, teachers at a high school where students carried out independent research projects anticipated the development of more effective information-processing strategies as students searched the Internet for appropriate resource materials. Foreign language teachers predicted improved writing skills as students corresponded with pen pals overseas. Elementary mathematics teachers hoped for improved understanding of mathematical relationships and terms as students authored word problems to post on the Internet.

Teachers also believed network access could do more than provide specific course benefits. When asked by survey at training sessions "What is your opinion about the eventual consequences of Internet access for students?," teachers were somewhat more likely to suggest that Internet use would "result in educational experiences that they [students] would not have otherwise" than they were to indicate that Internet use would "enhance students' learning of traditional subject matter." Putting this another way during an interview with CK:P staff, a teacher stated:

> I mean, the Internet is from my view, is a tool for … is a tool … I hate to say a tool for life. It sounds like a GE commercial or something…. But, I mean it's really giving individual citizens a lot of power, either to organize socially, organize politically, or to develop economically … so I think that, you know, learning the Internet to finish a research project in the 12th grade is going to show up in that person's life in some way that you can't predict as they are an adult.

Educators' perceptions of benefits beyond classroom subject matter provided some of the motivation for their pursuit of network access. Citing the increasing pervasiveness of computers in daily life, many spoke of the importance of preparing their students for the world and careers of the future. A proposal submitted to the CK:P in the second year of the project clearly captured this sentiment, asserting:

> It is the goal of public education to produce citizens who are capable of success, people free of the anxiety of being ill-prepared to meet the demands of a modern workplace. In today's world, this means being computer literate and able to explore resources that are constantly expanding…. We must hurry to educate ourselves and our children in the many uses and benefits of technology in education and our daily lives. It is, perhaps, the greatest gift we can give our students.

For these teachers, introducing their students to computer technology in general and the Internet in particular was valuable in and of itself.

Many teachers believed that Internet access might reduce student isolation, particularly for those students marginalized socially, economically, and/or academically. For example, one team of educators wrote in their proposal for funding:

> Pittsburgh is composed of many ethnic communities each proud of their differences and heritages. A tradition among its citizens is to know only the area of the city in which they reside. Children with limited access to information and technology are isolated; their neighborhood becomes their "universe." It is also not safe for them to leave their neighborhoods because of the gang violence. Further limitations are placed on our students by an assignment to special education classes within their mainstream schools…. We must, therefore, enhance their academic world to broaden their horizons. We need to have our students prepared for inclusion in mainstream schools and society. One way to guarantee this adaptation is to provide access to the most current technology.

Arguing similarly, teachers at a school for the physically challenged lobbied for access based on the idea that "the project will promote life-long skills, through which [our] students would be on par with their non-disabled peers…."

Perhaps most important were beliefs related to the student–teacher relationship as perhaps the most salient workplace characteristic for teachers (Little, 1990; Powell, Farrar, & Cohen, 1985). CK:P teachers believed Internet access would increase student interest. For example, in surveys conducted after training sessions, teachers were asked to indicate whether they believed the Internet would enhance student interest and motivation. On a scale of 1 to 5, with 1 being very unlikely and 5 being very likely, the mean response from first-year project teachers was 4.6, and the mean response for second-year project teachers was 4.1. As one teacher put it in a written response to an open-ended survey probe: "I feel it [the Internet] will motivate students who may have difficulty in learning in a more 'traditional' setting. It will also offer an edge or 'leg up' to those students that don't have the support."

In end-of-the-academic-year interviews conducted with 28 educators who had participated in CK:P's first year, teachers continued to express optimism about the potential benefits of network access for students. For example, several teachers at a school where students used the Internet to correspond with pen pals overseas expressed their conviction that WAN access had improved students' foreign language-writing skills as well as students' motivation to express themselves correctly and appropriately in the second language. Similarly, teachers almost uniformly reported positive reactions from students with access to WAN and interest on the part of others. The following excerpts from interviews with network team members at two CK:P sites are representative of reports on these matters:

> I've noticed a great improvement in written Spanish. In spoken Spanish, that's like … really can't be improved [by the uses made of the Internet]. But their grammar knowledge has improved a little bit, and their letter writing skills have improved dramatically. One of the good things that I like is that most of the pen pals will actually write back and say, "I assume you meant *this* when you wrote *this*.… They expect corrections from me being their teacher, but when they hear it from somebody else, then they start thinking "Oh yeah, maybe I should have written it this way."

> I can't get to my machines most of the times during the day when I have free time because the kids are in here.… They're in here in the morning; they're in here after school. It's fantastic.… They just totally use every machine they can get on the network with … Kids … totally outside the (program using the Internet in class) say, "Hey! This is something that we can do that's extra" … It's like it's something special.

Teachers' perceptions of the benefits stemming from network access likely played a role in sustaining their efforts in the face of technical or other problems. In addition, this may have played indirectly into encouraging demand for technology because teachers were able to speak enthusiastically about their CK:P experiences to colleagues.

An Ability to Use Networking to Further Diverse and Valued Classroom Goals

Both Cuban (1986) and Schofield (1995) pointed out that teachers often are not convinced that technology will help them meet their classroom goals more effectively or efficiently; thus, they may resist the introduction of novel technologies. Consistent with these arguments, teachers who participated in CK:P found the ability to define and then tailor curriculum projects to their students very attractive. At the end of the second project year, 29 educators (teachers and librarians) were asked to describe the advantages and disadvantages of CK:P's grassroots approach to network implementation. All lauded the ability to control and direct their networking projects; one third referred particularly to the ability to tailor their projects to students, as did the following individual: "I think the school knows its population of students better than say another outside organization. So we know our students best. We know what they would benefit best from. So on that level it's definitely better that the school be the one that makes decisions as to how to implement all this."

In some cases, teachers said that network access enabled them to enhance activities that they currently carried out. In still others, network access allowed teachers to pursue a goal that was not possible before the project implementation. At one high school, for example, teachers paired high school seniors and juniors for one semester to work collaboratively, with seniors helping juniors master skills appropriate to completing a research project. Teachers linked their ability to experiment with this classroom approach directly to the presence of the Internet. Further, the teacher who developed this plan purposely sought a new instructional role, that of facilitator rather than transmitter of knowledge. As he explained in an email message, "This cooperative approach to research ... will also allow the teachers to be more supervisors of the process instead of getting involved in the passing of knowledge from one class to the next and the repetitive boredom of that tedious process."

In addition, almost half of the teachers spontaneously linked the ability to control and direct their networking projects to willingness to become involved in the project. Such opportunities, they argued, help to promote teacher acceptance rather than resistance. The following quote is representative of this perspective:

> Having worked for this district as long as I have, I know that when a program is brought in as a top down program ... it's very hard to get teachers committed.... If someone had come into our class and said, "Here's something we want you to do ..." everybody would have been very resistant.... But because it is something that ... faculty ... have said, "Yeah, this is a good idea.... This is something I'm interested in doing with kids," I think that means that we will have success.

Emphasis on Site-Level Change Agents and Their Expertise

A final factor encouraging interest in networking may relate to the fact that, for the most part, CK:P staff did not enter the project environment as outsiders proposing or requiring the use of technology. As noted previously, before CK:P's formal initiation as a project, Professor Carlitz and others had attempted to interest teachers in networking by providing them with accounts on the Internet. Over several years, these efforts created a cadre of teachers interested in the application of networking to classroom environments. These educators eventually became leaders and participants on a number of the project's network teams, creating a situation in which insiders facing similar challenges and time pressures lobbied on CK:P's behalf.

This cadre of educators helped to support and create demand for network access in at least two ways. First, it supported novice users who expressed some interest in networking but were uncertain about their technical skills. For example, one teacher explained: "I'm computer phobic. I always have been. I use the computer. I like the computer. But I don't trust the computer. It's going to do something ... you know, that's the mind set. So knowing that Shelly is here, and if I get in real deep over my head on the system, [there is an] advantage to knowing that that person here is a resource and Shelly will come and sit and walk me through." Knowing that help was available, some teachers engaged in exploration that they might otherwise have avoided out of fear or lack of confidence. Indeed, when asked in an online survey "What is your primary source of support for questions about software or hardware?," other teachers in the school district were the second most commonly cited response, with almost 22% of respondents selecting this answer.

Second, some of the cadre of educators who evidenced very early interest in network use became "second-order" stimulators of demand through their efforts to introduce colleagues to the Internet. One of the most striking examples of this phenomenon is a network team leader who was zealous in her efforts to spread interest in networking. Working before and after school as well as during lunch and preparation periods, this person held numerous 40-minute training sessions about email for faculty colleagues, as well as for the school administrative and clerical staff. She constructed a handout summarizing login and logout procedures for training sessions. She acquired a bulletin board for posting news related to networking and kept this bulletin board updated with messages from CK:P staff as well as materials from a variety of other sources. She reported setting up a list of the people she had trained and also writing to them periodically by email "to get them 'going' or even better to keep them hooked."

Perhaps it is not surprising given this person's efforts that her school was one of two first-year sites that submitted a proposal to the project to expand network access within the school building.

A Pro-novice Orientation

In accord with an emphasis on fostering teacher expertise and commitment, the CK:P staff made strong and concerted efforts to help novice users become more expert. Specifically, they granted requests for information, assistance, or accounts when at all possible, even when the information requested was of the most rudimentary sort or when it came from educators outside of the CK:P project. In addition, they proactively sought ways to facilitate educators' ability to use networking effectively. For example, knowing that teachers do not have a lot of free time at work during the school year and believing that time for exploration and skill development is crucial for the use of networks, the educational staff arranged for teachers to take school computers home with them one summer. In addition, they made visits to the homes of teachers and other school staff to do things like install new modems or set up SLIP (Serial Line Internet Protocol) connections to the Internet. These activities took place in addition to the wide variety of formal training opportunities previously described. The efforts of CK:P staff were almost uniformly praised by the 28 first-year project educators interviewed. In some cases, teachers also linked their interactions with staff to a growing sense of confidence and expertise, as did the following individual:

> It's been fantastic. All I have to do is pick up a phone and I get my answers. If I can't get the answer then, they'll send an electronic mail message and within a day or so I've got the answer. It's come to the point where I am now able, when we have one of our power failures, to go in and change scripts and codes necessary. I know what to check and which area of the computer to see if, when the power went out, how the file was altered.

Though the ready welcoming of even the most neophyte computer users probably did not actually create initial interest in networking, it appears that it contributed to developing and sustaining interest and motivation on the part of project teachers. Further, this orientation may have contributed indirectly to increased demand. Positive experiences and interactions with CK:P staff at training and informational workshops, for example, may have mitigated initial anxieties and concerns in teachers who were considering applying to the project's competition and in educators who sought ways to establish individual connections to the CK:P network.

ISSUES ARISING WITH A GRASSROOTS APPROACH

Although CK:P's grassroots approach fostered teacher interest in networking, this approach also had several drawbacks.

Widespread Inexperience and the Need for Expertise:
A Chicken and Egg Problem

Many teachers participating in the CK:P project had relatively little prior experience with either networks or curriculum design. Some of the proposals submitted failed to take advantage of the special attributes of networking in the proposed curriculum projects. Indeed, a few proposed to use it in ways for which it did not seem ideally suited. Many teachers did not understand the specifics of the operation of file servers and various forms of Internet connectivity, both of which can have substantial implications for classroom activity.

Teachers' lack of knowledge about networking led to a project decision to focus much of the CK:P training on skills that the network team members would need in order to work productively on the Internet and to locate resources useful to their work. However, the ability to use the Internet in some at least rudimentary way was clearly not all that was required of teachers in the project. Finding ways to implement network-based curricular ideas poses a whole host of practical issues and problems, and an emphasis on learning the Internet takes time away from the specifics of planning Internet curricula. Furthermore, issues such as the location and clustering of computers are difficult to resolve without an idea of how the computers will be used in the curriculum. Also, decisions related to long-term usage, which affect the initial wiring of classrooms, were very difficult for novice users to make.

Equity Issues

After the proposal selection process for second-year sites, one school board member complained that this process had exacerbated an already inequitable situation. The process, this member complained, led to a situation in which the educationally rich grew richer and the educationally poor grew, relatively speaking, poorer. Teachers who had had experience writing proposals for other sorts of projects or who had a history of participating in special programs were better positioned to write winning proposals than others less experienced, thus bringing still more extra resources to their students. In fact, the large majority of sites receiving funding for the second year were either magnet schools or schools that had been given district financial support for restructuring. Although this outcome may have been due partly to the fact that CK:P received comparatively more applications from magnet and restructuring schools than it did from the other schools, it nonetheless meant that those schools that were already in some way special in the district were more likely than others to end up with a network project.

The Hazards of Customization

As discussed earlier, one of the very attractive features of the grassroots approach is that it allows teachers to design and customize projects in relation to their curricular and pedagogical goals. However, responsiveness to the desires of particular teachers also can be inefficient. To the extent that equipment deployment is responsive to the special situation at each school, administration cannot be centralized and changes in personnel require another, nonstandard adjustment. To illustrate, if a particular room is given wiring to support numerous network connections and user devices and the teacher who initially made good use of that configuration leaves the school, there is no reason to expect that the next teacher using the room will make equally good use of this unusual concentration of resources.

Also, although teachers are the persons who must implement a technology plan, they are not the only interested constituents. Parents and community members as well as district personnel also have visions for children's educations and needs. Teachers' visions and perspectives are necessarily limited by virtue of their location in a specific school and environment as well as by their professional position, and it may be that the curriculum projects proposed would differ in scope or intention were others with different viewpoints also involved in their design.

CONCLUSION

It is too soon to tell if the Internet will have the far-reaching and transformative impact on education that its proponents anticipate. It also is too soon to tell if the specific project that is the focus of this chapter will be successful in the long term. One thing we can assert, though, is that interest in using networking in educational settings is coming not only from school administrators and technology advocates, but from classroom teachers as well. Our data indicate that many hundreds, not dozens or scores, of the roughly 2,800 teachers in the district are willing and eager to explore the *idea* of using wide-area networking in their classes even without much in the way of concrete examples from peers about exactly what it will entail or what they are likely to accomplish.

One cannot assume that all individuals who evidenced interest in networking were in fact deeply committed to using the Internet in their work. Given that there had been a moratorium on technology purchases in the district for several years before the CK:P project came on the scene, some teachers were anxious to acquire computers through whatever means available. Having heard so much about the "information superhighway," teachers were curious about the Internet and were motivated to use it for personal reasons. Much of the data we gathered, though, also suggests that many teachers do believe that network access should be an integral part of education in the 1990s. The teachers interviewed, for example, almost uniformly believed network access would benefit students, and several had fairly sophisticated visions of how students' education and future work lives would be transformed by the ability to access resources and communicate with people around the globe. We have argued that aspects of the Common Knowledge grassroots change model were relevant to encouraging and stimulating teachers' interest in using network technology for classroom activities. In particular, the ability to define network-based curricular projects assured teachers that involvement in CK:P would not prevent them from pursuing valued educational goals; rather, teachers were able to define projects that enhanced or enabled previously established goals. An emphasis on site-level change agents allowed teachers to serve as CK:P advocates; thus, more experienced teachers supported colleagues as they began to explore the Internet and also worked to sustain and to stimulate interest. Finally, CK:P's pronovice orientation assured teachers that prior computer knowledge and affinity were not prerequisites for project participation.

The conclusions drawn from this study may not be applicable to other districts, because certain contextual factors have influenced attitudes toward CK:P. In fact, it is reasonable to expect that different approaches to networking, as well as the varied social contexts found in different districts, are likely to lead to very different process issues and to varied outcomes. However, a close look at the experiences of CK:P is instructive, both because it begins to lay out what the first few years of implementing such a project are like in a set of relatively varied schools, and because it suggests the importance of paying careful attention to how technology is introduced within public school settings.

ACKNOWLEDGMENTS

The research reported here was funded by Contract No. RED-9253452 with the National Science Foundation and Grant No. 42-40-94032 from the U.S. Department of Commerce. All opinions expressed herein are solely those of the authors and no endorsement of the conclusions by the National Science Foundation or the U.S. Department of Commerce is implied or intended.

REFERENCES

Bacharach, S. B., Bauer, S. C., & Conley, S. C. (1986). Organizational analysis of stress: The case of secondary and elementary schools. *Journal of Work and Occupations, 13,* 7–32.

Carlitz, R. (1991). Common knowledge: Networks for kindergarten through college. *Educom Review, 26,* 25–28.

Cohen, D. K. (1987). Educational technology, policy and practice. *Educational Evaluation and Policy Analysis, 9,* 153–170.

Corcoran, T. B. (1990). Schoolwork: Perspectives on workplace reform in public schools. In M. W. McLaughlin, J. E. Talbert, & N. Bascia (Eds.), *The contexts of teaching in secondary schools: Teachers' realities* (pp. 142–166). New York: Teachers College Press.

Cuban, L. (1984). *How teachers taught: Constancy and change in American classrooms, 1890–1980.* New York: Longman.

Cuban, L. (1986). *Teachers and machines: The classroom use of technology since 1920.* New York: Teachers College Press.

Dawson, J. A. (1985). *School improvement programs in thirteen urban schools: A report of a four year documentation study.* Philadelphia: Research for Better Schools.

Grant, G. (1988). *The world we created at Hamilton High.* Cambridge, MA: Harvard University Press.

Hodas, S. (1993). Technology refusal and the organizational culture of schools, v. 1.2 [Online]. Available: ftp.u.washington.edu, directory/pub/user-supported/horsehorse, filename refuse_1.2.

Hunter, B. (1992). Linking for learning: Computer-and-communications network support for nationwide innovation in education. *Journal of Science Education and Technology, 1*(1), 23–34.

Hunter, B. (1994, April). *Collaborative inquiry in networked communities: Alice testbed Phase 1.* Paper presented at the annual meeting of the American Educational Research Association, New Orleans.

Little, J. W. (1990). Conditions of professional development in secondary schools. In M. W. McLaughlin, J. E. Talbert, & N. Bascia (Eds.), *The contexts of teaching in secondary schools: Teachers' realities* (pp. 187–223). New York: Teachers College Press.

Newman, D. (1992). Technology as support for school structure and school restructuring. *Phi Delta Kappan, 74,* 308–315.

Newman, D. (1994, April). *Costs and benefits of Internet-to-the-desktop: Observations of the national school network testbed.* Paper presented at the annual meeting of the American Educational Research Association, New Orleans.

Olson, S. (1976). *Ideas and data: Process and practice of social research.* Homewood, IL: Dorsey.

Pea, R. (1994, April). *The CoVis collaboratory: High school science learning supported by a broadband educational network with scientific visualization, videoconferencing and computing.* Paper presented at the annual meeting of the American Educational Research Association, New Orleans.

Powell, A. G., Farrar, E., & Cohen, D. K. (1985). *The shopping mall high school: Winners and losers in the educational marketplace.* Boston: Houghton Mifflin.

Sarason, S. B. (1990). *The predictable failure of educational reform: Can we change course before it's too late?* San Francisco: Jossey-Bass.

Schofield, J. W. (1995). *Computers, classroom culture, and change.* Cambridge, MA: Cambridge University Press.

U.S. Congress, Office of Technology Assessment. (1995). *Teachers and technology: Making the connection* (Report No. OTA-EHR-616). Washington, DC: U.S. Government Printing Office.

Part VI

DIFFERENCES IN ACCESS AND USAGE

Many of us have a friend who is an Internet "junkie," know others who use the Internet strictly for work, and still others whose purchase of a computer (or time to use one) is inconceivable. Business and government are spending billions on an infrastructure for the networks of the future, yet little is known about this variability—why some people want to use a computer or electronic communication and, if so, what they want to accomplish (conversation? fooling around with programs? getting information for their work?). Social scientists are studying these questions, for example, asking which people use online services, and how they do so. Also, studies are just beginning to appear on the personal and social consequences of differences in use of electronic communication (Kraut et al., 1996).

This section is headed "access and usage" because these are not the same; access pertains to whether a person can use online services whereas usage pertains to whether the person actually does use them. Access and usage are intertwined, of course, since without access a person cannot have usage. Access barriers are important for us to understand to interpret differences in usage. For example, children of wealthy parents use computers more, and have more skill, than children of poor parents. However, economic status clearly affects whether parents can buy a computer in the first place. There is some evidence that when you remove the income effect on access, poor people like computers as much as wealthy people do. In one case, poor students were put in a classroom with really good technology and trained teachers (that is, with access), and they showed impressive gains in motivation (e.g., Schofield, Evans-Rhodes, & Huber, 1990). Similarly, a group of poor disabled persons who were given access to electronic communication and support (that they would not otherwise have had) gained confidence in themselves and enthusiasm for the technology (Earls, 1980). A new study shows that when families were given computers and online access as part of a field trial, income did not predict differences in their usage (Kraut et al., 1996).

Usage can be culturally conditioned as well as economically determined. For example, if people look down on members of a group for developing computer skills (e.g., for being "nerdy"), the group members soon may have less desire to develop computer expertise. Researchers who studied girls' use of computers in the 1980s proposed that social pressures discouraged many from even trying to be experts. Groups also can develop certain kinds of expertise that other groups don't have—and never learn because the groups don't have many connections with one another. John Walsh and Todd Bayma in chapter 18 describe how scientists in different disciplines work in technological "islands" created by their work practices and close communities. This leads to their using electronic communication quite differently.

Tora Bikson and Constantijn Panis present a review of computers and online electronic communication services in households. Their chapter can be interpreted as a demonstration of how the increasing income gap is affecting people's access to goods and services, including computer technology and electronic communication. This chapter represents what we know so far about changes in the last decade in differential access to electronic communication.

The chapters in this section represent an important topic for future research. Because groups create culture, generalizations about the culture of the Internet will certainly be wrong if they aren't accompanied by a better understanding of how the Internet is, and can be, used by different groups. Further, social policy and business investments surely could be better informed by knowing what different groups really want from the Internet.

REFERENCES

Earls, J. (1990). *Social integration by people with physical disabilities: The development of an information technology model based on personal growth and achievement.* Unpublished doctoral dissertation, The University of Wollongong, Wollongong, Australia.

Kraut, R., Scherlis, W., Mukhopadhyay, T., Manning, J., & Kiesler, S. (1996). HomeNet: A field trial of residential Internet services. *Communications of the ACM, 39,* 55–65.

Schofield, J. W., Evans-Rhodes, D., & Huber, B. R. (1990). Artificial intelligence in the classroom: The impact of a computer-based tutor on teachers and students. *Social Science Computer Review, 8,* 24–41.

18

COMPUTER NETWORKS AND SCIENTIFIC WORK

John P. Walsh
University of Illinois at Chicago

Todd Bayma
University of Georgia

This chapter explores the incorporation of electronic communication in science. From interviews with 67 scientists in four fields, we find that computer network use differs substantially by field and explain these differences in terms of the different work and work organization of each field. Fields with tightly coupled but geographically dispersed work groups (e.g., particle physics) use electronic communication more heavily than those whose work is performed within relatively autonomous groups (e.g., experimental biology). Also, fields that are more buffered from the market (mathematics) tend to use informal electronic communication, whereas those more tightly linked to commercial markets (chemistry) tend to limit use to formal electronic communication. This study, like previous research, shows that the form of technological innovation is dependent on the social context into which new technology is embedded.

Electronic communication is becoming increasingly important to the work of large numbers of people. Among the earliest users of this technology were research scientists. Scientists used these networks to communicate with distant colleagues, access remote databases, share computing resources and distribute research results to others in their field (e.g., Committee on Science, Engineering and Public Policy [COSEPP], 1989; McClure, Bishop, Doty, & Rosenbaum, 1989). In this chapter, we discuss the uses of these networks across fields and suggest some reasons for the tremendous variation in use across different groups of scientists. We argue that differences in use are due to the nature of work and work organization across fields.

SOCIAL STRUCTURE AND TECHNOLOGY

Technological determinists argue that once a machine has been invented, its ability to fundamentally transform social relations is only a matter of time (Beniger, 1986). Others argue that social organizations operate on an internal logic, ruled largely by the existing normative order and its ideological underpinnings. From this perspective, new technologies either are not adopted, or are modified to fit with the existing social structure (Perrin, 1979; Ellis, 1986; Noble, 1984; Thomas, 1994; Walsh, 1991). Because of the flexibility of computer-based technology, we might expect to find social factors playing an important role in influencing how computer technology gets incorporated into work systems (Calhoun; 1981; McClure et al., 1989: Kling, 1991).

Much of the research on electronic communication focuses on its impact (e.g., Hesse, Sproull, Kiesler, & Walsh, 1993). In science, some have argued that electronic communication is leading to a fundamentally new form of work, the "collaboratory" (Finholt & Olson, in press; Lederberg & Uncapher, 1989; National Research Council, 1993). However, impact depends on use, and there has been little comparative research on how electronic communication use differs across settings (see Mantovani, 1994; Rice, 1994; Rice & Tarin, 1993; Ruhleder, 1994). Two U.S. government reports suggest there are differences in use across scientific fields (COSEPP, 1989; National Research Council, 1993) but these reports do not explain these differences. Developing such an understanding is a central focus of this chapter.

DATA AND METHOD

This chapter analyzes the use of computer networks in four disciplines: mathematics, physics, chemistry, and experimental biology. The analysis is based on structured interviews with 67 scientists (15–19 from each discipline), who were chosen using a snowball sample with random starts. These interviews were conducted from January 1991 to October 1992. Also, we drew on archival data for broader information and to balance the subjective interviews.

Given the rapid pace of technological change, this method yielded a snapshot of a moving target. Our design does allow cross-field comparisons. However, the results must be checked against the current state of each field.

MATHEMATICS

Mathematics is a diffused community made up of relatively isolated, independent members (Fisher, 1973). A typical mathematician works alone or with one or two other people. Relatively few people work in each specialty, and they have little shared understanding across specialties. Several respondents noted that it would be difficult for a mathematician to comprehend a talk from someone in a different specialty. This communication problem is exacerbated in written work. Respondents said that transferring mathematics ideas requires informal face-to-face communication, generally in front of a blackboard:

Q: It seems that mathematicians travel more than other fields.

Mathematician: Yes. They have to. The way mathematicians write and talk are two different things. We write very proper, formal, very abstract. We think informally, intuitively. None of that is in the publication. When we get together we ask, "What does that mean?" I pity the fool who is off by himself reading the journals. The dean asking him, "Why can't you do it." Unless you're in a new area of your own. You don't write insight, intuition, what got left out because of lack of room. That is very critical. Travel is our lab.

Another reason for emphasizing direct communication over formal (published) communication is that published work is often hopelessly behind the times. As one mathematician explained: "If [a paper] is significant, you want it out early. Math journals have a horrendous backlog. We rely on preprints. You write a paper and then send a copy to everyone who is interested. Actual publication counts as an archival record. It's important for promotion; you need the publication. For the field, it's already known."

Table 18.1 gives the publication lags for each field. The other fields all had lags of 8 months or less. Mathematics, on the other hand, had a publication lag of over 19 months. Although the dependence on preprints is a well-known phenomenon across fields (Garvey, 1979), the publication lag in mathematics is substantially longer than in other disciplines studied (see also Hargens, 1975; American Mathematical Society [AMS], 1991).

Frequent travel to conferences and visiting positions are quite common and help in the transfer of knowledge. According to one mathematician: "Sometimes, you're the only one at your university who does your kind of work. They hire you because they need one of those, and you have no one to talk to. Even at prestigious universities, those people are isolated."

Table 18.1 gives the average number of authors and institutions for samples of articles from each field. Mathematics articles had, on average, the fewest authors. On the other hand, the ratio of institutions to authors was highest for mathematics. Biology, chemistry, and physics collaborations frequently included two or more scientists from the same institution, but only one mathematics publication in our sample involved a local collabo-

Table 18.1

Co-authorship and Publication Lag, by Field

Field	Authors per Article			Author Institutions per Article			Publication Lag (Months)		
	Average	*Median*	*Range*	*Average*	*Median*	*Range*	*Average*	*Median*	*Range*
Math	1.4	1	1–3	1.4	1	1–3	20.4	19	3–42
Physics	4.0	2	1–79	1.7	1	1–17	7.3	6	4–25
Chemistry	3.8	3	2–11	1.5	1	1–5	8.2	8	4–16
Biology	3.8	3	1–10	1.4	1	1–4	6.5	6	4–12

Note. From a sample of articles from 1990, *Journal of the American Chemical Society* (*n* = 96 articles), *Journal of Biological Chemistry* (*n* = 96), *American Journal of Mathematics* (*n* = 40) and *Physical Review D* [Particle Physics] (*n* = 114).

ration. Further evidence of the geographic dispersion of mathematics is found in Table 18.2, which shows the percentage of published papers with collaborators from more than one country, by field. Mathematics papers have the highest number, with physics having somewhat fewer. Chemistry and biology have substantially fewer international collaborations.

In sum, in mathematics, information is contained not in the published literature, nor in the equipment and materials found in a research lab, nor with local colleagues. Information is found in the persons in one's specialty at other institutions and in the interactions among remote colleagues: "Travel is our lab."

The following statement of a heavy user of the networks summarizes the tasks for which electronic communication was commonly used by mathematicians:

Q: How do you use electronic networks?

Mathematician: I can't live without email. I get about 20 messages per day. I send email to researchers in other areas, mail administrative messages. It beeps when I get something. It's quite important.

I just sent a manuscript a few minutes ago to a colleague to get his reaction. I'm writing a paper with X at University of Michigan. We communicate via email. "How do you do this?" "This is what I do." It's a critical component of my work. I can't remember what it was like before. It was like before we had word processing on computers. I use it to keep in touch with research. Gossip. Ask a question about the literature. Ask questions of collaborators. I use it to send referees' reports. Use NSF line to send reports to NSF. I'm an editor for a journal and I use it to send manuscripts, and sometimes to get referees' reports. Or, use [postal] mail for the manuscript and they email me the report. I communicate with the editorial office. I'm trying to get one journal I work with to accept papers in TeX. People email me a manuscript. I can run hard copy if I want. Then I email it to a referee.

Table 18.2

Percentage of Publications with International Collaborators, by Field, 1981 to 1991

Field	1981	1986	1991
Math	8.8%	13.4%	17.1%
Physics	8.5%	10.5%	16.1%
Biology	4.8%	6.5%	10.0%
Chemistry	4.7%	6.1%	9.1%
All Fields	5.5%	7.5%	11.0%

Note. From Appendix Table 5-24. National Science Board. 1993. *Science and Engineering Indicators-1993*, Washington: US Government Printing Office. An international co-authorship is defined as a paper where at least one author's institutional affiliation is in a country different from that of the other(s). The data are from the *Science Citation Index* list of journals, representing over 3,500 U.S. and foreign journals.

Although this respondent was one of the heavier users, other respondents tended to use the networks for the same tasks, or some subset of these tasks. The overwhelming use of electronic networks was for electronic mail. Electronic mail was seen as particularly useful for facilitating collaboration with distant colleagues. Mathematicians incorporate networks into a cycle of collaboration that generally begins with a face-to-face meeting during a visiting position or at a conference. This meeting allows intensive interaction to determine the potential for a fruitful collaboration and to develop the shared intuition that respondents argued was necessary for sharing mathematics ideas. Once the two have decided that they share common interests and have some interesting ideas to pursue, each goes to his home institution and pursues the collaboration via electronic mail, as in the following example:

Q: Are you collaborating online?

Mathematician: Not now. I have. I did some work recently, someone who was visiting Princeton IAS. We sent papers back and forth [electronically]. He was from Poland. I met him at an international meeting. We got talking. We found some common interests. Said, "Let's pursue this." We pursued it completely by email.

This type of collaboration seems feasible in mathematics, because the only equipment most mathematicians need is paper and pencil, or their electronic equivalents. One problem is transmitting mathematics symbols over networks, which tend to have limited and nonstandard graphics capabilities. Mathematics has largely solved this problem through the adoption of a standard technical word-processing language called TeX. The adoption of TeX as a standard was a combination of a problem–solution match (TeX was one solution to the perceived problem of representing mathematics symbols), history (TeX's author was a mathematician), and institutional factors (the American Mathematical Society adopted TeX as standard).

Several mathematicians also mentioned belonging to electronic mailing lists (distribution lists) or electronic newsletters. These were often associated with computer equipment or software. Many were aware of bulletin boards such as sci.math on the Internet netnews system. Most respondents felt these public bulletin boards had a very low signal-to-noise ratio, but a few had received assistance or assisted someone else through these public bulletin boards. New results would occasionally be announced via these public bulletin boards. Wiles' proof of Fermat's Last Theorem was quickly disseminated on sci.math.research, with an outline of the proof sent out within a few days of the conference where the result was presented. However, electronic distribution of results was not nearly so institutionalized as in physics.

PHYSICS

Modern physics, particularly high-energy experimental physics, is in some ways the polar opposite of mathematics. High-energy physics experiments require elaborate equipment costing millions of dollars and requiring years to design, build, set up, and test, with more years required to collect and analyze the data (Traweek, 1988; Taubes, 1986). Research on this scale requires the collaboration of large numbers of institutions and researchers. Projects typically have 50 or so collaborators, even several hundred from dozens of institutions across the globe. Table 18.1 gives the number of authors and institutions for a sample of physicists' articles. On average, four researchers from 1.7 institutions authored each paper. But there are papers with up to 79 authors from 17 institutions.

Large collaborations are generally experiments involving extensive divisions of labor (Swatez, 1970; Traweek, 1988). Working groups of 5–10 people are responsible for one piece of the experiment, for example, a certain detector, or some software, or a particular type of analysis. The whole project must coordinate much more closely than is the case in mathematics or chemistry or biology (Knorr Cetina, 1995), as explained in the following:

Q: How many people are working on your particular part of the project?

High-energy physicist: Here we currently have two faculty, two postdocs, three grad students. We constructed a portion of the apparatus. That $50 million is split into lots of pieces. We built one piece of the apparatus. We maintain it and keep it going. The detector is split into groups. Depending on how the detector is constructed, there will be four or five groups. Each has to be responsible for tracking part of the reaction. Ours is close to where the interaction occurs. We try to track where the particles go. There were teams from Saclay, Stony Brook, LBL. Each made a detector for tracking. I had to coordinate everything, make sure it was done on schedule. Make sure we had the resources we needed. We had weekly meetings and endless computer mail.

In particle physics experiments, the actions of one part of the group directly and immediately affect those of the other parts of the group and vice versa. Thompson (1967) used the term *reciprocal interdependence* to describe this type of close linkage. He contrasted this with *sequential interdependence* (serial dependence where the output of one group becomes the input of the next) and *pooled interdependence* (where each group must independently perform as expected or else the performance of the whole organization is threatened). These latter forms of interdependence better describe the links among research teams in a biology or chemistry collaboration. According to Thompson, pooled interdependence can be coordinated by standardization and sequential interdependence can be coordinated by scheduling, but reciprocal interdependence is best coordinated by mutual adjustment, a more communication-intensive form of coordination.

Most high-energy physics experiments are conducted at one of a handful of labs, such as Fermilab in Illinois and CERN in Switzerland. Because of the large group size and the geographic dispersion of the collaborators, coordination is especially difficult. For particle physics experiments, electronic communication has become a central component of this coordination system. Swatez (1970) noted that meetings, particularly the group seminar, serve an integrating function that facilitates scientific cooperation and dampens some of the alienating effects of large-group research. The use of electronic mail to coordinate the group and set the agenda to make group meetings productive is illustrated by the following example:

> Experimental particle physicist: We have a collaborators' meeting every two months. We have 100 people there from all over the world. Email is essential. The success of the meeting depends on the organization and the effective use of the Net. The two experiments I'm on use different techniques. For the collision experiment they have set up [an electronic bulletin board]. All collaborators (except the Russians, Chinese, and Indians) are on. News goes on that. Then all can access it and find out. The agenda is sent around this way.

> The other experiment I'm in doesn't use [e]mail as effectively. It's a personal trait of the organizer. As a consequence, the collaboration is less effective. People aren't as organized. They don't know what they are supposed to do.

> We use the nets for agenda items. Weekly meetings. Make announcements. With the test beam data, we discuss procedures, data. We use it to tell someone to do this, or maybe we should get together and discuss X. That way you know ahead and can come prepared.

Mobility is an important factor in using email for coordination. We compared the percentage of biologists, physicists, and mathematicians who gave their phone, fax, and email numbers in recent membership listings. We hypothesized that physicists and mathematicians, who are relatively mobile, would be more likely to give email addresses, whereas biologists would be more likely to give a fax number. Table 18.3 gives the results. For biology, 57% gave fax numbers, but only 9% gave email addresses. In contrast, only 14% of physicists gave fax numbers, whereas 24% gave email addresses. For mathematics, 2% gave fax numbers and 34% gave email addresses. Fax and email are differently suited to scientists, according to their mobility. Biologists are tied to their local labs, and often want to send pictures; fax is both technically superior and is likely to get to the recipient. Physicists are highly mobile and so a fax is not as likely to get to the recipient (who may be at a distant lab or at his home institution on an erratic schedule), but email—which is sent to a virtual location rather than to a geographic location—is much more likely to find its recipient, because he

Table 18.3

Percentage of Scientists Giving Phone, Fax and Email Numbers, by Field

Field	Phone	Fax	Email	N=
Biology	98%	57%	9%	125
Physics	86%	14%	24%	125
Math	53%	2%	34%	125

Note. From *Membership list of the Federation of American Societies of Experimental Biology* (1991)—sample was of members of American Society for Biochemistry and Molecular Biology and the American Society for Cell Biology; *American Physical Society Membership List* (1991), and *Combined Membership List of AMS, MAA and SIAM* (1991/92)—sample was of members of American Mathematical Society.

can check his mailbox from anywhere in the world. As one experimental condensed matter physicist put it, "Networks are bringing us together. We can't live without them. This guy in Austria. He was traveling the whole time we were writing this proposal together. I sent him the proposal [via email]. But, I knew it would get to him, because it goes to a central system. Wherever he is, he can access his account." Mathematics results are similar to those for physics, and for similar reasons.

Although there were variations in the particulars of use, all respondents depended heavily on the networks as an information source. Even people sitting in the same room sometimes use email because it allows the quick transmittal of extensive information. For example, two physicists working on a computer program to reconstruct the particle data might pass code back and forth to fix some bug. Much of physicists' (and also mathematicians') email is internal, unlike that of chemists or biologists. These two statements illustrate:

Q: Is most of your email internal or external?

Mathematician: Both. I don't go next door, I send email. For one thing, there is a paper trail, so we can keep track of what was done. I just sent a message to X, who is two doors down. He's chair of the hiring committee. We're friends. We still send email. Even if we're both in the office.

Q: Are any of these [email messages] with persons in the department?

Chemist: No. If I want to talk to 'em, I'll walk down the hall and talk.

The contrast in the preceding statements shows how institutionalization of electronic mail affects its use. Once email becomes a regular part of one's work, then sending and receiving email becomes a low-cost, fast, high-certainty means of information exchange. Scientists who had not institutionalized use scoffed at sending email to a colleague down the hall. Scientists working where email was institutionalized noted its lower interaction overhead (greetings, pleasantries, and good-byes; see also Merz, in press).

The American Physical Society (APS) is encouraging people to use the networks. It now allows electronic submissions to APS journals, and even rewards electronic submissions by waiving the typesetting fee. Further evidence for the greater penetration of email in physics over biology is that the 1991 APS membership list included an 11-page guide to using email, whereas the 1991 FASEB Directory (for biologists) had no such help. Like the mathematicians, the physicists have adopted TeX as their standard word-processing program. Although any of a number of text processors may have worked, TeX is becoming institutionalized in part because, in addition to its technical capabilities, organizations such as APS and AMS have adopted TeX as a standard. *Physical Review* began publishing its electronic address for submitting articles in July 1991. Thus, institutional pressures from powerful actors (the editors of a major journal) have begun to facilitate the spread of computer network use (Powell & DiMaggio, 1991; also see Ruhleder, 1994).

Physicists (particularly, particle physics theorists) have also institution-alized the electronic distribution of preprints. Preprints are an important channel of informal communication in science. Garvey and Griffith (1979) noted in the 1970s that the distribution of preprints had been increasing to the point where it could become quite burdensome for authors. They also noted that "those who need preprints most—young scientists, workers at small institutions, and researchers in less developed countries—are fre-quently not the recipients" (p. 150). Recently, a theoretical physicist at Los Alamos set up a preprint bulletin board (Taubes, 1993). This bulletin board provides subscribers with abstracts of all the new papers and allows subscribers to send an email request and receive the full paper, with graphics, electronically. Service started in August 1991, and by December 1992, there were 8,000 subscribers. The database currently receives 1,000 new papers per month (Taubes, 1994).

Although there is some concern over the value of papers that have not been peer reviewed, this is mitigated by the small size of the high-energy physics community. According to an APS editor, such a system "works beautifully in a small community of people who work in harmony with each other and who know each other's reputations" (Taubes, 1993, p. 1246). Because this system simply automates what was already a "preprint cul-ture," there are fewer problems with the appropriateness of a computerized preprint database as a medium for scholarly communication. Before this bulletin board began, it was common for physicists to distribute hundreds of preprints when they submitted a paper to a journal:

Q: When do you send a paper out?

Theoretical physicist: As early as possible. I know in other fields they are reluctant to send out their papers. But we [theoretical high-energy physics] send out as soon as possible. At the same time as we send it to a journal. The information is already spread around the community long before it is published. Now [with the preprint bulletin board], we can know the same day. Six months, a year, maybe two years later, it will show up in print. But, the results are available now. It's really great.

The high acceptance rate for physics papers (about 80% for *Physical Review*) means that there is less fear that the papers sent out will not be forthcoming as journal articles (Hargens, 1988). This information gets incorporated into new research quickly, with preprints citing other preprints. Theoretical physicists have incorporated these preprint archives into a cycle of work that allows them to build on each other's findings without relying on the formal gatekeeping function served by print journals (Crane, 1967).

CHEMISTRY

Chemistry is perhaps the largest discipline of the natural sciences. The American Chemical Society (ACS) has about 140,000 members. Chemistry is a very heterogeneous discipline. There are several major, distinct subfields, with varied work modes. We try to summarize the core of chemistry's work organization, but there are important exceptions. In chemistry, major research is being conducted at a large number of institutions. Thus, unlike physics or mathematics, it is not crucial for chemists to have immediate access to one of a few major institutions in order to be current in their field. Also, unlike mathematics, lag times for chemistry journals are fairly short (Table 18.1). Shorter publication lag times reduce the pressure to get information through informal channels (Garvey, 1979).

Chemistry is mainly a bench science. Chemists work in labs with small teams of mostly graduate students and postdocs, and occasionally undergraduates. Research groups are usually in the 5-to 20-person range. But, the larger groups are often split into parallel experiments, with little need for tight coordination among them. One biochemist when asked "Is your current research a group project" replied as follows: "They're all group projects to some degree. They're sufficiently independent that they don't need to share each other's data."

Several respondents suggested that remote collaboration was uncommon. As Table 18.1 shows, there are more collaborators than institutions for both chemistry and biology. In other words, collaborators tend to work locally. In contrast, mathematicians who collaborated almost always collaborated remotely. Chemistry groups are relatively independent (i.e., linked by pooled or sequential, rather than reciprocal, interdependence). This lower interdependence among collaborators puts less pressure on coordination mechanisms (Thompson, 1967; Lawrence & Lorsch, 1967).

Physical chemists (chemists who study the physical properties of compounds) and theoretical chemists are much more computer literate than those in the other specialties. They use computers to model the phenomena they are studying. In the past, this meant limiting problems to what could be studied using the university mainframe, or going to the supercomputer centers or collaborating with someone at the supercomputer centers. With the development of electronic communication, physical chemists and theoretical chemists have incorporated these new resources into their work. For example, they are now likely to access supercomputers remotely. One respondent suggested that the networks have reduced collaboration, because they remove the need for collaborating with someone because he or she has special access to some equipment (like a supercomputer).

Because of the different structure of work in chemistry (compared to mathematics and physics), chemists have a very different use of computer networks. One of the most common uses of networks among chemists is accessing the online Chemical Abstracts (CA) database. STN, a for-profit subsidiary of the American Chemical Society, operates CA and some 40 other databases. CA contains abstracts in English for chemistry papers back to 1967 (including those published in selected foreign language journals). About half the respondents said that CA was a useful resource. CA not only facilitates staying current, but also expands access by allowing chemists to more easily keep up on research in other countries. However, other respondents felt the online version was not significantly more useful than the paper version, and that its cost was prohibitive. As one organic chemist explained, "I don't really use networks at all. At the moment I don't feel the need to. If I did, about the only thing I'd use it for is the Chemical Abstracts, but I haven't gotten around to that yet. Also, those are pretty expensive to run. We've got Chemical Abstracts in the library, and though it might take longer to send a student over to research them, it's less expensive." This statement suggests that electronic communication spreads, or does not spread, from a perceived need for which the technology is seen as a solution. This respondent (and other nonusers we interviewed) knew that electronic communication technology existed (although the extent of knowledge varied). But, given the work organization of his research team, electronic communication did not seem to solve any problems.

Email use was much less common in chemistry than in mathematics or physics. Just over half of the respondents used email. The others claimed that email is too limited for several reasons. First, a big proportion of chemists do not use email. Many are not connected to BITNET or Internet, with industry chemists (about half of all chemists are in industry) being cited as one large group. One physical chemist we interviewed explained it this way: "I have a colleague in industry who I wish was on it, but his company won't let him. They're worried about security and outsiders getting access to their files. A lot of industrial scientists are not on it. Primarily it's the academic scientists and those at national labs."[1]

---

[1] We were unable to get concrete information on email use from ACS because it does not collect such information. We take this as one more piece of evidence on the lack of use, or at least on the lack of institutionalization of use. A spokesperson at ACS told us, "[Generally] all academics are on it and no industry people are."

Also, many who are connected do not read their email. Seven out of 15 people interviewed volunteered that people not being on or not reading their email was a problem, and only 2 said this was not a problem (the others did not mention this problem). In contrast, no mathematician and only one physicist made this complaint. Also, respondents, particularly those in organic and biochemistry, complained that they cannot transmit pictures online, a serious drawback for their work. This was one reason for preferring fax over email (cf. Table 18.3), as this biochemist explains: "There's a central fax machine in the office, by the Xerox machine. It has one advantage over email—for simple graphics, you can send that over fax. A lot of chemistry and biochemistry is pictorially oriented. Things you can't send by text. As far as I know, you can't send pictures by email." This respondent also suggested email would be less of a problem for physical chemists, whose work consists largely of equations, rather than pictures or structures. Similarly, several respondents complained about the difficulty of sending papers via Internet because of formatting problems. None of the chemists mentioned using TeX.

Physical chemists and theoretical chemists are much more likely to use the networks (almost all use email, some quite heavily). They attribute this distinction to their greater familiarity with computers in general, when compared to, for example, organic chemists. As one physical chemist put it, "Some say the networks are a burden, having to answer memos, check their mailbox. Personally, I don't understand that, but many people are also computer shy, the older more than the younger chemists might be more computer shy. The exception would be the physical chemists, who've used computers all along. But, some people just see the networks as harassment."

This difference seems due in part to the nature of the work. Physical chemists and theoretical chemists are much closer to mathematicians or theoretical physicists than are bench chemists. However, none of the chemists felt one had to be on the networks to do good chemistry. In contrast, several physicists noted being on the networks was an integral part of being on a research team. This second point suggests that disciplines or departments also influence technology use, in part by organizing perceptions of what is viable and by providing institutional supports for particular technologies.

Similarly, we found no evidence of using electronic preprint databases. Chemistry, and biology, have much less established preprint cultures. An editor of the *Journal of the American Chemical Society* noted that his colleagues in electro-chemistry are likely to send out only a half a dozen preprints to those doing closely related work (compared to the hundreds sent out by physicists). Similarly, Joshua Lederberg, Nobel Prize-winning geneticist, claimed that in molecular biology, preprints "are not a well-honed formal mechanism" (Taubes, 1993, p. 1247). An ecologist, in response to an online posting on developing a similar service for ecology, responded: "I think having preprints of ACCEPTED articles (NOT POSTED!! [submitted]) would be great. Submitting unaccepted manuscripts does not make sense in our field. The work should be 'citable' once it hits the public, by whatever means. Submitted manuscripts are not [emphasis in original]."

There was also no reported use of mailing lists or bulletin boards like those found in physics or mathematics. What was a standard use of the networks in theoretical physics (and increasingly, in experimental physics and mathematics) was hardly touched in chemistry and biology.

One factor that may contribute to the low level of network use in chemistry is that networks tend to spread information. Once information is put on a publicly accessible electronic source, it tends to travel quickly throughout the networked universe, which, as one chemist explained, could cause problems: "You can imagine doing things [on the networks], but everyone wants their money. If you put together a database and put it on FTP [the network], people will just download it, and you won't make any money." This spread of information is a major drawback in a field where control over information has important commercial consequences, as in chemistry. Questions of patent rights and access to information are major problems in biology and chemistry. Ceci (1988) noted that those in biotech fields were likely to cite financial considerations as a justification for their refusal to share data.

The fact that CA is so expensive and that other chemistry databases also cost is a reflection of this difference in attitude toward information sharing in chemistry (and biology) as compared to physics or mathematics, where the immediate payoffs are less likely and where databases like the preprint archive do not charge for use. American mathematicians' and physicists' work is largely buffered from the direct effects of the market economy (Thompson, 1967). Chemistry and experimental biology, on the other hand, are much more directly tied into the market economy and its emphasis on commodification of the products of labor and impersonal relations between producers and consumers (of information in this case).

EXPERIMENTAL BIOLOGY

Biology is perhaps the most heterogeneous of the disciplines in its work arrangements. We concentrated on those biologists who do experimental work. Unlike physics, the necessary instruments and materials for experimental biology can be located at any geographic location, and the work does not require equipment so huge or expensive that only a limited number of labs can be maintained. Echoing the chemists, a recurring comment among biologists was that "[my type of] biologists are all over—all major universities will have at least one." In general, although they recognized prestige differences among labs, biologists did not point to a handful of labs where research in their specialty was concentrated.

The methods by which experimental biology is carried out are those traditionally associated with "laboratory science." The work is generally performed in a single lab or a group of labs located near one another. Research groups are of moderate size, generally four to seven people, including students and technicians (see Barley & Bechky, 1994). Communication within the lab is informal, although weekly meetings do lend some structure. Materials have to be obtained from outside, but the experiments themselves are self-contained. When a particular experiment involves a number of separate stages, each stage is relatively independent, in contrast to the highly interdependent experiments of the particle physicists. Although collaboration between colleagues at different labs is not uncommon (about half of our respondents reported current participation in such collaborations—see also Table 18.1), such collaborations tend to take the form of parallel or sequential experiments, reducing the coordination difficulties, as this biochemist noted: "In most collaborations, you don't need to be in constant contact. The division of labor is pretty straightforward. Everyone knows what to do; goes to do it. And, this isn't stuff that can be done overnight. These experiments can take months. So you just need to say, 'Here's the result. Let's see how to tie it in.'"

These less interdependent groups are able to work without constant access to information on the activities of colleagues. Because there is less interdependence between groups (compared to physics), respondents felt that phone, fax, and even regular mail worked as well as email, in most situations. Thus, like chemistry, and unlike physics, biology groups are fairly independent in their daily tasks, and hence there is lower pressure on the existing communication mechanisms.

As we would expect given biologists' work organization, use of email was less extensive than in mathematics and physics. Only 5 of 19 respondents used email in the course of remote collaborations, including 2 of the heaviest email users. Of those biologists who used email at all, only about half reported using it at least once per day. The others measured usage in times per week or less. In contrast, of those physicists and mathematicians who used email, all but one in each field reported their usage in terms of messages per day. And, like chemistry, but in contrast to mathematics and physics, complaints of others not reading email or not being on the networks were common among biologists.

As seen in Table 18.3, the percentage of experimental biologists reporting email addresses was substantially lower than in mathematics or physics. Our respondents noted that, with all researchers physically present in the lab and aware of their duties, there was little advantage in using email to coordinate work. Biologists tend to use email as one of several options that includes phone, fax, and post. Email is seen as being a convenient alternative for certain types of routine communication, but not as being indispensable, as one geneticist noted: "You can't guarantee that people are going to communicate by BITNET. If they do, that's fine, but that's why fax is sometimes good, since not everyone uses [email]."

Use of electronic bulletin boards was quite limited. Most respondents who were familiar with these networks reported that they were generally set up by someone in their specialty who was a network enthusiast and were of minimal utility. Use was mainly limited to distributing and exchanging information related to computer use (e.g., structural biologists used them to exchange computation programs and bug notices on these programs) rather than for exchanging substantive information.

The most important network resources used by biologists are the repositories for nucleic acid sequences and proteins that have been accessible on server machines via Internet for about 8 years. GenBank, run by the National Institutes of Health, is now accumulating nucleotides at a rate of over 20 million per year (Cinkosky, Fickett, Gilna, & Burks, 1991). Access to these databases is free and software is available online to facilitate searches. In addition, several commercial databases are available, serving more specialized areas. The ability to make sequence comparisons between materials produced in the lab and those in the databases has become a basic tool for biologists studying gene expression, determining sequences, and synthesizing new genes. Currently, newly sequenced genes are deposited into a database as a prerequisite to journal publication,[2] and sequences in the library are searched as a step in the preparation and analysis of experiments involving gene alteration and mutation. Most significantly, molecular biologists in general (those not specializing in genetics) have increasingly been using sequence comparison in their work, according to this geneticist: "There's been an enormous population explosion, tens of thousands of persons doing sequence work. There are all kinds of biologists who want to study the molecule via nucleic acid sequencing. It's been synergistic: As the sequences became available, more people started doing that sort of research, which in turn added more to the information base."

Electronic network access has made these databases generally useful. For geneticists, being able to deposit and recover sequences as files over a network greatly improves the speed and reliability, compared with such alternative methods as disk or magnetic tape transfer, where the problem of incompatible formats becomes salient, or typing, where error rates are high. About half of the respondents mentioned using sequence databases in their work. One possible reason for the widespread use of sequence databases is that they can be incorporated so easily into the established patterns of work in biology. In the other fields, there is no equivalent large and central domain of data that needs to be shared.

Biologists have also made use of Medline or similar online literature reference databases. Half of the respondents mentioned using electronic reference services either online or at their university library, citing their importance for moving research forward in an information-saturated environment. For at least some biologists, these databases have greatly expedited research, eliminating long hours doing searches by hand.

---

[2]*Journal of Biological Chemistry, Journal of Molecular Biology*, and *Genetics* all require that sequence data and crystallography data be deposited into electronic databases such as GenBank at Los Alamos or Protein Data Bank at Brookhaven.

Given the low level of email usage among biologists, the following quote is not surprising. In it, a biologist mentions his dilemma in wanting access to a literature database, but not knowing whether it is worth learning how to access it electronically:

> Neurobiologist: I used to get Current Contents on disk. But, that's $400 per year to subscribe to that, and I don't want to spend that much off a grant. Now I've found out that the library gets Current Contents on disk and there's a way to use the computer to get on there and use it. What I don't know is if I'll have problems—I can get on there and look at it, but can I download it to my computer, can I shift it into my data storage? I don't want to have to sit there with pen and pencil—I need a way to quickly utilize it. So, I'm trying to find a faculty member who wants to split the costs; or else I'll find out how to use the library.

Like chemists, biologists also perceive drawbacks to the increased flow of information produced by networks. Genetics and molecular biology are fields where competition is high. This has affected attitudes toward networks:

> Biochemist: One thing that happens is people say, "Can you get us your sequence?" and you say, "Yes, as soon as it's published!" [laughs] Then you can fax them if it's important. If it was someone else working on the same project and asks for a sequence, you have to let them have it, but the question is how quickly you will do it. It depends on how long it will take to get the paper out. So networks might not—you hate to say it, but there is a good deal of competition, and priority of publication is important in terms of recognition. This can mean a lot when it comes time for grant renewal.

The contrast between this comment and theoretical physicists' comments on their preprints database sums up the difference between these fields. *Journal of Biological Chemistry* and *Journal of Molecular Biology* both allow authors to request that sequence data deposited in electronic databases not be released for 1 or 2 years (respectively) after publication. This suggests that the desire to prevent the information from being spread extends even to "published" data. Hagstrom (1974) found a positive correlation between competition and the degree of secretiveness within a field. As in chemistry, networks in biology may be seen as a risk to the extent that they reduce the time delay for data sharing (see also Star & Ruhleder, 1996).

COMPUTER NETWORK USE AND THE ORGANIZATION
OF SCIENTIFIC WORK

Our results suggest significant differences in the use of electronic communication across disciplines. Electronic mail and group mail (bulletin boards, distribution lists) are quite common in mathematics and physics, and much less common in chemistry and experimental biology. Electronic communication in chemistry and experimental biology seems largely limited to using online bibliographic databases, such as Chemical Abstracts, or using online genetic or protein databases, such as GenBank. Mathematics and physics use electronic communication for informal communication. We think four factors may be responsible: size of research field, market penetration, locus of critical information and degree of interdependence between research units, and technical limitations.

Size. Mathematics and physics are relatively small fields. For example, the AMS has 27,000 members whereas the ACS has 140,000 members. Several respondents in these fields noted how small their fields were (Traweek, 1988, Taubes, 1986). In an article on the online preprint databases, Taubes (1993) noted the smaller population in particle physics allows users to filter the papers deposited through their knowledge of authors. Our respondents echoed this sentiment. In contrast, chemists and experimental biologists noted how big their fields were. Given that informal communication is more tenable in a smaller population, we would expect mathematicians and particle physicists to use networks more for informal communication.

Market Penetration. Property rights and the financial rewards attached to those rights, are important issues in biology and chemistry, more so than in mathematics and physics. Biology and chemistry also are commodified in the sense that scientists are more likely to purchase equipment and research materials. Scientific journals are filled with ads targeted to biologists and chemists for research instruments and materials, including brand-name genetically altered organisms. Thus, both the inputs and outputs of chemistry and biology are more tied to the market than is the case for mathematics and particle physics. Several of our biology and chemistry respondents mentioned problems of having their results stolen, and the problem of industrial scientists who do not want to share information. The large money returns that can potentially accrue to the "owner" of information suggests one reason for avoiding informal electronic communication. Because informal network use tends to spread information, chemists and biologists were reluctant to adopt this technology, at least in its more informal forms. They were willing, however, to contribute to and use commercial databases like CA and formal databases like GenBank. Use of these forms of electronic communication was also facilitated by institutional protections and inducements by professional societies and journals in these fields.

Locus of Information and Interdependence. Particle physics experiments consist of reciprocally interdependent research teams spread over a vast area. The need to closely coordinate this diverse group leads to a demand for communication links that are quick, direct, and inexpensive. Informal electronic networks have become institutionalized (in the form of email, bulletin boards, and distribution lists within the experiment) to link members of these large experiments. In mathematics, the critical information (a like-minded colleague) is likely to be far away, and information is more easily transmitted via electronic mail. In contrast, in the bench sciences of experimental biology and chemistry, the critical information is located primarily in the local lab. Collaboration occurs, but often it requires little ongoing coordination.

Technical Limitations. A communication medium may not fit well with the messages sent in each field. Biologists and chemists frequently complained that they could not send their kinds of messages electronically. There is some basis for this complaint. Photos and drawings can be difficult to send electronically. However, many of the messages sent are text messages and these also were not sent electronically. Several biology and chemistry respondents complained that the computer networks would not allow them to do things that were in fact done routinely by physicists and mathematicians, such as sending a formatted paper and not losing the formatting. Still, biology and chemistry messages may be more difficult to translate electronically than mathematics and physics messages are. This would also explain the higher use of fax machines by biologists. Related to this match thesis is the idea that those who use computers for other tasks find it easier to use electronic communication. In chemistry, scientists in those subfields that are most computer oriented (e.g., physical chemistry) are also the heaviest users of the networks. However, mathematics is a counterexample. Email use in mathematics was at least as, if not more, pervasive than in any field studied, yet much of mathematics work makes little, if any, use of computers (Hubbard, 1989). Still, it is worth developing this argument to see if there are synergies among computer applications and to see the paths these synergies typically take.

CONCLUSION

In science, work groups have adopted electronic communication that fits with their existing organization and environment. We have described several attributes of the organization of work in different scientific fields that may explain their differential adoption of electronic communication. We also found strong institutional effects. In each case institutional mechanisms, such as allowing electronic submission of papers, have spread the dominant use (Powell & DiMaggio, 1991). This suggests the final form of an innovation results from an interaction between work structure and institutional factors. Once a given use is seen as practical (i.e., fitting a field's constraints), institutional forces engage that make that use seem common sense. For example, any of several word-processing programs would solve mathematics's need for equation editing. But once TeX was adopted as a standard, it seems only common sense to use TeX. The problems with sending formatted documents noted by biologists results in part from the lack of an institutionalized word processor and accompanying support that facilitates new users taking advantage of the new opportunities provided by existing technology.

One fruitful follow-up to this research would be to expand the number of fields studied, and to use longitudinal data, to see if electronic communication use develops in the ways suggested by our data. Can we find support for our suggestions that the more market-penetrated fields limit use to the formal domain (or adopt informal electronic communication much later), whereas the more buffered fields make more use of informal electronic communication; and that the more highly interdependent but geographically dispersed fields are heavier users of electronic communication? It also would be useful to examine the adoption process at an individual level to develop an understanding of how a potential user learns of the technology and comes to adopt it. Finally, institutional arguments suggest that there may be links between disciplines, such that some disciplines follow the lead of others leading to patterns of adoption that mimic these influence patterns.

More advanced technology and diffusion of technology over time may overcome some of the limitations that have prevented electronic communication use by scientists in some fields. But our results suggest that there will continue to be important differences in use across fields. New technologies will result in some changes in scientific work practices, but we do not expect to see a convergence to a common use. Rather, our findings suggest that each field will take advantage of those aspects of electronic communication that best fit with its existing social organization and each will endeavor to institutionalize these uses of electronic communication into standard work routines. If this is the case, it will be further evidence for the importance of understanding the role of social structure in technological change.

ACKNOWLEDGMENTS

This chapter is an abridged version of Walsh, J. & Bayma, T. (1996). Computer networks and scientific work. *Social Studies of Science, 26,* 661–703. Adapted by permission. We gratefully acknowledge support from the Office of Social Science Research and the Campus Research Board at the University of Illinois at Chicago, and the Midwest Sociological Society's

Scholarship Development Fund. Helpful comments on earlier drafts were provided by Sara Kiesler, Lee Sproull, Bradford Hesse, and several reviewers.

REFERENCES

American Mathematical Society. (1991). Backlog of mathematics research journals. *Notices of the American Mathematical Society, 38,* 373–375.

Barley, S. R., & Bechky, B. A. (1994). In the backrooms of science. *Work and Occupations, 21,* 85–126.

Beniger, J. R. (1986). *The control revolution.* Cambridge, MA: Harvard University Press.

Calhoun, C. J. (1981). The microcomputer revolution. *Sociological Methods & Research, 9,* 397–437.

Ceci, S. J. (1988). Scientists' attitudes toward data sharing. *Science, Technology and Human Values, 13,* 45–52.

Cinkosky, M. J., Fickett, J. W., Gilna, P., & Burks, C. (1991). Electronic data publishing and GenBank. *Science, 252,* 1273–1277.

Committee on Science, Engineering and Public Policy. (1989). *Information technology and the conduct of research.* Washington, DC: National Academy of Sciences.

Crane, D. (1967). The gatekeepers of science. *American Sociologist, 2,* 195–201.

Ellis, J. (1986). *The social history of the machine gun.* Baltimore: Johns Hopkins University Press.

Finholt, T., & Olson, G. (in press). From laboratories to collaboratories: A new organizational form for scientific collaboration. *Psychological Science.*

Fisher, C. S. (1973). Some social characteristics of mathematicians and their work. *American Journal of Sociology, 78,* 1094–1118.

Garvey, W. D. (1979). *Communication: The essence of science.* New York: Pergamon.

Garvey, W. D., & Griffith, B. C. (1979). Scientific communication as a social system. In W. D. Garvey (Ed.),*Communication: The essence of science* (pp. 148–164). New York: Pergamon.

Hagstrom, W. O. (1974). Competition in science. *American Sociological Review, 39,* 1–18.

Hargens, L. L. (1975). *Patterns of scientific research.* Washington, DC: American Sociological Association.

Hargens, L. L. (1988). Scholarly consensus and journal rejection rates. *American Sociological Review, 53,* 139–151.

Hesse, B. W., Sproull, L. S., Kiesler, S., & Walsh, J. P. (1993). Returns to science. *Communications of the ACM, 36,* 90–101.

Hubbard, J. H. (1989). Computers in mathematics. Report submitted to the National Academy of Sciences Panel on Information Technologies and the Conduct of Research, Washington, DC.

Kling, R. (1991). Social analyses of computing. In C. Dunlop & R. Kling, (Eds.), *Computerization and controversy* (pp. 150–166). Boston: Academic Press.

Knorr Cetina, K. (1995). How superorganisms change: Consensus formation and the social ontology of high-energy physics experiments. *Social Studies of Science, 25,* 119–147.

Lawrence, P. R., & Lorsch, J. W. (1967). *Organization and environment.* Cambridge, MA: Harvard University Press.

Lederberg, J., & Uncapher, K. (1989). *Toward a national collaboratory: Report of an invitational workshop.* Washington, DC: National Science Foundation.

Mantovani, G. (1994). Is computer-mediated communication intrinsically apt to enhance democracy in organizations? *Human Relations, 47,* 45–62.

McClure, C. R., Bishop, A. P., Doty, P., & Rosenbaum, H. (1989). *The National Research and Education Network (NREN).* Norwood, NJ: Ablex.

Merz, M. (in press). Nobody can force you when you are across the ocean: Face to face and email exchanges between theoretical physicists. In J. Agar & C. Smith, (Eds.), *Making space for science*. London: Macmillan.

National Research Council. (1993). *National collaboratories: Applying information technology for scientific research*. Washington, DC: National Academy Press.

Noble, D. F. (1984). *Forces of production*. New York: Knopf.

Perrin, N. (1979). *Giving up the gun*. Boston: Godine.

Powell, W. W., & DiMaggio, P. J. (1991). *The new institutionalism in organizational analysis*. Chicago: University of Chicago Press.

Rice, R. E. (1994). Network analysis and computer-mediated communication systems. In S. Wasserman and J. Galaskiewicz (Eds.), *Advances in social network analysis* (pp. 167–203). Thousand Oaks, CA: Sage.

Rice, R. E., & Tarin, P. (1993, October). *Staying informed: Scientific communication and use of information sources within disciplines*. Paper presented at the annual meeting of the American Society for Information Science, Columbus, OH.

Ruhleder, K. (1994). Rich and lean presentations of information for knowledge workers. *ACM Transactions on Information Systems, 12*, 208–230.

Star, S. L., & Ruhleder, K. (1996). Steps toward an ecology of infrastructure: Design and access for large information systems. *Information Systems Research, 27*, 111–134.

Swatez, G. M. (1970). Social organization of a university laboratory. *Minerva, 8*, 36–58.

Taubes, G. (1986). *Nobel dreams*. New York: Random House.

Taubes, G. (1993). Publication by electronic mail takes physics by storm. *Science, 259*, 1246–1248.

Taubes, G. (1994). Peer review in cyberspace. *Science, 266*, 967.

Thomas, R. (1994). *What machines can't do*. Berkeley: University of California Press.

Thompson, J. (1967). *Organizations in action*. New York: McGraw-Hill.

Traweek, S. (1988). *Beamtimes and lifetimes*. Cambridge, MA: Harvard University Press.

Walsh, J. P. (1991). The social context of technological change. *Sociological Quarterly, 32*, 447–468.

19

COMPUTERS AND CONNECTIVITY: CURRENT TRENDS

Tora K. Bikson
Constantijn W. A. Panis
RAND Corporation

Email has swept the world during the last decade, but this revolution has not altered one fundamental feature of society: An information elite still exists, made up of those with access to and knowledge about computers and email. The gap between the information haves (richer, better educated people) and information have-nots has actually increased in the last few years even as computers and online services have become less expensive. We describe here how data from national surveys can be used to understand this important social issue.

The number of individuals who engage in computer-based communications in the United States has increased dramatically in recent years and is expected to continue growing well into the next century. Although its reach at present is far from universal, information technology is already woven into the fabric of the economic and social life of developed countries (King & Kraemer, 1995).

CONVERGING TRENDS

The trend toward growing use of computer-based communications stems from two mutually reinforcing influences. First is the often-cited history of improvements in price-to-performance ratios. That is, prices for equal amounts of processing power drop by about half every 2 years (Tessler, 1991). Having started at least two decades ago, such changes are viewed as the enabling force behind the widespread diffusion of computers to households and offices. Communication technologies are likewise beginning to show price/performance improvements while at the same time shedding their terrestrial and bandwidth constraints (Tessler, 1991; Benjamin & Blount, 1992; King & Kraemer, 1995). A second and related stream of influence has to do with the convergence of computing and communication technology within an integrated information medium (Eveland & Bikson, 1987). This integration, for instance, permits individuals to communicate information as readily as they create it, to one or many others, sometimes scarcely noticing that generating, editing, storing, and sending are distinct activities (Bikson & Frinking, 1993); conversely, this convergence preserves the "computability" or reusability of what is received via the medium (Steinfield, Kraut, & Streeter, 1993). Steinfield et al. contended that this property more than anything else accounts for the benefits of email over other contemporary communication media (e.g., voice mail).

In the past, the advantages of such convergence were generally confined to islands of disconnected interoperability (e.g., within particular organizations). However, the movement toward open systems has broadened the capability for interconnection, linking larger numbers of geographically dispersed organizations and individuals with heterogeneous hardware and software to one another through a common electronic infrastructure (Bikson, 1994). The result of these lines of influence is perhaps best illustrated by the phenomenal growth of the Internet in the 1990s (see Fig. 19.1).

WHY STUDY TECHNOLOGY TRENDS?

As indicated in the introduction to the report, this chapter provides a detailed look at trends in information and communication technology access for the U.S. population based on *Current Population Survey* (CPS) data. Specifically, we aimed to learn how evenly computer-based communications capabilities are distributed over the country's varied demographic constituencies and whether those groups exhibit similar trends in access to network services.

Before addressing these questions, however, it is appropriate first to indicate why they are important. That is, are there any reasons to view economic and social stratification of computer and network use differently from the socioeconomic stratification that characterizes the consumption of other goods and services (cf. Attewell, 1994). We believe there are at least four important reasons.

Information. Several well-designed studies have shown that individuals who use computer-based communications have more accurate informa-

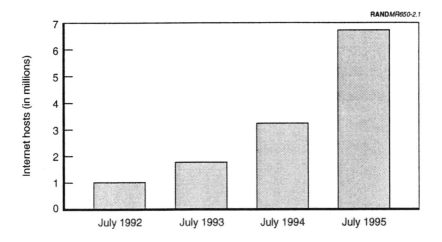

FIG. 19.1. Internet growth worldwide. Figures for July 1995 are estimates. Each Internet host represents from one to hundres of users; the total number of individuals it connects is not known.

tion about matters of political, professional, and organizational concern than peers who do not. For example, a nationwide Times Mirror survey of technology in American households (1994) indicated that 63% of adults who use computers and networks scored high on a current events quiz administered within the survey, compared to 50% of demographically equivalent computer users without network access and 28% of their counterparts who do not use computers. In another study, Kraut and Attewell (chap. 15, this volume) found that otherwise similar employees of a large international financial firm differed significantly in knowledge about the organization depending on whether they communicated via computers; network users knew more (see also Hesse , Sproull, Kiesler, & Walsh, 1990).

Different levels of access to computer-based communication technology, then, may further stratify individuals and create information have-nots alongside the "information elite," as the Times Mirror (1994) survey described those with computers, modems, and access to network services from home. However, the Aspen Institute's Information Bill of Rights (Firestone & Schement, 1995) argues that the emerging information society should have information openly flowing among all individuals and institutions, which in turn requires equitable access to an information and communication infrastructure (see also Denning & Linn, 1994). The policy significance of such potential information stratification can only increase as more public and social information is disseminated electronically.

Affiliation.   As Sproull and Faraj (chap. 2 of this volume) point out, policy discussions of the Internet and other electronic networks assume these media to be chiefly informational in nature. As a correlate, policy discussions cast users as searchers who want effective ways to browse and find the information they desire. Experience suggests a contrasting view of users as social beings who are looking for affiliation, support, and affirmation (Sproull & Faraj, chap. 2, this volume). Electronic gatherings, and not just digital documents, are what they seek.

That networks are not just information technologies but also serve as social technologies (or technologies for affiliation) is supported by the well-established tendency of users to turn what were initially designed as media for accessing and using remote data (e.g., ARPAnet and Minitel) into interpersonal messaging media (see Shapiro & Anderson, 1985; Sproull & Kiesler, 1991b; Lytel, 1992). These observations are corroborated by social science research results indicating that network use creates and sustains both strong and weak social ties (Bikson & Eveland, 1990; Feldman, 1987) and that those who use an organization's network feel more positive about their association with the organization than those who do not (Kraut, 1993; Huff, Sproull, & Kiesler, 1989).

This is not to say the two roles for electronic networks are in conflict; on the contrary, people often use other people as providers of information, pointers to information, and filters of information (Eveland, Blanchard, Brown, & Mattocks, 1995; Bikson, Law, Markovich, & Harder, 1995; Sproull & Kiesler, 1991b; Kraut, Dumais, & Koch, 1989; Bikson, Quint, & Johnson, 1984). Rather, it is to underscore that constraints on network access are at the same time constraints on affiliation. To the extent that civic and social alliances increasingly rely on computer-based interactions, constraints on association represented by less-than-universal access pose policy problems—and especially so if the constraints are unfairly distributed over socioeconomic groups.

Participation.   Study after study has found that electronic networks are significant predictors of the breakdown of status-based social structures. Networks also are related to increased participation in discussion, decision making, and task processes by those who typically are politically or economically disadvantaged. Although explanations for what Kiesler has called the "equalization" effect vary, the results are fairly consistent (see Dubrovsky, Kiesler & Sethna, 1991; Sproull & Kiesler, 1991a, 1991b; Rheingold, 1991; Bikson, 1994; Bikson & Eveland, 1990). That is, for online groups, ascribed and achieved status characteristics such as age, race, gender, formal position or title, and socioeconomic level are far less likely to determine interaction patterns, leadership roles, decision-making influence, and other outcomes in comparison to groups that meet in person. This finding holds true of professional societies, work groups, and social or political organizations.

As civic and political groups increasingly rely on electronic networks, these media could help them overcome status-linked barriers to full participation in social dialogue and public life. However, if access opportunities follow traditional socioeconomic lines, these barriers instead will be strengthened by the emerging information infrastructure (see also the Aspen Institute's Information Bill of Rights, Firestone & Schement, 1995, section A-II on nondiscrimination in "the information society").

Economic Advantage.   There is accumulating evidence that access to computers and communications technology confers economic benefits. At the individual level, for instance, a detailed examination of CPS data from 1984–1989 suggests that workers who use computers on their job earn 10% to 15% higher wages than otherwise similar workers who do not (Krueger, 1993). This conclusion rests on a variety of models estimated in the study to correct for unobserved variables that might be correlated with job-related computer use and earnings (e.g., recreational computer use, prior educational achievement, and economic health of the enterprise). Further, an assessment of payoff differentials for specific computer-based activities at work shows the most highly rewarded task that computers are used for is electronic mail (Krueger, 1993).

However, most studies of economic benefits associated with use of networked information and communication technologies have been carried out at the level of the enterprise or firm rather than at the individual or household level (see Computer Science and Telecommunications Board, National Research Council [NRC], 1994). At the firm level, the competitive advantages provided by interorganizational networks are widely recognized (e.g., Quinn, 1992; Rockart & Short, 1991; Malone, Yates, & Benjamin, 1987). More important, for purposes of this project, are findings from a well-designed comparative study of data from hundreds of small, medium, and large businesses in the United States and France carried out by Streeter, Kraut, Lucas, and Caby (in press). The study shows that national interorganizational networks (in contrast to proprietary networks) foster the formation of electronic marketplace relationships among businesses. Further, they diminish large organizations' inherent advantages (size, slack resources) in exploiting new technologies, making it comparatively easier for small- and medium-size businesses to enter the marketplace and benefit from it. Although we do not examine organization-level data in this chapter, these findings mirror some of the equalization effects observed at the individual level. They also call attention to the likelihood that policies affecting universal access to computer-based communications technologies are likely to have a disproportionate influence on the economic well-being of small- and medium-size enterprises.

There are significant reasons, then, for policymakers to become involved in the debate over universal access to electronic networks. Networks can influence the public's exposure to information. They can create opportunities for individuals and groups to affiliate and to participate in civic affairs. And they can create or shape economic opportunities and advantages. As suggested by King and Kraemer (1995), those who lack access to new communication technologies may be at risk of exclusion from the fabric of the nation's social and economic life.

COMPUTER AND COMMUNICATION TECHNOLOGY IN USE

Against this background of converging technology trends and their societal implications, we turn now to a more detailed investigation of access to computers and communication networks in the U.S. population. We rely chiefly on the October 1989 and October 1993 CPS data.[1]

The CPS is a large-scale random sample survey of households, conducted monthly by the Bureau of the Census. It is the source for much of the official data published by the Bureau of Labor Statistics. The Bureau of the Census periodically adds supplements to the CPS base questionnaires to gain more insight into topics of interest. In this study, we initially examined the October 1984, October 1989, October 1993, and November 1994 supplements because they include questions on computer use by each individual in the household. The 1984 data are not always comparable to data collected in later years, and the 1994 data were released too recently for careful examination within the context of this project. Consequently we focus here mainly on the 1989 and 1993 data.

APPROACH TO THE CPS DATA

CPS data are suitable for analysis at the household level or individual level. This report treats the individual as the unit of analysis. Although some outcomes of interest (e.g., presence of a computer at home) are readily interpretable at either level, others (especially behavioral variables such as use of networked services) are not. Exploratory work suggests that for purposes of this study, where both levels of analysis are appropriate, differences between findings at the individual and household levels are negligible (see, e.g., Fig. 19.2).

At the individual level, then, the analyses reported later are based on 289,979 observations (146,850 in 1989 and 143,129 in 1993). The sample consists of noninstitutionalized civilians in the United States living in households. Both adults and children are in the sample, unless explicitly noted otherwise.[2]

---

[1]*Current Population Survey, October 1989 and 1993: School Enrollment* [machine-readable data file], conducted by the Bureau of the Census for the Bureau of Labor Statistics, Bureau of the Census [producer and distributor], Washington, DC, 1990 and 1994.

[2]The analyses are done using individual weights that approximately equal the inverse of the probability of being in the sample, adjusted for interview response rates and normalized to add up to the sample size.

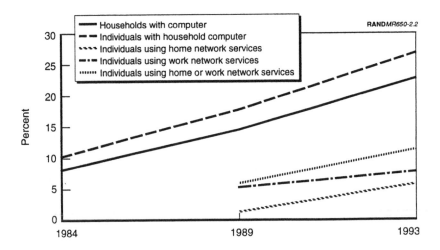

FIG. 19.2. Household computer access and network use.

Outcome Variables.   To represent access to information and communication technology, we employed two binary outcome variables. One, access to a computer at home, is a single-item measure; it receives a positive value if there is at least one computer in an individual's household. At this level of analysis, penetration of computers refers to the percentage of individuals with household access (rather than the percentage of households that have computers).

The other outcome variable, use of network services, represents use of a computer either at home or at work to connect to an electronic network. A derived measure, this variable receives a positive value if an individual uses a computer in any one of the following ways: (a) at home or at work for electronic mail, (b) at home to connect to bulletin boards, (c) at home to connect to a computer at work, or (d) at work for "communications" (this is distinct from word processing, desktop publishing, newsletter creation, etc.).

An alternative approach would be to define this outcome in terms of having or using a modem (compare Times Mirror, 1994). However, preliminary reviews of CPS data and other studies suggest that individuals do not always know whether they have or are using a modem.[3] Further, we

---

[3]Sometimes when computers have built-in modems, the respondents may not be aware of using a modem to access network services. In other cases, respondents are using computers linked to local area networks or hardwired to organization-wide networks that provide access to broader network services (e.g., Internet) without necessitating their use of a modem.

decided to include connectivity in the workplace as well as from home in the definition because it provides a more complete picture of the degree to which individuals use electronic avenues to communicate with others. At present, more people use network services from work than from home, often for both work-related and personal or social purposes; and networks are sometimes used by individuals doing part of their work from home (Fig. 19.2). Thus, the distinction between work and home use of network services could not be made reliably in the CPS data.

Unfortunately, no questions were asked of students about how they use computers and networks at school. This implies that our network outcome variable underestimates the actual use of network services among students. For most determinants of interest, this underestimate is inconsequential. However, results on variables that are highly correlated with student status (such as age and, possibly, household income) need to be interpreted with this caveat in mind. As background, Fig. 19.2 shows home computers as a percentage of both households and individuals in the CPS data; it also shows network use at home and work.

Predictor Variables.   Six predictor variables constitute the core of our study: income, education, race/ethnicity, age, gender, and location of residence. Income, a categorical variable defined by quartiles, refers to the total income of the individual's household. Location, another variable defined at the household level, reflects whether the individual lives in an urban or rural area. Remaining predictor variables refer only to the individual. (Each explanatory variable is further defined in the discussion of results later.)

In investigating the CPS data, our goal was to learn whether and how socioeconomic characteristics are correlated with distribution patterns and diffusion trends in access to computers and electronic networks.

Analysis Plan.   Figure 19.2 presents aggregated CPS data representing the two outcome variables of interest for the U. S. population in 1993 and 1989 (and, for access to a computer at home, 1984). The analysis was designed to answer two questions about these outcomes at the individual level.

In 1993, in comparison to their proportion of the population, are any socioeconomically defined groups significantly underrepresented among those with computers at home and those who use network services any-where?

How have recent trends contributed to the distribution of outcomes? That is, have differences between socioeconomically defined groups in access to computers and communications technology narrowed, remained constant, or widened between 1989 and 1993?

Answers to these questions were tested statistically in several ways. First, we examined differences in access to a computer at home and use of network services across socioeconomic groups in the 2 years separately. These differences follow from cross-tabulations and are shown in bar graphs for each socioeconomic dimension of interest. Because of very large sample sizes, in every cross-tabulation presented, and in both years, the differences between groups are generally statistically significant.[4] (When they are not, we make note of it.)

For purposes of policy analysis and intervention, however, these "gross" differences may be misleading. Socioeconomic status variables are likely to be intercorrelated, meaning that an effort to investigate any one of them should control for the potential influence of all other covariates of interest.[5] Therefore, we held the other socioeconomic variables constant and recalculated computer and network penetration levels to obtain such "net" percentages.[6] Net figures can be interpreted as representing differences between individuals with otherwise equal characteristics (where those equal characteristics are a weighted average of all characteristics found in the data). The same general pattern of findings emerges from the net data but between-group differences are generally reduced. The analysis are discussed more fully in Panis and Bikson (1995).

RESULTS OF DATA ANALYSIS

In what follows, findings from the data analysis are presented first for each of the six predictor variables. We conclude with a discussion of their combined influence on access to computers and communications technology.

---

[4]Statistical significance is determined here on the basis of the Pearson chi-square test. Note that all weights are normalized to add up to the sample size.

[5]For example, suppose that equal use of network services across socioeconomic groups is a political goal. As we see later, African-American individuals tend to use network services to a lesser extent than Whites. This may prompt policymakers to direct efforts to increase use of network services to African-American communities. However, as we also see later, low-income individuals too tend to make less use of network services than high-income individuals. As is well known, the average household income among African-Americans is lower than among Whites. It may well be the case, then, that part or all of the racial difference is due to income differentials. To achieve equal use of network services, public funds may then be more effective when directed toward poor communities generally, rather than to African-American communities specifically. Statistical controls aid interpretation.

[6]The procedure is explained in detail in Appendix A, Panis and Bikson (1995). For example, consider the effect of household income. We distinguish four income categories, corresponding to four income quartiles. First, we estimate a multivariate regression model for, say, presence of a computer in the household. Then, for all individuals in the sample, we predict the probability he or she has a computer in the household, under the counterfactual assumption that everyone falls into the bottom income quartile. The average, over all individuals in the sample, is the predicted fraction of low-income individuals with a computer, *controlling for all other covariates*. Then we assume that all individuals fall into the second income quartile, again compute predicted probabilities of owning a computer, and average over all individuals in the sample. This is repeated for the third and fourth quartiles, yielding a total of four average probabilities ("net" fractions).

Differences by Household Income.   Figure 19.3 presents the percentage of individuals who report that there is a computer in the household and that they have access to network services, as a function of household income category. We distinguish among four quartiles; for example, the bottom quartile includes the 25% of the population with the lowest household income. In 1993, the quartile cutoff income levels were $15,000, $30,000, and $50,000 per year. As is immediately clear in Fig. 19.3 (left half), there are very large differences in household computer access across income categories.

In 1993, just over 7% of the lowest income households had computers, whereas nearly 55% of the highest earning quartile had computers at home. Four years earlier, the respective figures were nearly 6% and 35%. Hence, although the income-based gap in household computer access was very large in 1989, it was even wider by 1993.

The net disparities, controlling for the other key socioeconomic characteristics remain substantial. For example, in 1993, on net, individuals in the top income quartile were four and a half times more likely to have access to a computer in the household than those in the bottom quartile. This net income gap is smaller than the gross figure, mainly because low-income individuals tend to have lower than average educational attainment. About a third of the income disparity is thus attributable to a concomitant effect from educational differences. The net income gap in 1993 represents a significant widening relative to 1989.

Although use of network services either at home or at work is far less than availability of household computers (see Fig. 19.3), generally similar

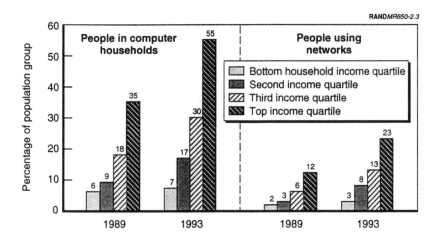

FIG. 19.3.   Household computer access and network use, by income.

patterns appear for network use as a function of household income level.[7] Again we find large differences between quartiles that are becoming even larger over time. In 1989, close to 2% of the lowest income individuals used network services at home or work, whereas over 11% of the highest income individuals used them. By 1993, these fractions had increased to nearly 3% and 23%, respectively. As before, the gross disparities are in part attributable to correlation of household income with other demographic predictors, notably educational attainment. The net gaps remain very substantial, though, and have widened significantly between 1989 and 1993. Interestingly, the net differences are smaller for network usage than for household computer access. This may be due to broader access to network services in the workplace, where no investments in hardware on the part of the individual user are required.[8]

These results are congruent with the Times Mirror (1994) survey's conclusion that the spread of technology through American society is quite uneven. Although that survey examined data from only 1 year (1994), it investigated a broad range of technology to find that these disparities were greatest with respect to computers and on-line capability. Rapidly improving price-to-performance ratios in recent years thus seem not to have narrowed (or even held constant) income-based gaps between information technology haves and have-nots.

Differences by Educational Attainment.   Figure 19.4 (left side) shows household computer access fractions for individuals without a high school diploma, for high school graduates, and for college graduates. (Children under 15 years of age are not included in this part of the analysis.) Persons with some college education, but without bachelor's degrees, are included among high school graduates. As may be expected, there are large differences in household computer access by educational attainment. Among persons without a high school diploma, only about 8% had a home computer in 1989. College graduates, by contrast, had a penetration rate of about 32%. All groups acquired more inhome computers between 1989 and 1993, leading to penetration rates of about 13% and 49% in 1993 for those without a high school diploma and college graduates, respectively. Controlling for other socioeconomic characteristics, the differences are substantially smaller but still highly significant statistically in both years.

---

[7]Recall that our measure of network use includes use at home or work, but not at school, because no appropriate questions were asked from students. This implies that we are likely to overstate differences in network use across income categories, because students who live away from their parents tend to have low household incomes.

[8]As may be inferred from Figure 19.2, there is no large overlap between use of network services in the home and at work. Use of network services at work by low-income individuals may partially explain why the net disparity in network service use is smaller than in access to a computer in the household.

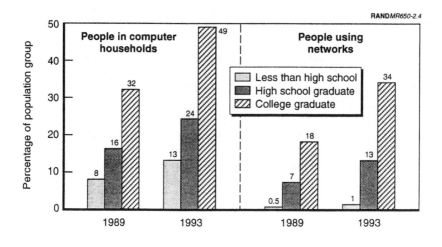

FIG. 19.4. Household computer access and network use, by education.

Figure 19.4 (right side) presents differences in network usage by education category. Network services are dominated strongly by well-educated individuals. In 1989, a mere .5% of individuals without high school diplomas used network services, compared with over 18% of college graduates. Both groups strongly increased their use in 1993, to over 1% and about 34% respectively. The net differences in network use by educational attainment widened significantly between 1989 and 1993. Interestingly, the divergence was entirely due to an acceleration of the adoption of network services among college graduates; the gap between high school drop-outs and high school graduates did not change significantly.

In summary, we find large differences in access to information and communications technology by educational attainment that are increasing over time. Given the established correlation between use of network services and knowledge of current political, professional, and organizational affairs cited previously, these results suggest that disparities in access to electronic networks may well amplify differential knowledge produced by education differences alone.

The Times Mirror (1994) survey of technology in American households yields similar conclusions using 1994 data. It also draws attention to the effect of these patterns of technology access on children's educational opportunities. Among college graduates with children in that sample, almost half reported that the child used a personal computer; but among those with a high school education or less, only 17% reported that children used a home computer (Times Mirror, 1994). However, although large income- and education-based differences exist in children's access to computer technology, the survey found virtually no socioeconomic differences in how often and for what purposes children used computers if they were present in the home. These findings suggest that effects of parental educational stratification could be at least partially offset if it did not result in differential access to information and communications technology for children.

Finally, it should be noted that if more and more jobs at relatively low levels increasingly make discretionary use of network technologies (such as email) available, differences among adults in access to online information based on income and education could decrease in the future.[9] At present, such differences are problematic because they exacerbate differences in earnings as well as differences in general level of knowledge (see the previous introductory section).

Differences by Race and Ethnicity. African-American community leaders have recently expressed concern that African Americans are lagging behind in the use of computers (Williams, 1995). At least part of the race-based difference is due to lower average household income and lower average educational attainment among African Americans as compared with Whites. However, our analysis shows that those characteristics do not account for the entire difference in outcome variables. Rather, racial and ethnic characteristics exert an independent influence on home computer access and network use.

For purposes of this analysis, we combine race and ethnicity into mutually exclusive categories. We distinguish between Hispanics, non-Hispanic Whites, non-Hispanic Blacks, Native Americans (both Indians and Eskimos), and Americans of Asian descent (including Pacific Islanders). In subsequent comments we refer to non-Hispanic Whites as "Whites" and to non-Hispanic Blacks as "Blacks." A small fraction of respondents (.11%) are identified as "other" in the CPS data; we do not reflect the "other" category in Fig. 19.5. Figure 19.5 portrays the percentage of individuals with a computer in the household and access to network services at home or at work by racial/ethnic categories.

As Fig. 19.5 makes clear, the highest penetration rates for household computers are found among Whites and Asians. In 1993, over 30% of Whites and over 37% of Asians lived in a household with a computer. Hispanics, Blacks, and Native Americans, by contrast, all reported a penetration rate of around 13%. As we mentioned earlier, part of these differences may be due to average differences in other characteristics, notably, household income and educational attainment. Controlling for these characteristics, however, we still find substantial differences. In particular, Hispanics,

---

[9]To date, email use in general, and discretionary use in particular, has typically been limited to high-level positions in organizations (e.g., Krueger, 1993). The extent to which organizations in the United States permit or support access to external networks via internal email systems is not presently known.

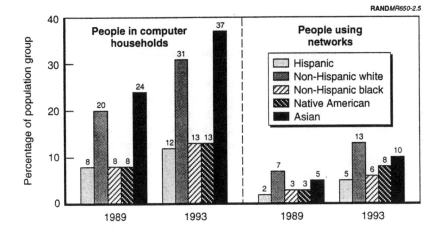

FIG. 19.5. Household computer access and network use, by race and ethnicity.

Blacks, and Native Americans are currently underrepresented among computerized households. Similar patterns of significant racial/ethnic difference in household computer access are also evident in the 1989 data. However, unlike income- and education-based differences, racial/ethnic gaps in home computer access have not widened over time.

Differential use of network services as a function of race/ethnicity also is apparent in Figure 19.5. Again, there are significant between-group differences, even when the influence of other socioeconomic characteristics is controlled. Net differences, however, are slightly smaller than for household computer access. Somewhat surprisingly, Asians have the lowest net rate of network use, even though they have the highest net rates of household computer access among the racial/ethnic groups we distinguished. Another striking finding concerns the relatively high use of network services among Native Americans. Controlling for other sources of effect, their net usage rate was not significantly different from the net rate among Whites in 1993, despite a much lower penetration rate of computers in their households.[10] Given the results of research on relationships of peripherality to network use (see, e.g., Hesse et al., 1990; Huff et al., 1989), it is worth exploring whether Native American usage rates are at least in part explained by their geographic remoteness. No statistical differences in these patterns emerged from our analyses; that is, the racial/ethnic gap in use of network services has remained constant between 1989 and the present.

In summary, we find rather large and persistent differences across race/ethnicity in both household computer access and network services

[10]Native Americans are oversampled in the CPS. In 1989, 1,408 Native Americans were interviewed; in 1993, there were 1,703.

usage. These findings are partially consistent with racial/ethnic differences reported in the Times Mirror (1994) survey, although that study did not include Asians and Native Americans as separate subsamples. There is no generally accepted explanation for these kinds of differences. For Hispanics, it has been suggested that language barriers may be partly responsible for the differences. For Native Americans, our literature review surfaced what seemed to us a comparatively large number of articles describing online educational, library, and other information-oriented services targeted to this constituency. For instance, in a recent *Boardwatch* ("Boardwatch 100," 1994) poll of favorite bulletin boards, a Native American entry emerged in the top 20.

Differences by Age.   We now turn to differences by age.[11] For purposes of this analysis we constructed four categories, distinguishing between individuals under 20 years of age, between 20 and 39, between 40 and 59, and 60 years of age and older. Boundaries based on age are admittedly arbitrary, and different studies employ different cutoffs, different numbers of categories or both (see, e.g., Times Mirror, 1994; "Boardwatch 100," 1994). Particular boundary choices do not, however, appear to affect analytic results in ways that would affect most policy decisions.[12] Figure 19.6 displays household computer access and network access as a function of the age categories defined here.

As Fig. 19.6 suggests, household computer access is distributed fairly evenly across broadly defined age categories up to age 60, where rates of penetration decline steeply. In 1993, around 30% of individuals under age 60 had access to a home computer, whereas only about 10% of individuals above age 60 lived in a household with a computer. Even when other socioeconomic variables are controlled, this difference is highly significant. The age gap appears to be headed for reduction, though; compared with the situation in 1989, older adults have higher relative penetration rates for household computers. However, this change is not large enough to reach statistical significance in the net figures.

Figure 19.6 also reveals the existence of large differences in the use of network services across the age categories defined, with disparities accumulating at both ends of the distribution. In 1993, only 1% of children and

---

[11]The treatment of age is determined by the objective of the study. Obviously, the decision to purchase a computer is in part determined by the size and the age composition of the household, but we wish to document socioeconomic differences in *access* to a computer, not in personal ownership or usage. The connection between presence of a computer in the household and access to it requires only the assumption that the computer is available to all household members—a relatively plausible assumption.

[12]In preliminary analyses, we distinguished as many as eight different age categories. We decided to collapse them into the four categories presented here, because the patterns that emerged were robust to this more parsimonious classification.

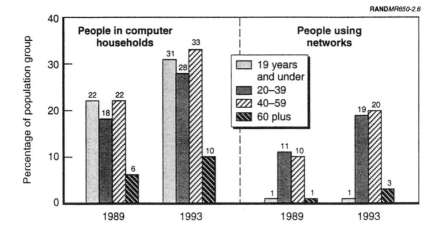

FIG. 19.6. Household computer access and network use, by age.

students under age 20 reported using network services, compared with over 18% among 20- to 39-year-olds, over 20% among 40- to 59-year-olds, and over 3% for people aged 60 and older.[13] Use of network services among very young children (e.g., those too young to read or spell) is likely to be near zero, which further lowers the average estimates for the group under 20 years of age. Also, a special issue of *Communications of the ACM* (CACM) on education reported very little use of networks at school, even in schools where students had access to computers (Soloway, 1993). On balance, then, those in the youngest age category are disproportionately likely to lack network access.

Older adults likewise make significantly less use of network services than younger adults do; the 3% access rate reported here coincides almost exactly with that obtained in the 1994 Times Mirror survey, in spite of differences in how both outcome and predictor variables were defined. But they may be catching up in the future—the data in Fig. 19.6 show that in 1993 older adults were about three and a half times more likely to use network services than in 1989. This growth rate is faster by far than that exhibited in the two other adult age groups during the same period, suggesting that age level per se does not determine either adoption or use of these new technologies. Their rapid diffusion among older adults now may be explained in part by the larger proportion of household income available for discretionary spending among older adults (Bikson, Good-childs, Huddy, Eveland, & Schneider, 1991). Nonetheless this growth rate

---

[13]It should be noted, however, that this measure of network use probably underrepresents students' access to online services because no CPS questions addressed network use at school (see earlier discussion).

has not yet produced a statistically significant reversal of trends; that is, although age gaps have not widened, they also have not yet narrowed significantly.

Differences by Sex. There is minor variation by sex in access to home computers and use of network services, as Figure 19.7 illustrates. Although the gross percentages shown in Figure 19.7 suggest a 2-point difference in 1993, that difference disappears entirely when the influence of other socioeconomic variables is controlled. This was not the case in 1989; controlling for other variables, men were more likely to have access to a computer in the home in 1989. The difference was small (less than a percentage point), but statistically significant. Between 1989 and 1993, though, the gender gap has closed. It should be noted that this outcome variable—having a computer at home—does not take into account which household member purchased the computer. CPS usage data for 1993 show that men make more frequent use of home computers than women; on the other hand, women are significantly more likely than men to use a computer at work (Times Mirror, 1994).

Use of network services also exhibits very little variation as a function of gender. We found differences between men and women on this outcome variable to be statistically negligible in both 1989 and 1993 when the influence of other socioeconomic variables is controlled. Paralleling the data for computer use, the Times Mirror (1994) survey reported that men engage in online activities from home more often than women; but women are more likely to go online at work. The reduction of the gender gap among adults, as evidenced in CPS data, seems also to be reflected in the behavior

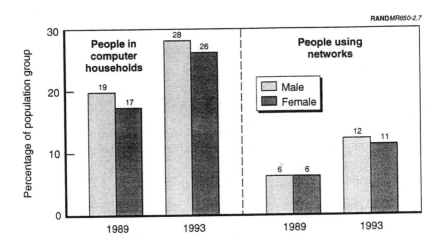

FIG. 19.7. Household computer access and network use, by gender.

of children in households with computers. Times Mirror survey data show that among all households with a computer and at least one child, one or more children are using the computer in 75% of them; and there is little difference between boys and girls in either likelihood or frequency of use.

The survey data indicate that girls may be heavier computer users than boys, at least for applications that assist them with their school work (e.g., word processing). Boys and girls are about equally likely to use a home computer for educational games and art, but boys significantly outpace girls in frequency of use of the home computer for playing noneducational games. On the whole, our analysis of gender differences in access to information and communications technology provides evidence that the gender gap among adults has decreased; we concur with the Times Mirror (1994) conclusion that it could disappear entirely in the next generation.[14]

Differences by Location of Residence.   Household computer access and access to network services as a function of residential location, the last predictor variable we explored in detail, are given in Fig. 19.8. Location is categorized here as rural or urban, where "urban" characterizes residences within standard metropolitan areas.[15]

Ostensibly, the household computer penetration rate in urban areas is much higher than in rural areas. In 1993, just over 29% of individuals living in an urban area had a computer at home, compared with just over 19% among rural residents. About half of the difference is due to correlation with other characteristics such as household income or education. The net gap is nonetheless statistically significant and narrowed somewhat between 1989 and 1993. There are substantial differences in the use of network services as well. In urban areas, over 12% of residents made use of network services in 1993, whereas for rural residents the figure is less than 8%. Again, roughly half of the difference is due to characteristics such as income and education. The gap has remained approximately constant between 1989 and 1993.

Interestingly, the use of network services is approximately proportional to the penetration of computers in the household; that is, rural residents show no greater deficit in network use than in home computer access when compared with urban dwellers. This finding conflicts with the expectation that "access ramps to the information superhighway" (Times Mirror, 1994) are likely to take longer to diffuse to rural homes. In contrast to urban modem users, who are often able to dial into the Internet or other networks with a local call (at low or even zero marginal cost), rural telephone connections may well involve nontrivial toll costs. Installation of a second line for computer access may also be more costly in rural than in urban

---

[14]This is not to suggest that gender differences in usage styles and preferences are disappearing. *BoardWatch* (1994), for instance, reported that its own subscriber poll indicates bulletin board usership is still overwhelmingly male.

[15]As defined by the Office of Management and Budget's June 30, 1984, definitions.

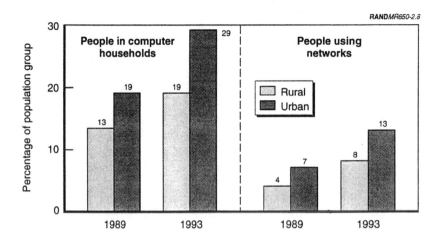

FIG. 19.8.   Household computer access and network use, by location of residence..

areas. Nonetheless, we find no greater urban–rural differences in use of network services than we do in household computer access. Motivation to use network services in spite of such obstacles may be partially explained by geographic remoteness (see Hesse et al., 1990).

Besides urban–rural differences, CPS data also show strong regional differences in distribution of information and communications technology. For instance, in 1993 about a third of the people in New England and in the Pacific and mountain states had a computer at home, and about 13% of people in these areas were using network services; in the east south-central states, by contrast, the corresponding figures are 16% and 7%. A review of specific cities and towns indicates further disparities that reflect other than regional differences. For example, in Michigan in 1993, about two thirds of people in Ann Arbor had a computer at home and 27% of Ann Arbor residents were using electronic networks. In neighboring Flint, 16% of the residents had home computers and 5% of residents used networks. These differences are likely to be at least partially accounted for by the influence of other socioeconomic variables (income and education, especially). Other factors (e.g., proximity to a major research university) need also to be taken into account in explaining location-related gaps in computers and communication technology.

CONCLUSIONS

Research reviewed in the introduction to this chapter provides evidence that access to computers and communications technology influences opportunities to participate effectively in a range of economic, social, and civic activities. If so, it is important to find out whether parts of the U.S. population are cut off from the emerging information society on the basis of their socioeconomic status. To address this question, the analyses described previously sought to learn whether significant differences in access to these electronic media existed in 1989 and 1993 and, if so, what had happened to the size of the gaps over time. Table 19.1 serves as a scorecard summarizing the results.

Although this scorecard does not do justice to specific variations along the socioeconomic dimensions studied, it brings to the foreground the main conclusions: There are information society haves and have-nots; membership in these two classes is significantly predicted by income, education, and—to a lesser extent—race/ethnicity, location, and age. Except for gender gaps, these disparities have persisted over a period when the technologies of interest have decreased dramatically in price and increased markedly in user-friendliness. More worrisome still, gaps based on income and education have not merely persisted but in fact have increased significantly. There is nothing in the data, then, to suggest that, without policy intervention, these gaps will close.

These conclusions, drawn from a national sample of the U.S. population, are disturbing because sizable demographic subgroups who remain in the have-not segment may be deprived of the benefits associated with membership in the information society. It is also appropriate, therefore, to inquire whether the quantitative data we have examined provide any evidence that the expected benefits are in fact realized. Most findings about benefits, such as those reviewed in the introduction to this chapter, come either from relatively small experimental research samples or from larger studies carried out at the organizational and international level.

TABLE 19.1

Summary of Findings

	Computers at Home			Use of Network Services		
	Major Gaps in			Major Gaps in		
	1993	1989	What Happened to Gap Over Time?	1993	1989	What Happened to Gap Over Time?
Income	Yes	Yes	Widened	Yes	Yes	Widened
Education	Yes	Yes	Widened	Yes	Yes	Widened
Race/ethnicity	Yes	Yes	Constant	Yes	Yes	Constant
Age	Yes	Yes	Constant[a]	Yes	Yes	Constant[a]
Gender	No	Yes	Narrowed	No	No	—
Location	Yes	Yes	Narrowed	Yes	Yes	Constant

Note. [a]Although the results are not statistically significant, the data suggest that those age 60 and older may be beginning to narrow the age gap.

For the most part, CPS data are suggestive rather than conclusive because the survey was not designed to address this question specifically. Times Mirror (1994) national survey data more directly bear on it. Results from studies of both datasets, however, tend to corroborate the view that access to computers and communications technology supports informational, affiliative, and participatory outcomes as prior research studies predict.

With respect to information gains, for example, CPS data from 1993 show that 21% of adults with household computers use them to access databases (34% do so from computers at work). Additionally, 15% of adults use home computers for educational programs, as do 39% of children with household computers. Even larger percentages of adults as well as children use computers at home to do school assignments. These findings are corroborated by Times Mirror data, which show information seeking to be one of the two most common activities pursued by people with computers and modems at home. This accounts in part for why such people scored higher on a political knowledge test embedded in the survey than a demographically equivalent sample of nonusers (see earlier discussion). It should be emphasized that such benefits appear not to be restricted to upper socioeconomic levels. Further, the Times Mirror (1994) survey also reported that younger children's use is almost entirely a function of access—among households with PCs, only modest differences were found across racial or income groups in use of computers by children. Results for the teenage survey were the same. The implication is that provision of the technology could go far toward equalizing information benefits across socioeconomic strata.

A second dimension of interest is affiliation, or the extent to which computer-based media yield social contact and support. Some evidence for this thesis comes from the CPS data, which show that apart from word processing, email is the single activity pursued by the largest proportion of adults with household computers. More direct evidence on this point comes from the Times Mirror (1994) survey, which asked more detailed questions about communicative activities. That survey found communicating with other people constitutes a distinct set of activities carried out independently of information seeking. Although acknowledging the importance of information seeking, the *Times Mirror* report concluded that perhaps of equal significance to society is the quieter revolution of computers facilitating communication between people. These findings give strong support to the view that electronic networks are social technologies that serve affiliative needs. It follows that lack of access can constitute a barrier to association in the information age, constraining opportunities for social interaction in ways that universal service policies could remedy. Further, that affiliation is demonstrably an independently significant function of these technologies gives rise to a "right to information" often cited in discussions of computers and connectivity.

A third key question is whether participation in civic and social life is likely to increase along with use of information and communications technology. No CPS items address this point. Times Mirror (1994) survey data are, however, highly instructive. Comparing computer and modem users with their demographic equivalents, the report noted that, aside from working at home more, the largest difference between them is engagement in groups and organizations. Specifically, the users are significantly more likely than their demographic counterparts to belong to a group in which they regularly take part. Further, controlling for other variables, users belong to more groups and are more likely to have worked for or attended a meeting of a group in the past week. Such measures have long been taken by sociologists (e.g., Havighurst, 1973) as indicators of engagement in civic life. These data are consistent with previous smaller scale research indicating that computer-based interactions supplement and extend, rather than supplant, social participation (Bikson & Eveland, 1990; Hesse et al., 1990; Huff et al., 1989; Kraut & Streeter, 1990). Broad access to computers and electronic networks, then, might help reduce if not reverse the trends toward disengagement in civic and political affairs.

The congruence of findings between national-sample survey data and social science research studies strengthens the conclusions drawn here. Although the social science research projects cited here are well designed and are better able to support causal conclusions than cross-sectional surveys, questions inevitably arise about whether the results will scale up to the national level. The survey data presented here are national in scope and representative of the U.S. population; but although they can establish clear correlations and reveal strong trends, they shed less light on causal or functional relationships over time. Together, the combined sources should be viewed as a robust policy foundation. Both kinds of information would, however, benefit from studies of real-world processes in day-to-day contexts. Understanding how outcomes are distributed over time when entire intact communities are networked with computers and communications technology would richly complement what has been learned from social science and from survey research.

REFERENCES

Attewell, P. (1994, November). *Computer-related skills and social stratification.* Paper presented at the workshop Universal Email: Prospects and Implications, Santa Monica, CA.

Benjamin, R. I. & Blount, J. (1992). Critical IT issues: The next 10 years. *Sloan Management Review, 33*, 7–20.

Bikson, T. K. (1994). Organizational trends and electronic media. *American Archivist, 57*(1), 48–68.

Bikson, T. K., & Eveland, J. D. (1990). The interplay of work group structures and computer support. In R. Kraut, J. Galegher, & C. Egido (Eds.), *Intellectual teamwork* (pp. 245–290). Hillsdale, NJ: Lawrence Erlbaum Associates.

Bikson, T. K., & Frinking, E. J. (1993). *Preserving the present: Toward viable electronic records.* Den Haag, The Netherlands: Sdu Publishers.

Bikson, T. K., Goodchilds, J., Huddy, L., Eveland, J. D., & Schneider, S. (1991). *Networked information technology and the transition to retirement: A field experiment* (Report No. R-3690-MF). Santa Monica, CA: RAND.

Bikson, T. K., Law, S. A., Markovich, M., & Harder, B.T. (1995). On the implementation of research findings in surface transportation. *Research Results Digest, 207*, 1–8.

Bikson, T. K., Quint, B. E. & Johnson, L. L. (1984). *Scientific and technical information transfer: Issues and options* (Report No. N-2131-NSF). Santa Monica, CA: RAND.

Boardwatch 100 readers' choice contest results (1994, September). *Boardwatch*, pp. 28–33.

Computer Science and Telecommunications Board. (1994). *Information technology in the service society: A twenty-first century lever.* Washington, DC: National Academy Press.

Denning, D. E., & Linn, H. S. (Eds.). (1994). *Rights and responsibilities of participants in networked communities, computer science and telecommunications board (CTSB).* Washington, DC: National Academy Press.

Dubrovsky, V. J., Kiesler, S., & Sethna, B. N. (1991). The equalization phenomenon: Status effects in computer-mediated and face-to-face decision making groups. *Human–Computer Interaction, 6*, 119–146.

Eveland, J. D., & Bikson, T. K. (1987). Evolving electronic communication networks: An empirical assessment. *Office: Technology and People, 3*, 103–128.

Eveland, J. D., Blanchard, A., Brown, W., & Mattocks, J. (1995). The role of "help networks" in facilitating use of CSCW tools. *The Information Society, 2*(2), 113–130.

Feldman, M. S. (1987). Electronic mail and weak ties in organizations. *Office Technology and People, 3*, 83–101.

Firestone, C. M. & Schement, J. R. (Eds.). (1995). *Toward an information bill of rights and responsibilities, communications and society program.* Washington, DC: The Aspen Institute.

Havighurst, R. J. (1973). Social roles, work, leisure, and education. In C. Eisdorfer & M.P. Lawton (Eds.), *The psychology of adult development and aging* (pp. –). Washington, DC: American Psychological Association.

Hesse, B., Sproull, L., Kiesler, S., & Walsh, J. (1990). *Computer network support for science: The case of oceanography.* Unpublished manuscript, Carnegie Mellon University, Pittsburgh.

Huff, C., Sproull, L., & Kiesler, S. (1989). Computer communication and organizational commitment: Tracing the relationship in a city government. *Journal of Applied Social Psychology, 19*, 1371–1391.

King, J. L., & Kraemer, K. L. (1995). Information infrastructure, national policy, and global competitiveness. *Information Infrastsructure and Policy, 4*, 5–28.

Kraut, R. E., Dumais, S., & Koch, S. (1989). Computerization, productivity and quality of work-life. *Communications of the ACM, 32*, 220–238.

Kraut, R. E., & Streeter, L. A. (1990). Satisfying the need to know; Interpersonal information access. In E. Diaper (Ed.), *Human computer interaction, Interact '90* (pp. 909–915). Cambridge, England: Cambridge University Press.

Krueger, A. (1993). Why computers have changed the wage structure: Evidence from Microdata, 1984–1989. *Quarterly Journal of Economics, 108*(1), 33–61.

Lytel, D. (1992). *Media regimes and political communication: Minitel and the co-evolution of democracy and interactive media in France,* Unpublished doctoral dissertation, Cornell University, Ithaca, NY.

Malone, T. W., Yates, J., & Benjamin, R. I. (1987). Electronic markets and electronic hierarchies. *Communications of the ACM, 30*(6), pp. – .

Panis, C. W. J. & Bikson, T. K. (1995). Additional information on computers and connectivity. Appendix A in R. H. Anderson, T. K. Bikson, S. A. Law, & B. M. Mitchell (Eds.), *Universal access to e-mail: Feasibility and societal implications* (pp. 179–188). Santa Monica, CA: RAND

Quinn, J. B. (1992). *Intelligent enterprise.* New York: The Free Press.

Rheingold, H. (1991, Summer). The great equalizer. *Whole Earth Review*, p. 5–11.

Rockart, J., & Short, J. (1991). The networked organization and the management of interdependence. In M. Scott-Morton (Ed.), *The corporation of the 90s*. New York: Oxford University Press.

Shapiro, N. Z., & Anderson, R. H. (1985). *Toward an ethics and etiquette for electronic mail* (Report No. R-3283-NSF/RC). Santa Monica, CA: RAND (Available to http://www.rand.org/areas/r3283.html)

Soloway, E. (1993). Technology education: Introduction. *Communications of the ACM, Special Issue on Technology in K–12 Education, 36*(5), 28–30.

Sproull, L., & Kiesler, S. (1991a). Computers, networks and work. *Scientific American, 265*, 116–123.

Sproull, L., & Kiesler, S. (1991b). *Connections: new ways of working in the networked organization*. Cambridge, MA: MIT Press.

Steinfield, C., Kraut, R., & Streeter, L. (1993, June). *Markets, hierarchies, and open data networks*. Paper presented at the meeting of the International Telecommunications Society, Gothenburg, Sweden.

Streeter, L. A., Kraut, R. E., Lucas, H. C., Jr., & Caby, L. (1996). The impact of national data networks on firm performance and market structure. *Communications of the ACM, 39*, 62–73.

Tessler, L. (1991). Networked computing in the 1990s. *Scientific American, 265*, 86–93.

Times Mirror Center for The People & The Press. (1994). *Technology in the American household*. Los Angeles: Times Mirror.

Williams, L. (1995). Computer gap worries Blacks. *The New York Times*, p. B4.

About the Authors

Paul Attewell
Professor of Sociology
Graduate School and University Center
City University of New York
33 West 42nd Street
New York, NY 10036.
(212) 642-2411
(Secretary/messages: 212-642-2401)
Email: PAA@CUNYVMS1.gc.cuny.edu

Paul Attewell is a Professor of Sociology at the Graduate School of the City University of New York. His research examines how Information Technologies affect work processes and organizational functioning. He has published on deskilling, on electronic surveillance, on the diffusion of new technologies, and on the "productivity paradox."

Nancy Baym
Wayne State University
Email: nbaym@cms.cc.wayne.edu

Nancy Baym (Ph.D., University of Illinois) is an Assistant Professor of Communication at Wayne State University in Detroit. She studies how language is used to create identity, social norms, and interpersonal relationships in computer-mediated communication. Her research also addresses the ways in which computer-mediated fan groups are altering mass media production and reception.

431

Todd Bayma
Department of Sociology
University of Georgia
Baldwin Hall
Athens, GA 30602
(706) 542-4320
Email: CMSTODD@UGA.CC.UGA.EDU

Todd Bayma is a graduate sociology student at the University of Georgia. His areas of interest include culture and social theory, urban sociology, and social change.

Tora Bikson
Rand Corporation
1700 Main St
Santa Monica, CA 90406-2138
(310) 393-7227
Email: tora@kiwi.rand.org

Tora K. Bikson, Senior Scientist at RAND from 1976 to the present, holds Ph.D. degrees in philosophy (University of Missouri) and psychology (UCLA) and has taught at both universities. Since 1980 Bikson's research has investigated properties of new information and communication technologies in varied user contexts in the US and Europe. For the past 10 years she has also served as technical consultant to the UN's Information Systems Coordinating Committee (ISCC, formerly ACCIS). Bikson has written numerous journal articles and book chapters, and is a member of editorial boards for Organizational Computing, Journal of Computer Mediated Communication, and The Information Society. She is coauthor of three recent books: Teams & Technology: Fulfilling the Promise of the New Organization, Universal Access to Email: Feasibility and Societal Implications, and Preservinv the Present: Toward Viable Electronic Records.

Irv Binik
Dept. of Psychology
McGill University
1205 Dr. Penfield Ave.
Montreal, Quebec, Canada, H3A 1B1
Phone: (514) 398-6095; Fax: (514) 398-4896
Email: binik@ego.psych.mcgill.ca

Irv Binik conducts resarch on psychosocial factors in chronic illness, human sexuality, and clinical uses of computers. Professor Binik has a bachelor's degree from the Jewish Theological Seminary, master's and Ph.D. degrees in clinical psychology from the University of Pennsylvania, and a clinical internship from Warneford Hospital at Oxford University. He is Professor of Psychology at McGill University and Director of the Sex and Couple Therapy Service, Royal Victoria Hospital. Also he is a Diplomate from the American Board of Sexology and is associate member of the International Association for Sex Research.

James Cantor
Dept. of Psychology
McGill University
1205 Doctor Penfield Ave.
Montreal, Quebec H3A 1B1
CANADA
Email: jcantor@psych.mcgill.ca

James Cantor received his BS in interdisciplinary-computer science from Rensselaer Polytechnic Institute and his MA in psychology from Boston University. Currently, he is completing his PhD in clinical psychology at McGill University, researching the interactions of hormones and neuro-transmitters during sexual behavior.

Peter Carnevale
Department of Psychology
University of Illinois
603 E. Daniel St.
Champaign, IL 61820
Phone: (217) 333-4899; Fax: (217) 244-5876
Email: pcarneva@s.psych.uiuc.edu

Peter Carnevale is a professor of psychology at the University of Illinois at Urbana-Champaign. He is co-author of "Negotiation in Social Conflict" (1993, Brooks/Cole) and "International negotiation: The structure and process of resolving international conflicts" (1998; Lynne Rienner). He was the recipient of the Erik H. Erikson Early Career Award from the International Society of Political Psychology as well as the Edwin E. Ghiselli Award for Research Design from the Society for Industrial and Organizational Psychology. He is President of the International Association for Conflict Management and Chair of the Conflict Management Division of the Academy of Management.

Terry Connolly
Department of Management and Policy, BPA
University of Arizona
Tucson, AZ 85721
(520) 621-5937
Email: connolly@aruba.ccit.arizona.edu

Terry Connolly holds degrees in electrical engineering, sociology, and organizational behavior and is currently on the faculty at the University of Arizona. His main research interests are in decision processes at individual, group and organizational levels and the impact of computer-mediated technology on these processes. He is a past president of the Judgment and Decision Making Society.

David Constant
Department of Social & Decision Sciences
Carnegie Mellon University
Pittsburgh, PA 15213

David Constant is a Ph.D. candidate at Carnegie Mellon University. He holds a degree in Systems Design Engineering from the University of Waterloo. His industrial experience includes management consulting in information systems and software development in real-time communications systems. He is a partner in Process Inc, a firm providing SEI-licensed software process assessments. His research interests include information and communications technologies in organizations.

Lisa Covi
Research Fellow
Collaboratory for Research on Electronic Work (CREW)
School of Information
The University of Michigan
701 Tappan Street
Ann Arbor, MI 48109-1234
(313) 647-7730
Email: covi@umich.edu
http://www.crew.umich.edu/~covi

Lisa Covi is a postdoctoral researcher in the Collaboratory for Research on Electronic Work at the University of Michigan. She completed her dissertation, Material Mastery: How University Researchers Use Digital Libraries for Scholarly Communication in September 1996 (University of California, Irvine). Currently, she is investigating work practices surrounding the use of information and collaborative systems in both field and experimental settings.

Pavel Curtis
Xerox PARC
3333 Coyote Hill Rd.
Palo Alto, CA 94304
(415) 812-4455
Email: pavel@xerox.com

Pavel Curtis received his bachelor's degree from Antioch College in 1981 and his master's and doctorate degrees from Cornell University in 1983 and 1990, respectively. He has been a member of the research community at the Xerox Palo Alto Research Center since 1983, during which time he has worked on aspects of the Smalltalk-80, Interlisp-D/Xerox Lisp, and Cedar programming environments and on other projects mostly related to the design and implementation of programming languages, including leadership of the SchemeXerox project exploring large-scale software development in the Scheme programming language. He is the founder and chief administrator of LambdaMOO, one of the most popular recreational social virtual realities on the Internet. Since 1992, as co-leader of the Network Places project, he has been working on bringing the benefits of network places to a broader range of users and applications.

Ann Locke Davidson Ph.D.
802 LRDC
University of Pittsburgh
Pittsburgh, PA 15260
(412) 624-7498
Email: adavidso@oberon.pps.pgh.pa.us

Ann Locke Davidson is an educational anthropologist and postdoctoral fellow at the Learning Research and Development Center at the University of Pittsburgh. Her work concentrates generally on the relationship between school environments and students' formation of academic identity, with a particular focus on working-class and minority youths.

Samer Faraj
MIS Department
School of Management
704 Commonwealth Avenue
Boston University
Boston, MA 02215
Phone: (617) 353-7057; Fax: (617) 353-6667
Email:samer@acs.bu.edu

Samer Faraj is completing his doctoral studies in IS at Boston University. He has 8 years experience in assessing energy and Information technologies. His current research focuses on work team coordination processes and the dynamics of electronic interest groups.

Gail Clark Futoran Ph.D.
Route 2 Box 170E
Marion, TX 78124-9522
(210) 914-3525

Gail Clark Futoran earned her Ph.D. in social psychology from the University of Illinois at Urbana-Champagne in 1987. She currently lives in San Antonio, Texas.

Rebecca Grinter
Center for Research and Information Technology and Organizations
University of California
Irvine, CA 92717
rgrinter@ics.uci.edu

Rebecca E. Grinter has recently received her Ph.D. from the Computers, Organizations, Policy and Society research area at the University of California, Irvine. She also has a M.S. from the Department of Information and Computer Science at UC Irvine, and a B.Sc. from the University of Leeds. Her research interests focus on the process of development.

Christopher Kedzie
Ford Foundation / Moscow
320 East 43rd Street
New York, NY 10017
kedzie@glas.apc.org

Christopher Kedzie's doctoral thesis at RAND analyzed effects of information revolution technologies in international affairs, particularly, on global democratization. Before coming to RAND, Kedzie acquired substantial overseas field experience using information and communication technologies to influence societal change. He was a Founder and Director of organizations in Ukraine and Uzbekistan that supported reform initiatives. Currently, Dr. Kedzie is the Program Officer in the Ford Foundation's Moscow office concerned with Russian democratic reform. A distinguished graduate from the Air Force Academy, Kedzie has also earned graduate degrees from the Massachusetts Institute of Technology and Harvard University. To date, he is published in English, Russian and Ukrainian on topics ranging from information technology to societies in transition.

Sara Kiesler
Department of Social & Decision Sciences
Carnegie Mellon University
Pittsburgh, PA 15213
Phone: (412) 268-2848; Fax: (412) 268-6938
Email: kiesler@andrew.cmu.edu

Sara Kiesler is Professor of Social and Decision Sciences at CMU. She is the co-author of *Connections: New Ways of Working in the Networked Organization* (MIT Press), and has published more than 45 research papers on electronic communication, and has served on 5 National Academy of Sciences panels concerned with technology.

John King
Dept. of Information and Computer Science
University of California
Irvine, CA 92717
(714) 824-6388
Email:king@ics.uci.edu

John L. King's research focuses on the ways in which organizational and institutional forces shape how information technology is developed (including what gets developed) and how the technologies that do get developed change the course of organizational and institutional behavior. This research draws on on the fields of economics and other social sciences as well as engineering and management. The practical goal is to improve the design of information technologies for both organizational and institutional usability, through better articulating the processes of requirements analysis, specification, and prototype creation. The work also informs policy and strategy development at the firm, sectoral, and institutional levels. Current projects include examining role of government and other institutional policies in shaping national information technology growth in 12 Asia-Pacific nations; a study of the evolution of systems requirements in intermodal transport and logistics; examination of California criminal courts as a venue of CSCW implementation; and study of the evolution of standards and technical infrastructure in the global telephony field. Dr. King is Professor of Information and Computer Science and Management at the University of California, Irvine, and holds a Ph.D. in Administration.

Rob Kling
Professor Information Science and Information Systems
& Director, Center for Social Informatics
School of Information & Library Science
Indiana University
10th & Jordan, Room 005C
Bloomington, IN 474005-1801
Phone: (812) 855-9763; Fax: (812) 855-6166
http://ezinfo.ucs.indiana.edu/~kling
Email: kling@indiana.edu

Rob Kling is Professor of Information Science and Information Systems in the School of Library and Information Science at Indiana University, Bloomington where he also directs the Center for Social Informatics (http://www.slis.indiana.edu/CSI). Professor Kling is Editor-in-Chief of *The Information Society* and has recently written and edited the second edition of *Computerization and Controversy: Value Conflicts and Social Choices*. Dr. Kling's research focuses on topics within social informatics, such as the roles of digital libraries and electronic publishing in improving professional communication.

Robert Kraut
Carnegie Mellon University
Pittsburgh, PA 15213
Phone: (412) 268-7694
Fax: (412) 268-6938
Email: kraut@andrew.cmu.edu

Robert Kraut is Professor of Social Psychology and Human-Computer Interaction at Carnegie Mellon University. He previously was Director of Interpersonal Communications Research at Bellcore, where he was responsible for a multidisciplinary study of residential telecommunications needs and where he designed and managed a field trial on the use of video telephony.

Jane Manning
School of Computer Science
Carnegie Mellon University

Jane Manning completed a Ph.D. in philosophy at Stanford University, and has developed World Wide Web pages for universities and industries. She was director of the HomeNet project, and now works in Australia.

Marta Meana
3455 Lebon Drive, #1625
San Diego, California 92122
(619) 677-9452
Email: mmeana@ucsd.edu (Marta Meana)

Marta Meana recently completed a Ph.D. in Clinical Psychology at McGill University in Montreal. She is currently doing an internship at the University of California, San Diego after which she will start a research post-doctorate at the Toronto Hospital in the Women's Health Program.

Michael Mehta
School of Policy Studies
Queens University
Kingston, Ontario K7L 3N6
(613) 545-6000, ext. 5636
Email: mm39@post.queensu.ca

Michael Mehta is an environmental sociologist who specializes in risk, environmental attitudes, social movements, and information and communication studies. His academic background includes a B.A. in Psychology, a Master in Environmental Studies, and a Ph.D. in Sociology - all from York University, Canada. He is co-founder of the Environmental Studies Association of Canada (ESAC), and co-editor of a new book entitled *Environmental Sociology: Theory and Practice* (Captus, 1995). He is presently a Postdoctoral Fellow at the Environmental Policy Unit of Queen's University, and is working on several things including a book on nuclear power plant safety, papers on the Internet and social control, and techniques for visually displaying three-dimensional models of risk data.

Kristin D. Mickelson
Institute for Social Research
University of Michigan
and
Department of Health Care Policy,
Harvard Medical School
Parcel B, 1st floor
25 Shattuck Street
Boston, MA 02115
(617) 432-2905
Email: mickelso@hcp.med.harvard.edu

Kristin D. Mickelson is a postdoctoral fellow in the Survey Research Center at the Institute for Social Research, University of Michigan. She received her Ph.D. in social psychology from Carnegie Mellon University. Her research focuses on stress and social support, psychosocial factors in health, communal coping, and gender.

Tridas Mukhopadhyay
Graduate School of Industrial Organization
Carnegie Mellon University
Pittsburgh, PA 15213
(412) 268-2307
Email: tm25@andrew.cmu.edu

Tridas Mukhopadhyay is an Associate Professor of Information Systems at the Graduate School of Industrial Administration at CMU. He has worked with leading corporations and agencies, such as General Motors and the United States Postal Service, in assessing the business value of information technology.

Eric Ochs
Department of Psychology
McGill University
1205 Dr. Penfield Ave.
Montreal, QC, Canada, H3A 1B1
Email: eric@ego.psych.mcgill.ca

Eric Ochs is completing a Ph.D. in clinical psychology at McGill University, focusing on attitude and behavior change in couples using Sexpert (an expert system). He also works as a clinical psychologist at the Allan Memorial Institute in Montreal.

Constantijn W.A. Panis
Rand Corporation
1700 Main St.
P.O. Box 2138
Santa Monica, CA 90406-2138
Email: panis@rand.org

Constantijn Panis is a labor and population economist with the RAND Corporation. His research focuses on many aspects of family life: child and adult health; mortality; Social Security and other forms of old-age support; education; fertility; marriage formation and dissolution; and more. His interests in the use of computers and network services are part of a broader research interest in the determinants of schooling decisions and the returns to education. In addition to conducting research at RAND, Panis teaches intermittently at the University of California in Irvine. He received his Ph.D. in economics from the University of Southern California in 1992.

Jeanne Pickering
Dept. of Information and Computer Science
University of California
Irvine, CA 92717
Email: pickerin@ics.uci.edu

Jeanne Pickering is a research associate with the Center for Research on Information Systems and Organizations at the University of California, Irvine. Her research investigates the problems of requirements definition for software development in socially complex application environments, including education, communications, and entertainment.

Dwaine Plaza
Department of Sociology
York University, Canada

Dwaine Plaza is a sociologist who specializes in migration, immigration policy, race and ethnic relations, and quantitative research methodology. His academic background includes a B.A. in Sociology and a Master in Environmental Studies from York University, Canada. He is completing a Doctorate in the Department of Sociology at York University. Currently, Mr. Plaza is a Postdoctoral Fellow at Cheltenham & Glouchester and Oxford Brookes Universities in Great Britain. He is working on a project which looks at the living arrangements, family structure and social change of Caribbeans in Britain.

Tahira M. Probst
Pscyhology Department
University of Illinois
603 E. Daniel St.
Champaign, IL 61820
Email: tprobst@s.psych.uiuc.edu

Tahira Probst is a graduate student at the University of Illinois. She received her MA in I-O psychology in 1995, and is currently pursuing her PhD. Her research interests include intra-and intergroup conflict and cross-cultural negotiation.

William Scherlis
Department of Computer Science
Carnegie Mellon University
Pittsburgh, PA 15213
(412) 268-8741
Email: william.scherlis@cs.cmu.edu

William Scherlis is Senior Research Computer Scientist at CMU doing research on software technology and information infrastructure. He is on the steering committee of an NRC study of information infrastructure. *Jane Aronson* is the Project Director.

Janet Ward Schofield Ph.D.
816 LRDC
University of Pittsburgh
Pittsburgh, PA 15260
(412) 624-7473
Email: schof@vms.cis.pitt.edu

Janet Ward Schofield is a professor of psychology and a Senior Scientist at the Learning and Research and Development Center at the University of Pittsburgh. She is a social psychologist whose research during the last twenty years has explored the impact of social and technological change in educational settings.

Candace Sidner
Lotus Development Corporation
One Rogers Street
Cambridge, MA 02142
(617) 693-5003
Email: Candy_Sidner@crd.lotus.com

Candy Sidner has been a member of the research staff since 1993. Before coming to Lotus, she had been a member of the research staff at Cambridge Research Lab (Digital Equipment Corporation), a visiting fellow at Harvard University, and a Division Scientist at Bolt Beranek and Newman, Inc. At Lotus, Candy is pursuing research in three areas: (1) studies of Email overload in order to produce better Email related tools, and (2) models of the tasks users must perform using currently available applications, and (3) collaborative interface agents. She has also been investigating the use of speech understanding with Lotus products. Candy serves on numerous program committees and journal boards for societies in artificial intelligence, and natural language processing. She is a past president of the Association of Computational Linguistics (1989), and is a Fellow and past Councillor of the American Association of Artificial Intelligence. Candy received a Ph.D. from MIT in Computer Science (1979), M.S. in Computer Science, from the University of Pittsburgh (1975), and B.A. cum laude Mathematics, from Kalamazoo College (1971)

Lee Sproull
MIS Department
School of Management
704 Commonwealth Avenue
Boston University
Boston, MA 02215
Phone: (617) 353-4157; Fax: (617) 353-6667
Email: lsproull@bu.edu

Lee Sproull is Professor of Management at Boston University. Prior to her current appointment she was a faculty member at Carnegie Mellon University for thirteen years. Her current research interests include the social dynamics of video communication and group processes in electronic groups.

Janet E. Stocks Ph.D.
815 LRDC
University of Pittsburgh
Pittsburgh, PA 15260
(412) 624-7480
Email: stocks+@pitt.edu

Janet E. Stocks is a sociologist and a Research Associate at the Learning Research and Development Center at the University of Pittsburgh. Her previous work includes a qualitative study of evangelical feminists and a qualitative study of an innovative elementary mathematics curriculum.

Warren Thorngate
Professor & Academic Advisor for International Students
Psychology Department
Carleton University
Ottawa, Ontario
Canada K1S 5B6
Phone: (613) 520-2600, ext. 2706; Fax: (613) 520-3667
Email: warrentccs.carleton.ca

Warren Thorngate received his BA in psychology and mathematics from the University of California, Santa Barbara in 1966, and his PhD in social and mathematical psychology from the the University of British Columbia in 1971. He is currently Professor of Psychology at Carleton University, Ottawa, Canada, and Carleton's academic advisor for international students. Professor Thorngate's research interests include the study of adjudicated contests, the economics of attention, and the development of higher education in the Third World. He is the former President of the International

Society for Theoretical Psychology, but is now working on the development of Internet facilities for university education in Cuba and Iran.

Professor Sherry Turkle
MIT/STS Program
MIT E51-296
77 Massachusetts Avenue
Cambridge, MA 02139-4307
(617) 253-4068
Email: sturkle@media.mit.edu

Dr. Turkle is Professor of the Sociology of Science at the Massachusetts Institute of Technology and a licensed clinical psychologist, holding a joint Ph.D. in Personality Psychology and Sociology from Harvard University. Dr. Turkle has written numerous articles on psychoanalysis and culture and on the "subjective side" of people's relationships with technology, especially computers. She is the author of *Psychoanalytic Politics; Jacques Lacan and Freud's French Revolution* (Basic Books, 1978; MIT Press paper, 1981; second revised edition, Guilford Press, 1992) and *The Second Self: Computers and the Human Spirit* (Simon and Schuster, 1984); Touchstone paper, 1985). Her most recent research is on the psychology of computer-mediated communication, including role playing on MUDs (multi-user domains). This work is reported in *Life on the Screen: Identity in the Age of the Internet,* Simon and Schuster, November 1995.

John P. Walsh
Department of Sociology
1007 W. Harrison St, 4112 BSB
University of Illinois at Chicago
Chicago, IL 60607-7140
(312) 996-4663
Email: JWalsh@uic.edu

John P. Walsh is an assistant professor of sociology at University of Illinois at Chicago. His research interests include studies of work, organizations and technology. He his currently studying the economics and organization of industrial R&D in the U.S., Japan and Europe.

Barry Wellman
Centre for Urban and Community Studies
and Department of Sociology
University of Toronto
Toronto Canada M5S 1A1
Email: wellman@chass.utoronto.ca

Barry Wellman learned how to keypunch at Harvard University, where he received his Ph.D. in 1969. He's now Professor of Sociology at the University of Toronto, based at the Centre for Urban and Community Studies. Wellman founded the International Network for Social Network Analysis in 1976 and served as its Coordinator for twelve years. His research investigates social networks of work and community, off- and on-line.

Steve Whittaker
Lotus Development Corporation
One Rogers Street
Cambridge, MA 02142
(617) 693-5003
Email: stevew@research.att.com

Interests include theory, design and use of systems to support computer mediated communication (CMC): including video, shared workspaces and lightweight communications applications. More recent work has addressed Email, Lotus Notes, "speech-as-data" and voicEmail, with a view to generating general principles for CMC.

Author Index

Subject Index